Liverpool, The Fifth Beatle;
An African-American Odyssey

by

P. Willis-Pitts

AM OZ EN
PRESS

Front Cover Photograph Courtesy Bill Harry:
The Beatles with (left to right) Joey Ankarah, Sugar Deen, Little Richard and Derry Wilkie

Front Cover Background Photograph Courtesy Glynn Parry (digitally manipulated composite):
The Liver Building from the Mersey River

Back Cover Background Photograph Courtesy Reflections:
The Liver Building, Liverpool

Visit the web site for *Liverpool, The 5th Beatle*: http://www.beatlesbook.net

Design Consultant, Cassandra Silk

Manufactured in the United States of America

This book is dedicated to:

My dear Vimal
Brendan McCormack, The Fey Celt
who went the extra mile—and more
Cassie, for her clarity of vision
Derry Wilkie who showed me what soul is
And all those Scousers and others
who gave so freely of their time and memorabilia
Rock on...

And
A special thought to the relatives
of two fine men, two fine musicians,
Colin Manley
and
Johnny Guitar
who kept the beat until the final bar

Acknowledgements:

For additional materials and invaluable assistance: David Abdulah, Margaret Avinyo, Tony Boase at Mersey Music, Barry Chambers, Patrick Cluskey, David Hillhouse at Wirral Museums, Spencer Leigh, Garrick Prayogg, Norman Williams, Bob Wooler and the Wallasey Library.

Lyrics from *In My Liverpool Home* by Peter McGovern by kind permission of Spin Publications.

Poems reproduced by kind permissions of Adrian Henri and Roger McGough.

Photographic Permissions:

Margaret Ainscough for the Harry Ainscough Collection
Colin Areety
Bluecoat Press, per Vanessa Chellembron
Ches Cherry
Patrick Cluskey
Combo Musical Weekly, per Matthew D'Arcy
Tony Davis
Sugar Deen
Ken Dodd
John Edwards
FAB, Fleetway Publications
Dave Forshaw
Gaz Gaskell
Johnny Gustafson
Peter Halligan
Neil Hamilton
Bob Hardy
Bill Harry
Karl Hughes
Professor Quentin Hughes
Charlie Jenkins
Michael A. Joseph
The Imperial War Museum, per Janice Mullen
International Guitar Festival of Great Britain, per Brendan McCormack
Spencer Leigh
Lewis's Department Store, Liverpool

Liverpool Daily Echo and Post, per Mr. Colin Hunt, Chief Librarian
Liverpool Libraries and Information Services, per David Stoker
Derek Massey
John McCormick
Mindscaffolding
Tony Myers
National Museums and Galleries on Merseyside, per The Board of Trustees
Glynn Parry
PEBE Splash Records & Casbah Promotions
Paul Pilnick
Private Eye, Ms. Hope Pym, Editor
Harry Prytherch
Reflections, per Carol Sharp
David Rushworth
Kingsize (Teddy) Taylor
Colin Thorpe
Wallasey News
Hank Walters
Weekend Daily Telegraph
Bernie Wenton
Mrs. Wilkie
Dave Williams
Norman Williams
Wirral Museums, per David Hillhouse
Bob Wooler

Liverpool, The Fifth Beatle;

An African-American Odyssey

Table of Contents

Introduction: 1

   Plate: **The Liver Building, Liverpool** (*courtesy Reflections*)

Chapter 1   In the Beginning Was Mathew Street 3

   Plate 1:   **Mathew Street, circa 1960** (*Author's collection*)

Chapter 2   Look For The Girl With The Sun In Her Eyes 7

   Plate 2:   **Slum Rooftops, Everton** (*courtesy Quentin Hughes*)

Chapter 3   The Beatles In Close-Up 13

   Plate 3:   **Paul McCartney at St. John's Hall** (*courtesy Patrick Cluskey*)

   Personal Anecdote: A Hard Day's Night* - 14

Chapter 4   Life In The Streets 19

   Plate 4:   **A Liverpool Street, 1965** (*courtesy Margaret Ainscough*)

   Personal Anecdote: Jimmy Mac—A Violent Way of Life* - 21

Chapter 5   Liverpool Clubs: The Scene Of The Crime 27

   Plate 5:   **The Harlems at the Cavern** (*courtesy Mindscaffolding*)

Chapter 6   Liverpool Music & The Irish 43

   Plate 6:   **The Irish Center, Liverpool** (*courtesy Mindscaffolding*)

Chapter 7   Drugs & Rock 'n Roll—Opening For The Beatles.................... 49

   Plate 7:   **John Lennon's Statue by Arthur Dooley** (*courtesy Mindscaffolding*)

   Personal Anecdote: Opening For The Beatles—Disaster Strikes* - 55

Chapter 8   The South Discovers Liverpool 67

   Plate 8:   **Beatle Street Sculpture by Arthur Dooley** (*courtesy Mindscaffolding*)

Chapter 9   The Lure Of America 81

   Plate 9:   **Ray Charles and Kingsize Taylor** (*courtesy Teddy Taylor*)

Chapter 10   Subculture and Pub Culture 87

   Plate 10: **The Baltic Fleet Pub, Liverpool** (*courtesy Mindscaffolding*)

   Personal Anecdote: It's O.K., I'm With The Band* - 94

Chapter 11   Pre-Beatles England & Class 101

   Plate 11: **Montage by Author** (*author's collection and courtesy Liverpool Libraries & Information Services*)

   Personal Anecdote: An Afternoon Session, Circa 1963, The Cavern* - 114

Chapter 12   A City Of Characters... 121

   Plate 12: **Montage by Author** (*Author's collection*)

Chapter 13   Sexual Attitudes, Mirth & Mayhem 133

   Plate 13: **Sir Jacob Epstein's Statue 'Liverpool Resurgent'** (*courtesy Mindscaffolding*)

Chapter 14   Football, Humor & Violence 143

Plate 14: **Riversdale Football Team** *(Author's collection)*

Chapter 15   Death & Madness In Liverpool 151

Plate 15: **Psychiatric Patterns** *(Author's collection)*

Personal Anecdote: Liverpool South Psychiatric Annex, The Acute Ward* - 160

Chapter 16   Crime As Play 167

Plate 16: **Up the Pole by Karl Hughes**

Chapter 17   Crime As Crime 171

Plate 17: **Kids** *(courtesy Margaret Ainscough)*

Personal Anecdote: The Great Candy Robbery: A Fully Felonious Event With A Modicum of Luck* - 173

Chapter 18   The Fey Quality Of The Celts 183

Plate 18: **Brendan McCormack and Lute** *(courtesy Colin Thorpe)*

Chapter 19   Liverpool Blacks 193

Plate 19: **A Liverpool Policeman** *(courtesy Tony Myers)*

Personal Anecdote: A Black Odyssey: From Lightest Coffee to Deepest Black* - 203

Chapter 20   The Blues & Liverpool 223

Plate 20: **Black and White Guitar** *(Author's collection)*

Chapter 21   The Slave Trade: Liverpool & Bristol 231

Plate 21: **Slave and Liver Building** *(Author's collection)*

Personal Anecdote: Bristol, Scrumpy & The Blues* - 234

Chapter 22   American Blacks & Liverpool Whites 239

Plate 22: **Chubby Checker and Kingsize Taylor** *(courtesy Teddy Taylor)*

Chapter 23   The American Presence In Europe 249

Plate 23: **American G.Is Arriving in Liverpool, 1942** *(courtesy The Imperial War Museum)*

Chapter 24   I Meet Little Richard & The Rolling Stones 265

Plate 24: **Little Richard and the The Roadrunners, a Liverpool group** *(courtesy Dave Williams)*

Personal Anecdote: Where Were You In '62? Little Richard Meets Two Liverpool Louts—And Smiles* - 267

Chapter 25   Strange Connections: Our Theme 273

Plate 25: **Montage by Author**

End Note   A Plea 280

Plate 26: **Liverpool Kids** *(courtesy Michael A. Joseph)*

Notes

Bibliography

*All personal anecdotes are courtesy of the book, *Tales of a Liverpool Lad* by P. Willis-Pitts

Introduction

"Liverpool is the pool of life."
Carl Jung

The details which form this book are drawn from my childhood in the Irish ghetto of Liverpool 8 and my first-hand experience of the Beatles and the rise of the Mersey Sound. Typical of my background, I was totally unaware of politics and the social movements which were taking place around me. However, after spending 18 years in the USA and getting myself two degrees, I now possess two languages: that of the street; and that of the educated researcher. The truth is, it is the language of the street which best illustrates the theme of this book. But by itself, though colorful, that would not communicate the message. So you will find the book is laid out in more or less alternating chapters: a "learned" chapter of social research is followed immediately by a real-life "street" anecdote from actual experience which fleshes out the more studied chapter.

When I first wrote the "street" anecdotes, modesty as well as self-preservation made me write in the third person—partially to conceal the identity of the not-so-innocent. My publisher persuaded me to change these anecdotes to the first person for the sake of the reader, and I do hope it doesn't come across as pure egoism. Some readers may find the language, the sex and the violence in this book disturbing. I cannot help this. It is not gratuitous. As black comedians from Richard Pryor to Chris Rock have demonstrated, violence, sex and obscenity are part of the ghetto experience—and you cannot enter into a description of ghetto life without them. Why this should be so is a basic tenet of this book. The fact remains that some of the world's finest music and humor have sprung unexpectedly from the most sordid conditions, whether it be in Liverpool, Harlem or Watts. This somewhat original format is an attempt to show how two very different oppressed ethnic groups on opposite sides of the globe "made a way out of no way" and, in doing so, changed the history of the world.

America and England

Even in the '60s, it would seem that America and England were very far apart. After all, America had been founded by rebels who would not knuckle under to the demands of religious persecution, and from the first historic Thanksgiving in Plymouth, Massachusetts in 1621, Americans have made their own way in the world.

In the '60s, as a Liverpool-Irish kid raised in a slum, the hows and whys of politics evaded me—except that there was little love in my community for the 5% of the ruling class that decreed that our thick accents were "common"—and so were we. As an adult, I read a little, researched a little into American history, and what I found was absolutely stunning.

The fact which bowled me over was the discovery that the poor whites in Liverpool had so much in common with the blacks in America. This extended to speech, aspirations, dress, habits, crime, culture and more. It was then I realized that the spark of life that had sprung up in the black ghettos of America and leapt across the Atlantic to ignite the Liverpool Beat was no accident. Usually it is the differences that are seen when English and American cultures are compared, but here was viable proof that the similarities are overwhelming.

The tale told in this musical history stretches far beyond Liverpool Rock or the Beatles. It is an ode to the fact that the human spirit, like boiling tar, will not be confined. And if you try to contain it, it will ooze from unforseen cracks or, even more dramatically, burst out from hidden crevices until, one day, the entire lid will blow off, spraying the stuff everywhere. It's hot, messy, scalding, but it's Life. And it won't be contained—else, beware.

The Main Theme

The conclusions and findings in this book are absolutely original. They have not, to my knowledge, been reproduced elsewhere. On reading this account, African-Americans, Beatles' fans and music aficionados will be exposed to a number of unexpected twists in the Beatles' tale, not the least being the relationship between American Affirmative Action, President Kennedy and Carl Jung, the Swiss psychiatrist.

What, you may ask, does Carl Jung have to do with the Beatles?

The answer is: quite a lot.

And by way of a brief explanation, we have to pay a visit to early '60s' Mathew Street, the home of the Cavern, the heartbeat of Beatle music...

In The Beginning
Was Mathew St

1

In The Beginning Was Mathew Street

On this damp Sunday morning in the early '60s, Mathew Street is quiet. Light from a grayish sky filters between the chasm of the narrow alley. On the right is a pub, The Grapes, not yet recovered from the excesses of the night before. To the left, on the opposite of the street is a narrow cellar doorway surrounded by crushed cigarette packets and empty drink cartons.

The serenity of the morning belies the hordes of fans, beehive-haired girls, musicians and hangers-on who crowded in a long line the previous night to catch the evening's rock session. Yes, this is the Cavern, the center of Liverpool rock.

Though the street is empty today, it will not be on Monday morning. Mathew Street, set in the heart of the business district, is a working street. The Cavern is but a cellar in a tall warehouse which is functional—an integral part of Liverpool's seaport life. Tomorrow, laborers will sweat to unload bales of goods from numerous trucks: apples; togo[1] from the West Indies; peanuts for the soap factories. Exotic goods transported by ship from the world over will be hauled onto the loading bays and stored in the high, echoing warehouses.

Further down the street is a puzzling sight. A building with an odd sign—*The Liverpool School of Language, Music, Dream and Pun*—and, alongside it, a statue set in the wall. Almost a shrine, it is dedicated to Carl Jung, the psychiatrist. The inscription reads: 'Liverpool is the pool of life'.

This odd proximity of the Cavern and the Jung Center is no coincidence. It stems from one of the strangest facts behind the Beatles' story—and is a crucial point in this account.

When The Truth Is Stranger Than Fiction

Carl Jung, the Swiss psychiatrist, revolutionized the world with his theories of symbols and the spiritual nature of man's psyche. He was born in 1875 and died in 1961, just as the Beatles were arriving. The existence of the the Liverpool School of Language, Music, Dream and Pun so close to the heart of Liverpool rock springs from a most extraordinary event. *Though Jung never ever went to Liverpool, he dreamed of it.* The dream was prophetic—as though he foresaw the rise of the Beatles:

I had a dream. I found myself in a dirty, sooty city. It was night and winter; and dark and raining. I was in Liverpool. The various quarters of the city were arranged radially around the square. In the center was a round pool; in the middle of it, a small island. While everything around it was obscured by rain, fog, smoke and dimly-lit darkness, the little island blazed with sunlight. On it stood a single tree; a magnolia in a shower of reddish blossoms. It was as though the tree stood in the sunlight and were, at the same time, the source of light   Everything was extremely unpleasant; black and opaque—just as I felt then. But I had a vision of unearthly beauty ... and that's why I was able to live at all. Liverpool is 'the pool of life'.[2]

Courtesy Mindscaffolding

A close-up of Carl Jung's statue in Mathew Street, early '60s

Jung's incredible statement found a strange echo in Alan Ginsberg, the American beat poet who, in 1963, visited Liverpool. He went to The Cracke Pub, The Philharmonic Pub, The Hope Hall club, haunts of the Beatles, the unemployed, the hopeless and hopeful—places we shall visit further in the course of our journey. Ginsberg, author of Howl and other such seminal beat works, made a remarkable statement: *"Liverpool,"* he said, *"is the center of consciousness of the universe."*

This may seem an odd start to a Beatles' book but, as the heading says, the truth is stranger than fiction. And this is what the two and a half years of research which formed this book revealed:

There was a tide of events set in motion by the great atrocity of the seventeenth century when thousands of Africans were torn from their tribes and sent to loneliness, despair and even death across the reaches of the ocean as slaves. A subjugated race, they could only express themselves in one way—through music. And the Blues were born.

Jung has said that the creative expression of any culture, like its dreams, reveals what he calls the 'collective unconscious' of that culture—and, of course, in this case, the Blues is about repression, pain and solitude.

In England there were no black slaves. They weren't needed. British society was still feudal; in other words, run by an aristocratic regime which used the lower classes as their own "God-given" slaves. After World War II, this aristocratic system began to weaken. Thus, just as the poor whites were throwing off their shackles in England, so were the former black slaves being emancipated in America through Civil Rights.

Courtesy Mindscaffolding
Carl Jung's statue set in the wall of the Jungian Center, in the 60s

A spark leapt across the Atlantic in the form of black music and was adopted by the British "subjects" as their own newfound expression.

Author's collection
Author outside the Cavern, Mathew Street, 1964

Author's collection
The Cavern Doorway, early '60s

The fact is, the atrocity of subjugation, white or black, is an event that is still rolling through the second millennium, and Jung talked about it like this:

What seems to be a wholly senseless heaping up of single, haphazard occurrences because we pay attention only to single events and their particular causes, is, for primitive man, a completely logical sequence of omens and of happenings indicated by them. IT IS A FATEFUL OUTBREAK OF DEMONIC POWER SHOWING ITSELF IN A THOROUGHLY CONSISTENT WAY.[3]

The "fateful outbreak of demonic power" is no less than the cry of human spirit—a cry reverberating around the world in Watts, in Kosovo, in Belfast, in Bosnia. The human spirit bursting out from its confines like scalding, black tar.

The four Beatles were being propelled forward on the crest of a movement they could not feel, could not see. The seed of dissent, hope and pain which was carried within black American music found its roots in the poverty and deprivation of 1960's Liverpool. And, incredibly, history suddenly took a right-angle turn.

Courtesy Mindscaffolding

The Liverpool School of Language, Music, Dream and Pun, early '60s

Courtesy Mindscaffolding

Carl Jung's statue as it is today in Mathew Street

In fact, the unique character of Liverpool is not just the *background* against which these events took place but an essential ingredient. Just as conditions in Harlem, Watts and Little Rock formed the background to the African-American character, so the city of Liverpool itself is a main protagonist, even a hero. Which is why the book is called *Liverpool, the Fifth Beatle.* You will see its sooty figure lurking behind every line of this book.

But it is time.

Our hero has waited long enough. So lets go and meet him. Yes, 'him'. Our hero could never be a 'her'. What lady would clad herself in filthy rags, dab her face with grime, and greet the world dressed in perpetual shades of gray?

6

Look For The Girl With The Sun In Her Eyes

2

Look For The Girl With The Sun In Her Eyes

...And She's Gone

Liverpool: Liva...pool. *From the Anglo-Saxon word, liva —*
dirty. Hence, dirty pool.

Oxford English Dictionary

Roofs. Row upon row of slate roofs merging with the monochromes of a gray landscape. Smoky gray; dark gray; charcoal gray. Slate gray.

Slate. A hard, dour material imbued with all the elements of a wintry sky.

Just fifty miles from Liverpool, the slate is quarried in the mines of North Wales. Half a mile below the surface, dour-faced Welshmen sit, as did their fathers before them, in a shadowy, flickering cavern, ill-lit like the mines of hell. With incredibly deft movements, these men tap the parallel cleavage planes: one tap, two taps, and a piece of the very earth, compressed by aeons of time, splits perfectly, opening like a giant, gray moth into double wings.

And so it is that the roof slate is manufactured on the very spot where Time formed it with its slow, slow grind. From these stygian chambers, the slate is hauled up into the bright blues and greens of the Welsh countryside; a veritable portion of underground darkness exposed to the light, destined to mantle the roofs of Liverpool houses.

The acid-polluted air nibbles voraciously at the brickwork, blackening it, shredding it with a constant, fretful grind. But not the slate. The slate, itself a subterranean creature of smoke and

Roofs of Liverpool, early '60s

A burnt-out Corn Exchange, Liverpool, after a 1941 bombing raid by the Luftwaffe

darkness, seems inviolable. Rather, it is an ally to the ashen air, and, bleeding what light there is, transmutes it, gray reflecting gray.

Liverpool 8. Ringo and John were born here and all four Beatles were to pursue their hopes, dreams and aspirations never very far from this area. They drank here; played here; worked here; and they were all schooled here, both formally and informally. Particularly Ringo; in that school which has been called euphemistically 'The School of Hard Knocks'.

It is a less than auspicious breeding-ground for such talent: Rows of dirty, terraced houses squashed shoulder to shoulder, flanking torn and badly-surfaced roads; alleys rank with bad sewers, dog turds and rats; whilst above it all rear the grim monoliths of chimneys gazing down in blank, brooding silence.

Huskisson Street, Canning Street: once home to poet Adrian Henry, painters, artists, musicians, would-be poets. A splash of color, a swirl of bright, bright words nestling in their hearts, they work their inner magic surrounded by the vast, peeling edifices of the once-gracious Victorian homes of the wealthy.

In cavernous, ill-heated rooms, the artists paint, play and write, teasing a little sunshine into surroundings that are slowly crumbling into sordid disarray: soot-blackened facades; ornate, rusted railings; grimy windows; and the slate, always the slate.

Behind grayish, lace curtains, watchful eyes calculate, compute and file. For Huskisson Street is also the home of prostitutes; blacks; poor whites; the unemployed; students.

In 1941, acting on orders from Hitler, Liverpool, a major seaport, was bombed mercilessly—a terrible and frightening period which left thousands homeless and even more dead and wounded. The scars still show.

Here and there whole sections of the street are missing, like the blackened stumps of diseased and rotted teeth. There is little life on these vacant lots: the crumbling carcass of a pram; the wheels of a rusted bike; and a few brave tufts of green poking through the rubble. And even the grass

Huskisson Street, Liverpool 8, the Black Area of Liverpool
(picture taken from author's doorstep, quite coincidentally)

is not a true green, as though it has been smeared with a film of dirty, gray powder that chokes the light and life from it. But still, somehow, is grows.

Soot-blackened facades; ornate, rusted railings; grimy windows; doors covered with corrugated iron; panes of glass replaced by squares of brown cardboard; and the slate, always the slate.

Liverpool, it can be seen, is extremely photogenic, but the reality does not match the drama of this monochromatic photo-essay—the reality is grim, shabby and sordid.

To the world, it would seem an unlikely beginning for the Beatles, the image and voice of an era. But not to a Liverpudlian. It is a known fact that dirty, impoverished Liverpool 8 periodically gave birth to poetry, music, dance and laughter, rather like spring flowers in a dung-heap.

Given the grimness of these surroundings, rock 'n roll was a ray of light in the gloom. Nightly, hordes of teenagers would make their way to the clubs of Liverpool, just as the blacks in New York or Detroit would go to their own "jive joints" and rock the night away fueled on drugs or alcohol. A brief respite from the early wake-up calls and grueling shift jobs in bleak factories or the relentless lines of the assembly plants.

And, of course, key figures in these nightly rock sessions were the Beatles themselves.

During the 1960s, I was one of a group of emaciated youths loosely termed "beats" who, in a period of widespread unemployment, haunted Liverpool's rock clubs and underground dens.

Courtesy Mindscaffolding

A Building in Liverpool 8

The Cavern and the Iron Door were the main venues. For a brief time, a motley group of musicians worked at the Iron Door, a cellar club in the basement of a six-storey derelict warehouse. Not only did we work and play there, with nowhere else to go we even lived there. We rarely saw any sunlight. We slept all day and worked the club at night in search of the Holy Grail—the rush of adrenaline that is raw rock played with gusty passion. This is an eyewitness account of one such night—a night when the Beatles were playing.

The Beatles In Close-Up

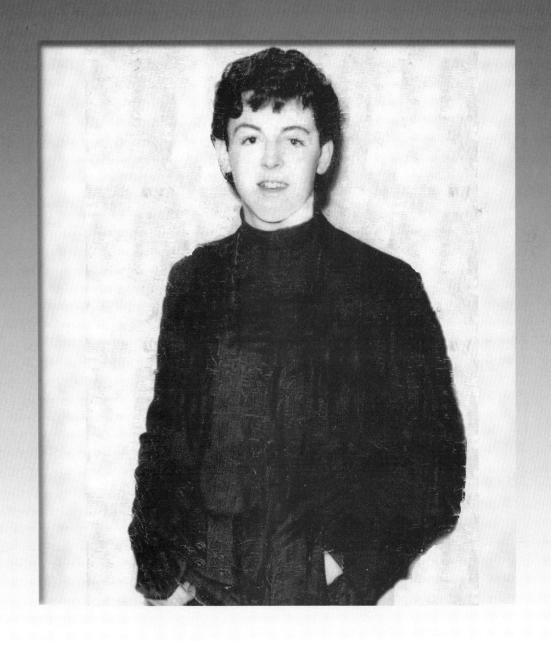

Courtesy Quentin Hughes
Early warehouse, Canning Street, Liverpool 8

A Hard Day's Night

—A Personal Anecdote—

The Iron Door Club, Liverpool, 1962: 9 p.m.

Imutter in my sleep, tossing and turning as something nudges my head.

I roll over on the dirty pile of blankets. My back encounters a loose board and I slowly come awake. Something nudges into my head again and, irritated, I open my eyes and realize where I am: above the Iron Door club sleeping on a makeshift mattress.

The warehouse floor is in darkness, but a feeble light filters in from the open warehouse door set in the wall. With its gray gibbet crane poking out into the ceiling, it resembles a wanly lit scaffold.

The light cuts across the dirty floor in a swathe, etching the ghostly silhouettes of the twelve-by-twelve pillars that recede off into the gloom at regular intervals, supporting the low-slung roof with its rusting eye-hooks, worm-drives and metal brackets, reminiscent of some mysterious function when the warehouse was a working unit.

The something nudges my head again. Awareness dawns: it's sound. Foggy brained, I recognize it for what it is: the note of a single E string amplified to horrendous proportions. It shears through the floor boards at my feet and soars through the air like a laser, slicing through metal, glass, wood, solids and liquids with equal disdain.

Courtesy Dave Forshaw

Paul and George on stage at St. John's Hall

My dull brain transfixed by the horrific volume, I have a brief hallucinatory vision of the note soaring through the roof, into the sky and streaming across the universe to boil the crust off some planet in a distant star system. Then I suddenly realize that what I am hearing is the riff from Ray Charles' *What'd I Say* played on the metallic twanging E string of an over-amplified guitar

The music pounds through the floor accompanied by vast, belly-quivering resonances which are the muffled notes of a bass guitar.

I realize I have overslept. The day has gone and the night begun; the music denotes the beginning of the evening session in the cellar two floors below me.

I yawn, stretch, and stagger to the locked doorway at the top of the stairs. I slide back the bolt. The noise from the floor immediately below hits me redoubled, accompanied by laughter, clinking glasses, the shrill sounds of girls' voices.

Zombie-like, I descend, staggering down the stairs like an extra from *The Night of the Living Dead*. On the ground floor, the babble from the crowd is incessant but not sufficient to drown out

the music. I push my way, dazed, through the crowd of brightly-clad girls and the motley-dressed youths; the evening's rock audience. I head for the open doorway which will take me to the cellar

I clatter down the crude, wooden cellar stairs, glad of the gloom on this lower level, and pause halfway to peer across the gloom, over the bobbing heads of the crowd to the brightly-lit stage on the other side of the dance floor.

Paul McCartney, his face bathed in sweat, has heaved himself up on the low slung rafters above the stage. Both his legs are wrapped around the beam, in one hand he holds a microphone, the other hand he uses to hang like a monkey from the rafter. George, clad in the ubiquitous black Hamburg leathers, is grinning broadly at Paul's antics. He has become the de facto Bass player, playing Paul's fiddle-bass upside down, while John chops out the vast laseresque riff on his 'ole Rickenbacker'.

In the low-ceilinged space, the noise is electrifying. Pete Best breaks into the drum beat for the call-and-response section of the number, and John and George stop playing, clap their hands and scream their

Courtesy Dave Forshaw

John, Paul and George on stage at St. John's Hall

15

responses into the stand-up mike, al cappella:

"Hey - ey - ey - ey!" screams Paul from his impossible position hanging upside down.

"Hey - ey - ey - ey!" the crowd roars back.

The hairs tingle on the back of my neck and I sit down on the cellar steps to watch the action from my vantage point above the crowd.

"Aaa - aa - ah!" screams Paul, jerking himself up and down in a series of contrapuntal pullups.

"Aaa - aa - ah!" screams the crowd.

Then comes the rapid build up, each cry punctuated by a vast bludgeon from Pete Best's bass drum:

"Oooh!" (Paul)

"Oooh!" (Crowd)

"Aaah!" (Paul)

"Aaah!" (Crowd)

"Oooh - ah - ooh - ah!" screams Paul, higher and higher as the drum beat rises to the crescendo. Then he screams: "Tell me what I SAY!!"

On the word 'say', the entire band swings back into action like the clap of amplified doom. Girls scream, men roar; the entire crowd goes berserk as the cellar walls shudder under the impact of the rhythm. Still hanging upside down, Paul jerks as if he is being electrocuted; screaming his heart and lungs out in an insane, inspired motion.

Involuntarily, I jump to my feet. I have to, as the whole crowd leaps up, surging around the stage in a

Courtesy Mindscaffolding
The Iron Door Club Entrance

frenzied dance, cutting across my view. The noise is deafening; blood pounds in my ears; adrenaline spurts; my mouth goes dry. I am suddenly very awake

The number ends on a tremendous crescendo.

Paul drops down to the stage his dripping face wreathed in a boyish grin, the famous smile which is to become his trademark. There is a brief roar of approval from sweat-drenched

Author's collection
Jam At the Iron Door
Author on left wearing major Phil Everly hairstyle

IRON DOOR NEWS

IRON DOOR CLUB · 13, TEMPLE STREET, LIVERPOOL

No. 2   MARCH, 1964

WILLKOMMEN ZU DEN NACHTLOKAL EISENTÜR!

(OR IF YOUR GERMAN ISN'T TOO GOOD.....)

WELCOME TO THE IRON DOOR CLUB!

THIS week-end the Iron Door Club is proud to welcome more than 70 members of the Famous Star Club in Hamburg to Liverpool, and in particular to their own club.

For several years there has been a strong link between the two clubs, and several well-known Liverpool beat groups who started their careers here at the Iron Door have played long seasons at the Star Club.

Plans for this visit started several months ago when members of the Star Club started clamouring for a visit to Liverpool—home of the big beat—and this is it.

During their stay they will be attending the all nighter here at the club and seeing most of the city sights. Many of our own club members have agreed to act as hosts for the German youngsters and to show them the city over the week-end. It is also likely that the Lord Mayor of Liverpool will be according a civic welcome to our visitors during the week-end.

Biggest news of all is that in a few weeks time there will be a return visit by Iron Door Club members to the beat clubs of West Germany in Hamburg and probably to a show in Berlin.

Details of the trip are not yet finalised, but it is known that the total cost will only be about £12—against £36 for the normal air fare.

Places on the charter flight will be strictly limited, and in fairness to our members they can only be allocated on a first come first served basis.

This really is the chance hundreds have been waiting for at a knock-down bargain price, so if you are interested (and who isn't?) leave your full name and address at the Club Office so that your name can be put on the list.

In the meantime—welcome from the Iron Door to all our German friends. We have been looking forward to having you with us, and hope you have a fabulous week-end.

Courtesy Harry Prytherch

Owing to Liverpool and the Beatle's flirtation with Hamburg's rock clubs, Hamburg was seen as a sister city. Events in the Iron Door were sometimes planned to bring the two "Rock Cities" closer.

crowd. Then the crowd disintegrates, as in a single, concerted action every male runs for the stairs where I am sitting. I just manage to lever myself up and over the stair rail and drop to the floor with an alacrity born of self survival, as they stampede up the steps to slake their merciless thirst in the bar.

As the last footstep dies away I turn to look at the band on the stage. Pete Best is preoccupied, fiddling away with some screw fitting on his drum kit oblivious to the others.

Paul has retrieved his fiddle bass from George and is leaning close to John. Their black leathers are dull and shiny in the stage lights. Paul says something to him, his face shining, his boyish smile even broader. John tosses his head and guffaws loudly, a horselike, braying laugh that is very familiar. It sounds dirty, brazen; it probably is. George smiles wanly although he could not have heard the joke. He fingers his black Gretsche as if to attract their attention and a plays a few bars of Chet Atkins' One Mint Julep. John pulls a comic face and plays a brief and stumbling accompaniment. A group of girls with impossible beehive hairstyles crowd around the stage blocking my view of the four lads.

I yawn. I am fully awake now. I saunter up the stairs to have a pint of beer for breakfast.

I've just had the doubtful honor of being awoken by the loudest alarm clock in the world.

Pushing through the crowd, I nod to Pete Best who has obviously dodged up the side stairs to the bar before me. Pete smiles; he is handsome, quietly self-assured. Little does Pete know he is soon to be fired and will miss his chance of becoming a universal icon.

Author's collection

The Iron Door, Early '60s
Vinnie Ishmael (center) was one of the few guitarists of color in Liverpool
Author seen on far right leaning on piano

Bobbing on the waves of history that were rippling through Liverpool unseen, little did anybody at the Iron Door know the fate that was destined for these very ordinary lads from Liverpool. On this night, Ringo was somewhere else smacking out a heavy 4/4 beat behind Rory Storm and The Renegades, little aware of his fate and future just beyond the horizon.

In retrospect, this seems like a Golden era, but it must be realized that the conditions which gave rise to such a bright, brazen burst of energy were not always desirable.

Affluence and comfort do not tend towards monumental works of art, music, literature. The real blood, bones and guts of artistic achievement seems to be deprivation, whether it be the colorful creativity of a Bronx Italian or the passionate outbursts of a New York Jew.

In an astute observation, mythologist Joseph Campbell said: "Violence is the shadow of sentimentality."

What does it mean? Why is there so much violence in a subjected race whether it be Italians, blacks or East L.A. chicanos? The answer is grim and simple: in any subject race, self esteem is fragile and it can only be established by resorting to a very Darwinian principle—the act of domination—which expresses itself physically. Sadly, those at the bottom can only ease their burden by violence on each other.

Life In The Streets

Life In The Streets: Violence

Growing up in Watts, Liverpool 8, Northern Ireland or Harlem is an education. But the "educatees" never know it until they have left. The conditions in which they live are, for the inhabitants, normalcy—no matter how extreme.

I slept in the same bedroom as my parents and my brother, who was three years younger. My two sisters, being in their teens, occupied the only other bedroom. We had neither hot water nor inside plumbing or toilets—and, at the time, never knew the difference.

The weeks' washing was done in vast, commercial "washhouses" provided by the authorities. In order to bathe, we had to go to a communal bath house and pay a small fee.

Violence was the norm by day and, more especially, by night when it was fueled by alcohol.

Oddly enough—an indication that the pressures of ghetto life transcend race or creed—I once experienced a very similar event to that which follows in a village in India, of all places. The point being, poverty means there is no escaping one's neighbors

Courtesy Reflections

Liverpool Womenfolk Returning from the Communal Wash House, early 1960

Jimmy Mac: A Violent Way of Life
—A Personal Anecdote—

The Outside Toilet

Jimmy Mac is surprisingly small; a square jaw, dark, wavy hair, bright eyes; clean-shaven. Undressed, his body is white; he never sunbathes. His arms seem to be the most prominent feature: they are long, almost Neanderthal. His body is the spare, taut body of a laborer, with none of the belly fat that denotes the heavy-drinking Irish trench digger.

The middle brother of a family of six, he lives opposite me in a cramped two-up two-down house in a gray, terraced street in the heart of south Liverpool. His occupation: coal man. He hefts bags of coal from the lorries eight hours a day, plunging them down the opening in front of the house cellars, to fuel the grate-fires of these primitive houses.

When he returns from work at night, he is coated in black soot. He scrubs himself clean at a brown-glazed sink—with cold water. Clean, or thereabouts, he dresses: a blue suit; narrow-ankled trousers; a white shirt; thick, crepe-soled shoes; long, well-oiled side-burns. He sweeps his hair into a greasy quiff and heads off to the Pub.

Jimmy, unassuming though he may be, is the most violent person in south Liverpool. In a city where violence is the norm, he is the 'cock' of Liverpool 8. Nightly he is challenged. Gangs come from other areas: the Bullring; the Docks; Scotland Road where the police have to walk in threes after dark. It is like being the fastest

on the draw. But though he is challenged frequently, he is never beaten. In the ghetto, there is no privacy, and I know this as fish knows fish in tide. I know the stories, I've heard the tales:

Jimmy lounges in the shadows of a derelict lot waiting for his girlfriend. He tenses as a couple cross the pavement and wend through the darkened mounds of rubble and the rotting carcasses of prams. He hears the tinkle of laughter; sees the flash of blonde hair. It is his girl. He tenses, picks up a house brick and beats the man into unconsciousness. Then he sets about two of the man's friends who came to his aid with such frenzy that they flee. The other man lays on the ground bleeding from head wounds, unconscious, perhaps brain damaged.

Alone with Jimmy in his backyard, I am awed as I

The Bullring, Liverpool 8

Courtesy Margaret Ainscough

Women selling fruit and vegetables in Liverpool, early '60s

recall the stories about him. But I am also puzzled: he seems nice; a quiet, soft-spoken person.. I am ten years old, he 19. I am a thin boy, all gangly arms, knobby knees and bony elbows. We are in Jimmy Mac's backyard working on a makeshift doghouse together.

The yard is white-washed and littered with half-finished projects—a rabbit hutch; a pigeon pen; half-sawn two-by-fours; three-quarter ply boards. It smells of piss and dog turds. This doesn't bother me, as all backyards in Liverpool 8 smell of piss and dog turds.

I help Jimmy make the dog house. Grave at age ten with the burden of my task, I comply to Jimmy's soft requests as efficiently as I can, aware of the awesome figure at my side—the Ruler of Liverpool 8.

Oblivious to my awe, Jimmy holds down a piece of wood with one foot and nails it with methodical, even strokes. His movements are precise, his hands nimble. I obey his commands quickly, a little fearful in case I do something wrong. So, naturally, I do. Wielding the hammer clumsily, I bend and mash a cheap nail, splitting the wood. Confused, fearful, I drop the hammer, my heart pounding, waiting for recriminations.

Jimmy does not bat an eyelid. Quietly, he takes the hammer, shows me how to swing it: "Use the weight of the head, hold the nail. Tap it once; set it; keep yer eye on the nail, not the hammer. There (swing, smack) it's easy." The nail is buried to the hilt in the wood. "Now you do it."

I try, fumble, try again and succeed. There is no applause, but there were no recriminations either. I breathe a secret sigh of relief. With an intense concentration, I follow every word, every gesture of Jimmy's, and the dog house is built without further mishap

That night.

I lie in bed on top of a bunk fashioned by my father. The room is dark. No shadows play on the ceilings—there are no street lights. No cars pass on the cobblestones outside. The room smells of piss. It always does; my younger brother in the bunk below is perpetually enuretic.

It is late—11 p.m. I should be asleep. Everyone else is. We are four in the room: two brothers, mother, father. My sisters sleep together in the only other bedroom. I can hear my father's deep breathing and the funny little smacking noises my mother makes with her lips as she snores. My brother is quiet, but he is asleep; he is always asleep, except when I prod him into wakefulness.

It is not quiet outside. It is Saturday night. It is never quiet on Saturday night. From the river comes the sonorous drone of a ship's fog horn. In the distance, the raucous "wah, wah, wah" of a police siren and the long, drawn-out "claaang" of shunting trains in the goods-yard at Edge Hill.

And the screams. Always the screams.

A woman's voice rises in the air—a stream of sibilant invective: "You bastard! You bastard!! You bastard!!" It is interspersed with the deeper grunt of a man's voice. Other voices are raised. There is a rending sound, a brief silence, then it starts all over.

I study the underside of the bunk above in the gloom, barely listening to the sounds but aware of them, comfortable in their familiarity.

Suddenly, a guitar chord cuts through the night air outside, and my senses are set athrall. It is magic; a drunken beauty that I cannot find words for, though strange emotions curdle and clutch at my heart.

The sound is just audible. It is an A chord strummed with more gusto than skill, as two home-bound drunks sing with all the joie de vivre of their alcohol-inspired hearts, Guy Mitchell's current hit:

> "I never felt more like singing the Blues
> 'Cos I never thought that I'd ever lose
> Your love, dear,
> Why do you treat me this way?"

My neck tingles, shivers run down my spine as the chords bite through the dank air like blades of light, dispelling the gloom.

The revelers pass beneath the window and the ratch-ratch-ratch of the guitar reaches its loudest. The guitar strum is executed with all the force and skill of a rotating crankshaft, but for me it is Nirvana. I drink in every nuance, half-raising myself on one elbow in the dark until the sound grows faint in the distance and then fades completely.

I sigh. The gloom crashes back in, but it is not silent. A woman screams, this time just

Courtesy Mindscaffolding

Berkley Street
19th century mansions of wealthy merchants have been made into apartments for poor blacks and whites

23

below my window. My ears prick up as the scream is closely followed by a staccato, guttural voice that is, without a doubt, Jimmy Mac's.

"No! No, Jimmy!! Don't—please don't!!" sobs the girl.

"Whore!!!" hisses Jimmy. His voice, familiar to me from this afternoon's work session together, is now edged with the razor sharpness of insane rage.

I clutch the sheets, stiff and tense. In my mind's eye I see deft hands, a hammer, hear another Jimmy Mac, quiet, sure: "Use the weight of the head, hold the nail, tap it once, set it (swing, smack)." The memory is strangely at odds with the savagery being enacted outside. I shiver in the dark and lay back listening intently.

Another scream of rage fractures the gloom. I squirm beneath the sheets wondering how this voice can belong to the quiet man who taught me how to nail wood this afternoon, an eternity ago.

In the dark, the room freezes. My mother stops making the smacking noises; my father stops snoring; only my brother sleeps on. In a concert of stunned silence, the family listens, each knowing that we are all listening.

There is a crash, then another, punctuated by Jimmy's screaming invective. The scene forms itself in my mind: Jimmy is picking up milk bottles from the doorsteps, lining them across the street like toy soldiers and venting his mad rage by decimating them with swift kicks. The kicks and crashes are laced with oaths. The girl's voice rises higher:

"Jimmy!! I didn't!! I didn't!!!"

"It's not my bleedin' kid!!!" screams Jimmy.

There is a brief pause. Jimmy Mac has run out of milk bottles to kick. Then the woman screams. This time it has a different quality—I don't know what, but I sense it is different. There is a dull thud; then another and another. The screams are now whimpers coinciding with the thuds.

The tension in the bedroom elongates, seems to swell around us all. I am dimly aware that no one is breathing—not me, nor my mother or father—as the girl's quiet whimpers of pain drift upwards as soft as torn lace, yet piercing the air like shards of broken glass. Jimmy's voice explodes, low and guttural, with each kick, with each whimper: "Whore! Whore! Whore!"

Eventually the noises stop, and this time, it's the entire street that holds its breath in dumb shock. No windows are thrown up. No doors fly open. This is Jimmy Mac. The street listens to this new outrage. No one will interfere. It has happened before; it will happen again.

There is a moment of aching silence outside suddenly broken by the rattling of a key in a lock; a brief curse; a front door is flung open; there is a dull thud, a heavy slithering sound; the front door slams shut. And then there is silence—a true silence, as heavy as lead. I let my breath out with a gasp. I hear my parents do the same.

Eventually, I fall into a restless sleep.

In the dim hours of the morning, I'm awoken again. I mutter and turn sleepily. Then I

The Chung-Wa Supermaket, Liverpool 8

Courtesy Sugar Deen

The Valentinos, a typical Liverpool do-wop group, early '60s
From left: Vinnie Ishmael, Sugar Deen, Tony Fayal and Laurence Areety

realize what has awoken me: Music.

Four young blacks returning home after a night of drinking and charas[1] at one of the local shabeens[2] are singing—stoned and drunk. This music is different from the staccato, mechanical grind of the strummed guitar.

I know that the boys are dancing; I can tell by their voices, the shuffling of their heels on the pavement echoing off the sooty, brick walls. They are dancing not simply out of joy, but as an act of provocation against the whites sleeping in the houses about them. I have seen them do it often, and I see them again in my mind's eye as they swagger along the narrow street, bopping, clicking fingers, cool, cool, proclaiming their message to the John Bull ofay white raas-clat[3] bastards in their beds. "This is how we do it," is their unspoken proclamation, "Wake up whitey." They dance, sway and pout; all shaven, ugly heads, muscular shoulders and aggro. They never miss a beat. Their music is another weapon in the armory of black supremacy.

I am moved, enthralled even, seeing them with closed eyes.

> "Little darlin' (boop wup up a doop bop)
> How I love you (boop wup up a doop bop)
> Oh I love only you ......"

Their voices rise in perfect three-part harmony. Two of them keep up the contrapuntal off-beat bop-wops with perfect timing, clapping their hands. The third begins to wail.

Poised, macho, hip, confrontative—the music is all of these things. There is something else, too, something which I do not have words for. At the time, it is only an feeling in my breast. Just as a soaring eagle does not know the poetry of its own motion, the four blacks do not even realize it themselves—it's beautiful. Yes, above all, the music is beautiful. And despite their aggression, so are they.

Though I don't know this word, my chest is open, raw with Jimmy Mac's violence. I am vulnerable to the sensual assault of the music. I strain my ears until the last de-wop fades into the distance.

Not knowing why or how, a sadness wells in my bruised, child's heart and I begin to cry softly. I cry myself to sleep, careful not to let my parents hear.

25

Epilogue:

Jimmy Mac's girlfriend recovered in the hospital. But she lost the baby. No surprise, as that's what Jimmy intended: despite the number of kicks, her face and legs were unscathed.

I did grow up and become a musician. I played in many bands, met many famous people. My origins—this peculiar mixture of brutal violence and sensuality—were essentially those of the Beatles, in particular Ringo, who was born just streets away.

Ringo was to pursue the same aimless, disenfranchised existence as I had, and even worked with my father as a laborer's assistant, making my Dad's tea on cold, blustery building sites in the Liverpool suburbs. It can be said that Ringo, being the most lower-class Beatle, was perhaps, more Liverpudlian than the other Beatles—although, this in itself is a misnomer, because the Beatles, themselves, represent different facets of the same city.

Courtesy Mindscaffolding

The Green Moose Cafe

Liverpool Clubs
The Scene Of The Crime

Liverpool Clubs: The Scene Of The Crime

And thus, just as I did, John, Paul, George, Ringo and Pete Best headed for the clubs in their teenage years, lured by the thrill of rock 'n roll. And it seems that when we did so, we were accompanied by almost all of the teenagers in this city of three-quarters of a million. There was definitely something afoot in the '60s.

At the time, I was a young seaman in the Merchant Marine on "coasters"—which meant my ship circled the British Isles, stopping off at the major ports. Of course, being a rocker, I would make a beeline for the nearest rock clubs. To my astonishment, being used to the plethora of clubs and groups in Liverpool, I found that there were hardly any in other cities. And those that did exist were playing instrumentals or Elvis Presley frontman clones.

The sheer number of groups in Liverpool was obviously something of an anomaly.

At the time, Bill Harry, who launched the *Mersey Beat Magazine*, was a student at the Liverpool College of Art where both John Lennon and Stuart Sutcliffe attended. He says:

> When I started the Merseybeat, I got together with Bob Wooler and we came out with a list of over 400 bands. I know that there was no other scene like it in the entire country, probably not in the whole world, and I thought it was very like New Orleans at the turn of the century.

Author's collection
Author (left) at Sea in the Merchant Marine, 1961

Author's collection
Author in the band room of the Cubik
one of the many clubs in the early '60s

A comparison of the figures for cities of commensurate size, such as Bristol or Newcastle, are significant in that there is *no* comparison. Obviously, whatever was taking place in Liverpool was not happening in the same way in other cities.

On the following page is a rough list of some of the working bands in Liverpool in the early '60s, followed by commensurate figures for Bristol.

With so many working bands, there had to be a lot of venues—and there were. The newspaper cuttings from the period illustrate just how many.

There was obviously some major factor at work here. To fully comprehend why Liverpool had so many groups and why it was they were playing such different music from that played in other cities, we have to go to the scene of the crime—Liverpool's clubs—and talk to the musicians themselves.

Some of Liverpool's Clubs in the '60s

With three hundred and fifty half-starved groups clinging to a tenacious existence in pre-fame Liverpool, music and clubs flourished and died out with the regularity of febrile mushrooms.

In the suburbs, there were many clubs: St. John's Hall; the Litherland Town Hall; the Cubik; and even Quaintways, an almost yuppie-style establishment in the lovely town of Chester nearby. In Liverpool town center was the Blue Angel run by Allan Williams, the man "who gave the Beatles away." His other not-so-genteel establishment was the Jacaranda with its tiny, dank and peeling cellar where the Beatles regularly assaulted the ears of late-night coffee drinkers.

But, undoubtedly, the king and queen of the clubs were the Cavern and the Storyville (later renamed the Iron Door), both set in darkened alleys in warehouses cradled on either side by the soaring monoliths of ancient buildings.

The Cavern, itself, originally featured mainly jazz. Trad was in and crowds of "beats" clad in bizarre clothes (one used to wear just a sack) would nightly stomp away to the happy-time music of Storyville Jazz. In comparison to the huge Iron Door, it was a small club consisting of just three low-arched chambers and a roof of dripping bricks that would have done credit to an Edgar Allen Poe tale. The Iron Door was within walking distance of the Cavern, and it occupied the first two floors of a huge building, while the

29

Some Liverpool Bands in the Early '60s

Aarons, The
Abraham & His Lot
Adam & the Sinners
Alamos, The
Alby & the Sorrals
Alibis, The
Almost Blues, The
Alphas, The
Ambassadors, The
Anzacs, The
Aristocrats, The
Arrows, The
Aztecs, The
Backbeats, The
Banshees, The
Barbara Harrison
Beatcombers, The
Beathovens, The
Beatles, The
Big Three, The
Billy Butler
Billy Kramer & the Dakotas
Black Cats, The
Black Diamonds, The
Black Knights, The
Black Velvets, The
Black, Cilla
Blackjacks, The
Blackwells, The
Blue Chips, The
Blue Diamonds, The
Blue Four, The
Blue Mountain Boys, The
Blue Notes, The
Bluegenes, The
Blues System, The
Bob Evans & the Five Shillings
Bobby & the Bachelors
Bobby Bell Rockers, The
Boot Hill Billys, The
Breakaways, The
Buddy Dean & the Teachers
Bumblies, The
Cadillacs, The
Carl Vincent & the Counts
Casey Jones & the Engineers
Cass & the Cassanovas
Cavaliers, The
Cavemen, The
Chain Gang, The
Challengers, The
Chants, The
Cheaters, The
Chentermen, The
Chessmen, The
Chick Graham & the Coasters
Cimarrons, The
Cirques, The
Citadels, The
City Beats, The
Clansmen, The
Clay Ellis & the Raiders
Clayton Squares, The
Cliff Roberts' Rockers
Climbers, The
Coins, The
Collegians, The
Columbians, The
Comets, The
Concords, The

Connoisseurs, The
Conquests, The
Conspirators, The
Corals, The
Cordes, The
Corsairs, The
Corvettes, The
Country Four, The
Creoles, The
Crescendos, The
Crossbeats, The
Croupiers, The
Crusaders, The
Cryin' Shames, The
Cy Tucker & the Friars
Dale Robers & the Jay Walkers
Daleks, The
Danny & the Asteroids
Danny & the Hi Cats
Danny Havoc & the Secrets
Danny Havoc & the Ventures
Danny Lee & his Stalkers
Dave Bell & the Bell Boys
Dealers, The
Dean Stacey & the Detonators
Deans, The
Dee & the Dynamites
Dee Fenton & the Silhouettes
Dee Young & the Pontiacs
Deerstalkers, The
Defiants, The
Del Renas, The
Delacardoes, The
Delemeres, The
Delmonts, The
Deltones, The
Demoiselles, The
Denems, The
Denis & the New Towns
Dennisons, The
Denny Seyton & the Sabres
Deputies, The
Derry Wilkie & the Others
Derry Wilkie & the Pressmen
Detours, The
Diablos, The
Dimensions, The
Dino & the Wild Fires
Diplomats, The
Downbeats, The
Dynachords, The
Earl Presont's Realms
Earl Preston & the TTs
Earl Royce & the Olympics
Earthlings, The
Easybeats, The
Eddie Lee Five, The
Eddy Dean & the Onlookers
Eddy Falcon, & the Vampires
Elektrons, The
Epics, The
Escorts, The
Excheckers, The
Executioners, The
Expressions, The
Eyes, The
Factotums, The
Falcons, The
Faron & the Tempest Tornadoes
Faron's Flamingos
FBI, The
Federal Five, The
Few, The
Fix, The
Flames, The

Flintstones, The Fontanas, The
Four Aces, The
Four Clefs, The
Four Dimensions, The
Four Jays, The
Four Just Men, The
Fourmost, The
Frank Knight & the Barons,
Freddie Starr & the Delmonts
Freddie

Starr & the Flamingos
Freddie Starr & the Midnighters
Freddie Starr & the Ventures
Fruit Eating Bears, The
Galaxies, The
Galvinizers, The
Gary B. Goode & the Hot Rods
Gay

Tones, The
Gene Day & the Jangobeats
Geoff Stacy & the Wanderers
Georgians, The
Gerry & the Pacemakers
Gerry Bach & the Beethovens
Ghost Riders, The
Gibsons, The

Globetrotters, The
Griff Parry Five, The
Group One
Groups Inc.
Gus & the Thundercaps
Gus Travis & the Midnighters
Hailers, The
Hammers, The
Hank Walters & the Dusty Road Ramblers
Harlems, The
Heralds, The
Hi Cats, The
Hi Hats, The
Hi Spots, The
Hideaways, The
Hillsiders, The
Howie Casey & the Seniors
Huntsmen, The
Hustlers, The
Ian & the Zodians
Incas, The
Inmates, The
Invaders, The
Jackobeats, The
Jaguars, The
Jenny & the Tall Boys
Jensons, The
Jet & the

Valiants
Jets, The
Johnny Apollo & the Spartans
Johnny Gus Set, The
Johnny Marlow & the Whip Chords
Johnny Paul & the Dee Jays
Johnny President & the Senators
Johnny Ringo & the Colts
Johnny Sandon & the Searchers

Johnny Tempest & the Tornadoes
Jokers, The
Kandies, The
Kansas City Five, The
Karacters, The
Karl Terry & the Cruisers
Ken Dallas & the Silhouettes
Kingpins, The
Kingsize Taylor & the Dominoes
Kinsleys, The
Kirkbys, The
Kruzads, The
Kubas, The
L'ill Three, The
Landslides, The
Lee Castle & the Barons
Lee Crombie & the Sundowners
Lee Curtis & the All Stars
Lee Paul & the Boys
Lee Shoudell & the Capitols
Liam & the Invaders
Lincolns, The
Liver Birds, The
Long & the Short, The
Mafia, The
Maraccas, The
Marescas, The
Mark Four, The
Mark Peters & the Cylones
Marlins, The
Marsden, Beryl
Masqueraders, The
Master Minds, The
Mastersounds, The
Mavericks, The
Memphis Three, The
Mersey Blue Beats, The
Mersey Five, The
Mersey Four, The
Mersey Men, The
Mersey Monsters, The
Merseybeats, The
Method, The
Michael Allen Group, The
Mike & the Explorers
Mike Byrne & the Thunderbirds

Mike Savage & the Wild Cats
Missouri Drifters, The
Mojos, The
Morockans, The
Motifs, The
Mr. Lee & Co.
Music Students, The
Musicians, The
Mustangs, The
Nameless Ones, The
Nashpool Four, The
Nocturns, The

NEWCASTLE
50 bands

LIVERPOOL
350+ bands

BIRMINGHAM
(a huge, extended metropolitan area)
100 bands

BRISTOL
30+ bands

LONDON
no figures

30

Some Popular Liverpool Groups in the Early '60s (continued):

Nomads, The
Notions, The
Ogi & the Flintstones
Others, The
Paddy, Klaus & Gibson
Paladins, The
Panthers, The
Pathfinders, The
Paul & the Diamonds
Paul Valence, & the Tremors
Pawns, The
Pete Best & the Original All Stars
Pete Best Four/Combo
Pete Picasso & the Rock Sculptors
Phantoms, The
Phil Brady & the Ranchers
Pilgrims, The
Plebs, The
Pontiacs, The
Poppies, The
Premiers, The
Press Gang, The
Pressmen, The
Profiles, The

Prowlers, The
Pyramids, The
Quarrymen, The
Quiet Ones, The
Quintones, The
Rainchecks, The
Rainmakers, The
Ramrods, The
Ray Satan & the Devils
Remo Four, The
Renegades, The
Renicks, The
Rhythm & Blues Inc.
Rhythm Rockers, The
Richmond, The
Ricky & the Dominant Four
Ricky Gleason & the Top Spots
Rikki & the Red Streaks
Riot Squad, The
Rip Van Winkle & the Rip It Ups
Rivals, The
Roadrunners, The
Robettes, The
Robin & the Ravens
Rockefellers, The

Rogues, Gallery
Rontons, The
Roray Storm & the Hurricans
Rory & the Globe Trotters
Roy & the Dions
Roy Montrose & the Midnights
Runaways, The
Sandgrounders, The
Sapphires, The
Savva & the Democrats
Scaffold
Schatz, The
Searchers, The
Secrets, The
Seftons, The
Senators, The
Sensations, The
Sepias, The
Shades, The
Silver Beatles, The
Skeletons, The Skylarks, The
Sneakers, The
Sobells, The
Sonny Kay & the Reds
Sonny Webb & the Cascades
Sorrals, The
Soul Seekers, The

Spidermen, The
Sportsmen, The
Squad, The
St. Louis Checks, The
Statesmen, The
Stereos, The
Steve Aldo & the Challengers
Steve Bennett & the Syndicate
Steve Day & the Drifters
Strangers, The
Sundowners, The
Swaydes, The
Swinging Blue Jeans, The
Syndicate, The
Tabs, The
Takers, The
Talismen, The
Team Mates, The
Teenbeats, The
Tempos, The
Terry Hines Sextet, The
Texans, The
Them Grimbles
Three Bells, The
Thrillers, The
Thunderbirds, The
Tiffany's Thoughts

TJ's, The
Tokens, The
Tommy & the Olympics
Tommy & the Satellites
Tommy Quickly
Tony Carlton & the Mersey Four
Tony Jackson & the Vibrations
Traders, The
Travelers, The
Tremas, The
Trends, The
Trents, The
Tuxedos, The
Undertakers, The
Valkyries, The
Vampires, The
Vance Williams & the Rhythm Four
Vegas Five, The
Ventures, The
Vic & the Its
Vic & the Spidermen
Vigilantes, The
Vince Earl & the Zeros
Vinny & the Dukes
Wild Harks, The
Wranglers, The
Wump & His Werbles

Popular Bristol Groups, 1960 -1964

Colin Anthony and His Beat Combo
The Blackhearts
The Blue Diamonds
Pete Budd and The Rebels
The Buddys
The Burlington Berties
Johnny Carr and The Cadillacs
The Casuals
The Chequers
Chet and The Triumphs
Danny Clarke and The Jaguars
The Comets
The Corvettes
The Cougars
Alan Dale and The Chevrons
Johnny Dee and The Diatones
The Eagles
The Echoes
Andy Grai and The Strangers
Bob Grant and The Democrats

Johnny Hastings and The Tributes
Lee and The Decoys
Sandra mcCann and Her Escorts
Dale Martin and The Mysteries
The Pentagons
Dean Prince and The Dukes
The R.B.Q.
The Re-Treads
The Riots with Paul Vernon
Dale Rivers and The Ramrods
The Roadrunners
Mark Roman and The Javelins
Johnny Slade and The Vikings
The Sheridans
Dee Starr and The Planets
Mike Starr and The Citizens
The Syndicate
Mel Taylor and The Trek-a-Beats
Mike Tobin and The Magnettes
Cole Young and The Graduates

**Cover of the Cavern Club Membership
Card, 1961 Season Booklet**

remaining floors reared up massive and echoing, filled with rubble and rat droppings. It was there that I spent many a night sleeping in the upstairs levels as described earlier.

The Cavern was originally situated in Matthew Street. Nowadays, it only exists in a restored version at a different location.

During the early 60s, each day at lunchtime a horde of mascara-eyed, beehive-

**Page from Cavern Club Membership Card
1961 Season Booklet**

haired office girls clad in very high heels and very short skirts would clatter down the cellar steps. There, for the sum of a shilling (about 25 cents) they could watch the Beatles and other local groups.

These sessions were the brainchild of Ray McFall, the Cavern's manager. Myself and others—the unemployed, the usual handful of beatniks and out-of-work musicians (all musicians were out of work then)—would stand under the stage arch a few yards from

The Terry Hines' Sextet playing at the Cavern, 1965
Ray Rens, sax, Pete Newton, bass, Terry Hines, vocalist, Dave Irving, drummer, Phil Perry, piano, Bob Hardy, guitar

During one of my Merchant Navy trips around the coast, I docked at Liverpool, much to my excitement. The thrill of actually being on a ship in my home port was quite something. I had to work on the ship from 9 a.m. to 5 p.m. in dock, but once the work day was over, I headed for my old club haunts. One night in the early '60s, I was asked by a shipmate whose name escapes me, if I could take him around the clubs. Of course, I said yes. One of our stops was the Cavern. My colleague, a ship's engineer, was a Cockney (i.e., from London), a pleasant, amicable sort of chap, completely harmless, and he was overwhelmed by the scene in the Cavern as group after group came on. Then, much to my joy, the Beatles came on and that scene must be for ever etched on my shipmate's mind.

The Cavern, Liverpool, 1962: 10 p.m.

The walls of the gloomy cellar are damp with condensation, dripping onto the sweat-drenched crowd whirling and stomping to the throbbing roar of the music blasting from overwrought Vox amplifiers. On the stage, the lead guitarist - a thin, pale-faced youth with delicate features - grins self-consciously as his long, slender fingers slide over the neck of an a black Gretsche guitar, wringing out bent notes and two-finger runs in a crude but exhilarating rock solo.

I stand below the stage, half-hidden in the shadows, equally thin, equally pale. I'm avidly absorbed by the lead guitarist, as I replaced him in the group he left to join this one. I stare, drinking in information with intense concentration, gazing intently at the youth's left hand, fascinated; the positioning of the long, sinewy fingers.

The song, Ritchie Barret's 'Some Other Guy', reaches a crescendo. The audience surges forward; chairs are overturned; girls scream as the four leather-clad youths hit the call-and-response refrain in a three-part, wailing, R&B harmony.

The atmosphere is hair-raising, almost orgiastic.

"Who are they?" whispers my companion, ill-at-ease in this tribal, Liverpool environment.

"Beatles," I say.

The screaming reaches a maddening pitch.

"God ....!" he exclaims, dazed by the hysteria around him.

"Not yet," I grin, proud that this drab, northern town could show the boys from the Big City something. At that moment it was a thin joke. Ten years later it was to become as near-as-dammit true.

It occurred to me later what a blessing it must have been to my shipmate. Shortly after that, the Beatles hit the Big Time and never played in the Cavern again. By sheer luck, my shipmate had stood in the Cavern, yards away from the Beatles, watching them as they should be watched - wailing away in a small cellar with amps cranked to bursting point. I was glad I'd been able to provide him with the memory.

the Beatles, enchanted.

In early '60s Liverpool, an out-of-towner, Adrian Barber, perfected a set of "coffins"—stacks of bass speakers—that he filled with all kinds of experimental substances: sand, polystyrene—cotton wool even. This produced a remarkable dead *thump!* and was used by the Beatles and The Big Three to give quite a sound. (The drummer of The Big Three, Johnny Hutchison, replaced his bass pedal with a door knocker to add a zestful thump to the bass note).

Ringo's drumming was in total accord with the bass sound produced by Paul's Hofner fiddle bass with its dull strings. Furthermore, in contrapuntal timing to the huge thump from Ringo's bass pedal and Paul's Hofner were the forcefully-expressed chords on John's rather high-strung Rickenbacker guitar, which had to be hit quite hard, unlike today's faster, sleeker models. Quite accidentally perhaps, it all worked: the dull thud of the bass drum and bass, the trebly, ratcheting chords, and the distortion of the over-wrought amps. While the rest of England's youth was busy emulating The Shadows or the solo-star lineup of a Presley or Britain's own Cliff Richard, Liverpool began to focus on a different kind of music altogether. Not that artists like Elvis and Cliff were not popular, but, the 350+ bands in Liverpool, having assimilated Elvis, The Shadows and other English musicians, turned their faces to America and, in general, began to eschew British models and eventually moved on to black music.

The fact is that even early '50s British music was derived from America. Skiffle, as it was called, was a watered-down version of the blues. But it proved too lame for the ebullient, violent Liverpool character and, through a series of historical mishaps, Liverpool moved towards the original American sources. Because there were so many new bands

There were many popular working bands in Liverpool in the early '60s. Faron's Flamingos was one of them.

actively seeking new material, because rivalry was intense, Liverpool in the '60s became an incubator for change. Of course, with 350+ bands there were many stylistic differences. But with the exception of a few, they all leaned towards aggressive, multi-vocal, hard-driven rock.

In the early '60s, the Liverpool pop magazine, *Combo Musical Weekly* ran a popularity poll, and this is what it revealed:

'60's Popularity Poll

1. The Beatles
2. Gerry and the Pacemakers
3. The Remo Four
4. Rory Storm and the Hurricanes
5. Johnny Sandon and the Searchers
6. Kingsize Taylor and the Dominoes
7. The Big Three
8. The Strangers
9. Faron and the Flamingos
10. The Four Jays
11. Ian and the Zodiacs
12. The Undertakers
13. Earl Preston and the T.T.'s
14. Mark Peters and the Cyclones
15. Karl Terry and the Cruisers
16. Derry and the Seniors
17. Steve and the Syndicate
18. Dee Fenton and the Silhouettes
19. Billy Kramer and the Coasters
20. Dale Roberts and the Jaywalkers

Courtesy Dave Williams

The early Jaywalkers, a popular Liverpool band

Courtesy Harry Prytherch

The Zodiacs, a popular Liverpool band that played at the Cavern, early '60s

Johnny Gustafson Interview

Courtesy Johnny Gustafson

The Big Three Performing at the Liverpool Boxing Stadium

JOHNNY GUSTAFSON of The Big Three was a wild, charismatic figure with a pounding bass style and a wailing voice. His ardent search for newer, more arcane R&B artists was something that began to inform the sets of the Beatles, Gerry and the Pacemakers and, on the trickle-down theory, eventually every group in Liverpool.

Johnny says:

> *This shot was taken at Liverpool Boxing Stadium—the event being a Gene Vincent show (we were 900th on the bill). I am shown in full Ricky Nelson stance, clutching a semi-acoustic.*

John was one of the most sought-after rock singers and bassists on the Liverpool scene. He went on to play with Roxy Music and scores of other bands as a very successful session singer/bassist. What is not so well known is how much he—and Adrian Barber and the friendly rivalry between The Big Three, the Beatles and other bands—shaped the whole of the Liverpool Sound. Johnny, a largely unsung, but key figure in the history of Liverpool Rock, told me the story in his own words:

> *When the band took off, we needed extra amplification to make up for the lack of the other guitar; we thought we should beef up the bass department 'cos you couldn't really buy commercial bass amps at the time.*

The Big Three
Drummer Johhny Hutchinson, bassist Johnny Gustafson and guitarist Brian Griffiths

Adrian made these speakers for The Big Three; he made one for himself and one for me. He built them in a basement in Canning Street underneath a flat he was living in. He built mine, a big fat thing with one 18" speaker.

Now later on when Adrian left The Big Three, he sold his rig to Paul McCartney—and McCartney used it as a bass amp. They worked very well. I'd never seen anything that big.

The 50 watt amp and these speakers caused a great deal of problems in the Cavern at the lunchtime sessions, with this heavy bass noise reverberating up through the floors of the offices above. People were forever barging in to complain.

Anyway, as the sound developed, so did the direction we wanted to take. It began to take shape as a response to the power we had available. We veered towards the heavier kind of music: R&B, Isley Brothers, Bobby Freeman, Ray Charles and all that. I already loved Little Richard and the other rockers. So all that kind of gelled into one solid direction: that super-powerful R&B rock. And that's the way we kept going until the death of it, really.

A lot of these artists, to this day, aren't that well known in America. James Ray did a really powerful version of If You Got To Make A Fool Of Somebody; Freddy and The Dreamers did a watered-down version; others were Arthur Alexander, Bobby Freeman, Barrett Strong. They formed the basis for our set.... You see, NEMS[1] had a small shop in Great Charlotte Street, and I got friendly with a guy in there because of my constantly poking my nose in looking for new releases.

Every week he used to set aside for me all the stuff that came in from North America—State side—and all the American R&B labels. I told him: "I didn't care how obscure it is, but if it's the kind of stuff you know I like, keep it for me, and if I like it I'll definitely buy it." And that's how it came to be. 'Stateside' and 'London American' were the main ones. You see, 'London American' encompassed a lot of labels from America, all lumped together under that one label. We did do other stuff: some Chuck Berry, Ben E. King, Johnny Bernette; we did quite a few off the Rock & Roll Album. One of the chief records that really blew us away was 'What'd I Say?' by Ray Charles. I think I heard it on Radio Luxembourg and I knew I just had to get it and get it off. It was a real happening;

I guess it came about in a funny way. It was just my own obscure taste, really. Coupled to that, Liverpool is a big sea port and somebody always knew somebody who'd been to America on the ships. They brought back stuff from obscure blues singers, gospel records, early soul stuff and, of course, all the Little Richard catalogue; and anything at all that was loosely connected with raucous sounding bands with saxes in them, especially if the vocalist was screaming. It was all so fantastic then. Little Richard, he's the king. I got to play on the same bill as him when he played the Tower Ballroom. What a blast! Little Richard is my vocal hero—always will be.

As regards people like the Beatles, we all shared early rock 'n roll as our influences, then we branched out in our own directions. But I know for a fact that The Big Three was John Lennon's favorite band. But, like I said, though we did swap lyrics and tunes with each other, eventually we branched in slightly different directions. The Beatles weren't as raw as us, though they did a lot of the same numbers.

As regards the stuff we used to do, and the Beatles, there was a kind of friendly rivalry between us and Lennon and McCartney. Many times I would go to NEMS and either Lennon or McCartney would be in there in those little listening booths where the staff would pipe in records. If I was in a booth, the Beatles would stick their heads in to see what I was listening to, to try to catch up on these obscure numbers. That's where I first heard 'Hippy Happy Shake' by Chan Romero. Paul McCartney was having it played to him and I said, "What's that? I'd like that...." and we both bought it on the same day, and there was a kind of race to see who would do it first at the Cavern—but it wasn't really heavy rivalry. Those were really great days, and that feeling between the bands made it even greater.

From Johnny's account, and others taken from Liverpool musicians, at least it becomes apparent why Liverpool was such a fruitful ground for American music to take root. The friendly rivalry—itself an aspect of the peculiar tribalism of the Liverpool-Irish—militated against solo artists.

If we take the number of clubs, and then compute this with the number of bands in Liverpool, the effect is staggering: hundreds of bands; scores of clubs—and each bonded together in a peculiar, friendly rivalry as bands raced to try out new material to keep ahead.

Liverpool became a clearinghouse for American music that screamed, yelled and howled emotion. As the cornerstone of three Celtic cultures—Irish, Scottish, Welsh—the Liverpool character was a volatile mix.

Furthermore, as English musicians were primarily white, they were able to emphasize the aggression which was somewhat subdued in imported black music. For example, Ray Charles' songs were rather jazzy and soft until they arrived in Liverpool. They were assimilated and returned to the public ear with redoubled force.

Black music is a kind of ritualization or imitation of nature, which can channel black aggression towards constructive and creative ends. It does not drain away that aggression but redirects it in a more highly articulated form, back through the black community.

Ben Sidran
Black Talk, p. 139

Interview with Gerry Marsden

Gerry Marsden (left) with Cilla Black

This refining of American music styles is a point made by a Liverpool musician who has made a career out of being a typical Liverpudlian, breezy, cocky, cheery: GERRY MARSDEN of Gerry and the Pacemakers:

Although there was not an aspirate H anywhere in the interview, the reader is spared a dialectic rendering (which would have been unintelligible.)

Ladies and Gentlemen! In translation, Gerry Marsden:

> At the Cavern, we used our own stuff. Now, when the Beatles got bigger stuff, so did we. We had speakers six feet tall with the bottoms of the boxes filled with sand. And they used to rock the bleedin' Cavern. The first one was made by a guy named Adrian Barber. He made them for a few people. They were great; we used to put our vocals through them as well. Everybody was going through the speakers—it must have sounded horrendous. After a while, though, once we'd got the idea from Adrian, we started building our own speakers...bigger and bigger. We called them coffins. In fact, we built one so big that when we got to the Cavern, we couldn't get it down the staircase of the Cavern.
>
> The kind of stuff we used to play.... Well, a lot of people were influenced by The Shadows, stuff like that, but not us really. For me it was Chuck Berry—he was my inspiration—and Ray Charles' keyboard playing which I converted to the guitar;
>
> The thing about Liverpool was, because there was not enough to do, you either became a boxer or a musician. And I boxed for seven years and I decided music was easier, so I went full tilt into music. Only, I think because of the

SIX

Gerry will go up when
he goes
down under

Gerry and The Pacemakers

Gerry

Gerry is a terrible prankster. When on tour with The Silhouettes, Gerry would yank at the lead singer's mike when he was in mid performance. To pay Gerry back the band obtained a full sized cardboard cutout of John Wayne from a cinema foyer advertising the western Rio Bravo. When Gerry launched into a very soulful rendering of *You'll Never Walk Alone* the boys slowly lowered the cutout onto the stage behind Gerry; John Wayne with both guns blazing. Gerry couldn't understand the gales of laughter coming from the audience.

▶ *state of Liverpool, we all had rummy work; we had jobs of a day, then we'd play of a night; or, when we got a bit better, we could take an hour from work and go and play at the Cavern and go back to work after two o'clock. I worked for the Kardoma Tea Factory, then I worked Woolworth's, then I worked on the railway as a can lad[2] I was actually working on the railway when I packed it in to go to Hamburg. I was 17½ then. We went out there just when the Beats (Beatles) came home because the Top Ten Club was just opening. We opened at the Top Ten just after the Beatles came back from the Kaiser Keller.*

We did a lot of different numbers, and to get the material, we used to go to NEMS, that's how we first met Brian Epstein. We used to go to NEMS and order the records from the States—like numbers by Arthur Alexander, Chuck Berry, Fats Domino, Ray Charles—and we used to get them sent in, and Brian Epstein said: "Why are you getting these obscure records?" And we said: "We don't like the British scene, so we play these." And that's why he came down to the Cavern to see what McCartney and I were doing, 'cos Paul and I used to go into NEMS regularly. When Brian came down to the Cavern, he fell in love with the whole scene. But it was 'cos we had Epstein bring in these records through NEMS—that's how we met him. He was knocked out. He signed the Beatles when we went to Hamburg and when we came back, he signed us. There was a great deal of rivalry between us and the Beatles—on stage, that is. But we were good friends off stage. Like, if we got a new number, we wouldn't let the Beatles hear it until we actually played it on stage. We had a thing: whichever of us got a song, it was ours 'til we did it, then they would say: "Cor, where did you get that from?" Like, in one instance, I swapped 'Roll Over Beethoven' with George Harrison for 'Jumbalaya'—that was a Hank Williams' number. We rocked it up and made a rock 'n roll song out of it. George loved it and he said: "You can have 'Jumbalaya' and I'll have 'Roll Over Beethoven' off you." So we never really pinched each other's numbers, we swapped 'em. It was friendly, really. Like I said, when the Beatles had their record 'Love Me Do' in the charts, we were as happy about it as they were; we were over the moon.

The funny thing is that all the other cover numbers we did, like the time we were getting people like Chuck Berry sent over, the people in America didn't even know him there; he wasn't famous. The Yanks didn't really know any of these artists.

What we did was, we heard these records brought in by seamen, brought from the States; these rock 'n roll numbers that we'd never heard. We got all the names and we thought, right, we'll send for that. Take Jerry Lee Lewis: we were doing 'A Whole Lot of Shakin'' by Jerry Lee Lewis even before people in the States itself knew about it, so we later went there and sold them all their own music back again!

Gerry's account underscores the point which which is very important to Liverpool rock: rivalry was so strong that a record bought in the afternoon would be featured that evening.

In Liverpool bands, everybody sang. The Beatles' set consisted of a round in which first John, then Paul, then George, and finally Ringo would sing—then the round would begin again, usually based on requests from the audience.

> The Beatles' best work was never recorded. We were performers…what we generated was fantastic. When we played straight rock, there was no one to touch us in Britain. As soon as we made it, we made it, but the edges were knocked off.
>
> John Lennon

There was something very tribal in the call-and-response system of the black R&B groups. Bands like the Beatles would hardly ever feature the singer as a solo performer; everyone would sing backup, as in Ringo's Boys (a Shirelles number which should have been sung by girls!).

With the clarity of 20/20 hindsight, it is now obvious why Liverpudlians leaned towards the arcane R&B of disenfranchised blacks: the Liverpudlians were disenfranchised whites with the same oral traditions.

Lee Castle and the Barons

Colin Manley Interview

Courtesy Dave Williams

Colin Manley (right) and The Remo Four

COLIN MANLEY of the Remo Four was a bright, highly-intelligent and multi-talented musician. He provided a great deal of insight into the roots of Liverpool rock:

> *George and I shared an interest in Chet Atkins early on. He came to our house a couple of times—George was good, he could handle it, though! He used to do that Bach number, 'Bourre'. He could play, George, but some of the earlier stuff on the records I thought was a bit hurried; but later on when he played some of his classic solos, when he put some thought into it, they were very good. Sometimes George would throw in a bit of 'Bourre' as a joke, like—the way the Beatles would sometimes do all kinds of things like that. You know, if we did Duane Eddy's 'Peter Gunn' at a lunchtime session*

and the Beatles came on immediately after, they'd play 'Peter Gunn' all out of tune, just to take the mickey.

George Harrison had an amp with his Hofner President before I did—I couldn't afford it until I left school. I always remember George playing 'Raunchy', a Duane Eddy number, through his amplifier in the music room at school. It sounded great. Then, after he left school, he was backing Johnny Gentle. He and Paul disappeared for a while, then they went to Hamburg and reappeared again in about 1960 as the Silver Beatles. About late '60-'61, they started to emerge as a force in Liverpool. I never wanted to be better than him, I just really loved him. But the Beatles weren't too fond of The Shads. They thought they were a bit twee, you know, and they went against the Fender sound, the clear sound—they had the beginnings of a dull sound. I think it was deliberate, you know.

Why the huge explosion of groups should take place in Liverpool, I don't know. Perhaps I am an indication of it in that I used to spend all my time at school, instead of studying, drawing guitars. But why, I don't know. People put it down to the Navy; people put it down to the American records coming over. The Mersey Sound was, in fact, American music with a natural Liverpool accent.

Maybe it was the Irish influence. You listen to the Beatles; they concentrate a lot on melody. They used to do plenty of rock 'n roll and bluesy stuff. You see, early on, they did more like the classical R&B stuff, and yet, when they started writing, it was very melodic, wasn't it?

I can remember as a kid, I wasn't allowed into the pubs in the early '50s, I was too young. But I can remember in the Dingle (where Ringo came from), in every pub, about 9:30 p.m. everybody would start singing. Every night of their lives these Scousers[3] would sing 'til they got kicked out. Now that didn't necessarily happen in a lot of places, did it?

It is a fact that Celts are given to drink and song. The other Celtic races who took to song are the Cornish and the Welsh; but it's very ethnic. Whereas, in Liverpool, it was different—it was Irish-Country in a way. Pub sing-songs took place around a lot of Hank Williams—it's sentimental stuff, isn't it? But then they'd lapse into the songs from the Olde Country, like, 'Now Is The Hour', 'Wild Mountain Thyme'. As well as that, they had the Irish quickness, the Irish humor.

Colin was making very important point here, because the debt owed by Liverpool musicians to the Irish is considerable, and deserves closer examination.

Liverpool Music & The Irish

Liverpool Music and the Irish

There is the biggest C&W following in England in Liverpool, besides London—always besides London, because there is more of it there. I heard C&W music in Liverpool before I heard rock & roll. The people there—the Irish in Ireland are the same—they take their C&W music very seriously. There's a big heavy following of it. There were established folk, blues and C&W clubs in Liverpool before rock & roll, and we were like the new kids coming out. I remember the first guitar I ever saw. It belonged to a guy in a cowboy suit in a province of Liverpool, with stars and a cowboy hat and a big dobro. They were real cowboys and they took it seriously. There had been cowboys long before there was rock & roll.

John Lennon
Rolling Stone Interview, 1971

Liverpool is known popularly as the "Capital of Ireland" —simply because there are so many Irish there. In the '50s and '60s, the music of preference for the Irish was not the haunting strains of Gaelic folk songs, but American country & western.

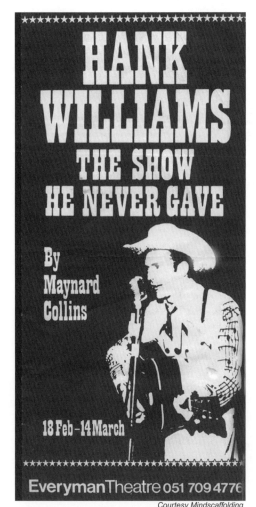

Courtesy Mindscaffolding

The show played at the Everyman Theatre near the Philharmonic pub

The sheer breadth and knowledge of American C&W and the reverence in which it is held by the Liverpool Irish is staggering. In the same way that the Liverpool blues' aficionados collected rare artists' albums and the jazzers collected Blue Note albums, the Liverpool Irish, during the Fifties and Sixties, amassed a collection of C&W that would have put Nashville to shame.

The Irish are great drinkers and, therefore, the most important faction in the pub scene. As the pub is the single biggest aspect of Liverpool cultural life, the average Liverpudlian (myself included) by contingent exposure, knows by heart the lyrics and music of all the great American C&W artists—and quite a few of the lesser known: Hank Snow; Hank Williams; Kay Starr; Johnny Cash. Nightly, these songs are immortalized in the Liverpool tradition of the drunken singsong.

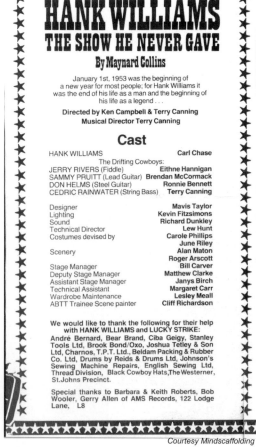

Courtesy Mindscaffolding

Program for the Liverpool musical show *Hank . Williams, the Show He Never Gave*, early '60s

44

It is no chance that the maudlin, sentimental angst of a haunted Hank Williams—the John Lennon of his time and the perpetrator of the 'white blues'—acted as a stepping stone to the Negro blues.

The C&W artists were greedily assimilated into Liverpool Irish culture and, of course, they overlapped into the music of the Southern whites, such as Jerry Lee Lewis and Carl Perkins. The genres often cross—there is a fine line between Elvis and, say, Arthur Cradip or some of Buddy Holly's material and the more traditional Country artists.

In particular, *The Carl Perkins' Dance Album* was the mainstay of rock bands in Liverpool and, along with Chuck Berry, Perkins can be accredited as one of the Beatles' greatest influences.[1] In fact, quite often the Beatles would plough their way through all the sixteen numbers on this album in one set, delivering the Country music with the shattering force of rock. Their fans for a long time did not realize that they were listening to sixteen

Courtesy Hank Walters

Hank Walters, the most famous C&W Scouser in Liverpool or, as his Japanese fans put it, "a libbing legend."

numbers all from the same album.

Thus, the Irish C&W scene was of tremendous importance in preparing the collective Liverpool consciousness for the influx of American music in the '60s.

Courtesy Mindscaffolding

Hank Walters Performing at the Everyman Theater, Liverpool, 1981

Author (left) in transcendent state gets in the C&W mode; his companion gives new meaning to "if looks could kill."

Lonnie Donegan: The Ultimate Celt, A Scottish Irishman

Lonnie Donegan's influence was momentous: Single-handedly, Donegan bridged the white tradition of C&W (and its implicit blues roots) with the blues' tradition from Africa America.

In the Fifties, Lonnie Donegan, with an inspired guitarist called Les Jackson, was busy adapting material from such early blues' artists as Leadbelly and transforming it into a sub-genre known as skiffle.

Lonnie Donegan was, then, the first white blues man (though no one acknowledged him as such at the time). His records swept throughout England and laid the foundation for a new genre that was the precursor to rhythm & blues and rock 'n roll: namely, skiffle.

The first Liverpool bands were largely inspired by Lonnie Donegan's nasal renderings of early black American material: prison songs; work songs; and watered-down Badman songs—all delivered in Donegan's unique, tonsil-twanging style[2]. Donegan, then, was an innovator whose influence upon the history of music is, to say the least, as profound as it is unsung. Donegan was adapting black music as early as the 1950s: *Rock Island Line* (a train song); *Staggerlee* (a version of the Badman toasts); *Stewball* (the race-course song); *Worried Man Blues* (simple blues); *Midnight*

Courtesy Mindscaffolding

Lonnie's skiffle album benchmark

Special (a prison song); *Whoa Buck* (a field holler).

Donegan's songs, though white and watered down, nevertheless, still contained the essence of the blues' spirit. An odd historical note is that Donegan's career followed a similar pattern to Chuck Berry's. Both started off as serious artists and both ended up as 'Rock-comics'.

Indeed, Donegan and Berry, major influences on the English Rock scene, have, at the end of their careers, both come to the same point. Chuck Berry's concerts have degenerated to massive, comic sing-a-longs with material like *My Ding-a-Ling*. Similarly so, Donegan eventually turned to comic songs like *My Old Man's A Dustman* and *Does Your Chewing Gum Lose its Flavor On the Bedpost over Night.*

Perhaps one explanation for this may be that the blues, in its original context of life-and-death had to be self-parodying to avoid punitive action; its very context gave it a mordant bite. Historically, as the situation changed and its context became less serious, all there is left, perhaps, is the self-parody—and this seems to be what has happened to Chuck Berry and Lonnie Donegan.

Courtesy Dave Williams

Note the mixture of Trad Jazz, C&W and Rock

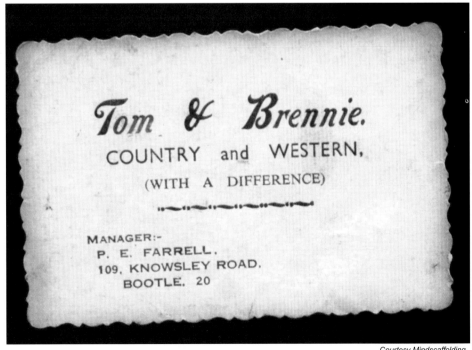

Courtesy Mindscaffolding

Invitation to a C&W Gig, 1963

47

Colin Manley, who brought up the point about the Irish influence in Liverpool earlier, went on to say:

We identified with American guitarists more than any other part of England did. Yes, other kids liked them—but it was something deep with us. It's funny, 'cos Liverpool is a black area and yet I hardly knew any black guitarists. **It wasn't racism: the blacks just didn't seem interested in the guitar**, *it was their choice. But for us, the guitar was everything.*

The first time I heard a 3rd string bent—when James Burton hit that 3rd string and bent it from B to C in Ricky Nelson's 'Mary Lou', for me, that was history in the making, Obviously somewhere down the line, James had got string bending off the American blacks—incredible! That was something that changed the way I thought about music forever."

The funny thing is that when people go on about race, we really weren't racial—we just treated everybody the same. There was no prejudice, certainly not among the musos. But the blacks were into singing and doing street corner harmonies. Remember the clubs? They were more into do-wop—nobody played a guitar.

The Chants
A popular Liverpool do-wop group

The forces which were at work shaping the white teenagers of England were not quite the same as those affecting the development of the transplanted black teenagers whose parents came to England from the Caribbean in 1952. Nor was it the same for those second-generation black kids who were born in England of West Indian parents. Their rite of passage was a different struggle for identity. Were they black, Liverpudlian, Caribbean? They never knew. They were caught between two cultures, England and America.

Their heros were the successful do-wop groups of America; swaggering, cool, finger-clicking harmony-mongers in sharp suits. What self-respecting English black dude would choose as a role model some clapped out old sharecropper from the Mississippi delta when there were successful blacks to choose from?

The real musical interface that took place between the Liverpool black kids and the Liverpool whites was shared, not over musical instruments, but drugs. Liverpool has always been a city of excessive consumption and when it came to drugs, it certainly didn't pull any punches—not then, not now.

It's incredible that the Liverpool blacks chose to go for the group identity of an oral medium - which is exactly what the blacks in the early South did in America, as it gave them a sense of group identity. Cf. to Ben Sidrans Black Talk

Drugs & Rock'n Roll-
Opening For The Beatles

7

Drugs and Rock 'n Roll—Opening for The Beatles

The influx of West Indian and Asian culture into Liverpool in the Fifties brought with it ganja, charas, tompy, spliffs[1] and all the other regalia, linguistic and otherwise, of hip 'blackness'; including cool Jazz, Milt Jackson, Roland Kirk and Miles Davis.

Not everyone took the same drug. There were definite lines of demarcation in drug taking, though, as usual, the musicians took them all:

The blacks in Liverpool 8—who sported exotic names like Paris, Bye Bye, One-Man—were definitely into ganja or charas and either Soul music or really cool jazz. This was the era of The MJQ; Kinda Blue Miles Davis; Dizzy Gillespie; and Jim Hall.

Courtesy Mindscaffolding

The Casablanca Club
This sweetie was snapped very recently. When told it was for an expatriate Scouser in the USA, she remarked: "Duz 'e wanna live-in luvver?"

Amongst the poor whites who became integrated into the black culture there flourished an amazing, eclectic knowledge of jazz, imbibed with vast amounts of seed-popping spliff smoke in the dour basements of Parliament and Canning Streets.

Black met white and the resulting color was blue.

Imported Blue-Note LPs from the U.S.A., the main source of avant-garde jazz, were sought after. The result was that some working-class whites were walking encyclopedias of jazz. Unemployed, uneducated, but streetwise and shrewd, they literally lived for the next import Blue-Note album—a little ray of gold, blue-gold, warding off the street gloom for an hour, for a night.

Arcane, esoteric, the music was assimilated greedily. Stanley Turrentine, Ornette Coleman, John Coltrane, Thelonius Monk, Jimmy Smith, Jimmy Guiffre—such artists were in the common parlance of smokers; smokers who, in the daytime, were the shift workers who disappeared behind the stacks in grim, gray factories to blast[2] during the lunch hour and talk, incongruously, of esoteric jazz or even more esoteric blues: Peg-leg Howell, Blind Lemon Jefferson, Etta Baker, Big Bill Broonzey; the knowledge of the black music phenomenon by these white boys was extensive.

Thus, the odd factor in Liverpool was that drugs were not the prerogative of the middle-class whites or the hippies, as was largely the case in Sixties' America, but rather the solace of the working class and disenfranchised—another factor which brought the Liverpool whites closer to their urban black American counterparts. Musical awareness was very high amongst the working-class smokers and it was also a bridge to communication with the blacks.

Although dope was used extensively for relaxation or listening to music, the drug of choice for working rock musicians, however, was definitely amphetamine. When it came to playing, what was needed was an

Courtesy International Guitar Festival of Great Britain

Chuck Berry was so taken with the Liverpool beat that he wrote an ode to Liverpool: *Liverpool Drive*

upper, a drive. Thus, the sheer power of rock groups like the Beatles, the Big Three, the Dennisons, Derry and the Seniors was founded on amphetamine.

All-night sessions at the Cavern or the Storyville (the Iron Door) were sweaty, noisy affairs in which groups would batter out rock numbers for hours on end. A staccato wall of sound was delivered by bright-eyed, lip-chewing amphetamine-loaded musicians whose drug-induced tachycardia elevated the beat to inhuman proportions.

Eyes sparkling like coals, musicians would hammer out explosive versions of arcane American R&B artists. The sound was horrendous; the treble on the guitar pumped up beyond the limits of distortion. Rapid-chopped chords ratcheted in contrapuntal rhythm to the huge whoombs of the bass speakers, matched beat for beat by the solid boom of a bass drum.

The result was electrifying. So much so, that Chuck Berry, the king of the twelve-bar, was overwhelmed when he finally visited Liverpool and was backed by Kingsize Taylor and the Dominoes. (Kingsize was a butcher by trade, and his ham-like fists could wield a guitar or swing a solid punch with equal alacrity. This primitive aggression was an additive power to the music.)

Berry was amazed. Here he'd been churning out this high-school rock for years, and here were these white cats who'd got it all, note for note, listening to tinny LPs on cheap record players. What's more, they had turned the music into something so raw and primitive that it blew Berry away.

Berry was to say later: "I spent years hacking out this stuff, but no one would buy it until these Liverpool guys showed up in America doing the same thing! Why?" He supplied the answer himself, and not without a modicum of sardonic humor: "*Why, no one else in America would listen to the stuff, good or bad, when it was coming from a big, black, sweaty spade*[3]. But when they saw the white boys doing it, they listened ... and they heard it and knew it was good.*" Berry was so overwhelmed by it all that he penned a number especially for Liverpool—*Liverpool Drive.*

Black or white, drug addict, criminal, child-molester or wife-beater, it made no difference to the Liverpool musicians: 'Bring me your poor, your downtrodden and let's hear their best rock' was the unspoken

When Chuck toured with The Dominoes, he wore a baggy Elvis Presley style silk stage suit. When the act began, Chuck always appeared on stage transfixed by a giant spotlight. He was overwhelmed by the vociferous audience response. Unknown to him, the reason for this massive accolade was that the spotlight rendered the silk suit virtually transparent.

51

Kingsize Taylor and the Dominoes, backing band for Chuck Berry's tour
Sax player, Howey Casey standing in back, second from right

motto, simply because their eyes were not blinkered by the three and a half centuries of racism that had oppressed America. Not only did they accept America's so-called low life—Jerry Lee Lewis; Gene Vincent; Carl Perkins; Chuck Berry; black or white—but, with amphetamine power, they turned it into "white nigger" music.

One-night stands, poor pay and bad food sapped a rock guitarist's fibre and enthusiasm and, faced with the rigors of an all-night session, amphetamine was the drug of necessity.

The Beatles ran on amphetamine power, as did all rock bands. Well-informed audiences would point knowingly at a guitarist on stage who was almost chewing off his bottom lip, shouting: "Pill head!" Lip-chewing was the first sign of self-medication, amphetamine style.

A Slight Geographical Aside: New Brighton

Courtesy Reflections

A Day Out
On the sand at New Brighton, circa 1960. Passenger ship in mid-center, New Brighton ferry approaching

The Tower Ballroom is situated across the River Mersey in a seaside resort named New Brighton. The term "new" Brighton, in this case, is somewhat synonymous with "New" Jersey. It is a rather ratty, cheap, fish-and-chip town which caters to the hordes of less-than-salubrious Liverpudlians who flock there at the weekend. It is all booze, fish 'n chips and "Kiss-Me-Quick" hats. It is reached by ferry—as immortalized in Gerry Marsden's song *Ferry Across the Mersey.*

At one time, the hordes of blue-collar workers who sought a momentary jaunt on the beaches would pack onto the sand, as in the photograph above. But now, most of the sand has been washed away and it is a muddy haven for scores of stranded jelly fish.

As an indication of "what you don't know you don't miss", my family's yearly vacation consisted of visiting New Brighton for *one day*, all that Dad could afford. My brother and I were dressed up in our one "good" set of clothes and taken to New Brighton. There, we ate out at what we thought was a posh café, 'cos it sold chicken *and* chips. And that was that for our year's vacation. Knowing nothing better, we looked forward to it as a middle-class family would regard going to the Bahamas—summer, vacation, bliss.

The Tower Ballroom and the rock sessions held there in the '60s was also invaded by the beery, fish-n-chip mob—this time, greasy-haired Teddy Boys[4] and their girlfriends. Of course, fights were the order

53

of the day (or night). Gerry, of the Pacemakers, once proved the superior quality of Fender guitars by wielding one like a battle axe during one such altercation, with no visible damage to the gui-tar—which was not the case for the would-be assailant it impacted.

But that is another story.

I was, at the time, a thin, over-active rock guitarist whose nights were demarked by the mood swings brought about by the inordinate use of drugs. But at the time I was young and strong and thought I could take it. So I did—amylnitrate; ephedrine; sparine; LSD; mogadon; and, of course, amphetamine. But the night I had to play at the Tower Ballroom, such excess proved my undoing...

Courtesy Glynn Parry

The Ferry Across the Mersey
A journey from downtown Liverpool to New Brighton

Author's collection

Author (right), Parents and Brother
on their yearly day's vacation to New Brighton dressed in their best

Author's collection

A Postcard Advertising the Wonders of New Brighton

54

Opening for the Beatles—Disaster Strikes
—A Personal Anecdote—

There were very few black guitarists in Liverpool. But there were a few solo singers. Derry Wilkie was the only black singer of prominence who regularly wailed away with the 350+ white groups playing rock. He was an ardent man, tall, thin, and a live wire on stage. He is, in fact, credited with being the first to go to Hamburg, thus paving the way for the Beatles who followed. Ironic that, again, it should be a black man who started it and whites—i.e., the Beatles—who followed and benefitted. Derry, a professional artist with his eye on fame, eventually left Liverpool and made it very big in Italy. He still sings to this day.

Living on Social Security as many Liverpudlians were at the time, I spent my days hanging out at the rock joints, especially the lunchtime sessions at the Cavern. I couldn't play in a group, even though that's all I wanted to do, because I didn't own a guitar—couldn't afford one.

Then one day, Derry, who had heard me play, asked me to front the band at the Tower Ballroom where his band, Derry and the Pressmen, was opening for the Beatles. I was stricken with fear and doubt as I was very under-rehearsed and out of practice. It was an occasion when the only sensible thing it seemed I could do was to stoke up on amphetamine, which led to a Tale of Disaster—though some would call it a tragicomedy...

Lunchtime at the Cavern

As porters and laborers shouted, swore and hauled sacks of brown sugar and apples onto the loading bays, female workers from the nearby office buildings, perfectly clad as though for an evening ball, picked their way through the litter of muddy cigarette packets and torn newspapers towards the door of the Cavern—a narrow fissure in the dirty brown wall.

From this hole-in-the-wall issued a steady pounding thunder; the sound of rock 'n roll from

Courtesy Mrs. Wilkie

Derry Wilkie (left), Freddie Starr (white shirt) and sax player, Howie Casey (second left)

the dripping cellar below.

One by one, the girls filed through the door, paid their shilling and, stepping gingerly in their high heels, negotiated the steep narrow staircase under the watchful eyes of the beefy bouncer, Paddy. Once below, they headed for the soup-and-sandwich bar, grabbed a bite, then returned to the stage for a noisy Rock-filled hour of music. Today, it was the Beatles and the Big Three—two extremely popular bands.

I stood disconsolate in the alley outside, my eyes flickering over the crowd of loafers and hangers-on that used this afternoon session as an assembly point. I recognized most of them by sight, some by name, and my busy mind computed, filed and categorized them: out-of-work musicians; would-be musicians; dole-ites; nuts; petty thieves; criminals; and—

Aha, it was Ming.

I sauntered over and slapped Ming on the back. Ming, a small, laughing, over-active Chinese listened intently as I explained the situation: I had a gig that night; I was on a downer; any purple hearts, dex, or what have you ?

No sir. Ming only had ephedrine, amylnitrate and a little Dr. Collis Brown's chloradyne (18%) opium which could be bought anywhere.

"Shit, you'll be trying to sell me Lady Esquire shoe polish next!" I said.

"Yeah, gives you brain damage, man," grinned Ming.

There was nothing for it—it was down to Traveling-By-Tube. I headed for the nearest pharmacist.

No luck. I tried three down Church Street before I hit pay-dirt in Whitechapel.

The pharmacist smiled thinly as he slid the card over the counter towards me. Some of the nasal inhalers had been removed, but there were still ten of the slim, bullet-shaped dispensers on the card.

"That's ten shillings," said the pharmacist, "Want them wrapped?"

I shook my head and stuck the card in my pocket. I handed over the crumpled one-pound note, took the change and turned to go.

Courtesy David Rushworth

Band in Whitechapel, Liverpool

Whitechapel

"Bad case of sinus trouble?" asked the pharmacist innocently.

I glanced back at him without smiling and said: "The whole family. Had it for years." And left.

I sat at the window of the Kardomah coffee bar, staring at the foot traffic that swirled by on the pavement outside. On the plastic tabletop in front of me stood a cup of coffee and one of the inhalers. A miniature yellow rocket ship, snub-nosed, two inches high, it was as bright as a child's plastic toy.

I unscrewed the top and, inserting the tube in my nose, sniffed. My belly contracted at the familiar, lavender bite of the nasal inhaler. The inhaler was ripe, man! Some of them were old and the volatile oils had evaporated, but not this one. Carefully I dissembled it, unscrewing the bottom and sliding out the center insert. Inside was a wad of cotton-wool soaked in volatile oils. As the container came apart, the smell rushed up to greet me and my belly contracted again. Quivering in anticipation, I broke off a large wad of cotton-wool and, taking a mouthful of coffee, swiftly popped it into my mouth. I swallowed quickly before I choked on it,

The Kardomah Coffee House, early '60s

then washed it down with the rest of the coffee.

I waited for a moment, fearful that the wad would stick in my gullet and make me vomit, as it had done on previous occasions. But this time it stayed down.

I glanced around the coffee bar. A shabbily-dressed workman with a deeply-lined face quickly averted his eyes; and the frizzy-haired female counter hand stared fixedly ahead through bottle-thick, pink-framed glasses. It did not matter, they thought I was nuts anyway—this emaciated, white-faced, black-clad youth eating a nasal inhaler in broad daylight. Neither of them knew what I was really doing.

I poked the rest of the cotton-wool back into the container, carefully screwed it tight and popped the top back on. I contemplated the tube. Each one contained three hundred and fifty milligrams of volatile amphetamine sulphate. I'd just taken the equivalent of about seventy milligrams, or fourteen tablets. Most people needed about four tabs to get off. But my tolerances were rather high. In an hour, I would be flying.

The Tower Ballroom: Rock Night

The crowd jostled in a muddy swirl between the gaudy primary colors of the tawdry side-shows. Yellow light flooded between gloomy islands of closed concession stands.

Courtesy Wirral Museum

The Tower Ballroom, New Brighton, early 1960s
(before it was burned down)

Courtesy Wirral Museum

Tower Ballroom Interior
Yes, though it appears salubrious in its pristine, empty state, its rock clientele was not

The night had succeeded day, and the last of the day crowd mingled with the fresh onslaught of beery night revelers, grabbing a little tinsel fun before the night's dancing at the Tower Ballroom.

Raucous music blared out from the side-shows. Couples giggled and fed each other candy-floss, sporting diminutive polystyrene cowboy hats that said, in defiance of man's restless search for the arcane and innovatory: 'Kiss me quick'.

I was half-way through a meal of my bottom lip.

I tried to stop but I couldn't. My jaw moved constantly and I chewed relentlessly into the inside of my mouth. It was a side-effect of the amphetamine. My brain reeled with flights of fantasy, delusions of grandeur and a silky sensation of excitement that found its way to the pit of my stomach, particularly when I thought about music.

Unfortunately, I was too high. I'd taken too much too soon and my thoughts moved too fast for me—too fast for those around me—and, more often than not, my mental uproar resolved itself in an involuntary lip-chewing—like the hapless man in H.G. Wells' story who moved too fast for the world around him and, hence, could not communicate.

No guitar.

I still had no guitar for the gig. But Derry would fix it—or so he said.

> **TOWER** BALLROOM
> NEW BRIGHTON
> WHIT "BEAT" SHOW
> Merseyside Sounds
>
> **WHIT MONDAY JUNE 3rd**
> 7-30— 11-30
>
> **DERRY WILKIE AND THE PRESSMEN**
> **RORY STORM AND THE HURRICANES**
> Ian & the Zodiacs The Nomads The Renegades
> PAUL FRANCIS & THE DOMINANT FOUR
> Admission (at door 5/-   Licensed Bars

Courtesy Wallasey News

Derry, a black, stick-like figure, tall and thin with an elongated face and jaw, stood a little distance away chatting animatedly to four dissipated-looking youths. They were half obscured by the shadow of the huge, ugly edifice that arose from the melange of side-shows, holiday crowds and fast-food stalls: It was the

Tower Ballroom itself.

Derry's band were unloading their equipment from a grubby van. The four dissipated youths in conversation with Derry were members of another band who'd played there the night before and were packing up their gear.

American rock singer at Tower tonight

LEWIS Buckley Entertainments Ltd. are presenting the American rock singer Gene Vincent, backed by his own group the Rockabeats, at the Tower Ballroom, New Brighton, today, at a dance from 7-30 p.m. to 11-45 p.m. This is Gene Vincent's first appearance in the Wirral area.

The City Slickers Jazz band and the Blue Genes will also be appearing. There will be licensed bars and late transport and tickets can be obtained at the usual agencies or at the door.

Gene is 21 years old and was born in Norfolk, Virginia, and his first singing success came when he was serving as a boiler tender in the U.S. Navy. On his demobilisation he returned to Norfolk, more determined than ever before to make singing his career.

He was auditioned for a local radio show, won his audition and quickly became the star of the show. Another important audition followed not long afterwards—with Capitol Records, and again Gene Vincent won through—this time being chosen from nearly 200 male rock 'n roll singers.

Since being signed by Capitol Records he has occupied a consistently high position in the popularity polls, and best sellers charts both in this country and in America.

Courtesy Wallasey News

May 5, 1962

Courtesy Dave Williams

Gene Vincent (center) with Dave Williams and friend

Eventually, Derry finished his gesticulations and sauntered over, giving me the thumbs-up. He'd fixed it. I was going to be lent a guitar by Rich, the lead guitarist of the departing band. Waving his arms animatedly, Derry explained the running order: Derry's band was to follow the Renegades; and next, on top of the bill, were the Beatles.

"Thanks," I muttered, biting into my bottom lip and resisting the urge to tell Derry about my mother, my father; the sensation of sheets against my belly when I was five; how I was getting on with women; the latest theory of the cosmic bang; the psychology of perception applied to Skinner Box-trained rats; and how much I loved Ray Charles—all in one sentence. The amphetamine was working overtime.

The lead guitarist of the departing band sauntered over and proffered the said instrument. "Be careful with it," he said with a warning note in his voice. He relinquished the guitar with all the tenderness due to a Stradivarius, "Any damage and....!" He walked away, leaving the sentence unfinished but understood.

Thoughts crowded into my mind thick and fast as I gazed at the guitar blankly, unable to register the feeling I *would* have felt without the amphetamine. It should have been despair. But it did not even touch my drug-addled emotions.

The guitar, in fact, bore little resemblance to a musical instrument at all. It did have strings, pick-ups, frets and so on. But each of the strings was raised at an impossible height above the fret board and appeared to have been fashioned from those steel hawsers used to haul tug boats.

I picked up the guitar and tried it. By gritting my teeth and breathing in sharply, with a superhuman effort, I managed to push a string against the fret board and produce a note. I released the string with a wince and gazed at the deep incision in my finger-tip made by the string.

A further examination revealed that matters were even more grave: The volume control had been jammed into its hole arbitrarily, so that any sudden movement would make it drop inside the hollow-bodied guitar where it was almost impossible to fish out.

I hefted the guitar in my left hand and nodded sagely. Flushed with amphetamine, I made my unwise decision: The guitar would be just fine...

I gazed down from the vast height of the Tower Ballroom stage, mesmerized. Below me washed a vast sea of greasy, sleeked male hairstyles and their accompanying satellites of blonde, domed, beehives, bobbing about like hundreds of maritime buoys. It reminded me vaguely of something I'd once read about in a horror story: the Sargasso Sea; a weed-choked section of the ocean which no man dare sail alone.

Faint stirrings pricked at my belly—which may have been stage-fright. But the emotion was thwarted by the amphetamine and, instead, I stared down abstractedly into the crowd-choked ballroom. The greasy, turgid flotsam rotated slowly in the color-spangled gloom as the crowd waited for some musical input. The oceanic illusion was highlighted by the huge, crystal ball that rotated in the spotlights, dappling the whole scene with colorful streaks, like tropical fish darting hither and thither amongst the greasy islets of hair.

My bottom lip was twice its normal size, so agitated was my chewing. The amphetamine had reached full rush, and my mouth was flecked with a fine foam which I removed with regular, darting swipes of my swollen tongue, fearing that it would reveal my condition to those who may not be sympathetic—particularly my musical colleagues. Contrary to popular belief, not all musicians are drug addicts.

But the band members were busy snaking out cables, plugging in plugs, cursing, tripping and making horrific amplifier noises—the usual motley sounds of a group setting up. Being new, I was implicitly excused from this chore and at a loose end until the set started.

I turned and examined the stage behind me. It was an unlikely rococo affair, reminiscent of those vast baroque structures of heavy ornate plaster that once graced the proscenium of the Music Hall are still to be seen in some of the older cinemas. A series of crescent shapes ascended to a diminutive platform, like tiers on a wedding cake. On the uppermost podium sat the drummer, transfixed by multiple spotlights.

I squinted at the drummer who was surrounded by vast arabesques of swirling gold and silver plaster. My vision blurred until the drummer resembled a diminutive, plaster figure on the top of a Christmas cake. It was all I could do to stop myself reaching forward and breaking off a portion of the white stuff to see if it was edible. I shook myself and jerked my gaze away, dimly aware that I was too, too high, and turned my attentions to the band.

It was formidable. In fact, I had never played in such an enormous band. They were strewn out in a line on the stage, seemingly scores of them—bass player; two saxes; back-up vocalists; percussion. I was separated from the farthest man by a good twenty yards. It all seemed very remote, as if I were viewing it through misted glasses.

Suddenly, the lights changed. The crowd roared and I chewed

Flyer advertising performances at the Tower Ballroom, May 25, 1963

Part of Gene Vincent's act was to lie on the stage clutching the mike and moaning. After his car accident, Gene wore a leg iron to support his weakened limb. On one such occasion, when he came to stand up again after flailing around on the stage, he immediately toppled over. Some of the Liverpool yobbos had loosened the screws on his leg iron while he had been lying on the stage screaming.

61

my bottom lip even more assiduously as I was plunged into an amber glow. Derry screamed into the mike and the sea of white faces below swung around of one accord and faced the stage:

"Are you ready?!!"

"Yeah!!!"

"Do you want it?!!"

"Yeah!!!"

Derry, already jumping up and down, turned and screamed at the band: "Let's do it!! A-one, a-two, a-one-two-three-four!!!"

There was a rumbling roar above my head on the second beat of the count-in as the drummer did a vast, syncopated roll and, right on the first beat of the bar, he slammed down two-handed as the bass, saxes and myself hit it with the force of a constrained explosion. It was *Lucille*, Derry's theme song.

Right on cue, I slapped out the riff, whilst Derry screamed and bobbed; an emaciated, black stick-man jerking and writhing convolutedly, mike in hand.

But something was wrong: because of the amphetamine, I had almost reached stasis. Like a tuning fork that eventually vibrates so quickly the illusion of motion is lost, my speed-freaked thoughts were so fast I was, in fact, playing the *Lucille* riff at about one quarter the requisite tempo. The rest of the band were following suit—even the drummer had slowed down—and the effect was rather like a 33 rpm record being played at 16 rpm.

Derry flailed and bobbed up and down like a maniac, whipping his arms around as though trying to spur a recalcitrant horse into action.

Gradually, due to Derry's efforts, the music picked up tempo like a rusty turntable and by the second chorus it was almost back at normal tempo. The sound crashed about me like the thunderclap of breaking surf. I knew the riff, knew it in my heart and my bones, and gave it my all.

The wave of sound flooded from the stage and raced through the crowd of dancers. The kinetic motion imparted into these floating particles was an improbable sight—an event beyond the laws of Newton's physics. The whole floor began to seethe and gyrate in a frenzied eddy as Derry wailed and screamed:

> "Luc-eelle!
> You don't do you daddy's wee-ill..."

I observed all of this with the passion of a well-oiled camera; my eyes, glassy twin black beads; cheeks hollow; lips flecked with foam. But my fingers fairly flew over the heavy strings of their own accord, chopping out the riff in contrapuntal timing to the blare of the saxes.

Something was wrong. I noted it dimly, puzzled. There was an odd sound melding with the vast, textured multi-chord that was the sound of the band. It wove in and out of the fabric of the song in a way that made me uneasy.

Then I realized that the bass player was leaning across and shouting something. Caught in the moment—the thunderous sound, the screech of saxes, the thrup and ratchet of the drummer smacking out the rhythm with all the force of a village blacksmith—I stared at the bass player's lips, trying to read what he was saying without losing my own riff.

Courtesy Wallasey News

Flyer advertising performances at the Tower Ballroom, April 1963
Note the spelling of the "Beetles"

Courtesy Dave Williams

Flyer advertising Jerry Lee Lewis performance at the Tower Ballroom, New Brighton, May, 1962

The bass player danced up and down in agitation. He seemed to be repeating a single syllable over and over. Then the music soared, the drummer did his out-roll and the number ended in a crescendo of wailing saxes and thunderous applause. In the relative silence that followed, it was only then that I realized what the bass player had been saying over and over again: "E...! E...!! E...!!!"

I had been playing in D.

The odd noise weaving through the dense matrix of sound created by the bass, drums and saxes had been my riff: I'd been playing in the wrong key.

I mouthed foam-flecked apologies to the irritated bass player. "Look," I said as soothingly as my stiff jaw would allow, "Do me a favor, eh? Don't just say the key. Say, like, E for Eric, otherwise I don't know what you're saying—not with this racket. C'mon man, what d'y expect...?"

The bass player, veteran of a hundred lousy lead guitarists, nodded wearily. Then Derry was into the next number, the Isley Brothers' *Twist and Shout* and there was no time for further objections. Once again, I was caught up in a tide of involuntary action as my fingers chopped out the riff of their own accord while I gazed in wonder at the frenzied gyrations of the greasy black flotsam and jetsam in the sea of swirling color. Time suddenly seemed to freeze to a stand-still as the moment overtook me and I was suspended in the sheer, exalted act of playing rock.

Without warning, the volume control fell into the guitar halfway through the number. I glanced about nervously as if it was my fault, but in the hiatus of noise and action, no one had noticed.

Suddenly Derry gave an impossible mid-air leap and fell to his knees, screaming, his voice rising higher and higher. Reaching a crescendo, he turned and with a dramatic gesture, flung out his arm and pointed at me: "Take it, man!!!"

Solo.

Adrenaline did not rush into my blood-stream. It could not; it was already over-saturated. It had been working at a maximum for hours, pumped relentlessly by the jetting tachycardia of a speed-elevated heart. But I responded. I whipped the guitar in the air, bent my knees and my fingers raced over the fret-board at eye-dazzling speed. Eyes closed, teeth bared, I bent notes impossible distances across the neck; ratcheted lower partial chords in stop timing; and screamed up the neck of the guitar into the higher octaves as I gave it my all, bleeding raw emotion across the strings.

I had never played so fast and furious in his life. But this was easily explained because, in fact, I wasn't playing at all. I was hitting the notes but I didn't know which ones as the volume control was now rattling around in the guitar and, if my solo could have been heard, it would have been a mere thin, discordant rattling of arbitrarily-plucked strings—the pathetic sound of an unamplified electric guitar.

The solo ended. The crowd never even noticed. But the bass player did. "Nice solo!" he shouted above the buzz of the crowd noise, "Next time, switch up a bit!"

Courtesy Wallasey News

Second set. I was flying. This time with emotion, not amphetamine—a Gibson! I cradled the smooth, designer neck in my left hand lovingly. A Gibson. I'd been lent a Gibson by the lead guitarist of one of the other bands. Oh joy!

At the back of my amphetamine-addled brain was the dim knowledge that, when normality returned, I would probably be deeply embarrassed by the wrong keys, wrong time, erroneous chord changes and faltering riffs that had been my contribution to the set so far. But now here was my chance to redeem myself.

Feeling ten feet tall, I stared across the ballroom like a warrior waiting for the next skirmish. I wielded the guitar like a loaded Uzi. With this, I could do anything!

The band lilted into a slow Ray Charles' number, *Drown in My Own Tears*, and I felt my way across the neck in an almost orgasmic delight. The notes purred out just as I would have them: gorgeous! I was playing my music: the blues. I was just getting the measure of the guitar when the number ended.

The crowd roared and stomped in approbation, and I flushed—my first normal sign of emotion—thinking, quite erroneously, that they had recognized that I was playing better.

"O.K.! O.K.!" screamed Derry, "You wan' it! You'll get it! And now, another number from the high-priest himself: *What'd I Say!!!*"

Despite my impending come-down, my synapses gave a final flare and my heart lit up as I soared into the riff which had been the cornerstone of Liverpool rock music since it started. The drummer's face lit up with a vast grin as he responded to my vibe, and he began belting out a rhythm that would not have shamed a steel mill punch machine.

My heart soared... I was there! My head was light, my face glistening with sweat. I felt that I could leap twenty feet in the air as I pumped out the rhythm, my heart full of the rightness of the moment. I closed my eyes and felt the wall of sound lick around me like honey.

"I gotta go. Can I have me guitar?"

The voice was an inch from my ear.

I turned, still intoxicated by the silky feel of the strings beneath my dancing fingers, the lilt and pulse of the music, the solid belly-thump of the rhythm. I found himself staring into the disgruntled face of the Gibson's owner.

"I said," the grim-faced youth repeated icily, "I want me guitar—now!"

I nodded, anguish contorting my features—but I did not relinquish the guitar. "Wait a mo'," I hissed, "Nearly finished."

Courtesy Wallasey News

But the number went on—and on. The bass player took a solo; each of the sax players took a solo—even the drummer. Still I would not give up the guitar.

Sour-faced, the Gibson owner thrust his face into mine as, frantic for this opportunity to redeem my lost kudos, I pumped everything I had into a guitar solo. "Look, I only lent it you for half an hour. You've had it an hour. Now I'm going to miss me lift home. Give it to me!"

I nodded desperately, but didn't stop playing.

Finally, the exasperated guitar owner grabbed the neck of the guitar and pulled.

I felt the whole tide of the evening's events in that pull. The hand clutching at the neck of the guitar was the grim hand of Fate as manifested by the precarious volume control, the impossible neck of the first guitar, the wrong chords, the wrong key, the wrong decision. And, in mid-solo, I dug my heels in and resisted the Fierce Tug of Destiny: Still playing, I pulled back on the guitar.

Courtesy Wallasey News

But the Gibson owner clamped his hands over it even more fiercely and thus began a struggle of life and death while, about us, the band members leapt and wiggled, playing their hearts out for the finale.

Bizarre chords rasped out of my amp, discordant and shrill, as three hands clamped around the neck: one hand, mine; the other two, the Gibson owner's. And still I played on, much as the orchestra on the Titanic had played on so many years before, ignoring the downward pull of dire Fate.

It is a curious, historical footnote that, in a few more years, with a few more wails, some extra distortion and feedback, the sound produced by the three hands on the Gibson's neck—rhythm perfect, melody arbitrary—would have set the crowd on fire, à la Jimi Hendrix. Unfortunately for me, the rock world of the early Sixties was not quite ready for such departures.

Discordant, squealing chords and rasping notes soared above the structure of the melody as in a kind of tunnel-vision trance, I played on, note for note, ignoring the other two hands around the Gibson's neck. I was going to finish my solo come hell or high water.

Finally, the Gibson owner won the tug of war. There was a final discordant jangle as I fell backwards onto the floor. The owner pulled at the cord with a vast amplified "pumph!", and, leaping from the stage with his possession tucked under his arm, disappeared into the crowd.

I sat down glumly on the edge of the stage and began poking into the F hole of the first guitar in an attempt to retrieve the volume control—and my lost glory—before the number ended. But, of course, I didn't make it.

The set finished. My confusion and dawning depression were momentarily occluded by the flurry of action as Derry's band folded down and four emaciated youths with greasy quiffs of hair leapt onto the stage, clad in black leather trousers that must have been, to say the least, uncomfortable under the hot lights. It was the Beatles, the next band.

I roused myself sufficiently to assist with the change-over, though I kept my eyes cast down, fixed on the floor, not daring to meet the eyes of George, the lead guitarist. George seemed curious about my approach to lead-guitar playing, but he was sensitive enough to see that I didn't want to talk about it. A grayishness was beginning to edge my thoughts and I didn't dare meet the eyes of my own band members, let alone those of another guitarist.

Finally, I climbed down from the stage while Derry stayed behind to announce the Beatles. Derry did a mumbling preamble and announced the Beatles, and the crowd clapped, stomped and whistled in approbation as the four leather-clad boys roared into their first number at twice the amplification of Derry's band.

As the dancers swirled and jostled around me, I stood glumly watching the other band, aware in retrospect of how badly I'd played everything in comparison to the way they were playing it.

Mesmerized by the Beatles, I became dully aware that my thigh itched. Then something ran up my leg. I jerked back and collided with a blonde girl, a virtual giantess by dint of the extra foot her bouffant hairstyle added to her height. "Sorry," I muttered distractedly, scratching at my thigh where the unknown thing still wriggled and writhed beneath my black pants.

"Don't be sorry! Be friggin' careful!" retorted the giantess, and whirled back into the crowd.

Panic surged in my breast, induced not by the girl's acid remarks but the sensation that something alien was crawling up my leg. Frantically, I dodged through the crowd and found my way to the toilets. I waited nervously in line with a score of beery, bucolic youths—all wearing blue suits, thick crepe-soled shoes and shiny ties—until one of the raw, evil-smelling toilet stalls was vacant. I dashed in, slammed the door, whipped my pants down and examined my thin, white legs feverishly.

Nothing. There was nothing there.

Then I realized what was happening: PMLD—post medication let-down.

I was on a come-down.

I was suddenly very aware of the horrific shadows of guilt, remorse and depression that were gnawing at the edge of my amphetamine-induced consciousness, only just held at bay by the residual shield of amphetamine. "Oh, Christ," I muttered despairingly and, pulling my pants up, I adjusted my fly and fled the toilet in the direction of the bar.

There I waited in line with (seemingly) the same crowd of acned, blue-suited, shiny-tied, crepe-soled youths until at last I managed to attract the attention of a barman, purchase a half a pint of bitter and hurriedly swallow down a large wad of amphetamine. Lost in my private nightmare, I choked down the cotton-wool. All around me the crowd swirled, the light twirled and the Beatles hammered out a fine version of *What'd I Say* with not a note out of place—much to my growing sense of impending doom.

Oddly enough, when I did collide (literally) with Derry, he said it'd sounded good and, despite my guilty protestations, Derry, ever the man of Fairness, paid me for the gig.

But I didn't go to bed that night—nor the next. In fact, I was awake for five days and five nights before I finally collapsed.

Don't try this at home

(as they say in Evil Knievel documentaries)

The fact is that, whereas marijuana is fairly benign, the taking of amphetamine in large doses is not. A price was paid for my '60s indulgence discussed here. In the short term, amphetamine psychosis struck me and my fellow musos. Most survived and moved on. Not all did. Three friends were hospitalized and one is a permanent resident in a long-term mental hospital. The chapter *Death and Madness in Liverpool* says it all.

Courtesy Mindscaffolding

The Liverpool Drugs Council Building

66

The South Discovers Liverpool

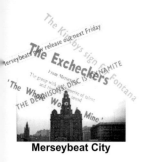
The South Discovers Liverpool

We were the ones who were looked down upon by the Southerners, the Londoners. The Northerners in the States think that the people are pigs down South. The people in New York think the West Coast is hick. So we were Hicksville

John Lennon
Rolling Stone Interview, 1971

As the Beatles suddenly shot to fame, the south of England, that had hitherto ignored the "hick" North, especially Liverpool, suddenly discovered it existed and hordes of producers,

The Kirkbys sign for Fontana

Courtesy Combo

newsmen and others looking for a fast buck descended on Liverpool and began signing up groups left, right and center, ad hoc. Recording sessions were set up in school rooms, ballrooms—and any other suitable spaces—as groups were hastily recorded as the "Next Big Thing".

Pop magazines by the score began articles on the "Pool" and the Liverpool accent—which sounds rather like a docker with asthma talking through a wet sock—suddenly became de rigueur with

THE VAMPIRES OF WALLASEY SIGN FOR COLUMBIA

DAVE and the Vampires from Wallasey last week rocked EMI recording men to their heels with the vitality of their new sound.

And now the group is expected to climb high in the disc world with their first record — "I'll Do What I Like" c/w "My Life" both penned and arranged by Kris Williams, the lead guitarist.

The record will be released on the Columbia label.

This group is so good that after a Scottish Television appearance they received 2,000 fan letters and their fan club was boosted to a staggering

Kris Williams (lead).

Mike White (bass).

membership of more than membership of more than 5,000.

TOUR
Now, the Vampires have undertaken a tour with Fosters Agency of London and they will appear at the Tetro Volturna in Rome followed by a tour of Scandinavia, Italy and Germany.

They will finish the trip in Copenhagen.

The lads are also booked to appear in London at the Two I's coffee bar, the coffee club which set many rock 'n roll stars, including Tommy

Steele, along the precarious tightrope to fame.

But the Vampires are already three-quarters of the way along the rope.

Dave (vocalist).

Mike Cooper (drums).

"Walking
The Dog"
(side A)

THE DENNISONS' DISC IS DYNAMITE

Merseybeats new release out next Friday

The Merseybeats were last week presented with a Silver Disc to mark the quarter million sales of their record "I Think Of You".
The presentation was made by Gordon Knowles, manager of the Locarno at Liverpool.
The Merseybeats' newest recording "Don't Turn Round" will be released next Friday, April 10 on the Fontana label, Combo learned this week.
Manager Alan Cheetham said last week he has so far refused to go on tour because the "Beats have not been top of the bill.
They will however, be topping the bill shortly at the Prince of Wales theatre in London.

Courtesy Combo

"You
Don't
Know"
(side B)

media types and debutantes alike.

Of course, the Liverpool groups were in seventh heaven. Who wouldn't be? In fact, in the light of posterity, apart from the British Invasion that followed the Beatles to America, very few of the groups that were signed got anywhere. Some did have a modicum of success at first, only to fall by the wayside later.

However, these were Salad Days for Liverpool, which was rolling on the crest of a wave of publicity. Pop magazines like Fab did in-depth articles on the phenomenon, such as the recording of the Merseybeat album, *At the Cavern*—which provided a memorable article in full "pop-esque" English.

SIDE ONE The Meranders (two numbers), the Fortunes, (two numbers), Beryl Marsden, the Dennisons (two numbers) and Heinz. A bumper bundle with the platter power that typifies the scintillating cellar of song.
All the torrid atmosphere of the Cavern has been captured by Decca A & R man Noel Walker in the grooves of this masterly LP with the Liverpool artists coming over exceptionally well-particularly on this side, Beryl Marsden, and also the Dennisons' with their number "You'd Better Move On".
This is great. This is the Big Beat sound stripped of its artificiality and laid bare to best effect. Play it — say it: "Decca — Live at the Cavern".

SIDE TWO: Heinz, Dave Berry and the Cruisers (two numbers), the Big Three, Lee Curtis and the All-Stars (two numbers), and Bern Elliot and the Fenmen (two numbers).
Once again, the Liverpool outfits, Lee Curtis and the All-Stars, and the Big Three, provide the power-packed punch of sound on this side. But the Fenman with the powerful beat that put cash registers ringing with their "Money" are not far behind and the unusual brand of Dave Berry's rythm and blues stamps an indelible impression on the listener.
SUMMARY: We shall be surprised, very surprised, if this doesn't leap to the top of the LP charts. But we won't be surprised if it becomes only the second LP to climb high into the single charts.

Decca LP : Biggest seller for the best cellar?

Courtesy Combo

Lee Curtis▶

singing raises the screams, (and the roof.)

Ready, steady, go! The Big Three's Faron is all set for the session, and what a session!

Maraccas and 'mood' music from Dave Berry.

The Merseyside miss scores a hit— Beryl Marsden.

The Cave-dwellers twist and shout their appreciation. The Dennisons have girls frenzied.

Testing time for Heinz, Noel (left) and Terry.

Heinz brings out the screamers at The Cavern.

Fab's June is in Liverpool with the lowdown

● So this is it. The Cavern. The Beatles have pulled out, so have Gerry and Billy J. But there aren't any ghosts here. It's a sunny Monday morning and Decca have moved in to record a "live" LP at the home of the Mersey beat

Ten thirty and not a soul in sight.

Let's take a walk. Let's soak in some of this atmosphere. The Cavern itself is cool, shadowy, comfortably shabby. Its stage tiny. The band-room lies next to the stage, and you'd better watch yourself because the floor is built on two levels—we don't want you to break your neck yet.

Noel Walker is already fiddling with the jam-packed-tight equipment and issuing instructions to technicians Terry Johnson and Gus Dudgeon. The LP is Noel's "baby". He's a neat, quiet young man who has a thing about the Liverpool sound. He should. He grew up with it. Although he works as a record producer for Decca in London, he's a Liverpudlian and since he recorded a hit LP here with The Big Three he's been rarin' to come back for a longer session. He's back.

Something's happening in the band-room. Surprise, surprise, it's The Big Three! Out in The Cavern, the first club members are arriving for the daily lunch-time shake session. The Cavern's resident deejay, Bob Wooler, gentle and helpful, says Hello to everyone and puts on a Sonny Boy Williamson disc as a "warm-up".

The Cave-dwellers are predictable. The girls usually have silky hair and leather coats; the boys are mostly mod. Many of them come here every day. A coke from the refreshment counter, and they're away. There's a Freddie-type doing a wild Mick Jagger shake on the floor while his girl friend does a mild shakedown of The Cavern Stomp.

Behind the scenes, Johnny Hutchinson of The Big Three is drumming gently to himself. Faron of The Big Three is not-so-gently stumbling from one floor level to the other. Paddy Chambers is just trying to push both of them on to the stage.

This is it, then. We're ready to put The Cavern on disc. Comes a slick announcement from Bob Wooler. Mersey beat from The Big Three, and the rest follow on. Sheffield's Dave Berry and The Cruisers are strictly on a U.S. kick with Bo Diddley and *Chuck* Berry faves—tailor-made for the r'n'b crazy Caverners. Liverpool's group-most-likely, The Dennisons get the crowd to fever pitch.

The beat bashes round The Cavern and slaps the bare brick walls like a fairground gone mad. The dancers are caught in the light for a second then shake back into the shadows.

They take a breather when a newish group called The Fortunes send a pleasantly folksy flavour around, but when Lee Curtis and The All-Stars take the stand, the scene is—er—wild again. A great crashing beat brings in *Jezebel*, and Lee (wearing, incidentally, an orange leather jerkin over a navy and white polka-dot shirt) gives *Jezebel* all he's got.

Ray MacFall, The Cavern's popular owner, smoothly threads a way through the stompers and disappears into the band-room. The reason soon appears in the form of Beryl Marsden, Liverpool's answer to Brenda Lee. Small girl, big, big voice. As she swings out, The Marauders come in with some belting American numbers.

The session is nearly all on tape, and the band-room is bulging with bods. Lee Curtis, and some of the boys from the groups that have already done their bit, are taking in the scene. Heinz, who has been around for most of the day, looks a bit nervous. With reason. He's brought more fans to The Cavern than you might see in a week here, and most of them are pressing against the flimsy door of the band-room, asking for him.

Bern Elliott and The Fenmen are on stage proving how underrated they are, with a Ray Charles fire-cracker *Talkin' About You*, and a beautiful arrangement of *All My Sorrows*.

Courtesy FAB

Article from Fab Magazine covering the recording of the album, *At The Cavern*

The "Posh" Papers Get in on the Act

LIVERPOOL 8:
The new culture
of 'Beat City'
Also this week:
READY FOR
'THE FLAT'

Eventually, even the "highbrows" stumbled onto Liverpool and learned musical critiques began to inform the population of the "complex modal structure" of the Beatles' songs. Even the Sunday Telegraph, a highly conservative, "posh" newspaper delved into the arcane mysteries of the dim-and-distant port and found, surprise, surprise, that not only was there a healthy music scene but that Liverpudlians were equally as adept at art, poetry, literature and even architecture.

Both photographs courtesy Weekend Daily Telegraph

Giant Beatles' Head

Sam Walsh, a 32-year-old Wexfod Irishman, came to Liverpool for the weekend seven years ago and stayed "for lots of reasons". He now teaches at the College of Art and makes his home in an attic pad in Huskisson Street. Walsh has been quietly building a firm reputation for his work up and down the country. Liverpool University has recently bought five of his paintings, and the city's Walker Art Gallery has two. Walsh paints large—the 5 ft 6 in head of Paul McCartney has been a contender for the world size title in portraits; The painting is whimsically called "Mike's Brother". One of the Walker's paintings is a huge head of Francis Bacon, who has clearly influenced a good deal of Walsh's work.

Walsh now wants to grow out into the third dimension, but the expense deters him. "They're doing great things in the States now with plastic and fibreglass and the only difference from us, like Hemingway said to Fitzgerald, is that they have more money."

71

The Weekend Daily Telegraph 1967

From a decrepit, decaying part of the Beatle City, a whole new Mersey Scene is ready to burst out; a scene that mixes local dialect, poetry, music, art and happenings. By SEAN HIGNETT.

One afternoon last summer the dolly girls in Bold Street, the smart shopping centre of Liverpool, had their eyes dragged from the minifurs in the shop windows by an extraordinary sight. Up the hill, on the steps of the blitz-blackened shell of St Luke's Church, a huge hardboard Ace of Spades was being hacked to pieces by a gang of beardies. Transparent plastic sausages, filled with multi-coloured liquids like the jars in a chemist's shop, were being pierced with darts by a litter of scruffy infants and a booming voice was declaiming across the heads of the attendant policewomen: "The daughters of Albion sleep in the dinnertime sunlight with old men looking up their skirts in St John's Gardens."

What was happening was a "happening" or, in Liverpool terminology, an "event", sponsored jointly by a local store owner and a black bearded, bespectacled, roly-poly poet, Adrian Henri. The "event" was one of several conducted in an attempt to bring an underground art into the open and bring Liverpool 8 down the hill and into the town.

Liverpool 8 postal district touches the city at the top of Bold Street. Behind St Luke's begins its grid of wide-open Georgian streets, where flaking stuccoed terrace houses stand silently in the light of gas lamps. Reasonably well preserved at the city end, where some of the houses are stone built and reminiscent of Edinburgh's New Town, the area decays rapidly after the first hundred yards and then, pock-marked by the demolition sites that have been added to the bomb sites of two decades ago, disappears altogether in a sea of rubble.

The first thing to strike one is the absence of cars, even where, in little islands, the multi-tenanted, multi-racial houses still stand. And then, as everywhere in Liverpool, the abundance of children: scrambling over the bomb sites, warming their hands round the watchman's huts on the demolition sites and playing in the wide streets themselves, where, with no threatening cars, they can kick a ball or make-believe with a battered pram or a wheelless bicycle. Stand still here and you will be asked for a penny, a sweet, have a ball thrown at you, be a threatened by Batman, menaced by dirty faces or just looked at. Stand still and you will be asked to settle a million arguments: who's biggest, best, oldest, toughest; Everton, Liverpool, the Green or the Orange. Stand still and you will be covered in children like St Francis was covered in birds.

At night the scrap from the derelict houses is gathered and every vacant site has its bonfire, attended by infant witch doctors and alchemists, baking potatoes, melting lead pipes in tin cans. The whole area is lit by the fires on the street corners that cast long shadows where the puny light from the gas lamps doesn't reach. The houses that remain have, in many cases, permanently open doors or no doors at all, windows are missing and boarded over with cardboard and cornflakes packets, and a united nations sits on the doorsteps in an area that, despite slogans such as KEEP AFRICA BLACK in letters four feet high, has little or no discrimination.

People like Viennese born Fritz Spiegl, flautist, musical joker and now cornering the market in Scouse publications (his recent *Lern Yerself Scouse* actually grabbed a leader in *The Times Literary Supplement*) have lived and created in the area for a generation. So has Quentin Hughes, an architect battling for Liverpool's dockland architecture and author of *Seaport*, an extremely sensitive photographic survey of the city. Others like Bill Harpe, agnostic director of a £50,000 festival that will this year open the new Catholic Cathedral, have arrived recently and find District 8 the only place to live. But it is the bunch of Liverpool poets now being published nationally and in quantity that depends most on and draws most from this ghetto of by-gone glories.

Half way up Canning Street—with Huskisson Street one of the main arteries of the area—at the top of a house teeming with artists, beat groups, poets and birds, lives Adrian Henri. Henri is the nerve centre of the area, tuned in to the comings and goings. Poets, painters and journalists looking for Liverpool turn up sooner or later in his attic pad. A painter by training and a lecturer at the Liverpool College of Art, Henri's pop-poetry is heavily dependent on Liverpool images—"Marcel Proust dipping marmalade butties in his tea in the Kardomah Cafe". Of the three poets that perhaps constitute a Liverpool school, he is the most articulate in explaining his progress and attitudes.

Poetry in Liverpool seems to have started in a coffee bar called Street's long before the beat scene developed. "The beat thing has simply focused attention on it. There wasn't even football—when we started Everton were in the Second Division. We used to go along to Street's after the pubs closed and there was this 15-year-old kid reading this marvellous stuff."

The 15-year-old kid was Brian Patten, now an old-in-the-head 20 and publisher of *Underdog*, an "underground poetry magazine". In June, Allen and Unwin are publishing his first collection, *Little Johnny's Confessions*, and he is one of the poets in *The Mersey Beat* being published by Penguin at the same time, along with Henri and Roger McGough.

McGough, too, is happening in the autumn when Michael Joseph's are bringing out, with his mini-novel, *Frink*, his series of poems, *Summer with Monica*.

Though these three poets have performed as a group and are being canonised by Penguin as the Liverpool school, they stress that their poems have little in common. "I suppose you could say that we simply cross-fertilise."

On top of his poetry and painting, Henri is responsible for the "events" that have been a unique feature of the Liverpool scene; unique in that, like the affair on St Luke's steps, they took the poetry and painting to the kids and mixed it up with the pop scene. "The really special thing about Liverpool poetry is the audience. The front row at Street's was practically the same as the front row at the Cavern."

Official Liverpool has not cut itself off from the developments in this uptown area. The Bluecoat Society, an old-established arts centre, recently commissioned a survey of the arts in Liverpool by author John Willett. Willett found that a great deal of his material came from Liverpool Eight, where the poetry and the pity, the painters, musicians and dancers are all mixed up together, living on top of each other in a small area and falling over each other every time they go out of the house. Liverpool Eight is where the new Mersey sound and scene will come from . . . provided it's left standing long enough.

Accidental Hit

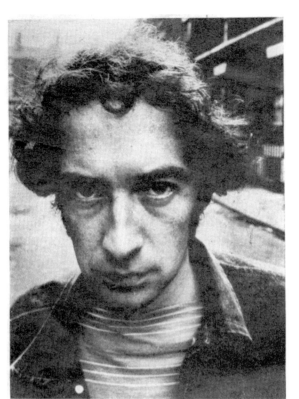

Courtesy Weekend Daily Telegraph

Roger McGough, early '60s

Roger McGough, one of the best-known residents of the district, lectures part-time in liberal studies at the Liverpool College of Art. But his serious time, he says, is spent writing poetry and performing with the off-beat Liverpool cabaret group, The Scaffold. The group grew out of a Merseyside Arts Festival organised by another Scaffolder, John Gorman—the third is Beatle-brother, Mike McCartney-McGear. Success came by accident. "When ABC-TV auditioned us, we never meant to be funny—it was just the way that Gorman read it."

McGough got into poetry via Street's coffee bar. "then there were readings at Hope Hall with Gorman. Henri joined us as a happeningist and the poetry became dialogues and trialogues. That's the thing here—there's no preconceoptions about what poetry is. The arts are all mixed up."

Mother, the wardrobe is full of infantrymen
i did, i asked them,
but they smiled saying it was a man's life

Mother, there is a centurion in the parlour
i did, i asked the officer
but he laughed saying Queens regulations,
and it was out of tune anyway

Mother, polish your identity bracelet
there is a mushroom cloud in the backgarden
i did, i tried to bring in the cat
but it simply came to pieces in my hand
i did, i tried to whitewash the windows
but there weren't any
i did, i tried ringing Candid Camera
but they crossed their hearts.

Roger McGough

It is difficult to avoid becoming involved with children in Liverpool 8. Kids play football in mid-road, behind them an upturned car and a derelict site. They spend little of their time indoors. Inside the falling-down houses, sometimes crammed a family to a room with a shared cooker on each landing, they will eat, sleep and glean enough from the telly to furnish their games with new characters. The street is their football pitch, the derelict ground their campsite and the wrecked car their Batmobile.

Courtesy Weekend Daily Telegraph

SOUVENIR PROGRAMME ~ 10 P.(2s)cheap.

THE 1st MERSEYBEAT REUNION

Courtesy Peter Halligan

The reunion was organized by Allan Williams of the Jacaranda Club in February 1971

The Cavern Reunion
Hosted by Bob Wooler

Courtesy John Edwards

The Cavern Reunion
Standing at back: Denis Swale, Ritchie Routledge, Steve Aldo, Finn Bradshaw, Alan Jones, Geof Bamford, Alan Lee
Sitting in front: Bob McGray, Mike Hart, Dave Williams, Rikki Cluskey, Brendan McCormack, Bob Wooler, John Edwards

Courtesy Bob Wooler
Bob Wooler on his DJ box at the Cavern, early '60s

Courtesy Bob Wooler
Bob Wooler, right, and Ray McFall, owner of the Cavern, 1964

Bob Wooler: Dr. Rock

No mention of the Liverpool scene could possibly omit a character who was not only larger-than-life but was way ahead of his time in his bombastic, tongue-twisting deliveries and pithy rock platitudes. That is, of course, the man who heralded the Beatles and many many more: the Cavern's famous D.J., Bob Wooler.

Below is an interview with Bob, conducted by Peter Halligan at the 1971 Reunion.

CALLING DOCTOR ROCK
BOB WOOLER INTERVIEWED BY PETER HALLIGAN

It was appropriate that Merseyside impresario Allan Williams should invite Bob Wooler to compere his Mersey Beat reunion event, for Bob Wooler and the Mersey Beat go together like salt and pepper.

Bob is Liverpool's first-ever disc jockey - he is known as the Beatles' dee-jay - and was very much in the swim of things in the Liver(pop)pool heyday. He now describes himself as "an amphibian who is more on dry land than in the water these days", although he still moves and grooves in pop circles.

When I asked him to name his favourite disc jockey he said it was Christopher 'Fibre Needles' Stone, adding "what a knock-out name for a dee-jay". This is all rather above my head and is either very, very 'in' or way, way back. Of the BBC in general he had this to say: "I'm at one with William Hardcastle's World At One but as for Radio One I still find most of it the biggest drag since Charley's Aunt! Personally, I think the local radio set-ups do pop much better".

Bob Wooler now calls himself a geological Musicologist and when I asked him what geological music was he exclaimed: "Rock, man, Rock!"

Like many other people I have wondered how he got the name Doctor Rock. He said: "Blame it on Ted Knibbs. He tagged me with it. This was way back in the early Sixties when Ted was very much on the scene as a talent spotter - he discovered Billy Kramer, you know. Ted was being interviewed by one of the musical papers and he described my 'prescriptions' for boosting flagging business at local dances and shows, and thus he labelled me Doctor Rock. To go with my 'practice' I had some business 'rave' cards printed bearing the legend: Bob Wooler - Rock 'n' Roll Consultant. I was made up when Stanley Reynolds did a piece about it in the Guardian.

"But that was many hit parades ago," Bob continued, "when our budding Mersey Beat scene was a comparatively innocent Garden of Eden with no sign of the Apple let alone the serpent!"

Then came the Beatles' breakthrough, and all of a sudden the Liverpool pop people were riding on the crest of a fantastic sound-wave of worldwide acclaim. TV, films, radio, the international Press, Fleet Street - they all came to investigate the amazing Merseyside pop explosion. As Bob Wooler puts it: "We had them all - from Akess to Zec - asking the same recurring questions: Just what is the Mersey Sound? Why here in Liverpool? Why long hair? What's with all this leather stuff? What does 'gear' mean? Has it anything to do with talking thgough your nose? And always the 64,000 dollar question: Is the Mersey brand of Rock the real thing - does it have Liverpool all the way through it?

"I guess the beginning of the end came when the cream of the scene sort of EMIgrated (sorry, but i've always wanted to slip that one in!). They became the nucleus of Brian Epstein's London-based pop Nempire; along with fellow-Merseysiders Tony Barrow and Derek Taylor".

So the limelight shifted back South and the British pop public developed a pronounced nausea for all things North West. Doctor Rock diagnosed it thus: "The nation was afflicted with an acute attack of mal-de-Mersey! Scouse was as 'out' as Strauss. You see, the whole Liverpool thing had been overdone, and what with the Beatles being strictly for export only and due to tour the moon or something like that nobody wanted to know any more. And when Hollywood manufactured the Monkees, we knew then we'd really had it. The fantastic Mersey Sound was stricken with scenile decay, and there followed more hang ups then an orgy of Roman crucifixions!

"So, you see, for some of us on the Mersey scene the good old bandwagon didn't turn into a gravy train after all. In fact it could be said (if you'll pardon another mixed metaphor) that those of us who stayed on the scene also missed the boat. All the same it was swell whilst it lasted, as Ray McFall used to say - Ray owned the Cavern Club when it was Liverpool's No. 1 tourist attraction. I think the Mersey scene's Napoleon.of Pop, Allan Williams, would go along with this philosophy too.

"About this time, some of our pop scene pioneers went forth to spread the gospel. People like Bill Harry, for instance, he was the founder-editor of the Mersey Beat pop paper, you know. He went to London to do PR work and he established a 'Little Liverpool' colony there. Agent Joe Flannery was pretty busy too, flying the Scouse flag for us on the Hamburg scene."

Bob Wooler maintains that Liverpool groups are still in the forefront of British pop culture. He insists that nobody can really challenge the supremacy of the Spinners for Folk music, the Scaffold for satire, the Hillsiders and Phil Brady for C & W, Adrian Henri and Co. for poetry, or of course the Beatles for Rock.

"You know," he mused, "before the advent of the Scouse Sound Sixties the nearest Liverpool ever got to a pop music mention was 'Mairzy Doats'. Amazing how the Beatles changed all that and really put us on the music map. Equally amazing is how the Beatles themselves were to change finally suffer the fate of Humpty Dumpty; You know, all the king's horses and all the king's men couldn't put them together again. George developed his own Guru-vy kind of love. Ringo decided all he had to do was act Nashville-ly. John indulged his penchant for full frontal assaults via LP (un)covers and turned Apple HQ into a kind of Phallus of Varieties. As for Paul, he did a pretty effective conversion job on their Rockumentary movie, 'Let it Be'. What started out as a joint effort, he made into a vehicle for himself and a hearse for the Beatles as a group.

"But whatever reservations we may have about the Beatles, MBE (in my book that stands for Mersey Beatsters Extraordinary!) if they had never 'come together' and achieved all that fantastic universal acclaim - the greatest in pop music history - then the Mersey Beat phenomenon would never have existed as the whole world knows of it today, and of course we would not be celebrating its exciting reverberations on this big reunion night."

The Fab Four's Favorite Group
A Report by Bob Wooler

"Over the years, I have often been asked by Beatle fans, especially at conventions, who were the favorite Mersey Beat groups of the Fab Four, when they were rubbing shoulders with them on the Liverpool scene.

The Beatles played lots of venues on both sides of the river at the beginning of the Sixties, notably the Cavern, where indeed, they did their last club gig in August, 1963. They also played in Southport, St. Helens, Widnes and Chester, and a number of other places in the North West. All in all, they were on stage here for about four years, sharing the bill with a whole host of local groups which they inevitably saw. They also made it their business to watch a lot of groups while they were doing lunchtime sessions at the Cavern, including those from Manchester like **The Hollies**, **Pete Maclean and The Clan** and **Wayne Fontana and The Mindbenders**.

There were then about 500 groups playing on Merseyside. About 50 of these were rated by punters and promoters as having any sort of following, and to boast anything worthwhile to offer, sound and presentation-wise.

This being a family newspaper, I can hardly quote some of the "assessments" made by the Beatles at the time about certain groups they saw. The most outspoken Beatle was, predictably, John Lennon, although George Harrison didn't pull any punches either in expressing his views. I was often belabored and blamed for certain groups being on the same bill with them. What they chose to ignore was that these groups were, in their own way, quite an attraction with some of the customers and as a result were a box office draw. Besides, their fee was so low it didn't cause the dance hall promoter to lose any sleep."

APPROVAL

"Generally speaking, the Beatles favored groups that didn't feature a front man. This meant that the likes of **Lee Castle and The Barons**, **Ray and The Delrenas**, **Cliff Roberts and The Rockers** or **Mark Peters and The Cyclones** didn't really get a look in with them. All the

Rory Storm and The Hurricanes (Rory is far left)

Courtesy Harry Prytherch

77

Earl Present and the TTs
Performing with Wendy Harris—an unusual sight at that time: a female vocalist

Kingsize Talyor and The Dminoes *(with Kingsize inset)*

The Merseybeats
Courtesy Mindscaffolding

more reason why, surprisingly, they were very pro **Rory Storm and the Hurricanes**. I think it was the type of numbers they used to play, which was raw rock 'n roll. "

"Another case in point was **Early Preston and the TTs** who met with the Beatles' approval.

Kingsize Taylor and The Dominoes was also a "front man" group, but you could hardly say Kingsize was a sex symbol. Although he did most of the singing, he was also an excellent guitarist, and once again specialized in true rock 'n roll numbers as originally done by the likes of Gene Vincent.

The group the **Merseybeats**, however, combined the image and the style of the Beatles, so much so, that when the Fab Four left Liverpool in late '63, they went a long way to filling the vacuum."

TOP 10

"**The Road Runners**, who hailed from the Wirral, were also much favored, being a typical non-conformist R&B band who didn't care about a "pretty boy" image. The Cordes, another local group of the time, similarly got their nod; and, although they were their arch rivals, so did **The Undertakers**.

The 4 Jays (later called **The Fourmost**) were always consistent favorites of the Beatles, and they actually chose them to be the other group with them on a special Fan Club night at the Cavern in April 1962. Later, The Fourmost were to record Beatle numbers and get into the U.K. Top 10 with them."

"**The Remo 4** was another highly-rated Liverpool group. This

Courtesy Dave Williams

The Undertakers

was chiefly because the Beatles always respected the musicianship of the act, although they tended to concentrate on duplicating numbers by the Shadows.

All these groups—and many others that I just haven't got space to mention—must be familiar to lots of Merseymart readers who were in their teens about 25 years ago.

It would be really difficult to pinpoint one particular group that got the seal of approval from all four members of the Beatles. This is because they each had different views and they often made these known in places like band rooms where there was some degree of privacy."

Courtesy Harry Prytherch

The Remo Four outside their first van

Courtesy FAB

The Fourmost

Courtesy Patrick Cluskey

Rikki and the Red Streaks
Brendan McCormack on left. The drummer was absent that day, which is why the drums sport the "Bob Evans" legend

EXCEPTIONAL

*"John Lennon is quoted as saying that a Litherland group called **Rikki and His Redstreaks** was his favorite, which has caused many Beatle fans to ask who on earth they were. They, in fact, mainly played north-end venues (like Lathom Hall and Litherland Town Hall) where they enjoyed a solid and loyal following.*

*Perhaps the group that always came into any reckoning was **The Big Three**. This combo comprised three of the most talented musicians on Merseyside: Johnny Hutchinson on drums and vocals; Brian Griffiths on guitar and vocals; and Johnny Gustafson on bass guitar and vocals.*
I know for a fact that Paul McCartney always regarded Johnny Gus as being an outstanding bass player, possibly the best in Liverpool.

Years before the London super group, Cream, came into being, we had up here The Big Three. If the Beatles were to settle for just one of the many exceptional groups that came from Merseyside during the Sixties, I believe from what they said at the time, that they would have chosen The Big Three."

—BOB WOOLER

Courtesy Johnny Gustafson

The Big Three
Johnny Gustafson, bass (left), Johnny Hutchison, drums , Brian Griffiths, guitar

Some of the pieces of the historical puzzle have been furnished by the musicians themselves in the previous chapters.

There were, however, other movements afoot which were unseen, as it was history-in-the-making. These were such that the conditions in England for the workers post-World War II were much akin to the position of blacks in America post-Vietnam.

But English whites knew little of the downside of America. For them, it was a distant land of glitz and glam...

The Lure Of America

The Lure of America

Life in postwar Britain was spartan, and to the Brits, America seemed to be the land of milk and honey—a colorful cornucopia of movies, music, money, glitz, glam and very hip people.

But though postwar Britain may have been austere economically, in terms of ideas and development it was one of the most exciting times in history. Working-class males had come to see England with new eyes; a green, idyllic isle for which they had fought and won (and, in some cases, even died). For the first time in history, the people of Britain were beginning to see themselves not as British subjects, the silent masses, but as the people of Great Britain. This found its greatest expression in British youth, and, as one, they turned their eyes longingly across the sea to the colorful, cheerful, affluent freedom of America.

Jeff Beck idolized everything that was American, from cars to guitars. The Beatles' music was a peculiar mixture of American and traditional British elements, from Harry Lauder to Hank Marvin, Americanisms peeked through its very original fabric: bits of Elvis, The Shirelles; the call-and-response of The Coasters; the rockabilly of Carl Perkins; the eclectic country of Chet Atkins; the down-home Southern riffs of Scotty Moore; the jump-swing of Chuck Berry; the hoarse harmonies of the Raelettes; the twang of Duane Eddy. Yes, in their music, all of America was there and, underlying it all was the underpinnings of the blues.

In postwar Britain, American black music was not simply accepted, it was revered. Touring black American musicians were greeted with something akin to awe, a fact which dazed and surprised them when they first came to England. Little Richard was the King; Chuck Berry was the Jack of Spades; Ray

Courtesy Mindscaffolding

T-Bone Walker Played in the Jazz Unlimited Program, early '60s

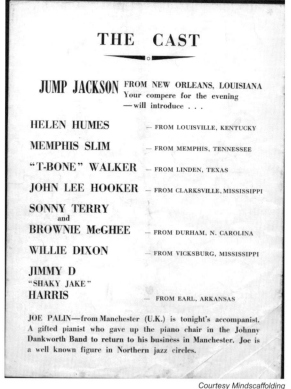

Courtesy Mindscaffolding

Program for Jazz Unlimited Festival

Big Bill Broonzey at the Temple Bar, Liverpool, mid '50s

The Liverpool musical connection with black America was already well established in the 1950s. The author's father, a poor plumber and talented pianist, attended Big Bill's gig at the Temple. He was later to comment to his son—as a disparaging comment about his son's fascination with the "three chord wonder" of rock and roll—that Big Bill Broonzey and Eddie Lang were the best guitar players he'd ever heard

Charles was the High Priest of Soul. Britain assimilated the blues wholesale, for everything to do with America had a charisma and an allure that made it larger than life.

LONNIE DONEGAN, the British Skiffle King spent a considerable time trying to get material from America. There was very little in evidence in postwar Britain. The BBC's policy on music was a rather stuffy leftover from the highbrow tastes of an aristocratic ruling class—they might feature a couple of hours of blues or jazz a week at the most, and that was that.

Donegan was to find his main source of supply in Collett's Book and Second-Hand Shop, Charing Cross Road, London. The material Lonnie culled from this small bookshop was to become no less than the starting point for the entire British rock scene that emerged in the '60s. Oddly, the bookshop was a Communist shop and it carried music by American traditional artists and blacks because it was "music of the people".

Music of the people.

This simple phrase underscores a crucial factor which ensured that an entire generation of Brit teenagers embraced American music.

To truly understand why it should be so, it is necessary to picture '60s England as an emerging nation toppling the final bastions of an ancient feudal system, its youth struggling for sexual expression and identity. To say the British Empire had disintegrated is too strong. But what is true is that, whereas youth in prewar Britain knew its place *unquestioningly*, postwar youth definitely did not and *questioned* everything. Coupled to this, the McCarren-Waler Act of 1952 meant that those Caribbean blacks who had been denied access to America began immigrating to England instead. Into the turbulent, postwar melange of Britain's crumbling social system poured these blacks, bringing with them the sun, Caribbean color and the rhythms and excitement of both West Indian and Afro-American music.

In a cycle that had taken years to complete, they ended up in those cities from which the slave

Courtesy Tony Davis

Pete Seeger at a gig in Liverpool with Tony Davis of The Spinners

Colin Areety

At last, record companies are again realising that there is still a great deal of talent in Liverpool, and over the past few months it has certainly been proved in the form of the record charts.

It will not be long before another 'star' will reach that destination - I mean of course Colin Areety. Merseysiders, in all walks of life, always have that certain determination to do well, and Colin, born Liverpool 1947, is no exception. On stage his determination and talent flow freely and his performance can be quite devastating.

From topping the bill at the North's leading venues, including the Hamilton, Birkenhead, the Wookey Hollow and Allinson's, Liverpool, his services are now well in demand throughout the U.K.

This L.P. which has been specially prepared for Colin to have with him on his travels, features a mixture of songs which Colin performs in his stage act, and I'm sure you will keep and treasure for many years to come.

I, personally, wish Colin all the luck in the world, and know in my own mind that this dedicated person will soon reach his aim.

Ben E. King

Ben E. King

SIDE ONE

1. I'VE GOT TO MAKE IT ON MY OWN (CARLIN MUSIC) 3.10
2. NEITHER ONE OF USE (CARLIN MUSIC) 3.28
3. YOU SEE THE TROUBLE WITH ME (SCHROADER MUSIC) 3.05
4. THE HUNGRY YEARS (WARNER BROS. MUSIC) 3.50
5. THE BEST THING THAT EVER HAPPENED (ARDMORE BEECHWOOD) 3.40
6. HEAVEN MUST BE MISSING AN ANGEL (BULL PEN MUSIC/LEVY MUSIC) 3.55

SIDE TWO

1. YOU'LL NEVER FIND ANOTHER LOVE LIKE MINE (CARLIN MUSIC) 3.20
2. I JUST CAN'T GET YOU OUT OF MY MIND (KPM MUSIC LTD.) 3.32
3. THE WAY WE WERE (SCREEN GEMS COLUMBIA MUSIC) 3.06
4. YOU'RE THE FIRST THE LAST (SCHROADER MUSIC) 3.40
5. MY WORLD KEEPS GETTING SMALLER EVERY DAY (WARNER BROS.) 3.50
6. WHEN WILL I SEE YOU AGAIN (GAMBLE & HUFF MUSIC) 2.45

Courtesy Colin Areety

Liverpool singer Colin Areety with Ben E. King of The Drifters' fame

COMBO   April 3 — April 9, 1964

TOP TWENTY

1. CAN'T BUY ME LOVE.
   (The Beatles).
2. LITTLE CHILDREN.
   (Billy J. Kramer).
3. JUST A LITTLE BIT.
   (The Undertakers).
4. ANYONE WHO HAD A
   HEART.
   (Cilla Black).
5. GOOD GOLLY MISS
   MOLLY.
   (Swinging Blue Jeans).
6. BITS AND PIECES.
   (Dave Clark Five).
7. DIZZY MISS LIZZIE.
   (Escorts).
8. DIANE.
   (The Bachelors).
9. I BELIEVE.
   (The Bachelors).
10. CINDY'S GOING TO
    CRY.
    (Mark Peters and the Sil-
    houettes).
11. I'M THE ONE.
    (Gerry and the Pacema-
    kers).
12. I THINK OF YOU.
    (The Merseybeats).
13. THAT GIRL BELONGS
    TO YESTERDAY.
    (Gene Pitney).
14. NEEDLES AND PINS.
    (Searchers).
15. JUST ONE LOOK.
    (Hollies).
16. NOT FADE AWAY.
    (Rolling Stones).
17. 5—4—3—2—1.
    (Manfred Mann).
18. STAY AWHILE.
    (Dusty Springfield).
19. FOR YOU.
    (Rick Nelson).
20. EIGHT BY TEN.
    (Ken Dodd).

TOP TWENTY

1. SHE LOVES YOU.
   Beatles.
2. I WANT TO HOLD
   YOUR HAND.
   Beatles.
3. TWIST AND SHOUT.
   Beatles.
4. PLEASE PLEASE ME.
   Beatles.
5. DAWN (Go Away).
   4 Seasons.
6. FUN, FUN, FUN.
   Beach Boys.
7. HELLO, DOLLY.
   Louis Armstrong.
8. SUSPICION.
   Terry Stafford.
9. MY HEART BELONGS
   TO ONLY YOU.
   Bobby Vinton.
10. GLAD ALL OVER.
    Dave Clark Five.
11. HI - HEEL SNEAK-
    ERS.
    Tommy Tucker.
12. KISSIN' COUSINS.
    Elvis Presley.
13. NAVY BLUE.
    Diane Renay.
14. JAVA.
    Al Hirt.
15. SHOOP SHOOP SONG.
    Betty Everett.
16. THE WAY YOU DO
    THE THINGS YOU
    DO.
    Temptations.
17. I LOVE YOU MORE
    AND MORE EVERY
    DAY.
    Al Martino.
18. STAY.
    4 Seasons.
19. DON'T LET THE
    RAIN COME DOWN.
    Serendipity Singers.
20. NEEDLES AND PINS.
    The Searchers.

Courtesy Combo

American Hit Parade as printed in Combo Musical Weekly, 1964

Courtesy Dave Williams

Buddy Holly playing the Philharmonic, one of Liverpool's popular clubs

Courtesy Dave Williams

Unfortunately for British musicians, American guitars were not available until after 1960. The above were cheap European imitations

85

Charlie and Inez Foxx visit the Cavern, mid '60s
Bob Wooler (standing next to Charlie Foxx), Spencer Davis (standing third from left) and Steve Winwood (far right), among others

trade had refurbished the colonies three and a half centuries before: Bristol, Liverpool, South London. By default, they were lodged and housed in poor areas with poor whites—Liverpool, Bristol, South London. The British band, The Police, for example, owe not a little to the West Indian music they absorbed in the black area of Brixton, South London—ska, reggae, etc. Caribbean influence was assimilated by British youth as part of the charisma of America. And nowhere did this find a greater expression than in the town of Liverpool…

Subculture & Pubculture

10

Subculture and Pub Culture: Drink

Pakistani Store, early '60s. The proprietor's wife instructed the author assiduously in the making of curry

As if the mix of four different cultures—English, Irish, Welsh and Scottish—was not enough, Liverpool was also to clash and merge with the cultures of India, China and West Africa.

And among these diverse cultures flourished subcultures. The focal point for these was the downtown area of Liverpool 8 and its multitude of clubs and bars—towards which most teenagers, including the Beatles, headed to escape the stultifying values of the predominantly white pubs in the suburbs.

The suburbs in question were not the yuppie-like suburbs of an American town, but were in fact very lower class. This stemmed from the fact that the Labour Government, in conjunction with an enlightened Liverpool Town Council, had rehoused large numbers of poor whites either in tract-type houses some way out of the town or in grim high-rises close to the original slums; very much like American 'projects'.

These council houses very quickly deteriorated, becoming a kind

Liverpool as a Cornerstone of Celtic culture

Liverpool's high-rise housing projects

of soulless, up-scale slum themselves, lacking the values of community cohesion which had existed in the earlier slums. They also began to take on their own social and cultural forms. And one feature of this was the mega-pub.

Drink, the opium of the working classes, was an immense source of revenue for the beer barons, and they spared no expense in erecting great barn-like, watering halls in which enormous amounts of beer were consumed nightly by a working class whose horizons were limited to the immediate gratification of their pleasures.

There is, in Liverpool, quite literally a pub on each street corner. Where Liverpool was bombed during the World War II blitz, often it's the pub that was left standing (the only building that would be repaired) and the houses were either blown down or torn down later.

The beer barons also built 'working men's clubs', not out of social conscience but because of the vast profits to be culled. These clubs are an amazing sight: vast, smoke-filled halls filled with hundreds of tiny tables, each table surrounded by four or five chairs. By nine o'clock, the pub is full to the brim with a chattering, jostling throng of men and women of all ages, united in one single purpose: to 'get merry' before the witching hour of ten thirty (last call for drinks).

Once I played in a working men's club that catered to the shift workers in local factories. It was an enormous hall with a 100-foot bar. The club opened at 10:30 a.m. precisely. By 10:15, a crowd of freshly-showered, thirsty workers was at the door. By 10:25, the barmaid had drawn up pints of fresh beer and placed them on the bar, four deep and 100 feet long. The door was opened and the crowd rushed in at 10:30 precisely. By 10:34, the bar was cleared, the pints were drunk and hundreds of empty glasses were shoved onto the

Great Homer Street Pub
the only building on the block left standing

Courtesy Mindscaffolding

Liverpool's Chinatown (today!)

90

bar waiting urgently for a refill by the thirsty throng. This is what generated the money for the beer barons.

At the heart of a Liverpudlian's or a poor American black's celebration lays a kind of desperation. Despite the attempts of a socialist government to bring about reforms, the class system was still as insidious as ever. There was, amongst the Liverpool working class, as with the ghetto blacks in America, a grim feeling of inescapable permanence; that this was their lot and they could do little to change it.

Despite the Liverpool Education Committee's enlightened attitude towards education in the 60's, the low-class Liverpudlians, as with American blacks, were statistically predestined to a life behind a brush, a hod[1] or churning away on the production line at the new Ford's factory in the suburbs. It was a rare person who stepped beyond the confines of the working-class ghetto. And when they did, they didn't come back.

> When a lower-class man squanders a week's pay in two days, it is not because, like an animal or child, he is present-time orientated, unaware or unconcerned with his future. He does so precisely because he is aware of the future and the hopelessness of it all.
>
> Charles Silberman
> *Criminal Violence, Criminal Justice*

This typically Liverpool-Irish ethos does not exist only in Liverpool, England. It was studied by Edward Barnfield in a very similar city in America - Boston. Barnfield made the rather pompous observation that the "inability to defer gratification was a central characteristic of lower-class life." Fortunately, another American writer, Charles Silberman, was to prove a more incisive observer of the human condition:

> "Orientation to the present is a realistic adjustment to a world which seems to have no future; a world in which it takes all the strength one can muster to get through each day."

Silberman hits the nail on the head. In the grim, gray streets of Liverpool and Boston cultures, the choice is not between immediate and deferred gratification - it is between immediate gratification and no gratification at all.

The similarities between poor whites in Liverpool and poor blacks in urban America are striking, the main difference being (fingers crossed) that the English counterparts don't have guns.[2]

Some working men, imbued with the ethos of their forefathers, did work diligently for a meager pension (if that) and no protection. The author's father was such. Billy Pitts worked thirty-five years on a building site, then the owner

Pub performers "getting down" in Liverpool
Jazz guitarists Les Bolger, left and Paul Mitchel-Davidson

of the firm promptly went bankrupt and shot himself and Billy was out on his ear at fifty-eight with a nominal and meager redundancy award.

At one period, Richard Starkey (Ringo, nonetheless) was the can lad on this very site, making tea and running errands for the laborers, my Dad included. Fortunately for Ringo, he got out; his career took him in another direction. Unfortunately for Billy Pitts, he didn't.

Strangely enough, the very purposelessness of the Liverpool working-class culture is its strength. It was Art for Art's sake; humor for humor's sake; music played simply for the sheer, uplifting glow it brought—a glow that would fade before the cold reality of morning.

For, despite the hostility of the second-generation blacks, blacks did not function as a totally separate culture. They still drank in the same pubs and, to a large extent, danced in the same clubs. The black clubs were not predominantly black, and the older generation of blacks (West Indian mostly) in particular were deferential and friendly to whites.

The blacks were integrated with the whites, not for any reasons of higher morality, but simply because everyone was in the same boat. The proletariat—blacks or whites—were lumped together and either sank or swam.

Artsy-fartsy stuff was not only frowned upon—it was jeered at. When a man in Liverpool stood up in a pub and sang, played the guitar or danced, it was not as an artistic statement or for money but sheer joie de vivre.

A laborer downing several pints on a Saturday night would spontaneously begin a passionate, melodramatic song; a group of lads would get together and start hacking at crude chords on cheap guitars.

They did it because they wanted to. They did it because they had to. The result of this was that working-class culture had a terrific exuberance because wat is a pure expression; without any other motive; fame, money or success. The same applied to the incredible styles of break dancing and hip hop are from the streets of black American ghettos.

Pub performers were highly colorful. I was introduced to one old man who was sitting with a galvanized iron bucket clamped firmly between his knees. He played this by dint of rattling the handle in skillful and enthusiastic contrapuntal timing, accompanying his singing. He showed me the bucket with all the ardor of a violinist showing off a Stradivarius, lamenting that this was "one of a kind and they weren't made the same anymore." I noticed some damp chamois leathers at the bottom and enquired if he was a window cleaner. He told me, in no uncertain terms, he was not, and that the leathers were there for reasons of tone.

In the early days of talent spotting, we were always beaten by a woman who played the spoons. She wiped the floor with us every time. We decided to knock talent contests in the head.

Paul McCartney

The Beatles Earn a "Fortune"

Courtesy Dave Forshaw

Dave Forshaw in his dual role as drummer, and, inset, with his faithful Black Book for bookings and, above, his business card.

Dave Forshaw was not only a musician himself, but also one of the most prolific agents in '60's Liverpool. He was a colorful figure, traveling from venue to venue on a 250cc BSA motorcycle wearing gauntlets, suede coat, a leather flying helmet and goggles. His main venue was St. John's Hall where he took the snapshots of the Beatles shown earlier. On Boxing Day, 1960, following a call, he went to the Litherland Town Hall to see the Beatles there. After seeing their act, he was convinced—and he went backstage to book them then and there for St. John's Hall.

The figures are astounding. He booked them initially for £6.10 for their first gig and agreed to hike it to £7.10 for the two subsequent bookings. On January 6, 1961, the Beatles drew a record 190 people—and their fee

92

increased to a dazzling £15. In other words, when the Beatles' fee was *doubled*, it worked out at something like $22 per night for the whole band!

And this was true, not only for the Beatles, but for the other three hundred and fifty groups that sprang up in Liverpool at the same time. Competition was fierce, standards were high, money was zero.

The Beatles' musical income was pitiful. The Beatles and the other groups in Germany had the gaunt looks and svelte figures associated with rock music—the result of amphetamines and a bad diet; in Germany, they were half-starved (with no Mum to scrounge a meal off).

No one, but no one was in it for Money, Art or Fame.

With an escapism born out of an uncertain future and a grim present, the Liverpudlian would drink with the intensity known only to those who awaken on a Monday morning to face the tawdry reality of a dead-end job or, even worse, the tawdry reality of no job at all. And in this we see once again an exact counterpart with the poor blacks of America. Is it any wonder that the Liverpudlians seized upon black music with such fervor? For, therein lies exactly the same passion.

The tale is told among Liverpool drinkers about the two unemployed Irishmen in Liverpool who decided to consolidate their social security so that it would go further. Mick does the shopping and returns with a crate of Guinness, a bottle of cheap wine, two six packs and a loaf of bread. When Paddy sees how the money has been spent, he is stricken. "You idiot?" he cries, "What are we going to do with all that bread?"

Courtesy Mindscaffolding

The Nook, Chinatown - a popular pub

Celebration, then, was the escape; a brief moment of laughter, light and music to push back the grayness of reality for an hour or two. As with gin in the England of Hogarth or crack in the American housing projects, in Liverpool the raw fuel was alcohol. What kind? Well, anything that can be afforded.

Obviously such a swirling pool of passion can be glamorized. Glamorous it was not. But it was all we had and knew nothing better. Nightly, I and others like me ran the gamut of violence in the search for a good girl, a good time.

To the average Liverpool-Irishman, I was an oddball beatnik. But the Irish are very forgiving, and if you can drink like them and with them, you're O.K. The following account is not an exaggeration. Nor is it allegorical. Scenes like this occurred in pubs in Liverpool every night. They did then and, sadly, they still do today.

Pub Music, Mirth and Mayhem

It's O.K., I'm with the Band
— A Personal Anecdote —

Courtesy Charlie Jenkins

Fat Johnnie's Club on Granby Street, Liverpool 8, 1959
A popular black club for both black and white Liverpudlians. Fat Johnnie is in front, third from right, with hat and moustache

*F*at Johnnie's, Canning Street, is a club—but the name itself is a misnomer. It is simply a ramshackle house with no carpets, little sanitation or amenities save an ugly, over-flowing toilet bowl filled with cigarette butts.

A shabeen, they call it, and, for such a hole, it is amazingly popular. After midnight, couples mill around on the dirty pavement outside the club; carloads of revelers roar up at frequent intervals, carrying sailors, drunken girls, blacks, Chinese, Indians and working-class whites. They pound at the door and yell through the letter-box; try to peer through the windows (it is useless, they are all painted black).

When the door opens, they are immediately silenced by the presence of a very large black man. This is not Fat Johnnie but a bouncer. The would-be patrons are either admitted or rejected, forcibly. The night has its own rules.

I t is the afternoon of Christmas Eve.

Poised on the threshold of the Holy Day, Christ's birthday, Liverpool already has a hangover. And no wonder. It began drinking some two weeks before. New Year looms, demarking coldly and definitively the end of the year—and the end of the celebrations. An air of grim desperation begins to nudge its way into the collective Liverpool consciousness as the Monday morning to end all Monday mornings hovers just a few more binges away.

But for now, there is still time to celebrate. Where to drink? The pubs close at 2.30 p.m. and are not open until the evening. Hung over, desperate, the residents of Liverpool 8 filter into the shabeens and black clubs. Racial and cultural barriers are eliminated by the need for alcohol. And the blacks, despite the efforts of a weary police force, never did pay any attention to rules, particularly licensing hours.

Fat Johnnie's in daylight looks very, very different from the way it is at night. The light probing through the cracks in the black-painted windows reveals that it is not a club at all, but simply a house with the inner walls knocked down. The score or so occupants drinking quietly in the sordid room belie the throngs that were jam-packed into the room the night before, wall to wall, guzzling down inordinate amounts of beer or dancing to the ratchety music blaring out from a tinny record player. The wall paper is green-gray; the floor carpeted with a thick layer of cigarette butts, empty packets, squashed cockroaches and the occasional dead mouse.

Enter me, stage left, a twenty year old youth. Pale-faced, black-clad in skin-tight, black corduroy jeans. At the time I sported an unlikely hair-do with a large, greasy quiff that denied the known laws of gravity. I am accompanied by an Irishman clad in the sober, rusty suit and white open shirt that is the trademark of the Irish laborer in his Sunday best.

And Sunday it is, so we are both drinking off our hangovers from the night before. An odd couple: I am chalk; the laborer is cheese; I am drugs and rock 'n roll; the laborer is The Chieftains, draft Guinness and Country & Western. And yet, there is a bond. Family. Paddy is my brother-in-law. Paddy is introducing me to the club. The pubs are closed, and we both need a drink to take us through the desert hours between 2.30 p.m. and 6 p.m. when the pubs will re-open.

Fat Johnnie is black and, of course, fat. He eyes me warily. The club's existence is completely illegal. He wants to know who I am. Paddy makes the introductions. I shift uncomfortably as Johnnie examines me shrewdly. Eventually, Johnnie is satisfied and he plonks two bottles on the counter and rips off the tops with a smooth motion. There are

Courtesy Mindscaffolding

The Nook, Chinatown
Note the sign posts are in Chinese

no glasses and, today, no choices (after the vast consumption of the previous night). Warm, bottled Guinness is all there is. There is never any ice.

I am in, accepted. Grateful, I down my drink and allow my gaze to shift around the room, careful to allow no criticism to show on my features.

The club is grim in the light that leaks through the multiple scratches in the black-painted windows. I eye a broad swathe of greasy gray that runs around the walls at a uniform height about four feet from the ground. I'm puzzled momentarily. Then it dawns on me what the line is: It was made by the nightly press of sweaty bodies. A tidal mark. It denotes the trapped flotsam and jetsam of humanity that has jammed into the club nightly. Their sluggish circulation has scoured this band of grease and dirt a foot wide across the walls. It is not pretty. But I'm not here for the view. I drain my drink and order another. The Guinness fills my belly with a warm glow and the grim surroundings of the club recede. The greasy line on the wall fades in significance.

"Goin' out drinking ternight?" asks Paddy tersely.

"Yeah," I grunt, "With Moo." My girlfriend who, with her page-boy hairstyle, short leather skirt and Grannie glasses, is denoted as a beat.

"Bit skinny, that one," comments Paddy absently, his mind probably already occluded by warm, beery thoughts of his companions down at the Irish Social Club, a night's C&W, foot stomping and Irish jigs. "'Case I don't see yer," says Paddy, clinking his bottle against mine, "Merry Christmas—when it comes."

"Same ter you."

The silence is cold about us as we down our drinks.

Christmas Eve, 8 p.m.:
The Fairfield Pub Three Miles Away; Down the Road from Moo's House

Courtesy Mindscaffolding

Andy Capp's Pub

The M.C[3]. for the evening reaches the microphone and, immediately, as though sensing the presence of an intruder, the alerted microphone begins to whistle and howl like a banshee.

So do the crowd. Tables rattle and the lights sway as the crowd jeer and boo good-naturedly.

"Hey, Harry, are you in the Musician's Union?!" calls out a wag.

"Get a licence for that thing!" calls another.

Eventually, Harry controls the mike and announces that tonight is a "star-studded Christmas Eve"——which brings more jeers and boos. Then he says: "By the way, the pies have come," which causes a minor stampede to the bar. When the stampede has died down, Harry announces that Kevin Whitehead is going to get up for them

At the back of the room, Kevin, a burly man with thinning hair and a red, bulbous nose, declines modestly. But the crowd will not let him have it:

"C'mon Kevin!"

"We want Kevin!"

Then they begin the slow hand clap known and feared by many a football team visiting Liverpool for the first time. The hand claps steady into a murderous, chopping rhythm, whilst the crowd chants poor Kevin's name: "KE—VIN! KE—VIN! KE—VIN!"

Grinning, Moo and I join in, punctuating the rhythm by banging the table with our glasses.

Eventually, Kevin capitulates and the rhythm breaks into thunderous applause.

Having achieved the maximum, dramatic effect by his initial, modest withdrawal, Kevin holds the mike with the grave expression of one about to deliver an ultimatum from the Russian premier. The pianist plays the opening chords in a sweeping arpeggio and Kevin glances respectfully at his feet—a gesture of professionalism he's copied from club singers.

The crowd falls into a reverent half-silence. Kevin leans his head back and opens his large mouth, revealing a row of white false teeth and a very mobile uvula. The piano's opening chords reach their trilling climax, and the pianist nods to Kevin.

The note begins at the back of Kevin's throat, washes around his trembling uvula and, whistling around the solid white barrier of his National Health teeth, cuts through the smoky air like the squeal of a rusty saw. He holds onto that note for an interminable period, obviously equating length with emotive quality:

> "Theeeeeeeeeeeeeeeere's an…"

(the pianist comes in with a crash of chords)

> "Ole mill by the stream, eh,
> Nellie Dean, eh,
> Where we used to sit down and dream, eh,
> Nellie Dean, eh…"

According to a well-established, Liverpudlian convention, the 'eh' is added arbitrarily to the end of each line, presumably to express the deep angst and emotional profundity of the singer's delivery.

"Hey," whispers Moo, tugging my sleeve.

I turn my mesmerized gaze from the singer's vast cavern of a mouth. Moo is pointing fearfully at two youths standing at the next table. Just then, they go for each other. The larger of the two, a greasy-haired youth, struggles with a much younger, crop-haired lad, yelling: "Cool it!! I don't wanna hurt you!"

I glance at Moo. She raises her eyes. "Here we go," she says wearily.

"Hey, cool it now! Cool it, man!" booms out a West Indian voice. A huge, black man appears from nowhere and grabs each of the struggling youths in a vast pink-black hand. The younger one is ferocious. He manages to get a swing in that catches the greasy-haired youth a glancing blow on the jaw.

"Hey!!" cries the youth, blood spurting from his lip, "Knock it off, man!"

The black man gently but firmly bundles the younger man out of the door, apologizing all the way. "Hey, man, I ain't taking sides—just keeping the peace. Just you go outside and cool off."

The incident doesn't even register with the crowd who are applauding Kevin's song. Moo claps enthusiastically and says: "Eh, look, there's a guitar over there. Why don't you get up?"

"Go on," I say, "Tell the M.C. then. I'll ask if I can borrow the guitar."

An hour later, after a motley collection of singers, the announcement is that it's my turn. Mellowed by the four pints I've downed in the interim, I stand by the mike as the M.C. harangues me mercilessly about my hair, much to the enjoyment of the crowd: "Well, sorry about this, folks, but the barbers went on strike last week, but the Charles Atlas course will be in next month's *Popular Mechanics* (my thin frame)!"

I take it all in good fun. Why not? I feel GOOD. The alcohol has diffused through my body and the

Courtesy Mindscaffolding

The White Star pub

97

room is filled with a mellow warmth, smiling faces, belly laughter and the tinkle of the piano.

I turn to the pianist, a dour-faced man in his forties who's obviously seen it all, and whisper: "*Lovesick Blues* in E." The man nods without a flicker of expression.

"So, we have him here, without Tonto, without his white horse, but with his guitar—Kemo Sabay, the Man-Who-Knows, singing an old Hank Williams' tune, *Lovesick Blues!*"

I edge up to the mike cautiously under cover of a round of applause. I find the optimum distance at which it doesn't feedback and launch into a yodeling rendition of *Lovesick Blues* in E.

Blinking in the stage lights, I see them come through the door at the back of the pub.

They push through the crowd. Replicas of the youth who was thrown out earlier, but older. They wear black suits, Italian style, small collars; their hair is cropped fashionably in a flat top. They jostle through the chattering, smiling crowd, three of them; grim-faced.

Still warbling Hank Williams' angst, I trace their path and see their destination before they reach it: the greasy-haired youth who struck the other in the face earlier.

Even through the smoke I can see that the guy is even more drunk now and even more loud-mouthed. He stands swaying, chatting to a group of girls who give him contemptuous glances or ignore him, bored expressions on their faces. His gestures are expansive. He is bragging; telling stories; telling jokes.

Suddenly, as if by magic, a space clears around the youth. He looks up, puzzled to find himself in a small pocket of emptiness. He sees the expressions change on the seated girls' faces, and his bragging speech fades on his lips. He turns as the three grim-faced youths reach him, his face a mixture of confusion and perturbation.

Courtesy Mindscaffolding

The Cracke pub

Moo stands to her feet swiftly, trying to catch my eye.

I see Moo rise. I smile and give the guitar an extra strum for her. But she does not smile back. Slowly she inverts her thumb and sits back down. My belly suddenly goes cold.

Moo was just a few feet from them when it started and was able to fill in the details to me later:

The three youths stand in front of the greasy-haired lad, legs splayed. Moo reads their lips: "Did you hit our John?" mouths one.

Greasy-Hair opens his mouth to speak, his face a study in obsequiousness. But he doesn't get the chance to mouth the first hypocrisy. The youth whips a Schweppes Bitter Lemon bottle out of his pocket and hits him in the face with it.

Moo told me she worked in the Schweppes factory once for a week—only a week, it was a terrible job. But she learned one thing: that these small bottles, perhaps four inches high by two in diameter, are practically indestructible. Many was the time she'd dropped such a bottle and made a frantic grab at it. But they never broke. They were so thick and tough in comparison to their size that they actually *bounced*.

She said that the bottle hit Greasy-Hair so hard in the teeth that the bottle actually shattered. She didn't have time to see what it did to his face because, simultaneously, the room erupted.

I see the fight erupt almost immediately to Moo's left. It spreads rapidly to the adjacent tables. Men who seem to be too old for what they are doing—old enough to be my father—suddenly turn on each other, pounding, punching, hurling glasses.

I stop in mid-chord and turn to see the pianist, completely deadpan, down his pint in one, close the piano lid and lock it carefully, as if packing up after a long, hard day. He sighs, gives me a weary glance and, veteran of a hundred bar brawls, says dourly: "Business as bleeding usual." Then he grabs a sheaf of music and disappears through the curtain at the back of the stage.

The M.C. is nowhere to be seen. I back away as two men roll onto the stage pummeling each other, their shirts pulled out of their trousers. One man's shirt is covered in blood. I stare as one man sits astride the other's torso, wrests off the man's shoe and begins smacking him about the head with it. A youth launches himself across the stage, grabs the microphone stand and whirls it through the air. It smacks across the shoe-wielder's shoulders and he falls flat across his victim, the shoe slipping from his hand.

I break out of my daze, lean the guitar between the piano and the curtain, leap off the stage and begin to thread my way through the crowd. A man rears up in front of me and falls instantly as a chair crashes over his head. I drop to all

Courtesy Mindscaffolding

Inside The Cracke

fours and begin crawling under the tables working my way through struggling bodies, broken glass, upturned chairs, searching for Moo.

The room is a seething mass of fists, screams, grunts, curses as the entire male community seem hell-bent on beating each other into the ground.

There are no women in sight. Where is Moo?

I find her crouching under our table clutching our back-pack. "You should've split," I say fiercely, "C'mon now, let's go."

"I couldn't leave you," says Moo faltering.

We begin crawling through the tables; a weaving path that follows their protective covering.

Suddenly I'm grabbed and hauled to my feet by a huge, fat youth in a torn, white shirt. Blood streams from the youth's nose; a bright red that matts into the hair on his chest. The youth's eyes are glazed with hate; his face contorted. He draws back a meaty fist, knotted, ready to strike. Then he pauses unexpectedly. "Oh sorry, mate," he

Courtesy Mindscaffolding

The Exterior of the Philharmonic Pub

Ma Egerton's Pub

Courtesy Mindscaffolding

says apologetically, "You were with the band, weren't you?" He turns away from me and is repaid for his act of mercy by a chair that whirls from nowhere and knocks him sideways. We do not wait to see more. A few more steps and we reach the relative safety of the doorway.

With a sigh of relief, we emerge into the cool air and push our way through a jostling crowd of sightseers who stand listening to the sounds of breaking furniture emerging from the pub.

"Sounds like a good night, mate," cracks one youth.

"Excuse me... 'Scuse me..." I mutter, pushing through the throng, pulling Moo closely behind me. Once free of the crowd, we run. We don't stop running until we're well clear of the street and onto the darkened perimeter of the park. Moo is panting; her face is red. It is quiet there. The trees sway gently in the wind and the air is filled with the smell of damp soil, leaves and grass. I look at Moo again.

She is sad. "It's always like this. Why?"

I have no answers. It is always like this.

For a moment, it is almost peaceful. The sky is clear and frosty; the stars are shining boldly. Suddenly a noise booms out in a vast, melodic chord. It is the boats on the river, each one sounding its horn. Then, all over the city, the church bells begin to ring. A lovely sound: the sonorous boom of the boats' horns; the pealing of the bells.

Despite her agitation, Moo is moved. "It's Christmas, luv," she says low-voiced, her eyes glowing in the starlight.

Staring into the sky, I listen to the ships' horns, my arm tight around Moo's shoulders. "Merry Christmas, Moo," I say, low-voiced, "I'm sad, too."

"Listen, luv," whispers Moo, "Promise me something, as a sort of Christmas Day promise"

"What's that?"

"When a situation starts like back there in the pub, promise me you'll always be with the band."

"Oh, that's easy...I promise. Merry Christmas, luv." We kiss.

She breaks away. A tear streaks down her cheek.

"Don't be sad," I say.

"I'm not," she says. "'Ave a Happy New Year."

Skinny, granny-glasses, small-breasted, straight-haired, mascara-eyed, she is to become a symbol of the Sixties. But what does she care or know of such things? For the moment she is happy. And the moment is all she knows.

Pre-Beatles England & Class

Pre-Beatles' England: The Class Phenomenon

Experience has shown that, although Americans know that the British are beset by class boundaries, this knowledge is, at best, superficial.

This is not meant to be a condescending statement, for an American cannot know of an institution that cuts to the bone—indeed, it is bred in the bones—if he is not born into it. Even the East Coast/West Coast old-money syndrome does not quite equate to what it is to be born into a society where all men are not equal.

The parallel with black Americans is not accidental. Black Americans will have no problem in grasping this particular phenomenon. For, if the slur of racism in America is color, then its English equivalent is accent.

When an Englishman opens his mouth, he is automatically categorized as to birth, education and area of origin—and neatly pigeonholed. Some accents are stigmatized more than others; and in pre-Beatle days, a Liverpool accent was an immediate sign that this person was:

a) potentially violent
b) definitely of the lower order of animals
c) stupid and violent (therefore dangerous)
d) to be avoided or exploited, depending on the relative proportions of (c).

This is by no means an exaggeration. There is a cruelly-incisive racial joke current in America which goes:

> *What do you call a black man with two Harvard degrees, and MIT research grant and a house in Manhattan?*
> *Answer: A nigger.*

Courtesy Mindscaffolding

Blackburn House
Built by business families wealthy from the wool or slave trade, now it is a Women's Center.

The same joke could equally be told substituting the term Liverpudlian for black man; and the punch-line would be: a Liverpool lout.

This is of course not to deny the class changes taking place in British society; nor is it to deny the dramatic changes that took place in the postwar years and gave rise to the Youth Movement, the Beatles and Swinging England. But something as deep as class cannot be eradicated in a single generation, just as racism cannot.

In the years immediately after World War II, we saw England without a welfare state, without an education system for the poor (schools were still private or charitable hit-and-miss institutions). MacMillan, a member of the aristocratic hierarchy, was Prime Minister and the vast British Empire, though still in existence, was sinking slowly in the sun. From then on, England was to be beset by some remarkable changes.

Courtesy Mindscaffolding

The Coffee Roaster
Catering to the doctors and lawyers in Liverpool

Within a decade, the British Empire finally sinks into the sea; the English get a Welfare State with both Labour and Conservative concerned (for different reasons) about the education of the working classes. Free secondary education for all is instituted; television arrives; so do over one million blacks and browns from the Caribbean, India and Africa.

The presence of such a large number of colored immigrants had a particularly unsettling effect on the staid British (though Prince Charles has always carried a personal torch for them, bless his altruistic heart). These changes brought about a significant emphasis on working-class vitality in Parliament. With the accession of Kennedy as the American President in 1960 the *New Look* ideas came sweeping across the Atlantic to inspire the rising generation of working-class British politicians.

During World War II, Hitler ordered a massive

Courtesy Mindscaffolding

This cafe is not closed. It's open for business, despite its appearance. NB: "Take away" means "to go".

103

assault on England's ports and, in 1941, Liverpool was battered mercilessly. Enormous damage was done and many lives were lost. But the war at least had the effect of uniting the public against their tormentors, the civil servants and revealed and confirmed social problems and fissures between groups and classes. The evacuation of poor slum dwellers from blitzed areas produced paroxysms of class hatred among well-to-do householders in safe areas who often tried to avoid billeting such riffraff. It was a case of working-class self-assertion confronting middle-class resistance.

In particular, Harold Wilson, a grocer's son, readily took advantage of the public disenchantment with the upper classes and made it to Prime Minister.

It was a period when the voices of artists were raised against the middle classes (despite the fact that the Arts were now widely supported by the State), as in John Osborne's *Look Back In Anger*. Gritty, social-realistic films like *Saturday Night and Sunday Morning* and *The Loneliness of the Long-distance Runner* found their way to the fore. It seemed that the working class was having its day (though, truly, the working class, themselves, didn't know this was going on).

The so-called rise of working-class consciousness in Britain was actually illusory. Ironically, it wasn't really a rise of working-class consciousness—the working class[1] plodded on largely as they had done before. Rather, it was a rise of consciousness of the working class by middle-class observers who had hitherto ignored it: journalists; sociologists; politicians.

The winds of change swept through the nation, short skirts and sexual permissiveness began to make a significant dent on public life. And, in a combination of fortune, fate and Jewish foresight, a lovelorn Epstein, with impeccable timing, launched the Beatles as the spearhead of the Sixties' youth culture.

It was the right time and the right place—the Beatles' music knocked the Americans' socks off. But what won their hearts was the Liverpool personality.

Liverpool: A Sense of Uniqueness

To explain why this was so, it has to be realized that the Liverpudlians regard themselves as a different race from the rest of England.

For a start, no one uses the very lengthy word "Liverpudlian". He or she is known far and wide as a "Scouser"—a word which comes from the Liverpudlians' favorite dish, a kind of meat stew. The term is alleged to come from "lobscouse", a Scandanavian word.

Just like the Texans—who regard Texas as the center of the universe and treat the rest of the U.S.A. as being at a disadvantage for not being Texan—the Liverpudlians regard themselves not just as a separate town with an individual character, but almost as non-English. To them, Liverpool is like a small country nestling in the larger context of England.

In the Liverpool shopping centers 'up country' people are readily identified by their accent. They are treated with a fair amount of courtesy but underlying it all is a faint amusement rather as one would see in New York if a couple of hillbillies walked into a department store. In actual fact these 'up country' folk live just ten miles outside of Liverpool.

Of course, Liverpool, as a city, observes all the laws, boundaries, rights and obligations of every other city in England. However, its natives ignore and reject totally attempts at compartmentalization, and the result is a sort of quasi Republic of Liverpool with a native language and native consciousness that is unique.

The Liverpool character is, in fact, unique—a mixture of vulgarity and incisiveness, streetwise cunning and sudden bouts of ingenuous friendship.

It is, in some ways, no different from that engendered in the Bronx or that displayed by the street kids of Columbia or the urchins of Paris—for the classroom of deprivation and survival is ever-present in such cities the world over.

The Liverpudlian may be small, fat or thin, but in general, he is quick on his feet and even quicker with his tongue. His rapier-like wit and, at times, cruel invective are fearsome. Couple this to an almost pathological aggression, and the resulting personality is a formidable challenge in any milieu. He is loud,

During the rivalry that occurred between taxi drivers in turf wars in '90s Liverpool, one man was awoken from his sleep by two men in his bedroom. He crashed through the window glass totally naked, and fled. Apparently they had tried to chop off his feet as a warning.

opinionated and domineering, with a shrewdness that assesses with incredible rapidity the prevailing values in any situation. And, by wit or sheer bravado, he will take control unless he is stopped. And beware those who try to stop him—for quite often, when meeting such resistance, he will resort to violence.

Since the World War II years, the Liverpudlian in the Army, the Navy or the Merchant Marine was known, feared and avoided, for to cross him meant instant reprisal—and TROUBLE.

He will talk fast; he will always move his hands, painting word patterns in the air, bombarding the listener with devastating street-metaphors, abusive wit and razor-sharp gutter analogies. His tongue is a weapon that sways, challenges and overthrows. It is inbred in the Liverpudlian to fight with words, with fists, with wit, with cunning—and, above all, to get one over on the opponent.

When the first tough American journalists lined up to shoot down the mop-headed Beatles, invaders at Kennedy Airport in 1964, within five minutes the Beatles had them eating out of their hands, charming the American nation forever. What the Americans didn't realize was that wit and repartee are the substance of Liverpool life and that a group of Liverpool bus drivers would probably have proven just as charismatic.

During Cup Final week in England when crowds of Liverpudlian football fans travel down to London, the streets are deserted, the police force tripled and the shop windows boarded up as a large section of the eight-million odd population of London retreat under threat of an onslaught by just a few hundred Liverpudlians.

This is not an accomplishment to be viewed with pride. Nor, it must be said, is the Liverpool character wholly desirable. At best, it is witty, entertaining, lovable, cheerful and supportive. But it can also suffer from narrowness and the limitations of chauvinism (i.e., the view that only a Liverpudlian is worth anything at all). It is also prey to the hypocrisy which afflicts both the lower-middle and working classes and, worse still, an aggression that, when nurtured by a ghetto mind, can be lethal.

Witness the streets of London strewn with broken glass, wrecked cars, rubble, filth and the carnage and destruction that is perpetuated by Soccer Specials in the name of sport: broken windows; torn seats; arbitrary violence; terrorism.

On the platform of London's Victoria Station, a drunken lout was berating a middle class Indian who was with a pretty blonde obviously his wife. It was an unpleasant scene of racist bigotry. A skinny youth of about twenty approached the drunk who was a burly man in his thirties. In a dour Liverpool accent the youth told the man to "fuck off." The minute the man recognized the youth's accent, his manner changed and he backed away and fled, mumbling profane apologies.
Yes, you're right—I was that scrawny youth, more incensed than common-sensed.

Perhaps it can be said that the Liverpudlian character can, like anything else, be a force for good or evil. It is, in essence, the volatile nature of street-survival skills coupled to a chameleon-like character. If this is coupled to a lack of social conscience, it can be pathological. As an adjunct to compassion and intelligence, it can be wonderful. It can even conquer the world—literally. And, as Liz Taylor has said: "Fame is a great deodorant."

But, in the pre-Beatles' era, as far as the rest of England was concerned, Liverpool STANK. When a Liverpudlian visited "The Smoke"[2] he was greeted by a range of reactions, which depended on the prevailing awareness of his potential. In the bars and pubs, where the class of the people was such that they would have come across the Liverpool character before, they were treated with all the fear and respect usually reserved for man-eating tigers. The equation was simple, Liverpool plus Drink equaled Major Trouble.

Just as a middle-class American white lady may fearfully hold onto her purse when a shaven-headed black American macho youth sits next to her, so was the reaction to a Liverpudlian. They are seen as thieves, criminals and potential psychopaths. And this is reflected in the comedy and T.V. jokes of the period, just as it is in the humor of black comedians like Chris Rock or Eddie Murphy.

I thought that the public image of Liverpudlians may have changed. But recently, when visiting Australia for the New Millennium, I met a drunken Welsh youth in a Sydney street who, realizing I was a *Scouser*, immediately launched into the following jokes:

> *What do you call a Scouser in a suit and tie?*
> *Answer: The accused.*
> *How do you show a Scouser how to make an omelette?*
> *Answer: First, steal five eggs...*

Plus ca que change c'est la même

Now, of course, in considering a city of three-quarters of a million, there is a spectrum—there are introverts; there are reticent, slow, dull-witted Liverpudlians. But, as the milieu is one of wit, of garrulousness, of pushy self-confidence, even a below-average Liverpudlian when placed in a less aggressive middle-class environment will, of necessity, take to the fore just as penniless European or Asian immigrants nurtured in want will quickly amass considerable sums when placed in the affluence of America.

During the late Sixties, the small, seaside resort of Hastings on the south coast of England was terrorized by a few Liverpudlians, who, having left their own city for the vast trek down south, quickly inserted themselves into key positions in this small town. Quickly, the Liverpudlians rose to prominence in all areas: drug dealing; bars; the music scene; and football. So significant was their presence, that any person with a Liverpool accent who approached a boarding house with a vacancy sign would suddenly and mysteriously find the notice being removed—myself included.

However, time told, and the Liverpudlians that stayed mellowed, adjusted, became a little blander, less aggressively idiosyncratic, and were absorbed into the local population—though always, in comparison to the quiet uniformity of the locals, they were still seen as colorful characters.

The Beatles, themselves, were a prime example of the Liverpool character released into a broader context. Here we have four, simple Liverpool lads, brought up in a tribal situation in which—no less than the Watsumi tribe or even the Mafia—a person is quickly categorized by a thousand signs and signals. With little experience of the world of show business other than a dank, cellar club, a few stage appearances and the doubtful pleasures of the Reeperbahn in Hamburg, the Beatles suddenly became International in a blaze of light.

Courtesy Mindscaffolding

The Philharmonic Pub
The Beatles' stomping ground

It was a unique phenomenon and a unique incident and, within months, the Beatles—at home in the dirty alleys of the Cavern and the cramped, sweaty pubs; used to jostling elbows with Irish laborers, blacks and working-class louts to get a pint of bitter—were rubbing elbows with presidents and politicians, film-stars and socialites. And, they not only survived, but emerged as cocky, witty and, apparently, unfazed by it all. Apparently. For, although it was by no means obvious at first, the strain of this transition was to take its toll.

The unflappable Liverpudlian is, in some respects, a necessary fiction: the Liverpudlian may be quaking inside, but in ghetto-land, this is a no-no, so an appearance of brash confidence is always maintained.

The greatest enemy the Liverpudlian has is the enemy from within—which manifested itself in one word: Class. Despite the social mobility and the vast upheavals in British economic power of the Sixties, class still existed.

An American can escape an unfortunate birth by amassing possessions. Not so in England. When a Liverpudlian opened his mouth, be he dressed from Saville Row[3], driving a Rolls Royce or on the way to his Chelsea penthouse, he is still a commoner. No amount of wealth could beat the elegance and casual, savior-faire confidence displayed by the upper classes. The languid aristocracy of the Oxford or Cambridge graduate shows even when he's wearing a tattered sports coat or driving a battered Ford; and the nonchalant, indolent charm of an upper-class Etonian[4] renders material ostentation as gross, rude and crude.

The Liverpudlian reacts to class in two ways: Initially, he laughs, he jeers, he blusters; he uses his rapier-like wit and aggressive charm to demolish, to dismiss, to belittle. This is easy from the safe platform of the home territory. But at heart he suffers a certain unease, and this is his downfall. Faced with the phenomenon of high birth and the Queen's English, despite his bluster, the working-class Liverpudlian feels inferior.

One reaction to this is political, and the pubs and the Art Colleges are full of educated Liverpudlian left-wingers who discuss philosophy and politics in extremely intellectual terms in the rough, crude tones of the working-class. They are aggressively hostile to any hint that their accent should be modified in the slightest, for this is seen as selling out to the middle classes—just as blacks in America talk in jive or rap and see correct English as the province of honkeys and Uncle Toms.

Exactly the same situation is described by Chris Rock—the pecking order of ghetto blacks:

"Who's more racist: black people or white people?
Black people.
You know why? Because black people hate black people, too. Everything white people don't like about black people, black people don't like about black people. It's like our own personal civil war.
On one side, there's black people. On the other, you've got niggers.
The niggers have got to go. Everytime black people want to have a good time, niggers mess it up. Can't keep a disco open more than three weeks. Grand opening? Grand closing. Can't go to a movie the first week it opens. Why? Because niggers are shooting at the screen."

Chris Rock
Rock This! p.17

The effect of this intellect expressed with gutter slang is often surprising:

"Jesus fucking Christ, Sartre was a bleedin' ass bandit! Look, bastard features, phenomenology was just a fuckin' copout, boy! He was a fart-faced, middle-class turd—who realized that with dialectic materialism he was fucked. Ontologically speaking—to use his own bleedin' obscurantist terms—he was not just fuckin' existentially unauthentic, he was phoney, and Genet was right when he said he was a cunt!"

(Overheard in a pub)

Armed with class wariness, motivational paranoia and information, the Liverpudlian politician is a formidable opponent, particularly with all the zeal of a Just Cause to add force to his arguments. Such a one was, of course, John Lennon.

The Beatles' Place in Liverpool

To some extent, the success of the Lennon-McCartney marriage appears to be a liaison between a working-class lout and a middle-class aspirant. John violently eschewed the values of middle-class living, while Paul was naturally drawn to them. It should also be emphasized that this does not make John the working-class hero and Paul the middle-class cop out.

In fact, the truth is much more subtle.

The word *middle-class* has become like *bourgeois*—a pejorative term. It is important to note that middle-class England is not the same as middle-class America. In fact, some of the better attributes of the British *are* middle-class, and these virtues can be exemplified by Paul, the ex-grammar school boy: He's quieter; less judgmental; takes control in a crisis; has a basic sense of honesty and decency; and just got on with it with the minimum amount of fuss.

Paul was a much smoother person socially, and, as the Beatles were a gestalt organism, John could no more do without Paul's poise and prettiness than Paul could do without John's rawness and rhythm.

Nevertheless, in England itself, each of the Beatles, by virtue of birth place, parents and background factors, were caught irrevocably in the spider's web of class. And the interesting thing about the Beatles is that, in some ways, they each represent a different aspect of this class phenomenon.

These fine gradations are very subtle to an outside observer—and it is to be remembered that to the rest of England these subtle distinctions do not exist. In

Paul spoke fluent German; I saw him teaching the Germans to speak English at the Star Club in Hamburg. He said, 'here's a good word: "BANANA" The whole crowd, all two thousand of them went "BANAAAAANA" you can imagine what it sounded like. Then he said "APPLE" and they went "AAPPLE". He said,'Now, here's a very hard one: "ORANGE" ' and they all went "OORAANGE" except for this one voice which went "BAANAANAA".

Bobby Thompson, The Dominoes

A typical Liverpool dwelling. Very different from the house where John grew up in (equivalent, class-wise, to the house where Ringo lived—see opposite page)

pre-Beatles' England, as far as middle-class England was concerned, *anyone* with a Liverpool accent was lowlife. Thus, the Beatles, as far as the rest of England was concerned, were all lumped together as John put it so succinctly, as "fuckin' peasants."

Even in the ghetto there are class distinctions. A street might be overrun with rats, but if someone has a window with a plaster vase in it or has painted their front door they are considered 'posh'[5].

The Beatles themselves, *within the context of Liverpool's own class system* occupy different positions on the social scale:

Paul, for example, although his origins were humble, aspired to something higher with his grammar school career, his eloquence, good looks and charm. Paul, had he not been a Beatle, would have no doubt entered into some comfortable career in the middle-classes with a wife not unlike Linda Eastman (minus the millions).

George, though he was born in an inner-city slum, had a fairly uneventful background. His family, by virtue of the slum redevelopment scheme, moved out to the slightly more salubrious suburbs of the Macketts Lane area, the same area my own family had been relocated to from the terraced slums of Liverpool 8. Though they were what Americans would call tract houses, for George it was a definite move up the social scale from the terraced house where he had lived before.

Whereas all three of the Beatles were raised in humble terraced houses, it is significant that John, the most vociferous and rebellious of the four, was brought up in Mendips, the house pictured on the opposite page. To the sensibilities of Liverpool 8, a house with a name might as well have been a mansion, so

In my own street there was one family, the Mortons that never had beds, they slept on the floor on thin mattresses. They also never bothered to buy cups—they used jam-jars instead. This was a widely known fact and their social standing entered into family parlance such that if a kid was doing something considered "low class" he was rebuked sharply, with the rejoinder "You're not at the Mortons now." The fact that the Mortons had THEIR Mortons to use as a term of admonishment is a mind-boggling indication of the fine shades of gray that exist in the ghetto situation.

far removed was it from the two-up two-down old terraced houses of the urban center. Yet, typically, it was John who becried being a "working class hero" and it was John who was most bitter about Paul's aspirations.

I noticed the same phenomenon at Sussex University, an educational establishment which, by virtue of its being designated as an alternate for the Royal family (Princess Anne—who never went), became the "in" place for politicians and movie stars sons and daughters (David Attenborough's kids were in my year). I was amazed to find that one particular militant socialist who walked around in tattered gear and a copy of *The Worker* under his arm, in fact, had a forty-bedroom manor. (I was one of the 2% of the working class allowed in under a

Mendips, John's house, a middle-class house with its own garden, internal toilet and bathroom

scholarship scheme).

The point being made here is that it isn't until you rise slightly above your background that you become aware enough to criticize it.

Our house was unheated save by a fire in the main room. It was usually dirty, as there were six people living in a space big enough for two. The outside toilet (the only one) stank, and there were rats in the alley.

When I moved to Huskisson Street in the black district, I came home one night and went down to the basement where my step-father-in-law (a black Trinidadian) lived with his white wife. I opened the door and stared, astounded, as I was not sure what I was seeing. In the absence of people, the cockroaches had emerged—and it was a ghastly sight. There was not a square inch of the entire floor uncovered by a seething carpet of cockroaches of every shade of reddy-brown, and the dog, asleep on the couch, was lying, unconcerned, as they ran over him.

Given these conditions and our lack of political or social knowledge, we simply thought "that's the way it is," whereas, a John Lennon, raised in the more salubrious surroundings of a Mendips (with a garden) was more in touch with social and political movements and thus more apt to be socially aggressive or vociferous about human affairs—though when I watched his sit-in with Yoko, I realized that his grasp of political affairs, though broader than mine at age 18, was still rather poor.

A house with a name *Mendips* would be totally alien to Ringo's sensibility and the values of the grim Park Road area where Ringo was born and raised.

Ringo's House

A two-up two-down terrace house in the Dingle/Park Road area, one of the worst areas of Liverpool 8. The house has been given a "make-over" in honor of Ringo's celebrity status

Courtesy David Rushworth

John and George, early '60s, checking out guitars at Rushworth's Guitar Center

However, John, who was raised at a slightly higher social level than the other Beatles, was typical of the vociferous working-class Marxist-Leninist politicos described earlier. By virtue of his troubled past, his artistic inclinations and his being at the Art College, John chose to frequent Peter Kavannaugh's pub, the Cracke pub, to rub shoulders with the leftwing clientele there and to deliberately flaunt the values and conventions of respectability—a status towards which Paul was probably headed before the Beatles' rise to fame lifted them *both* out of Liverpool and placed them firmly in the world at large.

It is a mark of the depth of early-life, cultural conditioning that each of the Beatles (despite fame, fortune and millions of dollars) ended up not being so different from the way they started—as is manifest in their choice of wives.

Paul aspired towards what might be termed loosely as yuppie-dom. George, the quiet, self-effacing middleman represents something in between the two extremes of Paul and Ringo. Ringo is and was right down at the bottom; a "peasant" by anyone's standards (this is not meant unkindly). George, in his intermediate position would probably have entered trade school or a polytech and become an adept behind-the-

During the incredibly long stints in Hamburg's Star Club, twelve-hour shifts 4 p.m.—4 a.m., two hours on, one off, alcohol and amphetamine abuse led to many strange scenes. John Lennon started acting very aggressively goose stepping up and down the stage shouting "Heil Hitler!" and giving the Nazi salute. One time he stepped up to the front row and kicked a youth in the face.

The way in which you walk in Liverpool is very important—as it is, indeed, in the black ghettos of America. It is a fine edge. If your shoulders swing too much, if it's too cavalier, the signal is that you're a "hard case and looking for a fight." The key is to walk in such a way that it signals you're not looking for a fight but that you're also not an easy prey. I remember once watching John Lennon walking down Matthew Street past a crowd of Scousers waiting to go in the Cavern. John's status as a Beatle, even pre-fame, didn't necessarily offer him protection from the arbitrary violence of the "mean" Scouser who picked fights just for the sake of it. John's walk was puzzling. It was the lolloping, toe first, feet-splayed forward bounce of the Art-College nerd which would normally have attracted undue attention from the potentially violent. Yet, he strode down the road with an aplomb that bespoke of total obliviousness to the consequences. It was only later that I realized that, as self-conscious any any 18-year old about his appearance, John always walked down the street without his glasses and, as such, he was as blind as a bat. His apparent indifference to the crowd was mainly because he couldn't see a thing!

scenes, back-room technical expert in something or other.

John was the typical Marxist-Leninist Liverpudlian; the Teddy Boy; the rebel and social commentator and (Beatles apart) was possibly destined for incredible success or incredible failure—and eternal angst.

George reflected his middle position in his first marriage to Patti Boyd, which was probably a wish-fulfillment fantasy; the wife he thought he *should* have, and an extension of his own dark-horse dreams. In a word, she was *his* Linda, a mimicking of his hero, Paul. Unfortunately, it was not successful and it is an indication of the very basic nature of the Beatles' liaison that when George broke with Patti, he made a desperate play for Maureen, the solid, Liverpool wife of "peasant" Ringo. It was an obvious choice, for Maureen represented everything with which poor George was familiar; a balm to his bewildered and bruised ego after being rejected by a girl above his station (Beatle or no Beatle). Thus, George was oscillating between the social polar-opposites of Paul and Ringo. When asked why he did it, he replied: "Incest." This simple statement speaks volumes when we consider the class that each of the Beatles represents and the inner struggles which they had. In other words, George, being denied access to the normal social outlets of Liverpool at large, was naturally playing out this social drama in the only arena open to a Beatle—within the Beatles itself. Eventually, George ended up with a wife from a different culture (Mexican-born Olivia Aries), a girl, in many ways, was not much

Courtesy Dave Williams

The Quarrymen were, of course, the precursor to the Beatles. Noting the various brass-band influences in their recordings (especially the Sergeant Pepper album), it should be realized that Paul was a trumpet player in school. Here, in the Liverpool suburb of Woolton, we see an indication of this influence: The Quarrymen played skiffle alongside the Liverpool Police Dogs Display and the George Edwards Band and, lo and behold, the Band of the Cheshire Yeomanry.

Courtesy Combo

different from the solid, northern Maureen but with the allure of cultural difference.

Paul on the other hand, with his outward-going ways and charm, was always was a public Beatle with an eye for the camera and Image. He was a readier candidate for cultural and social mobility than John.

John, who aspired to the anarchic traditions of the Liverpool Art College where Marxism and Revolution were ripe, resisted this pressure all his life. Yoko's iconoclasm was a perfect foil to this—and the perfect wife for him.

In a vast oversimplification it could be stated that Linda McCartney is the socially-mobile, Liverpool working-class boy's dream of success: rich, blonde, intelligent, erudite, well-connected and well-heeled; she could as well grace the arm of a Marin county socialite or be a status symbol at any social function on the East

Paul Beatle helps Freddie to star in Maggie May

PAUL McCARTNEY

Courtesy Combo

FREDDIE Starr, the 22 years-old pop star chosen for the third lead in Maggie May told Combo that a Beatle had made certain of his getting the part.

Said Freddie: It was Paul McCartney. When the producers and casting men were making up their minds who to select, Paul McCartney put in a good word for me. "It was shortly after that, I learned I had the part."

He went on: "I feel really great about this — it's something I've really wanted."

Freddie will begin rehearsals on July 1 after making his last tour with his group, the Midnighters.

A spokesman for the Northern Variety Agency, which handles the outfit, denied this week that the Midnighters will break up. He said that when Freddie leaves a new front-line singer will be found — it will probably be either Shane Corday or Tracy Martin a new female singer appearing in Germany at the moment, who is said to be Britain's answer to Brenda Lee — and the Midnighters will become a Sounds Incorporated-style group.

Coast. Careerist, intellectual, with the right connections, Linda—by the standards of the Liverpool left-wing, garrulous socialists—would be seen as a middle-class cop out.

It should also be noted that in his choice of wife and lifestyle, Paul was doing no more than follow the natural path and predilections of the grammar-school boy that he was before he met the loutish John and the Beatles changed all that.

Unfortunately for Paul, fellow Liverpudlians resent anything which smacks of betterment. And when Paul followed his natural inclination to modify his Liverpool accent and wear smart clothing, John was furious at Paul's reactionary lifestyle. It was these implicit differences which were manifested in their final split-up and the bitter, musical feud that ensued. The vituperation came largely from John, whose suffering was a great deal more public than Paul's.

The way in which they expressed their suffering was, itself, a mark of the differences between the two men and not at all an indication of their actual degree of pain. Paul, no doubt, suffered as much as John, especially as the public openly sympathized with John and not him. It should be remembered that his pain ran just as deep, but he never made a public spectacle of it. Whereas John's bitterness openly manifests itself in the running argument of *Imagine*.

There was, at one time, a public trend to hero-worship John and to denigrate Paul when he began to display a leaning towards the middle class—which infuriated not only John but some of Paul's fans. They were up in arms when Paul appeared on English television in an afternoon program as a host with Linda. The show was something like a poor man's *Oprah Winfrey Show*. It had Paul and Linda clad in casually-elegant attire standing by the mantlepiece of a comfortable, middle-class house with a fire blazing in the grate, while the happy couple, arm-in-arm smiled warmly at the camera. The fans claimed that Paul did not need the work, the money or the publicity. The image he presented was of a hybrid personality—a deodorized, sanctified Liverpudlian, so the argument went. As the show-host his Liverpool cockiness largely disappeared, and when it did reveal itself, it was a self-conscious effort which became a parody i.e, Paul *acting* as a cocky Liverpudlian, the edges neatly trimmed for afternoon TV.

To denigrate Paul like this is to do him a great injustice. What made the Beatles was their differences; and Paul's

One incident, in particular, stays in my mind as an example of Paul's kindness to his fans:

In the late Seventies, when Paul was living in north London, I was working as a producer for the BBC and I met a Liverpudlian in Camden Town, London. (Camden Town is a curious mixture of Irish, ghetto, Blacks, students, gays, and, right in the middle of it all, islands of outlandish wealth and ostentation.)

Well, this guy was a pitiful sight. He was an old, bombed-out Beat whose long hair was now completely gray-white. He was filthy and visibly had the shakes. Nevertheless, he was an open and honest character with his heart on his sleeve. And he told me that once he knocked on Paul's door in St. John's Wood and told the doorman he was a Liverpool guy who wanted to see Paul. Well, Paul actually came out to see him and talked. He told Paul he was an artist, and Paul actually went to his crash pad and bought three of his paintings for an exorbitant sum.

The guy took me back to the very same house to see his paintings. It was a sordid place; a derelict building with no heating; sacks for curtains; dank and filthy. I looked at his paintings. They were absolutely terrible by any standards—really awful—and when I saw them, I mentally saluted Paul, who had responded with his heart to a down-and-out fellow Liverpudlian.

attributes were no more dispensable than John's, George's or Ringo's.

Furthermore, the whole nuance of the above TV appearance could be read in another way: as an act of courage. Paul was putting himself on the line. When the Beatles split up, he was the first one to step outside the protective umbrella of the Beatles' name and go it alone. Because Paul was, primarily, a performer, he, of all the Beatles, wanted to keep on playing—and did so, under tremendous odds. Furthermore, Paul has manifested a quality of endurance under duress which is

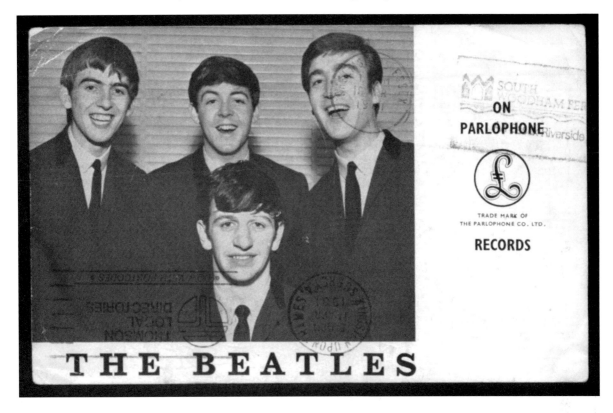

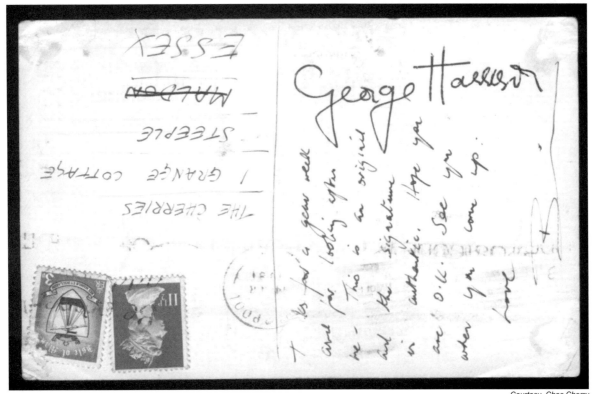

The postcard above displays George's own signature

not solely Liverpudlian, but one of the attributes of the middle-classes described above (they do have good points as well, you know).

Furthermore, Paul has always shown quite clearly that he realizes his debt to his fans; to perform, he must have an audience, and he has always been willing to go out to meet or to do things for his fans. And in the final analysis, all he ever wanted to do was to play—as was exemplified by the period when he would suddenly appear at no-name gigs in small towns in England without warning or publicity, just for the thrill of playing to an audience he could *see*.

So, as with all marriages—and the Beatles was longer-lived than most—it must be remembered that what goes on in between the sheets is something we'll never know. Paul, in his later (long and happy) marriage to Linda was only being the stable person he would have naturally been without the interference of the Beatles' phenomenon. Paul always was an ordering influence to John's wildness, both in life and on stage.

However, the point must be understood that neither Beatle was better or superior. Just as John needed Paul's ordering influence, so Paul needed John's rebellious fire.

The Beatles on Stage

Source unknown

A band unloading outside the Cavern door for an afternoon session. Note the girl on the right—short skirt, flat heels and unpermed hair. She was considered "weird" in an era dominated by beehives.

Always anarchic, disruptive, sometimes even on stage, during the afternoon or evening session at the Cavern, John would take time out to read the numerous notes that were handed to the group. He took great pleasure in satirizing the notes with a zeal and sense of the bizarre that was a forerunner of *Monty Python* or *Saturday Night Live* sensibilities:

An Afternoon Session, circa 1963, The Cavern
—A Personal Anecdote—

The Cavern is filled with scores of elegantly-clad, beehive-haired girls drinking soup and munching cheese and tomato sandwiches, scribbling frantic lovelorn

114

The Cavern Stage

notes to the four lads, requesting numbers or special favors or sometimes just being downright provocative.

John reads a note out loud, peering shortsightedly over his glasses while George (the quiet technician) grins shyly. Ringo whistles blithely, unaffected by it all. Paul hops about on one foot eyeing John with a slight frown; Paul is in charge—self-appointed—of crowd appeal and quality control, and if John begins to horse around too much, he will restrain him.

John clears his throat and says in his dour, flat Liverpool monotone: "We've gorra note 'ere from Emily Hutchinson of Aintree who wants to know if we'll sing Mr. Postman for 'er. She also says: 'Dear John, sumtimes you are very funny, sometimes you're daft; but have yer ever thought of including impressions in your act...?'" John pauses, his eyes gleam from behind his spectacles. "Where are yer Emily?"

His eyes search the crowd as Emily hides behind a group of giggling girls at the front of the stage, crying out: "Oh friggin' 'ell! I feel like a lemon, Mary! 'ide me! 'ide

The Cavern Toilets

me!" at the same time basking in the attention from her idol.

"Aach, there she is there—all ready to attack the crowd with her hairstyle!" (Emily's bouffant is improbable, to say the least).

Despite her awe, Emily is still possessed of her native wit and shouts out: "I thought you could do a pretty good impression of Dracula, or, even better, Frankenstein—but I could be wrong!" [Laughter]

Paul begins to hiss at John—he's taking too long. But John, on a roll, ignores Paul, saying: "Well, luv, I can do impressions. Here you go... This is my impression of a lead vocalist with TB [makes horrendous noise into mike]...with tonsillitis [makes another horrendous noise]...and, last but not least, cancer..." In hoarse tones, he whispers: "Oh God, I'm dying...!"

Paul finally manages to catch John's attention, and, with true show business aplomb, says smoothly: "And here for Emily is Mr. Postman..." He counts the band in and they swing into action.

Ever the showman, always aware of the camera, Paul was also wary in the presence of other rougher musicians. He felt the gutter nature of their origins and, with a Liverpool musician's sensitivity to the acerbic nature of street wit, Paul, the diplomat, trod carefully around them. In this way, he also served as a natural foil to John's rebellious recklessness.

Courtesy Mindscaffolding

The Cavern Wall of Rememberance

The Beatles: The Pressure To Go Under
Yoko Did Not Break Up the Beatles

The pressure on the Beatles was increased enormously by their isolation. They were not the first superstars but they were the first superstar group from a working-class background. They had no precedents; nor did they have anyone else to lean upon but themselves. The music business is notoriously unstable, and the parameters and social conventions of normal society completely missing. It is a fierce world of dog-eat-dog where the rules are made and broken every day; and, as such, it is easy for a performer, particularly one who rises quickly, to fall apart completely...

Tony Palmer made a series of films in 1975 which shows how Janis Joplin, Jimmy Hendrix and other stage performers who died are, in some ways, victims of a society which elevates them to a position of Godlike social isolation. There at the top, they have it all—materially. But, that in itself is valueless without the nurturing network needed by all people: peer approval; familial

Courtesy Mindscaffolding

Brass plaque in Mathew Street of John Lennon's poem, 'Liddypool'

support; purpose; motivation; and social sanctions. Without these, the performer falls apart and will resort to incredibly self-destructive behavior.

Unless the artist has something outside of show business to maintain him through the vacuum formed by total material freedom, he perishes. Bob Dylan, for example, has the support of his religion.

For the Beatles, the pressures were enormous, and their reactions manifested in their music; in their constant experimentation and search for identity: psychedelics; the Maharishi; George's excursions into Krishna Consciousness; John's clinging onto Yoko; Paul's clinging onto Linda; John's romantic delusions of peaceful revolutions; and Ringo, who, like any working-class lad with unlimited resources, got drunk for twenty years and watched telly. Their search was for *meaning* in a world where the only value is money which, particularly for them, by itself was meaningless.

The Beatles have each paid a tremendous price, but they did survive—apart from the senseless tragedy of John's death. And for these reasons:

First; the natural defenses and protective reflexes of Liverpool which go very deep. If the Beatles had been from disparate cultures, they might not have survived. Ethnically, the four Beatles reflected four very different facets of Liverpool in a microcosm. And this not only kept them together for so long, but was what made their music so juicy and colorful.

Secondly, the Beatles had themselves. The very different attitudes of Paul and John which have been detailed here can be seen, without value judgement, to be a necessary component in the Beatles' music; no yin without yang; and no earth or water (Ringo and George) without air or fire (Paul and John).

Whether you prefer John's raw, aching honesty to Paul's showmanship, Ringo's earthiness or George's quiet, technical expertise, all of these were needed to make up the total sound of the Beatles. It was their *differences* as Liverpudlians which gave the Beatles their unique quality. And it was their shared origins that kept them going—a tiny island of communality awash in the glitz-infused world of show business.

Two Liverpool Lads Who Lost Their Mums

In the description of the first meeting between John and Paul, the remark "a lout who smelled of drink" is attributed to Paul. But what is often missed is that the most significant cornerstone of the Lennon-McCartney duo was the mutual loss of their mothers.

Tragically, for Paul it was breast cancer that took his mother, just as it took his beloved Linda—a cruel twist of fate. Following his mother's death, a distraught Paul plunged himself into the world of guitars.

John's mother was crossing the street to Mendips when she was struck by a car driven by an off-duty policeman rumored to be "under the influence".

What brought the strange duo of John and Paul together was this shared tragedy. Paul says:

> *There was one rather funny incident that happened a year or so after Julia (his mother) had gone. I remember us meeting up with someone who happened to ask how my mother was getting on. "Well, actually, she died a few years ago," I replied. "Oh, I'm awfully sorry, son." Turning to John, they asked him the same question, only to be told precisely the exact thing. We somehow found their deep embarrassment rather amusing. Actually, it was a wonderful way of masking our true feelings, and it gave us both a bit more of a bond.*[6]

The fact is, it's not a question of why the Beatles broke up but how on earth they managed to stay together—and this bond was one factor that made them ride through the bad times.

In this context, the bitterness which manifested itself between John and Paul when the Beatles broke apart is understandable, for, without this familial bond, it can be seen that the love turned volte-face—just as it does in all broken marriages. For the Beatles group was, indeed, a four-way marriage.

This was never more apparent than in the music which each Beatle produced immediately following their breakup. Like fledglings fresh out of the nest, they took their first, tottering steps and launched themselves back into show business to face the world as themselves—alone.

Paul—the handsome youth whose images of grace and elegance and social acceptance manifested

Parlaphone & E.M.I. Recording Artists

THE

BEATLE'S ★

★ MERSEY BEATS

AT

ST. JOHN'S HALL,
ORIEL ROAD,
(Opposite Bootle Town Hall)
★

ON MONDAY
30th JULY 1962
7-30 p.m. to 11-0 p.m.

Courtesy Dave Forshaw

themselves both in his appearance and his music—initially brought out a series of tinkling, pretty, melodic and slightly schmaltzy songs.

John, all raw emotion and rhythm, with little melodic sensibility, brought out a series of aching, thumping, gut-wrenching songs with vast thumping beats and gaps, as though recorded in a barn.

George flirted with Krishna, dabbled in this and that, seeking to perfect not just his music but to find his own identity.

Ringo simply retired for twenty years and got drunk, apart from brief excursions into sentimental albums.

Of course, accomplished performers as they were, these songs worked, more or less, but initially each piece was only a fragment, a part of the whole. Like an exploded diagram of a functional machine, these separate productions were an indication of how the Beatles' songs had worked.

John's raw, thumping emotion and anarchic rhythm had been a perfect foil to Paul's pretty, showcase music and trilling melodic sense. We see these at their best in their earlier masterpieces together.

George, is must be said, was ever the technician, and his most important contribution was just that. Each of his guitar pieces drew on a wide range of influences from Mississippi Delta Blues to Chuck Berry, Indian ragas to Fats Waller, and were always totally original. However, George's music was *never individual*. In other words, George was able to supply a lead guitar backing which was always tasteful, appropriate, inventive and original, but of no particular recognizable style.

Unlike a Hendrix or a Clapton whose style is immediately recognizable simply because they can only play one way, George was an unusual phenomenon: a lead guitarist with a sideman's ego—in other words, no ego. George did not possess the desperate flair to be out front and impress his style on the whole group, which is the main (and necessary) attribute of most lead guitarists: flowery, pushy, assertive and dominating.

George was, and is, a craftsman. Eclectic, appropriate, working away quietly in the background to meld together the two extremes of Paul's prettiness and John's raw power. He functioned in a superbly innovative way always supplying exactly what was required. Oddly enough, this is normally the role of the bass player in a group. And there we have it: George was a lead guitarist with a bass player's ego, whilst Paul was a bass player with a lead guitarist's ego.

Ringo laid it down, and, unlike most drummers of the modern era, did not blend with Paul in that symbolic marriage of drummer and bassist, which is the mark of power in later jazz-rock groups, but rather, Ringo laid it down for the whole group.

In the bizarre gestalt that was The Beatles, Ringo's contribution was indispensable.

Ringo, the Saving Grace

Ringo (second left) performing with Rory Storm (left) and the Hurricanes
A rare moment, Ringo strikes out on guitar. Obviously everyone was having a lot of fun-viz Johnny Guitar waving the hi-hat (right)

Without Ringo, the group would have fallen apart much earlier. For, though they were all so very different—a difference which manifested itself in the tug-of-war which took place between John and Paul (Marx vs. capitalism) or Paul and George (kid brother vs. elder brother; sideman vs. spotlight grabber)—the one thing they had in common was Liverpool, and, if anything, Ringo was Liverpool: flat; ugly; down-to-earth; common; lovable; easy; witty; gregarious; what-you-see-is-what-you-get Ringo.

George once said: "Whenever I get any fancy ideas about being a Beatle, I just look at Ringo's nose once and it brings me back to earth."

And that was it. The Beatles loved Ringo as they loved Liverpool. He was the common bond that helped them stay afloat in a hostile world among a sea of strangers.

Ringo's role in the Beatles was never more apparent than in an early interview on the *Eammon Andrews Show*, an English version of the *Johnny Carson Show*, hosted by a smiling Eammon Andrews who was very charming but not too bright. Ringo was interviewed first, and he talked about his marriage to Maureen and his newborn son.

Wolf Makowitz, another guest—a composer and classical musician—poured out wrath against the Beatles, their music, their taste, their vulgarity and their plebeian values whilst John and Paul (who had just seen a James Bond film) made chopping karate motions and barked and growled at him, shouting: "Wolf!! Come boy! Good Wolf! Down boy! Woof! Woof!" Mankowitz was furious, and his vituperation increased, as did John and Paul's scathing wit.

The situation was fast getting our of hand, and Eammon Andrews, desperate for a solution, turned to Ringo who was calmly sipping his drink. Hoping to turn the tide, Eamon said: "Ringo Now you, Ringo, what do you make of all this?"

"I dunno, Eamon," said Ringo dryly in his flat, nasal monotone, "I stopped listening after 'babies'..."

In a way, Ringo *was* Liverpool itself. He was the common ground over which the other three roamed metaphorically and literally. Ringo was predictable, reliable, earthy, sentimental, unswayed by outside forces and pressure; his relationships were real, characterized by a down-to-earth sensibility.

With his big nose and his easy humor, Ringo was the oil in the machine. He possessed the easy relaxation of someone who doesn't need to excel because he knows he can't. His drumming was average but competent, his looks mundane, his intellectual power ordinary. In fact, Ringo's vast gift to the Beatles—and one which carried them through many a crisis—was his *ordinariness.*

John could rack his soul and beat his chest; hold his sit-ins; rant and rave; exhort an unfair, unkind world to "make love not war", crippled and tortured by his own inner angst. Paul could duck, bob and weave; smile cheerfully, eternally cute for an Eternal Camera. George, cool and methodical, would take frequent excursions into the mists of Enlightenment, Karma and the Eternal goal of Truth...

But, when they wanted to come back Home, Ringo was there, with a ready Liverpool grin and a no-nonsense wit. More at ease with himself than all the others, Ringo was the typical Liverpudlian who would say "well, what can you do?" to the worst of fates, and quietly get on with it.

One song alone sums up the Beatles' love for Ringo's ordinariness and all that he represents of their common heritage. It is *A Little Help From My Friends.* The song takes its form in a question and answer dialogue between Ringo and the other three Beatles and is a wonderful acknowledgment of their debt to Ringo.

Ringo served his time making tea for dour Liverpool laborers on my father's building site. I saw my father heading off to work every morning at 6 a.m., and it was no joke: Cold, empty building sites in the drab outskirts of Liverpool, under vaulting, gray skies the color of dirty linen, it was a world that could crush a man's spirit and, coming from this world, Ringo never lost his sentimentality. He, more than any of them, knew that he was Joe Ordinary. And the other Beatles turned to him because he was all that Liverpool had been for them before the rug had been pulled from beneath their feet by success.

Here we have it...for Ringo; singing *With A Little Help From My Friends*—with a little help from his friends John, Paul and George. The song *is* Ringo; each verse is almost a list of his attributes—and his simple honesty—'cause all of them knew he couldn't sing and they *didn't care*

Ringo:	*What would you do if I sang out of tune*
	Would you stand up and walk out on me?
	Lend me your ear while I sing you this song
	And I'll try not to sing out of key
	What do I do when my love is away?
John, Paul, George:	*Does it worry you to be alone?*
Ringo:	*How do I feel at the end of the day?*
John, Paul, George:	*Are you sure that you're on your own?*

And Ringo, most emphatically, answers "no." With his friends John, Paul and George, he's never alone. "No," he says, "I'll get by with a little help from my friends."

"Would you believe in love at first sight?" ask the other three Beatles.

And Ringo replies: "I'm certain that it happens all the time."

"What do you see when you turn out the light?" they ask.

And Ringo replies in his simple, uncultured, fashion: "I can't tell you but I know it's mine."

And, at the end of the song, finally the Beatles ask him: "Well, do you need anybody?"

And Ringo replies: "I *just* need someone to love."

"Could it be anybody?" is the mischievous retort.

Firmly, Ringo reiterates his point: "I *just* need someone to love. Oh, I'll get by with a little help from my friends. Mmm I'll get high with a little help from my friends. Yes, I'm gonna try with a little help from my friends. I'll get by with a little help from my friends..."

And he certainly did.

A City of Characters

There are so many colorful characters in Liverpool that they deserve their own book. In fact, the characters which are reported in this brief section are purely random, being no less than those encountered while collecting photographs in a couple of weeks from some of those involved in the early '60s Liverpool beat scene in one way or another.

Adrian Henri

Is a poet, artist, lecturer at the Art College, friend of the Beatles, inveterate drinker, humanist and a propagandist for the Liverpool Scene. Here is the manifesto he drew up with Sam Walsh (the painter of the large McCarney face in the chapter *The South Discovers Liverpool*) in the early '60s:

> We would rather paint like Cannonball Adderly than Picasso.
> We would rather paint like Charley Mingus than either.
> We oppose megaton bombardments with Persil packets, dead birds and strange apparitions with fixed painted smiles.
> We would like children to find our paintings at the bottom of cornflakes packets.
> If Frankenstein's monster didn't exist, it would be necessary to invent him.

Adrian's poetry became a very dynamic part of the Liverpool scene, much aclaimed by Alan Ginsburg.

Adrian Henri, early '60s

Albion's most lovely daughter sat on the banks of the Mersey
dangling her landing stage in the water

The daughters of Albion
arriving by underground at Central Station
eating hot eccles cakes at the Pierhead
writing "Billy Blake is fab" on a wall in Matthew street
taking off their navyblue schooldrawers and
putting on nylon panties ready for the night

The daughters of Albion
see the moonlight beating down on them in Bebington
throw away their chewing gum ready for the goodnight kiss
comb their darkblonde hair in suburban bedrooms
powder their delicate nipples wondering if tonight
will be the night
their bodies pressed into dresses or sweater
lavender at the Cavern or pink at the Sink

The daughters of Albion
wondering how to explain why they didn't go home.

ADRIAN HENRI

Arthur Dooley

A true member of the working class, son of a docker and himself an ex-factory hand, parking bobby and nine-year veteran of the Irish Guards, Arthur is also a gifted, self-taught sculptor. My earliest memory of him is sitting in the Jacaranda club with Allan Williams' pristine and rather socially conscious wife, and I was amazed at how often Arthur used the "f..." word in front of this lady, both with impunity and total lack of self-consciousness.

Courtesy Weekend Daily Telegraph

Arthur Dooley, early '60s

Courtesy Mindscaffolding

Arthur Dooley's sculpture of the Beatles in Matthew Street

Courtesy Mindscaffolding

Arthur Dooley's sculpture of the Crucifixion

Harry Prytherch

. . . . Is a fine drummer. Pictured here both in his youth and present day. Harry has the most amazing collection of Merseyside and music memorabilia—and, with a generosity as deep as the shades of black on the sooty Liverpool buildings, gave of his collection for this book. Here is just a brief view of his vast and varied collection.

Courtesy Mindscaffolding

Harry Prytherch in his museum

Courtesy Harry Prytherch

Harry as a young drummer, early '60s

Courtesy Harry Prytherch

One wall of Harry Prytherch's Beatle Museum

Dave Williams

Another Scouse musician who gave most generosly to this book is Dave Williams, whose pictures of the Beatles graced the pages earlier. Dave not only has the distinction of being a collector of Beatles' and Merseyside memorablia, but the amazing accomplishment of being in the same Liverpool band for 40 years. Indeed, he still plays to this very day.

Courtesy Dave Williams

Dave's guitar

Courtesy Dave Williams

Dave Williams, early '60s

Harry Ainscough

Some of the nicest photographs in this book are from Harry's collection. Harry, a Scouser, moved to Sheffield and, for twenty years, came back to Liverpool every weekend to take his compelling photographs. His widow, Margaret, gave most freely of his fine collection for this book. His collected works can be found in the book *Ainscough's Liverpool.*

Courtesy Margaret Ainscough

Harry Ainscough

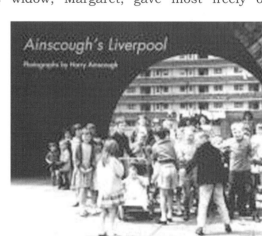

The cover of Harry's book *Ainscough's Liverpool*

125

Quentin Hughes

Is an architect and lecturer at Liverpool University. Some of his lovely black and white photographs of Liverpool buildings are used herein. They were taken from his book, *Seaport, Architecture & Townscape in Liverpool,* pictured below.

Courtesy Weekend Daily Telegraph

Quentin Hughes, early '60s

Defence of Dockland, 1967

Quentin Hughes was Senior Lecturer in architecture at Liverpool University. "I hated Liverpool as a child. I hated its untidiness. Now I think it's the untidiness I like." His liking for the untidy city is celebrated in a beautiful photographic survey Seaport. He is probably more than anyone responsible for the upsurge of interest in Liverpool's dockland and commercial architecture and, in particular, the Albert Dock and warehouses which are threatened with demolition and development as a complex of office blocks. For the moment, the dock sits silent and empty and this is its attraction to him, an attraction that any kind of preservational change of use would destroy. "You know what I think they should do with Liverpool? They should let it be a depressed area. It would balance itself out. Industry might as well move to the South-East. We've got no tradition of manufacturing here anyway. It's completely alien. We should simply let Liverpool run down in a natural way and we'd end up with somewhere like Venice, somewhere that was nice to live in."

Courtesy Bluecoat Press

The cover to Quentin Hughes' 1964 book, *Seaport* and 1999 book, *Liverpool City of Architecture*

Gas Gaskell

Is one of the few sax players on the Liverpool scene, along with Howey Casey (pictured with Derry Wilkie in the Chapter 7, *Drugs & Rock 'n Roll—Opening For The Beatles*). Gas, shown in full western regalia and as he is in present day—hardly changed in 50 years and still blowing up a storm. A fine musician and a delightful man.

Courtesy Gaz Gaskell
Gaz Gaskell as an "urban cowboy" lured by the

Courtesy Gaz Gaskell
Gaz Gaskell today, one of Liverpool's finest sax players

Courtesy Gaz Gaskell
Gaz (far right with glasses) and his band, early '60s

Liverpool's Rag and Bone Men

Liverpool Joke:

Tonto:	We are lost, Kemosabe. This desert is vast. Even my tracking skills are of no use.
Lone Ranger (hears sound):	Wait! A bugle! It's the cavalry!
Tonto:	No, Kemosabe, it's the Ragman. He's lost as well.

Courtesy Weekend Daily Telegraph

The local ragman plying his trade at the bottom of the author's street, early '60s

Indeed, some of the ragmen did carry bugles, but most of them had their own distinctive cry. They would travel the streets in their horse and cart, giving away trinkets and toys in return for rags, which they would sell by the pound to paper manufacturers. Each ragman's cry was haunting and memorable. I remember the one that plied the jiggers[1] at the back of my home. He was, in fact, shouting: "Your rags, oh! Your rags, oh!" But it was delivered in a long, drawn-out cry as "Jerankooh! Jerankooh!" which immediately identified him to all and sundry.

Courtesy Ken Dodd

Ken Dodd, early '60s, well-known Liverpool comedian

Ken Dodd

Ken Dodd is a sweet, shy man whose stage presence belies this. He made his name as a Liverpool comedian bringing to national consiousness such rare and delightful items as jam butties (a jelly sandwich) and often talked about "the diddymen" who tirelessly worked the "black pudding" fields in "Knotty Ash"—in other words, an arcane, self-made Liverpool world around which Ken wove his comedy. The fans loved it.

Stan Hugill

Stan Hugill was born in an old coast-guard station early in the 1900s. He came from a sea-going family, both his father and grandfather having served their time at sea. Stan sailed in his first sailing ship when he was four years-old, being taken aboard by his father who was investigating the allegation of cruelty in the case of a cabin boy's flogging. Years later, when Stan joined his first ship, a steamer, he was shipwrecked off the coast of New Zealand on his first trip, whereupon he joined the sailing ship, "Saucy Kate" which was used for coasting around New Zealand. After many adventures, Stan went on to become one of the foremost collectors of sea shanties and ballads in England.

Courtesy Tony Davis

Stan Hugill, collector of sea shanties

129

Those In The Firing Line

Reports from social workers and teachers who deal with the arduous task of helping non-English-speaking migrants to assimilate into the culture reveal that conditions haven't changed much. Kids are sometimes under-nourished, homes are overcrowded, sanitation minimal. In other words, all the old problems continue to flourish like Hydra the Gorgon, the mythical beast which, having one head cut off quickly grew two more in its place.

Courtesy Mindscaffolding

Tiber Street, the author's former school

Having considerable experience in this field, I know how harrowing a job this can be. I have nothing but admiration for those brave souls who put themselves in the "front line", often for very little in the way of financial remuneration.

One such person is Margaret Avinyo (known to her best friends as Maggie). A Liverpudlian born and bred, Maggie is a multi-talented girl representative of a new breed of language teacher. Not only is she fluent in Spanish, French, Italian, Greek and Welsh(!) but she is a also a performing singer of some note.

Maggie recounts many colorful stories in her duties as Home Teacher for the Liverpool Education Department, and the following show that she has not lost her sense of humor, despite the grind of the job. Maggie is, indeed, a lovely girl, as her picture shows, both inside and out.

Courtesy Mindscaffolding

Margaret Avinyo

Tiber Street school, now an Islamic Center

The front entrance of theTiber Street Islamic Center

Maggie was on a home-teaching visit to a young dyslexic boy. The boy told her that he was epileptic. She made careful note of this. Later in the lesson, as though remembering and changing his mind, he said earnestly: "Sorry, Miss, I'm not epileptic, Miss, I'm dis-electric."

Maggie, when substituting for other teachers, would often invite pupils to make a temporary register by writing their names on a list. It's not unusual for real names to be transposed and the class to be filled with names from the movie and pop industries. When Maggie glanced down at the completed list, she saw that one of her pupils was named Madonna. Thinking of the singer, Maggie asked 'Madonna' to stand up. She gently inquired if the girl had any other names. "Yes, Miss, Madonna Jones, Miss. Me Mam loves the Beatles and called me that because she wants me to marry a Lord and be a Lady."

131

WHO ARE THEY THEN..?

Mr. Murphy Sports Master | **Jim Guitar Salesman** | **Moo Craft Teacher** | **Frith** Future Teacher **Anna** Future Hairdresser

Rita Restaurant Owner | **Quentin Architect** | **Freddie Comedian** | **Brian Poet**

B.J. Arranger | **Pete Adventurer** | **Florrie Irish Chanteuse** | **Ms. Singleton** Herself - always

JUST ORDINARY PEOPLE - IN LIVERPOOL,
EVERYBODY IS A CHARACTER...

Sexual Attitudes
Mayhem & Mirth

13

1963: Sexual Attitudes, Mirth and Mayhem

Lewis's Department Store and the Statue *Liverpool Resurgent*

"We talk with an accent exceeding rare
Meet under a statue exceeding bare
In my Liverpool home..."
The Spinners
(courtesy Pete McGovern)

I n 1956, a statue was commissioned to stand outside Lewis's, the Nieman Marcus of Liverpool, opposite Liverpool's largest and poshest hotel, the Adelphi. It was meant to represent the spirit of Liverpool. To the shock and delight of Liverpudlians, Jacob Epstein, an American sculptor, responded with the 18½ foot statue of a naked man, arms aloft, one leg thrust forward, his eyes fixed on a remote horizon. He called it 'Liverpool Resurgent'.

This pose was a lot more revealing of the naked man's natural assets than the prudent fig-leafed sculptures of a Michelangelo. In fact, it was anatomically correct in more ways than one.

The average Liverpudlian responded with unbridled mirth—and the statue is still there to this day. In fact, *In My Liverpool Home* by the Liverpool Spinners has immortalized the statue for ever in song. The statue has entered into common parlance and is usually refered to as "Dicky Lewis" or "Nobby Lewis". It has even become an idiomatic phrase. When someone is being idle, stupid or just a plain dork, a Liverpudlian will remark "'e was standing there like one of Lewis's..."

In the '90s, the news that fired the public's imagination was the sexually-titilating gossip about the wayward aristocracy, i.e., Charles and Diana or Clinton and Monica Lewinski. Similarly, sex was the final factor which toppled the British Empire and the Conservative's reign of power in the '60s; namely, the Profumo scandal.

There is a historical echo here which shows how remarkable single events may reflect the tenor of the time. The impact which Diana's tragic death will have upon the future of the British monarchy is still playing out. It may be that, as an individual, she reflected a change that was imminent anyway. Once again we are back to Jung's collective consciousness.

The so-called shock with which the British public greeted the Profumo scandal was, as is often the case, a staged reaction by vested-interest power groups rather than a genuine, widespread indictment of upper-class sexuality.

The odd fact is the upper classes and the lower classes, though separated by an enormous gulf, have more in *common* than is generally thought. There is, and always has been, a wide acceptance of sexual deviation and personal idiosyncrasy amongst the English aristocracy. After all, many of the kings of England were homosexuals. Similarly, but for quite different reasons, the lower classes find little in sexual life to be shocked at. It is usually the upward-aspiring middle-classes who are most prudish. A typical Liverpudlian is not only virtually unshockable but actually revels in the gory details of the vilest sexual atrocities.

It was a tragic affair for Profumo, and the truth of the matter is that he was sorely misused. The facts are simple: in August 1961, the War Minister had a brief fling with Christine Kieler[1]. Brief is the word——it only lasted a matter of a few weeks. At the same time, she was having relations with the Russian attache, Ivanov. Of course, in black and white, this could be seen as a 'security risk', though nothing of that nature transpired. But two years later this affair was connected to the trial of Steven Ward, a London osteopath charged with living off the earnings of prostitution (the infamous Christine Kieler and Mandy Rice-Davies). Although there was little evidence that these two were any more than good-time girls and that Ward was a mere sexual opportunist, the English press was fired with a blaze of self-righteous wrath that burned for weeks, proving the old adage: Hell hath no fury like a vested interest posing as a moral principle

Thus, the news that Profumo—the British War Minister—and associates had been caught dabbling with some ladies of pleasure was received with great amusement amongst the working classes.

Investigative journalists, the middle classes and those with a political investment in the downfall of the aristocracy were suitably shocked. With great alacrity, they generated enough flack over the incident to oust the Conservatives. Of course, exactly the same thing happened with President Clinton. Whatever your personal view of his conduct, it's obvious that his enemies seized upon his sexual indiscretion as a political crowbar.

In the case of Britain, Harold Wilson, the Labour man (read Democrat) stepped into power with a very narrow majority in 1964.

A cartoon appeared in the May issue of *Private Eye* which summed up the furor. In Hogarthian style, it depicted England in a state of debauchery and moral collapse. Written in Olde English, it was entitled, *"Britain Gets Withe ITTE 1963."* It showed various public figures standing before a huge crowd in Trafalgar Square. The crowd sported an improbable banner saying "Hang The Queen", while each of the public figures uttered appropriate street cries (such as: "Come stare at ye breasts of a Duchess"; "Come buy my sweet, pornographic pictures.") The Royal family sat in a fairground platform alongside a sign which summed up the whole sexual circus: "Get Snapped With The Royals."[2]

Liverpool, of course, loved it, seeing it as a bit of spicy fun rather than a moral issue. And yet Profumo's coequals used it against the entire upper class.

The true nature of the campaign was an attempt to oust the Conservatives. This time, it worked.

The Profumo affair was a sad misuse of the power of the press. In truth, the upper classes in England have always revealed an innate tolerance and gentleness, a respect for individuality and eccentricity and a wholehearted rejection of coercion and uniformity which would have, under normal circumstances, quietly swept the Profumo affair under the carpet. The Profumo affair is not a true indication of the sexual attitudes of the British nation, upper or lower class.

Tim Birdsall's cartoon *Britain Gets Withe Itte, 1963*

136

137

Sex and the Liverpudlian*

The truth of the matter is that when it comes to sex, the Liverpudlian not only leaves little to the imagination, but revels in shock and disgust. Should one of his hair-raising anecdotes turn the face of a listener green with nausea, he is delighted. This is probably what Paul McCartney meant when he said in a TV interview: "Oh, we like cruel, sordid things."

Liverpudlians living in two-up two-down houses with no bathroom and an external toilet did not readily leave the warm sanctuary of their bedroom for "rest room" niceties. At 3 a.m. on a cold wintery morning with two inches of snow outside, not many would brave an unheated room and a half-naked trip down the sordid, dark backyard just to urinate in privacy. The "po"—or chamber pot, as it was called in posher societies—was an absolute necessity in bedroom life. Even in my relatively small family, we were four in one bedroom—two boys and Mum and Dad—it can be imagined that in larger families, sexual and toilet privacy was at a minimum.

One half of my relatives were actually Malaysian, so that my cousins were all yellow-skinned and slant-eyed. At the age of ten, I knew all the other boys in my street, aged 10 to 15, were regularly engaging in sexual intercourse with one of my 12-year-old cousins. "Jockey and Rider" was the name of the game. I refused to go along on this particular ride—pun intended—not out of morality, just a sense of unease about the whole thing which was wordless to my 10-year-old sensibility. The girl eventually became pregnant and, lo and behold, her father was arrested for incest and jailed. He was freed and some years later. When the next daughter came of age, she, too, became pregnant and the father was charged again. The fact is, he probably *was* having sex with his daughters. However, had DNA testing been in force at this time, charges may not have been brought at all as, amongst the six or seven children who were regularly having sex with these girls, some of the boys were fertile.

However, as with all working-class values, there is within these excesses a certain ambivalence. Working-class children are still brought up in Liverpool to regard sex as dirty, and there is a vague rule that women should be excluded from graphic, sexual conversations. However, these are tenuous sanctions at best and soon break down under the sheer attrition of work, drink and the sometimes bloody and violent vicissitudes of daily life.

For the lower classes, sex, like life, knocks insistently at the door at a very early age. Most children in Liverpool 8 were sexual connoisseurs by the age of fifteen at the latest:

Two children, brother and sister, at the age of six and eight respectively, repeatedly (and innocently) tried to copulate on their front doorstep opposite me. Group and private investigations into biological differences were carried out in real earnest from the ages of three upwards, in alleys, entrances, behind outhouses and in derelict buildings.

In this respect, the sexual development of the lower-class English children takes place much earlier than their middle-class peers. John Money, the famous sexologist from Johns Hopkins University pointed out, "it is crucial to healthy, sexual growth that all mammals (including homo sapiens) carry out an earlier period of sexual rehearsal play." This, unfortunately, is taboo in middle-class society. Money commented sadly, when showing a reporter a photo of two young children coupling: "I've just broken the Law."[3]

In the cozy, frowzy intimacy of the slum or ghetto, whether it be Liverpool or New York, a child's sexual initiation is simply a matter of exigency; living close to the bone, and even more pertinent, living close, period; one of the facets of overcrowding.

The result is that a Liverpudlian's conversation is so explicit and graphic that it is often repellent to other Englishmen. For a Liverpudlian, the level of sexual conversations starts at the gutter—and work downwards. No corner of human sexuality, deviation or excretive faculty is considered too delicate to discuss in vivid detail.

The Liverpudlian will take the vilest situation and worm out the most sickening, disgusting, putrescent aspect of it and take great pleasure in discussing this in detail.

Many years later as a seaman coming into Liverpool, I was accosted by a young lady of pleasure outside a notorious watering hole called the Lucky Club. It might have been more accurately named the "Get Lucky" Club. The girl who accosted me was almost 18 with yellowish skin and slightly slant eyes. She was dressed most provocatively and wore a huge pair of filter sunglasses modelling herself after some movie star or other. During her attempts to cajole me inside, she seemed quite amused and mischievous during the whole interchange. When she realized I was not going to partake of her pleasures, she asked me if I knew who she was. I didn't, of course. Then she told me, with much mirth, that she was one of my cousins. She had only been eleven the last time I saw her, so I didn't recognize her.

* Do not read this chapter if sexual descriptions and language offend you

THE FINEST FOLK IS ON FONTANA

Don't miss the SPINNERS NEW LP

AN other LP BY THE SPINNERS

DRUNKEN SAILOR · GO DOWN YOU BLOOD RED ROSES · SALLY BROWN · LIVERPOOL JUDIES
LINSTEAD MARKET · · SWEET WILLIAM'S GHOST · · GUNGU WALK · · NAVVY BOOTS
PLEASANT AND DELIGHTFUL · · JUG O'PUNCH · · ROTHESAY-O · · THREE JOLLY BOYS
STILL GROWING · · MINSTREL BOY · · SLY MONGOOSE · · THE LEAVING OF LIVERPOOL

AN other L.P. BY THE SPINNERS   STL 5431

a brilliant follow up to their LP releases:

THE SPINNERS!	TL 5201
FOLK AT THE PHIL!	TL 5219
MORE FOLK AT THE PHIL!	TL 5234
THE FAMILY OF MAN!	TL 5361

FONTANA RECORDS, Stanhope House, Stanhope Place, London W.2

The Spinners, early '60s

The Spinners Today

Liverpudlians and Upper-Class Sex

When the Profumo affair hit the headlines in 1961, the average Liverpudlian was not shocked or disgusted, but grateful. The aristocracy is so remote from gray, working-class Liverpool, and the Royal family so aloof—whiling away their time in a world of dignified estates, tea-on-the-lawn, cucumber-and-cress sandwiches—that Liverpudlian kids would spend hours discussing whether or not the Royal family "did it" at all. It was beyond our imagination to think that these cool, distant figures of State could stoop so low as to indulge in a practice which is all sweat, secretions, excretions, rolling eyes and flailing limbs.

The factual reality is, of course, that the upper classes do, in fact, reproduce, but it is quite a problem for a Liverpudlian to visualize them in the actual act of copulation. The jokes around the topic are endless:

> *Duke of Edinburgh (in mid-coitus; gasp, gasp): "I believe the poor people call this screwing, Your Majesty."*
> *Queen (oh, ah!): "Oh Gawd! It's much too good for them!"*

A living example of the tolerance of individual sexual deviation is manifested in Dame Margaret Rutherford. Dame Margaret was not merely an actress famous for her eccentric character parts, but who was quite eccentric in her private life as well. A bizarre incident was reported by the British press in a small, local paper (the Brighton Evening Argus). Apparently her nephew, an American writer, had had a sex change. Not only that, but the Negro mechanic came to the house one day and on seeing the nephew (whose name was now Dawn), instantly fell in love, returned with one dozen red roses and pleaded urgent and ardent desire to the bashful Dawn. Dawn succumbed and they were soon to be wed. When Dame Margaret was asked by a voracious and salivating press to comment, her sole reply was: "I do wish Dawn wouldn't marry a Baptist."

Thus, contrary to the reports in the newspapers, when Profumo's indiscretions were made public, Liverpool was not only amazed and titillated but delighted to find out that the icebergs of the aristocracy actually did possess carnal appetites—just as the Russians responded to Clinton's indiscretions by saying: "At last we know the man has balls."

The news of upper-class sexual dalliance was greeted with the same joy that the Liverpudlian experiences when he hears that the aristocracy actually swears. For, one of the most notable (and ill-reported) aspects of the Liverpool character, shared by all and sundry, including John, Paul, George and Ringo is the penchant for using the word 'fuck' every three words (a linguistic trait common to the working class in most countries but taken to excessive lengths by a Liverpudlian). The effect of such a conversation upon a refined sensibility is devastating, and often induces a state of nausea and momentary paralysis which is a source of great satisfaction to the Liverpudlian.

And, if you think this is an exaggeration, it is not. Liverpudlians will even break syllables to insert the word: "Don't you fucking well under-fucking-stand what I'm fucking well saying?"

American ghetto blacks use crude language as shock value to upset their more restrained white neighbors in exactly the same way. Similarly, Liverpudlians, aware of the refined sensibilities of the English middle class, used vulgarity as a weapon against them deliberately.

The American public, when reading derogatory stories about the Beatles' sordid sexual exploits—John did this and Paul did that—should bear the Liverpool character in mind. The truth is, yes, the Beatles probably did do everything they have been accused of sexually—and more. *Any* Liverpudlian would act the same way, given an unlimited supply of groupies and money. The only limit to the scope of their activities are the heights (or depths) to which imagination can lead.

The Beatles did it all—and far worse—without guilt. In fact, like many others, they had started their own sexual exploration around about the age of ten.

There is even a joke which exemplifies this:

A Liverpudlian is taken to court, charged with rape. His language is so colorful that he is stopped every two or three words for 'contempt of court'. Eventually it is explained to the judge that as this is the only mode of expression that the man knows, perhaps it might be best to clear the ladies from the court and to let him speak naturally, as this will speed things up considerably. The judge agrees, and this, then, is the accused's statement:

"I was walking down by the fuckin' park, Your Honor, 'oping to catch one of those birds who walks around with her tits hanging out, and, fuck me if I don't see this girl with these fuckin' big knockers and a fuckin' mini skirt halfway up her thighs. So, I asks her for a kiss and she's so fuckin' high and mighty that I get fuckin' well pissed off like, so I grab her by the fuckin' scruff of the neck, drag her to the fuckin' bushes and 'ave sexual intercourse with her."

One indication of the affection which Liverpudlians hold for sexual waywardness is the fact that the unofficial national anthem of Liverpool is a sea-shanty which recounts the doubtful charms of one of Liverpool's favorite characters, Maggie May, a prostitute who plied her trade in Lime Street, downtown Liverpool. So much so, that, as a joke, John Lennon, on the *Magical Mystery Tour* album, sang the song in true Scouse' pub style with guttural accent exaggerated.

Here she is, Ladies and Gentlemen, Liverpool's favorite Lady of the Night:

Chorus:
    Oh dirty Maggie May, they have taken her away
    And she'll never walk down Lime Street anymore
    Oh that judge he guilty found her
    Of robbing a homeward-bounder
    And she'll never walk down Lime Street anymore

Verse 1:
    I was paid off at the 'Pool
    In the port of Liverpool
    Three pounds ten a week, that was my pay
    With a pocket full of tin
    I was very soon taken in
    By a girl by the name of Maggie May

Verse 2:
    Now the first time I saw Maggie
    She took my breath away
    She was cruising up and down in Canning Place
    With a figure so divine

Verse 2 (cont.):	*And an accent so sublime*
	Well, being a sailor I gave her a chase
Verse 3:	*In the morning I awoke*
	I was flat and stony broke
	No jacket, trousers, waistcoat did I find
	And when I asked her where
	She said, my very good sir
	They're down in Kings Pawn Shop No. 9
Verse 4:	*To the pawn shop I did go*
	No clothes there did I find
	And the judge he took that girl away from me
	The judge he guilty found her
	For robbing a homeward-bounder
	Now she'll never walk down Lime Street anymore

A Brief Linguistic Aside

The fact that people are judged by accent in England is particularly relevant to Liverpool, as the Liverpool accent is totally unique. So much so, that when I took my post-graduate degree in linguistics at London University, I found that there is a special symbol for the unique and guttural manner in which Liverpudlians pronounce "t" as in "cat". It is sounds like "tz", where the "z" is halfway between a "z" and an "s".

When I began work as a producer at the BBC (a rare position for a Northern working-class boy), I was interviewed by a 60-year-old woman who put a red sticker on my personnel file. When I asked my colleagues what it meant, I was told it was a marker to indicate I was not eligible to read the news "because of my accent".

There are a few phrases unique to Liverpool which are needed for an understanding of this text, in particular, the word "Scouse" or "Scouser" which refers to a Liverpudlian. This is used ubiquitously in England and not "Liverpudlian". Another word which distinguishes a Scouse immediately is his use of "lar" as in "are you all right, lar?" or, more colloquially, "ar yer or righ', lar?" which is used for another person, i.e., a man (whereas a woman is a "judy").

All of this is fully recorded in a book intended to spread the wisdom of the Liverpool idiom to the world—'Lern Yerself Scouse'.

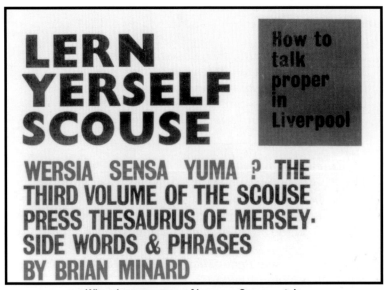

Where's your sense of humor—Scouse style

Football
Humor & Violence

Football, Humor & Violence

No discussion of the Liverpool character would be complete without a mention of football and humor, both of which are closely linked to the phenomena of Drink and Violence.

The Liverpudlian cliché is that everyone in Liverpool is a comedian: "Yer have to be to live here..." Humor, like drink, is a safety valve, a release, and the verbosity of the Liverpool character can, in part, be viewed like that of his black equivalent in the ghettos of America, as a natural way of diffusing violence.

Football is an almost instinctive tribal response and the fervor with which it grips the average Liverpudlian is incredible. It has become a form of group expression with its own criteria, its own catch phrases and songs (not to mention the inclusion of some of the Liverpool groups' hits: *You'll Never Walk Alone* by Jerry Marsden and an *Eee-Aye-Addio* followed by the Beatles' *Yeah, Yeah, Yeah*).

This bizarre pastime takes place between late August and May when the Liverpool supporters follow their team's Away Games. Wearing the team colors, young men, drunk and violent roam the streets of a foreign city and with great delight smash windows, tear up fences and literally assault the supporters of the rival team (and anyone else who gets in the way).

Courtesy Margaret Ainscough

Ghetto residents were relocated to high-rise dwellings like these early '60s redevelopment areas

Aggro, they call it. And the only difference between this and the Los Angeles phenomenon of 'colors' is that, fortunately, the Liverpudlians don't have guns. But they do have fists, steel-tipped boots, clubs and knuckles. And sometimes the outcome is fatal.

Englishman Bernard Nossiter, like Charles Silberman his American counterpart, sees this violence as an unfortunate side-effect of emancipation:

> *Only now is it widely understood that slums are organic communities where people feel some sense of responsibility for each other; where all can see what is happening on the street; more or less orderly and self-policing places.*[1]

The point being made is that because of social programs, rehousing and social mobility, the alpha males and females from the ghettos move out, causing a radical imbalance in self-leadership.

In America, a similar phenomenon is occurring in black ghettos where emancipation has resulted in the more highly motivated blacks moving out, disrupting the natural, ordering process.

The same thing happened to the Liverpool 8 slums. Due to the rehousing policies of a liberal government, the residents were relocated to the council estates or high-rises—as was George Harrison to suburban Macketts Lane. Often they were removed against their own wishes, because family and group ties were broken and a very strong but unseen matrix of social connections was torn asunder.

A social worker friend reporting on the doubtful consequences of rehousing tells of a visit to one Liverpool 8 family's new quarters resplendent with hot and cold water, inside toilet and, luxury of luxuries, a bathroom. When he went to the toilet, he found the bath was full of coal.

When the rehousing began in Liverpool 8, entire families barricaded the streets and refused to leave. After all, some of them had been born, married and reproduced all on the same block and the promise of an indoor toilet and a bathroom hardly compensated for the entire disruption of their normal lifestyle, no matter how sordid it may have seemed to outsiders.

The resulting changes were to have far-reaching consequences. Teenagers, in particular, became more and more unruly. In the wake of these social disruptions the Liverpool football supporter was to become much feared and hated. This less than admirable profile was to achieve international status after the particularly horrific incident which took place at Heysel Stadium, Brussels, April 29, 1985. It was the occasion of a European Cup match; Liverpool vs. Juventus. The events were so ghastly that they led to a complete ban on English teams in Europe.

The violence that erupted included hand-to-hand combat; supporters attacking each other with iron bars. 39 people were killed, trampled or crushed to death against a retaining wall. The waves of shock

In a peculiar way, the Welfare State may have built a hothouse for these youths. In the rush to throw down the old slums and throw up new housing, postwar Britain built towering blocks of subsidized, equally unaesthetic council estates.

Bernard Nossiter
Britain: A Future That Works

Courtesy Mindscaffolding

The street opposite the entrance to Anfield Football Stadium

145

which radiated through professional football are still resounding. As it turned out, only one of the 39 killed was an Italian, and only half those arrested had any connection with Merseyside. Fourteen Liverpool fans (but not all Liverpudlians) were convicted of manslaughter with jail sentences of three years each.

But as far as the world was concerned, it was a Liverpool-perpetuated atrocity in its entirety, such is the reputation of the city.

This incident was to have direct repercussions which reveal the opposite side of tribal violence: the urge towards tribal unity as a positive force.

Because of the Heysel Stadium incident, what may have been a simple incident at the Hillsborough Stadium in Sheffield, England on April 15, 1989, became a major tragedy.

This match was the Football Association Semi-Final between Nottingham Forest and Liverpool. A fire in the stadium caused panic in one particular area, the Leppings Lane end. The result was horrific, and many a fan is still in trauma, trying to recover from these terrible events which have been literally burnt into his memory.

Because of the fences erected in the stadium after the Heysel incident, the terrified spectators found themselves penned into a confined area, unable to get out. Hundreds of fans were injured, scrabbling for their lives and 96 died. Such was the reputation of the fans that, in many international newspapers, photos used to illustrate Liverpool hooliganism were, in fact, pictures of Liverpool fans, dead or dying.

The response of the supporters was amazing. Without any official organization, they broke up into self-governing groups; marshaling help, administering aid and providing stretchers for the injured.

It was a moving sight; and a Liverpool doctor, seemingly one of the socially mobile with his sympathies still firmly-rooted in the working class, made a wholehearted plea on TV, with tears in his eyes. He asked that the incident should not result in football being taken away from the Liverpool fans. "They haven't got

The rioting youth seek a pleasure, a joy... that they do not find during the week at jobs or school or on the weekend in the drab, city quarters from which they come. They are the children of *A Clockwork Orange* whose inarticulate grievances are gratified by a blood lust.

Edward Barnfield

Courtesy Mindscaffolding

Hillsborough Stadium Memorial

much," he said, "Don't take away the last vestiges of their struggle for identity."

This underscores the action of many of the Crips and Bloods in America, who, when given a chance, volunteered to go out to Bosnia. Many ghetto children, no matter how aimless they may appear, simply want something to believe in; something that accords with their own identity

Identity. This is the key, for it is not simply a matter of housing or poor parental control or any of the other problems claimed as the source of ghetto violence. It is a tribal urge to identity and respect, ill-conceived though it might appear.

The response of Liverpool fans to the tragedy has been a single-minded drive to assuage the wrong, to cleanse the blood.

Fans, stars, supporters, many of them living on the brink of poverty themselves, put their hands in their pockets. Gerry, of Gerry and the Pacemakers, offered his help, as did Paul McCartney, The Christians and Holly Johnson. With their help, Gerry recorded *Ferry Across the Mersey* which went to Number One. The fans and supporters raised £14 million, (about $25 million) for the victims of the disaster.

The National Football Association invited Gerry to sing *You'll Never Walk Alone* with the voices of 80,000 supporters who attended the all-Liverpool Cup Final. The mass sing-along was televised worldwide and went down in history as one of the most moving scenes in sports history.

Humor

These, then, are the two sides of the incredible tribal phenomenon of Liverpool football. There is, fortunately, a third: Humor.

Humor has always been an export from the Liverpool ghetto, as exemplified in the film hit, *A Letter to Brezhnev*.

Yet humor is one of the most difficult aspects of the Liverpool culture to convey to an outsider. Traditionally, Liverpool has supplied stage, screen and TV with an inordinate amount of comedians. But sometimes the humor is difficult to explain to the uninitiated because it is based on a particular lifestyle; the tip of the iceberg of an economically-depressed sea port with an historical tradition of crime, slavery, unemployment and poverty. It is, in many ways, exactly the same kind of humor as practiced by black American comedians.

The Liverpool humorist satirizes landlords; unpaid bills; workers who can't work; layabouts who won't work; professional hypochondriacs' exploitation of the social security system; drunkenness and crimes.

> One chap who worked as a motor mechanic had quite a lucrative career in spare parts. He regularly vacationed in the Canary Isles. He was apprehended when he forgot to pick up his wage packet three weeks in a row at a time when his colleagues were barely making ends meet.

"To be on the fiddle" is a common pastime in a world where the division between worker and boss is sharply felt, and the boss is often seen as fair game. Capitalists exploit workers, so, quite understandably, the Liverpudlian feels the worker can exploit capitalists.

When Ford's factory was opened in Hailwood, Liverpool, designed by American industrialists with American methods, it was manned by Liverpudlian foremen with an awareness of the potential for fiddling and not-so-petty thievery:

The security was extensive. The entire factory was surrounded by a chain-link fence with observation posts like a maximum-security prison. The gates of the factory were locked between shifts, and, as each shift changed, the workers had to go through a checkpoint which would have gratified the KGB. Random searches took place; surveillance was at a maximum. And yet, despite the intensive security, the factory still suffered heavy losses in stolen material.

One man even stole a whole car. He casually tossed car parts over a fence for a whole year, and, eventually ended up with a complete car. What he did when it came to the engine

> The humor of the Liverpool football fan was aptly demonstrated during an ITV special which portrayed the life of a 'typical' fan traveling down to London for the Cup Final. At first the program was scripted, as it was meant to be more of a comedy than a documentary. Eventually, the producer threw the script away because the actual comments of the Liverpudlians were funnier than the scripted version; viz:

> A Liverpool fan wearing a red and white hat and scarf is sitting open-mouthed at a London nightclub watching a well-endowed stripper do her thing. She wriggles out of her bra and her ample breasts flop out right in front of the fan's face. "Jesus!" he exclaims, "Bet yer don't get many of those in a pound!"

> During a football match, there are jeers at the Referee. A Liverpool wag shouts out: "Pull his leg off and hit him wid the soggy end!"

> A Liverpool fan, after a night of trouble and unbelievable alcoholic excess, groans: "Oh, friggin' hell, me nerves are like Shredded Wheat!"

block, is not quite known. However, the truth rests: the man stole a car; he still drives it.

No one who owns a Ford in Liverpool will ever leave anything in the car. Even when it's locked, it's unlocked, they say. Practically every kid in Liverpool owns a set of keys that will unlock any Ford car of any year or model.

Thus, the crime in Liverpool is not simply due to the presence of a criminal element. In a sense, everyone is a criminal because to 'take your share' is not seen as crime (though it is punished as such) but fair game. It is in this sense that the Liverpool humor about criminality is not always understood; for the 'criminal' is usually viewed with sympathy—as is the "bad man" of black America.

Humor: The Naming of Names

> Overheard: two elderly ladies at an exhibition in a Liverpool library during the time of the Japanese POW reconciliation a few years ago:
> "I'm sorry, Ethel, I don't care what you say, I can never ever forgive what the Japanese did to Alec Guiness during the war."

Another practice which seems to be indigenous to Liverpool is that everyone who works in a factory or on the docks is given a nickname; a name that is surprisingly pithy as a summation of the character's hopes and aspirations. And, needless to say, everyone uses and knows this name—except the person themselves.

In one engineering firm down the Dock Road, I was told that I would be apprenticed to the 'Convict', a thin pipe-fitter of about fifty.

I started work with him, and he maintained the usual terse conversation exclusive to working men all over the world—until he raised the subject of my length of stay at the works.

"Three months," I answered, "Just a temporary thing."

A Liverpool joke which is almost incomprehensible to outsiders tells of two Liverpool lads at a bar. One claps the other on the shoulder cheerily as they are about to order and says, "I'll get these; you're working." The joke is readily understood by Liverpudlians: the honest man who struggles away in a mediocre position earns far less than his companion who is involved in all kinds of shady deals.

"Three months!" he groaned, "Only three months!" He chewed his lip anxiously and looked around furtively—as if we were being monitored by the CIA, the KGB, *and* the FBI—then muttered: "I've gotta get outta here. I've been here too long. I've gotta get outta here!"

After a few days, I realized that this was his litany; he repeated this at least ten times a day. Hence, 'The Convict'.

Whatever it is or however it arises, humor oils the wheels of a drab and sometimes pitiless existence in Liverpool. Here are a few examples culled from random conversations in a pub—*in one night*:

> "So I went to the landlord and said: 'It's about the roof.' And he said: Well, what?' So, I said: 'Can I 'ave one?'"

The following are not just jokes, but actual events:

> *Two men were stopped for dangerous driving on a main road through Liverpool. Apparently, there was no steering wheel and they were steering with a pair of pliers.*

> *Two kids, four and six, were apprehended by the police for stealing a car. One of them was steering and the other was sitting on the floor operating the pedals.*

> *A man who'd left his brother at home while he went away for a few days, returned to find the house completely ransacked, drawers pulled open, contents strewn on the floor—and his brother had disappeared. He called the police and explained he'd been burglarized. Unfortunately, his brother returned at the same time*

as the police, and it turned out that it hadn't been burglarized at all—it was simply 'untidy'.

As a student, I worked in the Post Office at Christmas for the Christmas rush. It was a gleeful, wild, insomniac, drunken time (we worked nights). We were given instructions that the flood of mail addressed to John, George, Paul and Ringo (of which there were hundreds of letters from all over the world) was to be put in separate piles. Surveillance was very rigid in the Post Office, and tampering with the mail was a very serious offense; but the officials were a little more lax when it came to the Beatle's mail, as they couldn't quite take that so seriously. So, often, if someone came across a good letter, they would retire to the toilet and read it out to a drunken and appreciative audience. One I liked was a huge wad of a letter (forty pages, both sides). It had undergone a mammoth journey from Florida and been returned because it was under-stamped; the return postage had been paid, new pages added, and the girl had returned it again. The opening words were: 'Dear Paul, I'm sorry I didn't write yesterday, but...'

A sign in the window of a local Liverpool Chinese fish and chip shop: 'Free range chips'.

Actual statements written by job applicants on resumes:
"Reason for leaving my last job: maturity leave."
"Please do not misconstrue my previous 14 jobs as job hopping. I have never quit a job.."
"Personal interests: donating blood—14 pints so far."

Actual court room exchanges:
Q: What is the date of your birth?
A: 14th September
Q: What year?
A: Every year.

Q: Do you know what a vegan is?
No, I never watch Star Trek.

Q: What is your IQ?
A: 20/20. I can see perfectly.

Q: Tell me, doctor, is it not true that when a person dies in their sleep they don't know about it until the following morning?
A: Yes, in certain circumstances.

Q: What was the first thing your husband said to you the following morning?
A: He said, "Cathy, where am I?"
Q: And why did that upset you?
A: My name is Susan.

Q: This myasthenia gravis, does it affect your memory?
A: Yes.
Q: How?
A: I forget now.

Humor in Liverpool is inextricably interwoven with survival, poverty, hardship. It is that sudden gleam of silver that reveals itself in the heart of every cloud. The Liverpudlian will sense it, tease it out so that the monochromatic gray of existence can be shot through with flashes of light.

He has to; life would be unbearable otherwise. Not that the Liverpudlian thinks so. For him, poverty, grime, crime and penury are as common as the grass and thus not that remarkable.

In this, the Liverpudlian has his counterpart in the ghetto black in America who, living with deprivation and crisis, will never fully realize just how deep he is in the mire—until it is too late. A few drinks, a nice girl, a bit of coke and, "Hey, man, life is good!"

But statistics show a chilling fact that 25% of young blacks are in jail in America; that the rate of black homicide is far in excess of that of other ethnic minorities; and that the overall mortality rate is eight times that of whites.

"Why?" asks the uninformed observer, "This is America. There is food; there are jobs! This is the twentieth century—he doesn't have to *stay* in the ghetto!"

What the uninformed outsider doesn't realize is that the average ghetto dweller only knows the ghetto. His idea of social mobility is that he moves one block away to where people are only killed on Saturday night—and he thinks he's risen up the ladder.

At the age of twenty-five, I took a sociology course at Sussex University, England, and opened a book which described slum living. I'd always thought that slums were bad places and I didn't realize I lived in one *until that moment*; for, there right in the middle of the book, as a major research example of slums, was Liverpool 8. Well, I thought, it wasn't *that* bad... Then I began to think and slowly the statistics dawned on me, and that's when I realized that, though life is good in the middle, it is no bowl of cherries either at the bottom or top.

Courtesy Mindscaffolding

The Liver Building, Liverpool

Death & Madness
In Liverpool

15

Death and Madness in Liverpool

The typical Liverpudlian's response to adversity is humor which, perhaps, is why the converse is true: that the topic of much of Liverpool humor is grim adversity.

The net result is that sometimes the severity of a situation is lost. It is difficult to realize that life in Liverpool often exhorted a grim toll. Resilience is the keyword for survival. But not everyone did survive.

One particularly aggressive chap after a few drinks would invite his cohorts to a game of 'stab the copper'. The rules were simple: they would lie in wait until a policeman on foot patrol passed through a darkened area, then they would jump on him. The object of the game was to see how many stab wounds each assailant could inflict before they were interrupted and had to flee. Hilarious.

Such extremes of living as took place in Liverpool in the Sixties can only court disaster. And yet, no one thought so. It didn't seem *that* bad:

A Liverpool housewife on a good night out could easily drink 35 bottles of beer and her husband down 15-20 pints of Guinness, and yet they would have been very puzzled if someone had called them alcoholic. Gang beatings; street violence; stabbings and robbery were standard in Liverpool 8, but nobody thought they were living in a ghetto. In other words, when you're up to your knees in it, it doesn't smell.

Wired jaws were a common sight, an indication that someone had had the misfortune of repeated facial contact with a steel toecap.

But, in retrospect, the environment *did* claim its victims, and it is sobering when considering a small crowd—such as that which frequented the "scene" during the Sixties—how many did not survive. Tabloid critics of John Lennon, denigrating his so-called drinking and violence, should be aware of the world from which he emerged—because, many of his contemporaries did not. Given the roughness of the environment and the excessive nature of drug and alcohol consumption, this is no surprise.

The fact is, in all ghetto environments, whether it be Liverpool or black America, the toll on its victims is observed by a chosen few: psychiatric social workers, police, suicide intervention counselors, and so on. Within the society itself, people just tend to *disappear*. High-profile victims are just the tip of the iceberg.

Suicide was, of course, common in Liverpool, and one of the saddest and most prominent was that poor man out of his time and place, BRIAN EPSTEIN.

Brian was a homosexual from a genteel Jewish family at a time when the social repercussions were intolerable. Rumor was, he was being blackmailed by a laborer he'd picked up in a toilet encounter. Brian trod a precarious knife's edge, and it was his straight-laced background which made him fall in love with the rough and tumble, restless lifestyle of the Beatles. Socially, Brian lived through them vicariously until the time came when he realized nothing had changed—he was still himself. Poor man, how he must have suffered.

A less well-known suicide was that of RORY STORM, a sweet-natured man with an incredible stutter which disappeared as soon as he started to sing. He was the first Liverpool Rock musician to put his stage-name in the phone book; the first singer to be aware of 'Image'. Rory—the Beatles' peer and friend was the lead singer of The Hurricanes, the band in which Ringo Starr played prior to the Beatles. A part-time swimming coach, Rory committed suicide in a death pact with his mother. Rory, like many other Liverpool musicians, was left behind in the wave of Merseyside success that peaked in the '60s. Rory, unlike most Liverpudlians, including the Beatles themselves, had an unusual trait: he *wanted* to be a star and he took it very seriously.

An even sadder case was that of ROY WOOD, a genius guitarist who was so accomplished that he couldn't find

A musician friend tried to end it all by jumping off a bridge. He landed up to his thighs in mud and failed. Next try was to hold a saber he'd obtained from an antique store against his chest and, by dint of running at a wall impale himself. He failed the first time but seemed intent on trying it again. Horrified, I demanded that he give the sword to me for safekeeping. Quite missing the tragicomic nature of it all, he retorted dead seriously "Not on your life. That sword cost me a few bob!"

Rory Storm with one of his first bands and upright bass player John McCormick

anyone good enough to play with, even among the myriad guitarists who abounded in Liverpool at the time. A man ahead of his time like Epstein, Roy killed himself, leaving a note explaining that he'd done so because "he wasn't getting anywhere with his music."

Roy was just eighteen.

There is, and always has been, among subcultures a devil-may-care attitude about drug taking, a sort of "naughty-but-nice" syndrome. This attitude is prevalent because most of the victims just 'disappear' without the impact of their demise being absorbed by the general public.

BRUCE McGASKELL was a highly intelligent chap, one of the original Swinging Bluegenes. Bruce was a better engineer than guitarist and, as a result, went on to become a high-tech roadie for a number of big groups, including Eric Clapton. Eventually Bruce became manager of the Average White Band.

Unfortunately Bruce never lost his taste for potent drugs and I once visited him in London when he was working with Clapton, to find Bruce slumped in a chair, hardly able to speak. Apparently he was being treated by Dr. Roberts, the man immortalized in the Beatles' song of the same name. Bruce survived; just. But then last year he dropped dead in an American department store in LA, one more victim of an excessive lifestyle.

> Once at a Saturday night party, a friend of mine got into an argument with his own girlfriend. A group of youths at the party took exception to this and he mysteriously disappeared from the party. He turned up in hospital the next day with 43 stab wounds. He survived.

During the mid-Sixties, I was privy to an inside view of the effect of the ghetto lifestyle by virtue of the fact that I worked at the South Liverpool Psychiatric Annex which served the Liverpool 8 area.

The truth was sobering. Every day they rolled in: the cool, the esoteric, the musicians, the night people.

The toll of death and madness in the relatively small group of people which comprised Liverpool's musicians, poets, seekers and swingers was considerable. Here is a brief sample of some of the unfortunates that passed through the reception ward *in a matter of months*. Some of the names have been changed, as some of those who pulled through went on to become well known in the entertainment world.

Gus...was a wild one. Always unique. With bamboo glasses and a blonde mane, his adventures would fill a book on their own. Restless, arcane, at one time he was fired from working in a southern psychiatric hospital for breaking down the door between the male and female wards—for the sake of the patients. His colorful background made him the pick of the crop as Student Counsellor at radical Sussex University, England's most trendy college. Gus had formerly lived on a dose of barbiturates that would have killed an elephant. When he lost his girlfriend in a motorbike accident, he turned back to the barbiturates. Unfortunately, during his lay-off, his tolerance had changed, and the same dose that he took for his normal buzz was lethal. He died, age 25.

Bruce McGaskill (second right) with his early band, Groups Incorporated

Josh... A character amid characters, Josh was striking. Beats roamed the clubs of Liverpool with tattered clothes and wild, unkempt manes, whereas Josh wore a three-piece suit, a white shirt, collar and tie—always. His long blue-black hair was always clean and hung in an impeccable cut to his shoulders. In his right hand, he sported the class symbol of the British gent—a tightly-folded, black brolly[1]. Gus strode with impunity amongst the beats, drifters and drug addicts alike. He had charisma, class—and, unfortunately, asthma. Weakened by damp apartments, poor nutrition and too much charas, he died in hospital of an asthma attack, and the world lost a character. Age 22.

Phil the Pill... Thin, nervous, emaciated, prone to mood swings from excessive amphetamine consumption, he lost his true love and took a massive dose of mixed pills. Amazingly, the combination of uppers canceled out the downers and he lived—with a headache that lasted a month and a liver that was bloated to twice its size. Age 23.

Downtown Jake... A fearless foe of iniquity, collector of roots rock, Night-Prowler and Philosopher. He drank ten pints at a party which someone had laced with chloral hydrate. Unknown to the other revellers, he collapsed in the toilet. He tried to regain consciousness, repeatedly standing up and collapsing until his face was a lacerated mess. He lay unconscious in a pool of blood and urine for 48 hours—and miraculously survived. Age 23.

 P.J., famous guitarist... Prone to outbursts of anger on stage. He climbed to the top of the conservatory in Sefton Park after breaking in and was about to leap off when the police interceded. He was hospitalized in the Annex where, most curiously, the psychiatrists diagnosed him as being a "psychopath"!?? Age 26.

 Big Mel... Bouncer at the Iron Door. When his claims that he was being followed by the police, the FBI and the CIA disguised in laundry vans reached extreme proportions, he was hospitalized. Diagnosis: amphetamine psychosis. Age 27.

 Ed Flea... A street beat who lived in another time, another world. Manic, happy, erratic, he ended up in the Psychiatric Annex with his face a bloody mess, nose broken. Apparently, despite his pacifist mindset, he'd been "resisting arrest" by four policemen. Diagnosis: toxic confusional state brought about by drug abuse. Age 22.

 Mad Robbie... No one realized his ramblings were just that. He had a certain presence that inspired confidence in the listener that his insights were profound—until he went crazy in the Kardoma Cafe, claiming that a friend (me) had infected his head with crabs and ran amok. He was a long time pulling out of this. Age 22.

 Brian... Big, soft-spoken, a talented artist and friend of John Lennon. He would step on a bus and slide ominously and silently into the seat next to you without speaking. Then, after ten minute's silence, he would whisper such profundities as: *"They know, you know,"* and relapse into an even more profound silence. He grew worse, frightening everyone and eventually attacked a close friend. His career as a major artist took a devastating turn. I have no further news of him. Age 24.

The Unseen Pattern of Madness

Working in the Psychiatric Annex, I became aware of a singular fact: that the last people to realize that a person was slipping into insanity were always close relatives or friends. This often reached amazing proportions. You see, there were always personality factors in the person which were amplified by the dawning illness. These were always seen as "Oh, he's just a pain in the ass"—i.e., the normal character flaws somewhat amplified by the patient's illness—until it reached the point where the patient was hospitalized. Then the dazed relative would arrive at the hospital bewildered, overawed and frightened while a pompous, middle-class doctor would explain in terms that only confused them that their nearest and (sometimes) dearest was mentally ill.

I was no better—as in the following case of Mike Waddington.

The problem was that the life of Liverpool beats and musicians was so extreme that no one could see when it had gone too far. Such a one was Mike Waddington, a pleasant enough guy who liked a smoke, a girl, and rhythm & blues. Mike actually left the street and became a psychiatric nurse in the Liverpool 8 Annex. Then he started behaving oddly. For months, everybody assumed Mike was behaving the way he was because he was just stoned. Sounds all right, until you consider what he actually did:

- He attacked me with a carving knife a party.
- He was disarmed but not before he had broken my hand.
- He walked from London to Liverpool, nonstop (200 miles).
- He sat for three days and three nights on my doorstep, ignoring all attempts to get him to leave.
- He stormed into a math lesson uninvited one afternoon at the Liverpool North-East Polytechnic, his eyes staring, his hair disheveled, shouting obscenities (which didn't go down well with the teacher). When he was duly ejected, he went down into the school yard and began chalking foot-high obscene messages on the ground, much to the amusement of 900 day students.
- He followed me home and suddenly attacked me from behind.
- He began making bizarre phone calls to my girlfriend.

It wasn't until then that everybody began to realize that Mike *was not well*. Poor Mike ended up in Rainhill Mental Hospital, a huge Victorian establishment renowned for its brand of treatment called "thump therapy". (The patients were shaved, head included, their teeth pulled out, and their possessions commandeered). He entered at the age of 23 and was still there at the age of 40. He escaped twice, was captured in Ireland and given raw Electro-Convulsive Therapy (ECT) (no anaesthetic), and ever after perpetually complained of the "hole in his head".

Sadly, when Mike was hospitalized, he was apprended in his own home—wearing nothing but a pair of jeans, sleeping on a mattress—by his own boss from the Psychiatric Annexe, a mean-spirited man who enjoyed every minute of the 'apprehension'. Mike was drugged, straight-jacketed and bundled into a waiting ambulance.

This, then, is the dark side, not only of the Liverpool scene, but of all ghetto scenes in England and America. Any social worker in the Bronx, Watts or Harlem would no doubt be able to reel off an equally appalling list. And it is only the police, the social workers, and the patients' relatives who ever know where "Johnny went in the night".

But, as they say in Liverpool, if you don't laugh, you'll cry. And such stories, though they elicit compassion from close friends, just became woven into fabric of fantasy and hearsay. But the grim fact is that the truth of these matters is more bizarre than the fiction. Should you be wondering, the following anecdote (page 158) is quite factual. The raw details of death and madness in Liverpool are, to say the least, even more chilling—enough is enough.

Mike Waddington's story would make a screenplay in itself. He actually slipped into schizophrenia while still working at the Psychiatric Annexe. One day, his behavior was such that he was told to report to the matron. I escorted him to the matron's inner sanctum and waited outside her oak-panneled office in an aspidestra-bedecked corridor which smelled of lavender. Suddenly, the matron's door was flung open and the matron, an imposing women of 50 much decorated with hospital awards, ran out the door screaming. She fled down the corridor. I never found out what Mike had done.

Mental Illness as a Socio-Economic Factor

Yet, not *all* madness is so dark—nor were all mad people mad. Such is the case of Alcyd the drummer who, at one time, was considered by the Beatles as a replacement drummer for Pete Best. Unfortunately for him, Alcyd was gigging in France at the time and it was Ringo, not he, who became famous.

Alcyd, veteran of a hundred all-night sessions, was by no means insane—just another casualty of the lower socio-economic system. An honest, sincere, highly-sensitive youth, Alcyd was trapped by his birthright into his sordid surroundings, never to find a way out. Alcyd was liked by everybody, a fact which continually bewildered him. He was, in particular, friends with Cilla Black, the orange-haired, guttural-voiced singer who was one of the few girls Epstein took into his success stable (and his heart). Cilla is a warm, kindly, spontaneous girl with the flexibility and resilience shared by most Liverpool girls—in her friendship with Alcyd, she needed it!

One night, she was sitting in the Jacaranda coffee bar talking to John Lennon and Beryl Williams (the wife of Alan Williams who managed the Beatles briefly). Alcyd and his girlfriend Penelope had been having another of their interminable arguments, and Penny suddenly emptied a bottle of lemonade over Alcyd's head. Seeing which way the wind was blowing, John left and went to Alan's other

Alcyd and his drum, early '60s

club, the Blue Angel.

Not so Cilla. Like a fairy godmother, she ran after Alcyd, cajoled, chided and comforted him. This relationship, born out of Cilla's big heart and Alcyd's ingenuous nature, was to have a comic side-light.

Some years later, when the Beatles had made it and Cilla had attained national stardom as Epstein's (and the nation's) "blue-eye", Alcyd had definitely not made it.

Alcyd was living in a cold, damp flat in London, drumming in poorly-paid jobs in smoky London clubs; eating badly; living badly and feeling badly. By virtue of a visit to a doctor when Alcyd complained of ill-health and a total lack of motivation or interest in life, Alcyd ended up in Middlesex Hospital (a hospital at which no less than Patti Boyd's father was surgeon). Alcyd's complaint was assessed as clinical depression.

Of course, the cure would simply have been to have given Alcyd Mr. Boyd's salary, but no one in the medical field saw illness as socio-economic, so Alcyd was *treated.* He was given three meals a day and pummeled, prodded and, in a manner most agreeable to him, *pilled up* and taken on group outings by a psychiatric nurse.

Now, one of these group outings was, in fact, to the London Palladium, London's equivalent of the Hollywood Bowl. Cilla had made it and, in dazzling dresses, she was top of the bill, singing her throaty love-songs to an enraptured audience.

Alcyd's companions were, of course, the usual motley crew seen in psychiatric group outings: Epileptics; nose-picking confusional states; taut, drugged-up neurotics with glazed, staring eyes; the nominal, irascible post-syphilitic old codger—and Alcyd.

Unfortunately, once inside the London Palladium, Alcyd got into an argument with the psychiatric nurse, who was most amused when Alcyd told him that he and Cilla were friends. It was somewhat akin to him saying "Me and Barbara Streisand are friends." Alcyd was stung at his mocking disbelief. In wrathful defense of his veracity, Alcyd excused himself, ostensibly to go to the toilet. On his way to the toilet, he approached one of the ushers and asked him to pass a message on to Cilla saying: "Alcyd was up front with some friends. Could he come and see her?"

Cilla, bless her heart, was delighted. She sent back an enthusiastic "yes!". The psychiatric nurse was astounded, but he gathered his patients together and they set off

Alcyd with fellow musician Robbie Montgomery who had just been electrocuted by a microphone in a Hamburg club, early '60s

backstage to see Cilla. Cilla, for her part, received Alcyd most joyfully—until the sheepish psychiatric nurse filed into the dressing room with the rest of the patients. It is a mark of Alcyd's innocence and lack of guile that he simply introduced them as "my friends", while Cilla, trooper that she was, did her best to cope with this new turn of events. But, it was difficult for her. Alcyd says:

When one of the patients started picking his nose and staring at her, Cilla wrenched her eyes away from the group. Unfortunately, I was sitting with one leg up, revealing a vast hole in the sole of my shoe right through to the pink flesh. Cilla was mesmerized, caught between two fires: she couldn't look up, as then she was staring into the eyes of the patient; and she couldn't look down, as then she was staring straight at the hole in my shoe. So she looked sideways and tried as hard as she could to talk cheerfully with a crick in her neck, while staring at the wall.

Nevertheless, difficult and embarrassing though it was, Cilla brought it off—a mark of her own down-home heart and flexibility.

Courtesy Combo

Cilla Black, early '60s

The same flexibility enabled the Beatles to survive the single most pressured experience on the pop scene: Beatledom. In the context of the Liverpool from which they emerged, it will be more apparent that the Beatles were survivors when it is realized how many of their peers went mad or died. Whatever the tabloid papers say to the contrary, that the Beatles lasted so long is a mark of their incredible resilience.

A brief excursion into madness was then, in Sixties' Liverpool, rather more the rule than the exception. And a focal point for this was the reception ward for the area—the Psychiatric Annex of the South Liverpool Hospital in which I worked.

This "melting pot of madness" for Liverpool 8, the Psychiatric Annex, received at some time or other, many of the Liverpool characters—artists, musicians, painters, dole-ites[3]—who grace these pages. Some, like Mike Waddington, were never to emerge from the hospital system, but became life-long inmates.

Unfortunately, the Psychiatric Annex also drew upon Liverpool 8 for its staffing requirements—a bizarre situation, rather like the blind leading the blind. It was a motley crew almost as mad as the patients, and amongst their ranks, the nursing staff included two drug addicts; a child molester; a practicing felon; two transvestites; an alcoholic; a psychotic (yes!); and a former garbage trucker. That's the downside. The upside is that one went on to be a famous film actor; another a well-known poet; and a third, a BBC producer.

Such a bizarre mix precludes disaster. But, even disaster in Liverpool can be extremely funny, and the following story is a *factual* rendering of a few days in the life of the Liverpool 8 Psychiatric Annex.

The Psychiatric Annex of the hospital was staffed

Electro Convulsive Therapy was practiced widely in the Annex. Simple, uneducated parents were told by the doctors that their son would be receiving some "electrical therapy" and would innocently sign a consent form. As a result the poor psychiatric nurses would often have the unenviable task of dragging a screaming, kicking patient to the ECT trolley and strapping him down against his will, so that the doctors could send a jolt of electricity through the poor man's brain, which addled him for days, weeks and sometimes permanently..

Courtesy FAB

Cilla in full 1963 fashion flair

solely by men; a tiny island of masculine autonomy within the matriarchal structure of the large general hospital. This was like a cancer on the hide of the fifty year-old menopausal administrative staff. They ran the general hospital with all the precision of a sanitized concentration camp and were constantly at war with the males who staffed the disorganized and unseemly Psychiatric Annex.

The events reported in the following account are unembellished and factual. Other stories, would you believe, are even more hair-raising, but I resist the impulse to impart them as I am not a great fan of prurient sensationalism...

Alcyd after a major drum solo, sits with one of his many fans, early '60s

Liverpool South Psychiatric Annex, the Acute Ward: 9 p.m.
— A Personal Anecdote —

I had just finished cleaning up Paddy McCormack's hip. There was a hole in it so big that the shiny, white knob of the femur head could be seen poking through. Nightly, even more flesh sloughed away from the bone. It was a lost cause but he would not consider having his lower limbs amputated, useless as they were.

I stared dully at the bucket full of feces and blood-stained dressings and the neat, white patch of the new dressing—my last job before I went off for the evening. I was tired.

"You did a good job, kid," said Paddy, without taking his eyes off the magazine he was reading, "You always do."

"Thanks, Paddy," I said, "Boy, I need a pint. Where the fuck is Iglesi?"

Iglesi was a Nigerian student who relieved the day shift. Unfortunately, Iglesi was more concerned with studying for his engineering qualification, which was why he worked nights. As a result, we all suffered.

I yawned, covered Paddy carefully with a blanket, shoved aside the screen with a click and peered down the darkened ward.

Most of the patients were in bed, heavily sedated, though a few of them sat around the television screen, their faces pale in its blue-white glow. They *all* smoked incessantly, as if it was their last, desperate link to some form of identity.

I sighed, sensing the loneliness and alienation of the ward. "You want your light off, Paddy?"

"Naah, I'll read a bit. Say g'night before you go."

I looked at my watch, frowning: Iglesi was late again. I wheeled the trolley out into the corridor and into the sterilizing room where I began to dump the content of the soiled containers methodically into their respective bins.

My job was almost impossible. There were two wards in particular which required supervision constantly: the upstairs ward for geriatrics; and the downstairs ward which housed potentially dangerous patients. There should have been at least two staff on each ward—three on each would have been normal.

I was on duty *alone*, working the geriatric ward and the floor below. Not only did ward routine have to be maintained—TPR, routine medical checks, dressings, injections—but some of the patients were supposed to be under continuous surveillance. Patients like Cecil Jones who was dangerous.

Only the day before, Cecil had begun diving off the bed onto his head. He was big and his head made a lot of noise when it hit the floor. Finally, we'd had to give him another injection of paraldehyde, a sedative. There was a limit to how much we could give him, but there was also a limit to what the staff could take. I had helped to administer the injection with Mr. Kingsley, a big, gentle West Indian black, but Cecil had socked Mr. Kingsley in the teeth with a meaty paw and knocked out a tooth. Mr. Kingsley had walked away without a word of recrimination, blood streaming between his long, black fingers which cupped his mouth.

"You shouldn't have done that, Cecil," I had whispered and then had almost bitten off my tongue, thinking that this would precipitate a furor of rage in Cecil. But Cecil had merely looked puzzled, crawled along the floor and curled up, hiding under his bed.

Cecil had no visitors and he smoked even more incessantly than the other patients. This meant that his supply of cigarettes was, at the least, meager. He would make roll-ups from the butts, then from the butts of the butts. Sometimes he would end up smoking something that looked like dried-out molasses with a tar content of about 200%.

As Cecil was hiding under the bed like a naughty child, despite my chagrin, I had given him a cigarette, overwhelmed by a compassionate whim. Why not? He was mad but aren't we all, I had reasoned...?

Well, tonight Cecil was quiet, as was the upstairs ward. But the ward pressures had taken their toll. I stood in a haze of fatigue waiting for the release that would come when Iglesi took over for the night.

A noise aroused me from my fatigued reverie and I whirled rapidly, thinking it was Cecil. But it was only Old Joseph.

Old Joseph was an anachronism: an ex-sea captain of eighty-five; a Member of the British Empire[4], and a true English gentleman who even in his dotage seemed out of place with the rest of the men in the ward. Senile Dementia had stricken a fine brain. But he was the ward favorite, as, no matter what age or period his disintegrating brain regressed him to, he would always behave with the principled gentleness of E.M. Forster's mandates: Humanity and Reason.

"Joseph!" I cried, "You gave me a fright! Now, what are you doing out of bed?"

Joseph began to cry, clutching at my clothes pathetically, demanding to know where his wife was.

Tired and weary, my heart softened as I looked at this rheumy-eyed old man who, despite his bald head and large nose, still managed to look dignified in distress. Old Joseph once had had hundreds of men beneath his command; he'd even met the Queen of England. Now he stood blubbering, dressed in a shoddy, terry-toweling bathrobe and an old operating gown flapping open at the front.

I took Joseph by the hand and muttered soothing words, telling him that his wife would be "on board ship" in the morning. (Joseph kept addressing me as 'garcon' because of the white coat). Sadly, Joseph's wife had been dead for years, but by the morning—perhaps within the next ten minutes—Joseph's mind would drift into some other time zone.

I steered Joseph towards the stairwell and left him clinging there for a moment while I returned to lock the door of the Acute Ward. Where the hell is Iglesi?! I thought, irritated by the onslaught of fresh duties. It was nearly ten o'clock; Iglesi should have arrived.

I returned to the stairwell and began guiding Joseph up the stairs. When I took his elbow, this time Joseph slid his arm around my waist and turned to kiss me, whispering: "G'night, my dear."

"Sssh! Joseph, I'm not your wife. Now, c'mon," I said, grinning in spite of myself, and steered Joseph gently up the stairs towards the darkened zoo of the Geriatric Ward and the coughs, wheezes, groans, chirrups and bleating cries that were the sounds of the night.

Unfortunately, I didn't notice that, during our progress up the last few stairs, Joseph's bowels, laboring under the strain of age, fear and distress, had finally relinquished their hold on propriety. I didn't have time to do anything because at that very moment the alarm bell went off in the Acute Ward.

I flew down the stairs (missing Joseph's excretions by inches) and had the door of the Acute Ward unlocked and open in seconds.

I took in the scene at a glance: A short, white-faced patient with glasses, Jimmy Turnbull, was pressing the alarm button in agitation while two emaciated, stick-like figures wrestled and beat at each other in the middle of the darkened room. Those patients watching the television didn't even turn their heads, as *Mystery Theater* had reached a particularly gripping point. The remainder of the patients huddled under their sheets ignoring the racket, which was by no means unusual.

I raced down the darkened ward. "Now Jimmy, what is this?" I said frowning at Turnbull who ran along at my side. "Why did you ring the bell, eh?" Turnbull was constantly trying to attain some kind of authority as he deemed himself superior to the other patients, being an epileptic and not a "madman".

"They'll kill each other! They'll kill each other!" whined Turnbull, his bottle-thick glasses reflecting the light from the TV.

"Christ!" I said, "Those two?! I'd be the first to applaud!"

The two old men should have been in the Geriatric Ward, but despite their advanced years they were so tough that they had to be kept in the Acute Ward. One suffered from Senile Dementia; the other, from GPI (an archaic term for those whose general nervous system had been damaged by long-term syphilis—General Paralysis of the Insane).

If I hadn't been so tired, I would have laughed. The two men flailed and ranted at each other, naked; hairless; emaciated; and ugly, rather like two cadavers who had been miraculously revived, then set at each other's throats.

"Mr. O'Hara!" I roared, "Stop this!!"

I strode in between the two men to be rewarded by a thump on the side of the head that rattled my teeth. "Mr. O'Hara! You *should not* strike the staff, or, for that matter, anyone else!" I cried in my best bedside manner.

Both of the men were beyond reason, but I always kept up a semblance of propriety. I thought (a) it might ignite some tiny rational spark within each of them, and (b) it was good morale for the other patients.

"'Ee mpissed im me mshoe!" slobbered O'Hara in rage, his leathery, ancient face contorted like a distressed Fagin.

Practice enabled me to follow O'Hara's garbled speech. To a novice, however, it was almost unintelligible. O'Hara's voice started in the back of his throat and was shunted through a dense plug of phlegm in his nose to become a peculiar chugging sound. It sounded rather like an elephant snorting.

"'Eem mpissed in me mslippers!!" screeched O'Hara in rage. He flailed his skinny arms so rapidly that he momentarily broke free from my grip and his bony fist smacked into Mr. Turnbull's jaw with a sound like ceramic hitting marble.

"You bastard! You bastard!" snarled Turnbull. He whirled his arm like the prop of a Spitfire Fighter until it collided with O'Hara's bald pate, setting O'Hara roaring again.

"Ehoouw!!" screeched O'Hara, "Mnurse! Mnurse! 'Im's the mbastard!!"

"Fuck off!!" yelled Turnbull.

"Mmmshut your m-mouth!!" screamed O'Hara.

With all the strength I could muster, I grabbed them and held them apart. I stood there wearily, arms locked around the scrawny, naked bundles of taut energy, wishing the door would open; wishing that Iglesi would walk in; wishing I could just walk away and hand this matter over to someone else for another twelve hours; wishing I could catch the last hour in the pub and down four very therapeutic pints very quickly.

The door swung open. I let out a long sigh of relief. "At last."

But it wasn't Iglesi. It was the Brown Owl.

She was only five feet tall but her bosom protruded in front of her with all the grim authority of a Nautilus missile. Laden with badges, pens, nursing awards, scissors, thermometers, it was a formidable sight—and so was she. Her eyes glittering fiercely from behind bottle-thick lenses, her mouth pursed in a tight-pruned 'O' of indignation. She didn't walk, she *cleaved* through the air, prow-first, like a massive battleship.

"*Mi*-ster Pitts!" she cried, "What is going on here?!"

The two patients, mad as they were, were instantly subdued. Even *their* glazed minds recognized the Brown Owl as a superhuman force. Sheepishly, O'Hara and Turnbull dropped their arms and fearfully backed away.

The Brown Owl, keeping her eyes primly averted from their spindly, obscene nakedness, transfixed me with a gaze that would have pierced an armored tank. "And, not only that!!" she shrieked, her voice quivering with self-righteousness, "But why are those patients, sitting around at this time of night watching television!! They should be in bed—NOW!!"

"But Matron, I'm here alone ..."

"*No* excuses, *Mr.* Pitts!" (She kept emphasizing my gender as if that in itself were a cause for recrimination—which, in fact, was for her quite true.)

"But you don't understand. The night staff haven't turned up—I'm here alone. I should have gone off an hour ago."

"Should have, Mr. Pitts?!" she said coldly, her eyes gleaming with ice-fire, "*Should* have? Mr. Pitts, why my girls on the general ward would never say such a thing. It is your duty to maintain this ward, Mr. Pitts and there are no *shoulds*. Why, some of *my* girls have worked two double shifts in a row in times of need—and been glad to do so. Should have, indeed!"

I fell into silence as the Brown Owl's voice modulated into an acid, insidious drone which was worse than her shrieks. Her eyes flashed as she ran through a check-list of my misdemeanors: "The beds—look at them! A disgrace! The whole ward looks like a flea-market. And, Mr. Pitts, I assure you that neatness without hygiene is not my aim. But on the stairs outside, I saw what looked remarkably like feces! Feces, Mr. Pitts!! Have you ever heard of cross-infection, Mr. Pitts? Feces in a public ward!!!"

I stood wearily while she ranted, my mind full of murderous thoughts aimed at the creature in front of me. Why, she wasn't even meant to be here! She must have got a pass key and sneaked in, hoping to catch someone doing something wrong. Well, she had, indeed. The bitch!

"So, are you listening?!!"

I jerked back to attention.

"Report to my office when you finish your shift tomorrow morning!"

"Matron—"

"Tomorrow morning, Mr. Pitts!" And she turned on her black, hospital shoes with a squeal of rubber that set my teeth on edge and stormed off towards the exit like a wrathful tug boat.

I sighed glumly. Well, she wouldn't listen: I had not been relieved by the night man and, as I was due to start the morning shift at 7.30 the next day, I'd have to work right through—so the visit to the Brown Owl's office would cheerfully occupy my one free half-hour tomorrow morning—breakfast. Shit, no food, no sleep!

I swore and kicked the door. Then I swore some more and kicked the bed, then the desk, then the wall. The patients turned over and went to sleep. Such sounds were a normal accompaniment to their nightly retirement.

Twelve hours later...and I was still on duty.

I stared down the ward hazily. I was worried. Cecil was the object of my concern. Cecil was striding up and down grunting and muttering to himself. Occasionally, he would stoop, pick up a cigarette butt, then begin pacing again. His footsteps made heavy thuds on the parquet floor. The other patients—some sitting in chairs reading, some lying sleepily on their beds—kept well away from him.

He was "sparking up" again, I knew it. Cecil usually started acting like this just before the onset of a bout of violence that might take up to two or three hefty nurses to restrain.

But I couldn't afford that. I had no help apart from Mike Waddington, a thin, emaciated day-nurse who was even more neurotic than the patients. Mike was well-liked and well-intentioned but his thought processes didn't always coincide with what the world would loosely describe as Reality. I often had to make a lot of decisions single-handedly that I would sooner have shared.

When I'd finished giving out the medicines, Mike staggered over to me and whispered:

"Can I see you in the office?"

I nodded and, waving the patients away from the steel trolley from which I was dispensing medicines. I wheeled it into the tiny, cramped office at the end of the ward, and leaned on the door with a sigh. "What is it?"

"I can't make it," said Mike, leaning against the opposite wall, "I've had no sleep for forty-eight hours."

"Jesus, Mike, I've been on duty for hours!"

"It's no use. I've been taking amphetamines."

"Go to sleep then," I said, annoyed, "Go into the padded cell. I'll lock the door."

"I daren't," moaned Mike. "The Brown Owl has got it in for me. She'll be over on inspection today; she's just looking for trouble. Can't you give me something to keep me awake?"

I stared at the tray and shook my head. "Naah, none of these things are really uppers—not even the pertofrin or the tofranil. You need amphetamine or plain caffeine ..."

"Can't I take a pertofrin?"

"Well you could, but the effect is unpredictable. It will probably make you feel worse."

"If these doctors took half this garbage themselves, they wouldn't prescribe it so light-heartedly."

"Look," I said, "Just go upstairs to the Geriatric Ward—I'll screen the bed off—and sleep, man. If the Brown Owl comes, I'll be up and we'll hustle you into the toilet before she does her rounds."

Mike's expression was uneasy, but fatigue pulled him towards the vision of a soft bed. "O.K., you'll keep watch?" he said.

"Sure, don't worry," I said, "I'll be there."

Next afternoon, I sat in the office, hurriedly finishing the day's reports. Like me, Mike was due off in half an hour, 2.30 p.m., and, so far, the Brown Owl hadn't shown. He was safely tucked away in bed in the upstairs ward surrounded by screens.

"Mr. Pitts!!"

I started and dropped the pen at the cold familiarity of the voice. I brought my head up slowly and my worst fears were confirmed as I stared into the pellucid bottle-green of the Brown Owl's spectacles.

"M-matron," I said, trying to compose myself, "How did you get in...? I hope no one left the outside door unlocked!"

"No, Mr. Pitts," said the Brown Owl throwing her armored bosom out fiercely, "It was not open. I opened it with my personal key."

My mind was racing. All the time I was wondering how I could steer her away from the upstairs ward before she discovered that Mike was sleeping.

"Mr. Pitts, there is something very, very wrong in the upstairs ward," said the Brown Owl.

I quaked inside. I hadn't realized she'd been upstairs already. But she had—her pursed lips gave it away.

"Follow me," said the Brown Owl.

"Mr. Pitts!! Mr. Pitts!!!"

They lay there in blissful repose like two identical spoons curled up in each other, snoring: Mike with old Joseph alongside him, his gnarled, old head nesting on Mike's shoulder, his wrinkled, thin arm thrown around Mike's waist. Of course, to add to the total effect, old Joseph was completely naked. He obviously thought Mike was his wife.

"Not a pretty sight for a professional, is it, Mr. Pitts?" said the Matron contemplating the bed.

Though not accustomed to the ways of bureaucratic normalcy, for once I couldn't have agreed more.

"Both of you, come to my office at 3 p.m.!"

"But—!" I protested.

"No buts!"

The period passed in a haze of remorse, tension and anxiety for Mike but, finally, he was restored to duty with the backing of the whole ward. After all, we claimed, he had stayed on duty two nights and had run the ward single-handed (an outright lie) … fatigue had taken its toll. The lie worked—just. It had been a narrow margin and a fiercely-fought battle. The Brown Owl had given it everything she'd got. But the male staff had won and Mike was back on duty. But we knew that the Brown Owl was gunning for him. From now on, Mike's life was going to be even more precarious.

Mike's reaction was typical: faced with the need for caution, restraint and the middle path, Mike became reckless, flamboyant and openly courted disaster.

A week or so after Mike had been reinstated, I was working nights—with Mike again. It was a troublesome night. Cecil Jones had been acting up again and both Mike and I were tense and anxious because we knew the Brown Owl was on duty at the main hospital. If she could find some way of giving us trouble, she would.

I was in the autoclave, the room where we sterilized the instruments, a few yards down the corridor from where Mike was supposedly on duty watching the Ward.

A sudden pounding and a cry made me turn abruptly, just in time to see Cecil Jones flash past the door, closely followed by Mike.

With a clatter, I dropped the stainless steel bowl I was clutching and sprinted after Cecil, just in time to see him reach the front door and snatch at the pass-key. I groaned at my own stupidity: I'd left it in the lock.

With a snarl, Cecil wrenched at the key. There was a crack, and Cecil jerked backwards, holding the shank in his hand, the head still in the lock.

"Oh shit!" I cried, "He snapped a three-eighth steel key!"

Cecil flung down the head of the key with a snarl and headed in the only direction left—the bathroom. Cecil dashed in, rebounded off the wall, and, finding no exit, he began to pace up and down snarling, his face contorted in fear and rage.

Mike and I peered around the corner cautiously.

"Oh Christ," muttered Mike, his face white, his eyes drawn involuntarily towards Cecil's meaty fists which were clutching and unclutching. "What do we do now?"

"We'll have to get some help," I said, "He's long gone. You keep an eye on him while I draw up some paraldehyde."

"Hey, you keep an eye on him—I'll draw up the paraldehyde," muttered Mike.

Then I saw what Cecil was doing and I involuntarily shouted out loud: "Cecil! Oh no, Cecil!!"

The sink by the bathroom cabinets was laden with urine samples—tall beakers, each labeled with a patient's name. Some of the samples were evil-looking, long fermented, cloudy, green deposits. The urine tests were the last tasks tackled by an over-worked staff and some of them had been fermenting for a week. Cecil was drinking down these doubtful beverages one by one with great relish, as though he were quaffing prime beer.

"Cecil!!" I yelled, "Don't do that!! What d'you think you're doing?!"

"Poison," said Cecil significantly in one of his rare moments of lucid speech.

"Oh Jesus! You're bleeding mad, man!!" I yelled.

Mike groaned, expecting some physical retaliation for this prime case of over-stating the obvious. But, instead, Cecil finished the last of his unsavory beverages and then lay down on the floor under the sink.

"Hey, Cecil," I said in exasperation, entering the bathroom, "What's happening?!"

"Careful!" hissed Mike, but he followed closely, watching Cecil's every move.

I knelt down by Cecil who lay staring at the ceiling, his face immobile, his arms by his side. "Cecil," I said, tugging gently at the man's sleeve, expecting, any moment, that Cecil would leap up and belt me, "C'mon now, you can't lie there."

But Cecil, presumably awaiting his death, closed his eyes wearily.

"What now?" said Mike standing up and scratching his head.

164

"Any time soon I reckon he's going to puke all over the place." I shrugged. "Let's just cover him up. Take anything out of the room he might use to hurt himself."

Mike glanced at me with a feral grin and said sarcastically: "Oh yeah? Like he wouldn't touch us with it, would he?!"

"You know what I mean. Let's get some blankets and pillows and cover him up. We'll switch out the light, and maybe he'll just sleep."

"You want some paraldehyde?" asked Mike. For him, all solutions were chemical.

"Well, you draw it up," I said, wearily aware of my position as the senior member of staff, "But I'm not going to give it to him just yet—that shit hurts. He'll be up and raging all over the place—then we'll have to try and rush him. Nope. Just keep it at the ready—we don't want to give him any sudden pain—we just couldn't handle him the way he is."

"I'll say," said Mike thoughtfully, "Twenty cc's! The way we shove it in so fast, when it goes into the tissues it just pushes them apart in a big bubble—that's what causes the pain. Christ, you know how long it takes to give an intra-muscular injection if you want it to absorb as you inject it? Forty-five fucking minutes!"

I didn't ask Mike how he'd acquired this tasty morsel of information. I just stood and watched Cecil while Mike went and got the blankets and pillow. When he returned, we covered Cecil up, wary of any sudden movements. But as far as Cecil was concerned, death was nigh, so he didn't move.

I sat staring at the TV screen. Save for the TV and the glow of a few night lights, the ward was in darkness. The white bed sheets were pale and wan in the gloom and at the end of the ward, the outline of the ward door glowed faintly. The patients were largely silent, but from the bathroom came a noise like a rip-saw. It was Cecil, snoring loudly. I was keenly aware of distances and the time it would take to spring into action should Cecil cease snoring and suddenly lumber through the door towards me.

I let out a sigh and glanced around the ward. For a moment, everything was peaceful; a temporary interlude in a crazy day and a restless night.

Mike sat opposite me, his fingers drumming on the arm of the chair—Mike was never still. "Fucking assholes!" he said vehemently, "The Brown Owl—stupid bitch! If she knew what it was like to work here, she wouldn't bother with her stupid rules! Christ, they can't get any good staff—people who care. And I know you care and so do I and all we get is shit!"

I nodded glumly. It was true.

"Sshh!" I said, sitting bolt upright in the chair. I'd heard something outside.

"It's Cecil," said Mike rising slowly, "Shit, this is all we need."

"Naah...sit down," I whispered, "Listen,"

There was a furtive scraping sound then a metallic tinkle.

Mike furrowed his brow and I leaned forward and whispered: "The Brown Owl! She's pushed the broken key out of the lock—she must have a pass key!"

At that moment, the rip-saw snoring stopped and I went rigid. "Cecil! Christ! She's got the door open—he'll get out!!"

Mike put a restraining arm on mine. "No," he whispered, "Listen." The faint, metallic rattle came again. "She's locking the door behind her."

"C'mon!" I hissed, "She'll probably make a bee-line for Cecil. She's trying to catch us asleep on duty! She'll think it's one of us!"

Mike tugged gleefully at my sleeve again, "No. Sit down, man!" My heart was pounding as I stared into Mike's face. Etiolated by the light, it was demonic; a mixture of Mephistopheles and Pan. "Human reaction time is slow," he whispered cryptically with a grin that made his face even more devilish.

"Cecil is already awake!" I blurted, listening fearfully. "With his reactions he'll hear her—!"

"Not his—ours!" interrupted Mike, "This is our chance."

I got it. I stared at Mike's face and made my decision. "Yeah," I said, "It's quite normal for us to be momentarily startled, to wait a bit, like we don't know what's going on. We wouldn't run out without appraising the situation first, would we?"

Mike grinned. "No, of course we wouldn't."

I settled back into the arm chair and waited, ears cocked.

Above the snores of the patients, we could hear faint noises: the creak of the bathroom door; the "ruff ruff" of a starched skirt. Then, silence...

The moment seemed to elongate. I gazed at Mike; Mike gazed at me—and we both had to stop ourselves giggling nervously.

A piercing screech rent the air, followed by a heavy crash, then another. I began a countdown: "Ten Mary-anne; nine Mary-anne; eight Mary-anne..." Another shrill scream pierced the air, followed by a guttural roar. "Four Mary-anne; three Mary-anne; two Mary-anne; one Mary-anne—let's GO!!"

We sprinted down the ward together and dashed into the corridor. I thumbed on the lights and we entered the bathroom just in time to see a diminutive figure being upended into the bath tub by a roaring, wrathful Cecil. The Brown Owl's face was obscured her skirt: Cecil was holding her upside-down by her ankles and rattling her like a money-box. Watches, thermometers, nursing badges, pens clattered into the porcelain bath, their noise mingling with the Brown Owl's piercing screams.

We both stopped, momentarily stunned by the sight of the Brown Owl's thighs encased in a vast and voluminous pair of camiknickers, like two dun wind-socks flailing in the breeze. Then I flung myself on Cecil and, without ceremony, wacked the 20cc syringe through his nightgown straight into his meaty buttock, and depressed the plunger.

Cecil roared in pain and dropped the Brown Owl. She fell into the bath on top of the accouterments of forty years of nursing glory. Cecil whirled around and grabbed at Mike who turned and ran out of the bathroom and straight into the padded cell. Cecil followed Mike until he could go no further. Mike backed up against the quilted-covered wall, the floor spongy under his feet. He sidled away from Cecil, talking rapidly all the time:

"You've done it now, Cecil," he said, "That was the Matron, d'y' hear me? The Matron. C'mon, now, pack it in hey? You can't go on like this."

Cecil wavered uncertainly for a moment, his eyes full of confusion.

Standing at the door, I reached into my pocket. "Hey Cecil," I said, "Want a cigarette?" I showed him a full packet of cigarettes and then casually threw them on the floor of the padded cell.

Cecil's eyes turned from Mike followed their trajectory. Mike was up and around him in a flash. We put our shoulders to the heavy door and heaved. It banged shut with a rush of air. I turned the lock shut and let out a gasp.

"Oh Christ!!" cried Mike, half in hysteria, half in euphoria. He leaned against the door, eyes half closed, allowing his panic to subside. "What a rush! What a rush!"

A moan behind reminded us of the Brown Owl's fate and we tip-toed cautiously into the bathroom to peer down at the sorry spectacle that was the Brown Owl laying in a disheveled bundle in the white bath tub.

"Well, what do you reckon?" said Mike, "She's fainted. A little cold water would sure bring her around."

"Mike!" I said, "We can't do that!!"

But Mike, obviously less inclined to compassion than I, had already turned on the cold-water tap. "In a world of contingent realities, all things are possible," he said cryptically, "And—"

The rest of his most philosophical speech was drowned by the Brown Owl's shrieks.

End Note

I included this here rather than break the flow of the anecdote, but a strange incident occurred right at the height of the activity. It was a moment that will be specifically significant to all Americans. As we were sitting in the darkened ward, lit only by the glow of the TV set, there was a news bulletin and an announcer said: "Ladies and Gentlemen, the President of the United States has been assassinated."

None of the patients even looked up.

I had no time to react because, at that moment, the Brown Owl entered the building and I was caught up in the chain of events. It wasn't until several hours later when I was at home that the full significance of the situation hit me, and I reacted as everyone else in the world did—with total shock.

Crime As Play

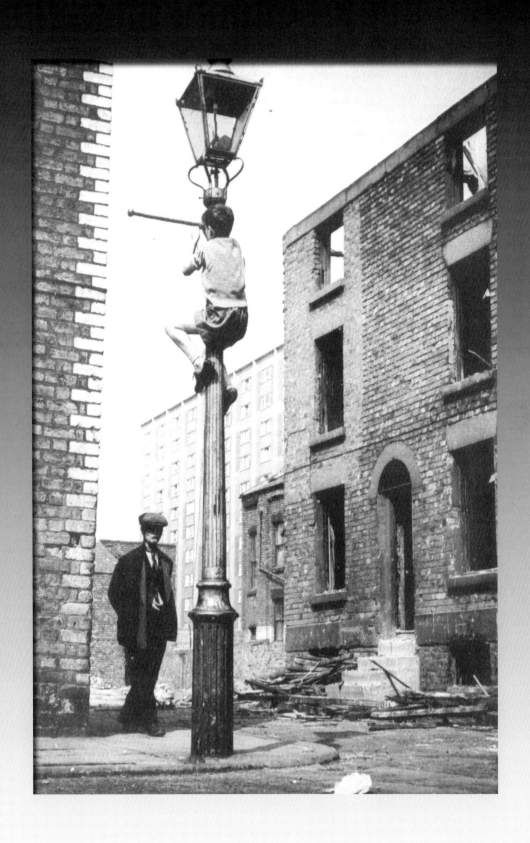

16

Crime as Play

Everyone's got their favorite criminals. Mine are pimps. We can all rob a bank, we can all sell drugs. Being a pimp is a whole other thing. Why? Pimps have it all together. They do real well with women. You never see two pimps at a party and one pimp saying, "Go over there and talk to her. I think she likes you." Pimps are cool for so many reasons. You know what else I love about pimps? They don't change. The same pimp who was out on the street in 1972 is out there right now. I'd like to know where he found that lizard jumpsuit. In green. You can't get a green lizard jumpsuit anywhere that I know. There must be a pimp boutique somewhere in New York.

Chris Rock
Rock This!

Police fighting crime in high-density crime areas like the Bronx, Detroit, Oakland, are up against a single factor: Crime is not just a greedy desire to possess material goods in the most rapacious and immediate way. In the urban landscape, crime is a lifestyle with its own parameters, hierarchies, kudos, status and rewards.

Courtesy Margaret Ainscough

The streets were our hills and dales, the roof tops, our mountains

"The frowsy intimacy of the ghetto" — George Orwell

One of the difficulties of interracial crime is that the victim is not seen as a victim, but as a source of revenue, like a fertile field waiting to be harvested. The criminal is often seen by his peers as a charismatic figure of glory. His fall from grace—i.e., being caught—is thus viewed as a sign of his profession; scars of battle bearing witness to his boldness and his daring accomplishments.

Each gang of kids had a secret hideout which totally excluded adults by virtue of the climbing feat involved. One of our regular pastimes was to steal stone flagons of ginger beer and dandelion and burdock from a soft drink brewery, we did this regularly but in small quantities so that the supply remained permanently available. A rival gang discovered our hideout and began drinking our supplies. The next batch we stole, we all drank half from each one-gallon stone bottle then pissed methodically into the remainder. We let the other gang steal it. Shortly after, we stood next to the felons and discussed our act in great detail. They tried to maintain innocent faces but to our delight ended up gagging and retching, thus betraying their guilt.

As a child sitting around with my peers who discussed, at great lengths, their probation officers, the various judges in Court, comparing sentences, penalties and records, I felt as deprived as if I were being forced to admit that I'd never scaled a tree, ridden a bike, smoked a cigarette or been in a fight. I was relegated to the bottom rung of the social scale. While my friends compared their crimes and their penalties like warriors showing off tribal identity marks, I felt guilty and inadequate simply because I had none.

Not that I'd never committed a crime. Everyone, at some time or other in urban Liverpool, has stolen

A reporter from the prestigious Daily Telegraph newspaper came to Liverpool 8 to write an article on crime in urban areas. He noticed one shop window was boarded up and the counter inside was heavily reinforced. He asked the shopkeeper what other measures he had taken against stealing, and the shopkeeper told him that he had bought the biggest meanest German Shepherd he could and kept it behind the counter half starved. The dog was nowhere in sight and when the reporter asked its whereabouts the shopkeeper said wearily, "The kids stole it."

or committed a burglary. But I just didn't have any 'war scars': I'd never been caught. (Actually, I was caught twice in petty thieving, but in each case I was let off.)

Thus, robbery was not seen as a sin. In fact, there is a certain genuine honor amongst thieves and, by and large, they didn't steal off each other. But anybody who *owned* something, be it a car or small shop or a business, is seen as very fair game. And anything *corporate* is more than fair game—its very ostentatiousness is an open invitation to be robbed.

For the kids in Liverpool's South End during the Sixties, robbery was part of the vast adventure of growing up. In the urban landscape, their trees were factory walls; their playgrounds, the roofs and valleys of warehouses; their dales and glens, the hidden territories found by scaling impossible heights, surmounting the obstacle of precarious roof and rafter; their meadows, the acres of sheet roofing above the factories—virgin gardens of glass and stone with groves of ventilators, oases of air-conditioning plants.

It was exciting, it was often nerve-racking. And on these jaunts, the distinction between boyhood adventure and crime often became blurred. A thrilling, daredevil climb over a large building could easily become a cat burglary—just as something to do at the other end. I mean, if you'd just scaled Everest and found a pot of gold at the top, would you leave it there?

As criminals, not many of the kids were accomplished. As a result, many were caught and sent to establishments, erroneously termed rehabilitation centers, where their criminal skills were honed to perfection by warden abuse, indifference, hostility, ignorance, cruelty and the educative value of older criminals. These institutions roped in boys playing games of wonder and awe on rooftops and turned them into criminals.

This is not an accusation, but a simple fact. As night follows day, it seems that these urchins of the rooftops, children of the stones are transformed during this process of 'remedial custody' from boys into men. And they end up possessing that fine instrument of social disruption: the Criminal Mind.

> Sometimes I think I need to go back to school. But the problem is that if you're black, you get more respect for going to jail than for going to school. You come out of jail and you're the man. You come out of school, nobody cares.
>
> Chris Rock
> Rock This!

Courtesy Margaret Ainscough

Workers' homes in front of the magnificent Anglican Cathedral which still stands with bullet holes in its walls where Nazi planes strafed it in World War 2

Crime As Crime

Crime as Crime

There is a myth prevalent amongst the middle classes of both American and England that the working class who resort to crime are lazy, dissolute or morally decadent. This betrays a total lack of understanding by middle America and middle England of how the transition into crime takes place.

There is also a myth that there is a group of "bad guys" and once these are removed, society will function. This is what led to the founding of Australia—an attempt to get rid of the criminal class by transportation.

In the urban environment, what starts off as fun and adventure can easily become serious crime. Furthermore, fueled by unemployment or the quasi-employment of standing behind a fast-food counter wearing a silly hat for minimum wage, with overbearing bosses and lack of prestige and respect, it is patently obvious that the quick money allure of crime and drugs cannot be resisted.

TV makes it worse. During the blackout of 1965 in New York when the whole town ran riot, one black said: "It gets to be unbearable, the difference between your own life and the life in the TV commercials. You just feel like reaching inside the TV set and grabbing it for your own."

Well, crime as crime is just that. And there are two factors which aggravate this situation.

Firstly: The inequality of opportunity. Many Americans and Englishmen don't realize that the working class in England and the blacks in America do *not* have equal access to the opportunities of society; a hundred barriers block them daily; not laziness or moral decadence.

The second factor is alienation. It is only when you are *outside* of the society that you can cheerfully rob, plunder or mutilate because alienation means that your fellow man is no longer your fellow man but an object. This is dangerous. In order for a fellow man to be violated, he *has* to be perceived as an *object* by his violator. Now, by definition, for the blacks, white men *are* objects because for centuries, blacks have been objects to the whites. And, like it or not, in order to rape, murder and pillage whites, they *have* to be seen as objects by black people.

In America, skin color is an incredible line of demarcation in this objectification of an entire class. Initially, blacks were no more unfairly treated than the first-generation Irish or poor Italians or poor first-generation anything in America. Traditionally, as an ethnic group enters into a society (any society), it is mistreated for the generation before it is absorbed. This is a sad-but-true generalization about human nature. The second generation are treated more equally than the former as they rise up the social scale.

But for the blacks, something else has happened: The history of slavery and skin color has led to a lack of social mobility which is simply not comparable to the economic repression of other subgroups—because it has continued from generation to generation. They have not been absorbed as have the Irish and the Italians.

Given these conditions, play often transitions to crime in the black ghetto and unpremeditated violence can occur; the perpetrator is locked into the punitive-reform system, branded as a criminal by society, and so the cycle is complete. And crime becomes a way of life.

I was very lucky. I was as involved in as much petty thieving as my peers but I escaped jail or reform school. At one point I hooked up with Lonny Mac, a wiry Liverpool Irishman with a criminal record and a history of violence. He was a professional Cat Burglar—and I was a very good climber. We decided to team up to do some jobs. It didn't turn out the way I expected. Thank God.

> Our gang hideout was called The Hidden Valley as German WWII bombing had left a chasm in the middle of a group of buildings which was only accessible by a tortuous roof top climb. On one occasion, an overzealous night watchman from a nearby factory propped up a ladder spotted us in the dusk, and blew a police whistle. One of the lads panicked. A burly kid, he picked up a large roof slate and threw it at the man, more to scare him away than with any intention of harm. The slate, measuring 3' by 3' with a razor edge skimmed through the air like a frisbee, narrowly missing the man. Had it struck him it would have near decapitated him. We escaped; the man was unharmed. Unfortunately all such escapades do not have the same happy outcome.

The Great Candy Robbery: A Fully Felonious Event with a Modicum of Luck
— A Personal Anecdote —

Courtesy Karl Hughes

The Bobby on His Beat

It was settled. Lonny had picked the target, I had approved the master plan and now the Arch-Criminal and His Apprentice were fortifying themselves with a few pints before they began their assault. We were in a nearby pub down Park Road—Ringo's birthplace and romping ground which, even by Liverpool standards, was grim..

Music blared tinnily from an old-fashioned radio; the pub air was thick with tobacco fumes, the smell of damp clothing and stale beer. We were sitting in the corner of the King's Arms downing our second pint of black-and-tan Guinness.

I was excited. After our fortifying pints, we were faced with a monumental climb. Lonny for his part, though casual and nonchalant, seemed secretly pleased at this new angle to his illicit nocturnal activities. My high-spirited, amateur enthusiasm seemed a definite boost to this normally solitary affair of cat-burglary.

"Don't get pissed[1] now," warned Lonny, "We've got a long climb in front of us."

"Pissed?" I responded. "You know, it's funny, but on a couple of beers I climb better."

Lonny nodded. If one thing was true, it was that I was a good climber—he'd seen me in action. Lonny

Roof of the Tiber Street School
One of many roofs we played on as kids, graduating to more serious activities

glanced around the crowded, noisy pub cautiously and said: "O.K., let's do it then."

We exited out of the side door into the poorly-lit street of the Dingle area. Somewhere in the neighborhood Ringo was either drinking or playing music, perhaps even involved in some nefarious activity like us.

It was dark. Very dark. The lamp-posts stood at regular intervals; puddles of yellow light barely pushing back the gloom that swirled around the base of the building like dense fog.

We stood chatting nonchalantly as though we were saying farewell after a few pints while Lonny briefed me about the target. "O.K.," he said, "That's it across the road. We split up and meet around the back. O.K.?"

I glanced across to the scene of our crime. The shops on the other side of the road were dour and dingy; most of them were storage warehouses that were boarded up. In the middle was a jagged gap where one of the shops had either been removed or had fallen down. It was an extremely narrow gap and the two adjacent buildings were shored up by twelve-by-twelve timbers that criss-crossed the twenty foot space between them, rising up to the fourth floor, some one hundred feet in the air. It made for an easy climb—at least, for us.

"O.K. Pittsy," said Lonny, "See you." Lonny winked and we shook hands and parted on the pavement in front of the pub, going off in opposite directions.

By circling the opposite ends of the block, five minutes later, we met behind the building opposite. We were now gazing across the street from behind the trellised gap at the lighted pub we'd just left .

Weeds pushed up between the compacted rubble; feeble, bedraggled things that had gained a little foothold. But to my foliage-starved, urban eye, it looked like a veritable forest, and not without a certain beauty.

I craned my head back and stared upwards, tracing the criss-cross trestle beams to where they met at the roof tops. The trestle supported a vast, wooden beam bolted to the adjoining buildings with huge, rusting metal plates.

"Think you can do it?" whispered Lonny.

"Phah!" I snorted. "Piece of cake."

By way of an answer, I was up and over the first trestle in a matter of seconds. Lonny grinned appreciatively and, leaping cat-footedly onto the beams, followed me. We shimmied up the wooden beams using footholds and chinks in the worn woodwork and in a very short time had made very rapid progress upwards.

Half-way: I paused. The beer was warm in my belly, the air sweet and clean (a totally subjective illusion). The lines and shadows of the timbers were etched out like a Buffet painting in the light from the pub. The chiaroscuro of light and shade gave me a delicate tingle of pleasure. I loved viewing the world from an angle that no one else would ever see. The illicit nature of the climb added a delicious thrill that made me linger to savor the moment.

"What are you waiting for, daft-ass?!" hissed Lonny's voice from beneath me, "Maybe you want to wait till breakfast time?"

My momentary spell of poetry broken, I cat-footed up the remaining timbers and up and over onto the slate roof. The roof was steep and, by sheer bad luck, the swathe of gloom ended and the grayish roof slates were clearly illuminated by the lights from the pub opposite. It would be a tricky matter to negotiate the roof unseen. If someone looked out of one of the windows in the pub?

Lonny gazed at me in unspoken agreement—it was too risky to break in through this side of the roof. "Bollocks," said Lonny, "Let's climb up the edge and get onto the other side. It's darker there, no one will see us."

I swung onto the edge of the roof after a cautious look at the pub below—I'd have to get up and over quickly. Fast as I could, I began worming my way up the roof. The roof angle was steep and my only grip was the jagged edge where the slates ended. I didn't look down. I didn't want to—it was a hundred foot drop to the ground. Cautiously, I inched my way up the roof, my left palm flat on the roof surface. I gripped the edge of the slate in my right hand—and hauled.

The chasm between the buildings on my right-hand side was illuminated here and there by the play of light on the wooden trestle beams. Intuitively, I noted the position of each of the beams, knowing that if I started to slide down the steep roof I could drop over the edge...and hopefully land on one of the twelve-by-twelves.

I reached the top of the roof without mishap, though my right hand was bloody and torn. I swung over so that my legs were astride the apex. I paused for a moment and looked out over this secret world. Below were the roofs and valleys of dockland Liverpool: the tall, jutting chimneys; the steep walls and odd chasms; the passages and tunnels hidden from the street-dwellers below, but forever mine.

Courtesy Glynn Parry

The rooftops of Liverpool

I inhaled deeply. It was my world. A huge piece of real estate in the midst of the city by the simple expedient of the climb.

I stared at the vast shape of the Liver Building in the distance, somber against the glow of the night sky from the Docks. It always reminded me of Gotham City or Metropolis and I almost expected Batman or Superman to come swooping through the night air to shake my hand and share my enthusiasm for this private, roof-top world.

"Bollocks, Pittsy, have you been taking pills?" muttered Lonny, arriving behind me. "C'mon, we haven't

A rooftop ripe for the picking

got all day. What are you sitting up there for?"

"O.K., O.K.," I muttered, a little abashed. Lonny did not share my poetic sensibilities.

Carefully, I gripped the apex of the roof in both hands and gingerly turned over onto my belly so that my legs were dangling down the slope of the roof behind me. I eased myself down the roof until I was sprawled out full-length with just my finger-tips hooked over the lip of the roof top. I let go with one hand and slid my other hand towards the torn edge of the slate roof, now on my left. Gripping the edge of the slate, I let go with my right hand experimentally, testing the friction of my belly against the roof.

I didn't move.

Cautiously, I began to worm my way backwards down the roof in successive grips with my left hand. It was difficult. Before, I had been hauling myself up the other side of the roof. This time, I was stopping myself sliding down the roof and I couldn't be sure whether I had enough friction to stop sliding backwards every time I released my grip.

I didn't. I suddenly tore free and began sliding down the roof, my chin battering against the slate. I let out a yelp of terror. Instinctively, I spread my legs and feet wide apart to increase the friction. I slowed momentarily but didn't stop. Then I picked up speed again and my head was filled with an awful vision of the gigantic drop to the street below. "Aaahhh!" I yelled, suddenly fear overwhelming my caution.

Then my heels hit something with a jar that rattled my jaw, and I stopped dead. My heart was pounding with fright, but I raised my head up cautiously and looked over my left shoulder. My feet had hit the edge of an ornamental parapet. Just six inches high, it jutted vertically upwards from the edge of the roof. It had stopped me shooting over the edge and saved my life.

I let my breath out with a whoosh and muttered over and over: "Oh suffering Jesus!" Until a noise at my side made me stop this panicked litany.

It was Lonny. He lay nonchalantly on his back at my side, his heels against the parapet, his arms behind his head, as though he were sunning himself on the deck of a liner. "Hey Pittsy," he grinned, "Good job the cornice held you, eh?" He winked and made a plummeting motion with his right hand like a fighter plane plummeting to earth.

I was not amused. "Oh funnee, Lonny," I said, "I nearly had it!"

"Naah," said Lonny, "Not you—you're a good climber."

The faint praise soothed me not a little and for a moment I lay on my back staring up into the hazy, night sky until I regained my composure. "O.K. Lon," I said, "What now?"

"Well," said Lonny, "This..." he pointed beneath us, "Is the top floor of the electronics' warehouse. It's packed up to here..." he held his hand at eye level, "With all sorts of goodies: transistors, test motors—expensive shit, man. What we do is get inside, pick out what we want and, whammo, we're off."

"How do we get in?"

"Ah, that's easy. Watch." Lonny rolled over onto his front, levered himself up onto his knees and, with the soles of his feet jammed against the cornice, he began to dissemble the roof.

I watched in admiration as Lonny took the roof apart with all the precision of a brain surgeon removing a section of a patient's skull. Within minutes, there was a large hole in the roof revealing strips of lath with plaster oozing between them like pink bubble-gum.

"Hey Lonny, that's great!"

"Yeah, now for the difficult bit." Lonny eased one leg over the hole and, with a quick, downward movement, thrust his foot through the lath. His foot broke through with a rending sound. Broken plaster and dust clattered into the building. Lonny withdrew his foot and rolled onto his back and waited for the noise to subside. Then he rolled over again and peered into the hole. He let out an audible groan.

"What is it?! What is it?!!" I whispered.

"Oh Jesus," said Lonny wearily, "Just put your head down there. No, be careful, don't put it inside, just look in."

The author on one of his many "urban" climbs

I lowered my head into the hole and peered from side to side cautiously. The room was stacked almost to the ceiling with brown cardboard boxes. "What am I looking for?"

"See those wires all over the ceiling? No, don't touch them. See them?" whispered Lonny. I could see them. They criss-crossed the ceiling like a cat's cradle, thin and black in the wan light from the dirty windows. "That's an auto-call system," whispered Lonny above me, "It's playing a record down at the Central Office now saying 'there's a break-in at so-and-so street'—you know. I tripped the friggin' thing when I stuck my foot through."

I jerked upright out of the hole.

"What are you doing?!" said Lonny in consternation.

"C'mon!!" I cried, scrabbling up the roof hastily, "Let's get out of here!"

"No," said Lonny firmly, "Shit man, we don't have a chance if they come and we're half-way down—that's it. We've got to sit still."

"Sit still?!!" I wailed, "Still?!! How can I stay still when the cops are on their way??!!"

"Don't worry," said Lonny with a resigned air, "I'm the one who'll get it, I'm the corrupting influence. You'll just be a first offender. You'll probably get probation."

This stylized speech made me even more agitated. "Fuck that!" I cried and was half-way up the roof when Lonny grabbed me by the ankle and hauled me back.

"Pittsy!" he said, "Sit still, you dickhead! I tell you, the cops'll be here any minute!"

Eventually, he persuaded me to lay on my back with my feet against the cornice and be quiet—and wait.

My already taut nerves grew even tauter. My over-active brain spiraled into multiple patterns of agitation as I lay in this frozen posture at forty-five degrees to the vertical. "What's that? What's that?!" I suddenly hissed, "What's that noise?!" I could hear a car in the alley below.

"Uh uh," whispered Lonny, "Be quiet now. Check it out. Here comes Ole Bill."

Ole Bill was a black police car; ominous and beetle-like from our overhead perspective. My chest was tight with fear as I levered myself up to see it cruise down the back alley behind the row of shops and slide to a halt. The lights suddenly died and all was dark again. It seemed even more threatening—like a predatory

Cammell Laird, the docks of Liverpool

Courtesy Mindscaffolding

The walls of the Dock Road in Cammell Laird have to be seen to be believed. Huge structures many feet thick, they are designed specifically to stop one thing: the ubiquitous robbery that takes place in all the dockyards of Liverpool. A docker's life (read stevedore) is hard and often bitter, and he often self-rewards his gruelling day's work by "broaching cargo", i.e., breaking into the cargo hold, as the dockers would steal anything. This has given rise to a spate of docker humor such as:

> *A docker approaches the dock gate struggling under a huge bale of cotton wool.*
> *Dock policeman: "'Ere, 'ere, what are you doing then?"*
> *Docker: "Oh, man, I've been sent home with the ear ache…"*

animal that has disappeared in the gloom momentarily, just before it leaps.

"What are they doing?" I muttered, anguished, "Why are they stopping like that? The fuckers are—"

"Shush! We've got a chance!" said Lonny, "The auto-call obviously doesn't register which part of the building it's in. It could've been set off by anything: a fault; the damp; sometimes the rats gnaw the insulation off the wires. Just cool it, Pittsy. We might do this. Stay put, stay still and for Christ's sake, shut up!"

I clamped my teeth together to stop them chattering and waited. The moments elongated. I became aware of the insistent pressure of a full bladder. I relaxed my jaw, but my teeth began to chatter again. My legs, stiff with the cold, began to ache. The air was beginning to clear and the stars were blossoming one by one.

"It's getting colder," whispered Lonny, "The stars are shining through."

"Great," I whispered in an agitated voice, "I've got frost-bite in my ass, my bleedin' legs are dropping off and he tells me it's getting cold! Thanks a lot."

Lonny giggled, betraying his own nervousness for the first time. In a nervous reaction, I responded with a high-pitched giggle of my own. I choked it back, trying to stop the noise. "Lonny! No—don't!" I said hysterically in between giggles, as Lonny began to heave with suppressed laughter.

Lonny clamped his hand over his own mouth. His eyes bulged, the veins stood out on his head as he tried to stop bursting out loud.

"Oh fuck!!" I hissed as something warm suddenly gushed between my legs, "Oh Christ! I'm pissing myself!!" I made a frantic grab at my fly, trying to stem the flood forced out from my pressurized bladder by my suppressed giggles. I spread my legs and pissed down the roof in a great stream and, involuntarily, let out a vast and vociferous fart.

That was that.

The night air was rent with a number of vast farts and Lonny's laughter burst out from between his clamped fingers in a high-pitched whine.

All thoughts of danger were gone. The supreme imperative was not to laugh, and yet we could not stop. Tears streamed down Lonny's face. He almost choked himself trying to hold in his laughter with both hands clamped around his mouth, while I giggled, gulped and, in spite of myself, let out vast, beery eruptions that tore the still night into evil-smelling tatters.

"Je-sus Christ, Pittsy!!" burst out Lonny, "The poor cops! They'll be poisoned, man!! Oh my God!!" This brought on a fresh gale of laughter.

Courtesy Quentin Hughes

The Dock Road Wall

The dock walls were designed by Jessie Hartley in the early 1800s. They isolated the dockland from the long thread of the Dock Road, and were immense. They were not just a luxury but an absolute necessity to restrain the ever-growing drain on shipping profits of pilfering. Some 18 foot high and 18 foot thick, they are pierced at heavy intervals by heavy wooden gates which slide with precision along iron guide rails deep into the walls themselves. Fort Knox could not be better defended. And yet the dockers still managed to pilfer. Human ingenuity knows no limits.

Then, suddenly, the car below us started.

"They've heard us!" I said, choking.

The car lights flooded on. Then, smoothly, the car moved off, rounded the corner and disappeared.

"No...no, they didn't," chortled Lonny wiping his eyes, "They've gone! Oh Jesus! You did it, man—they couldn't stand the smell!!"

We must have laughed for a full fifteen minutes more. My giggles began to fade as the chill wind bit into my wet crotch. I lay for a moment, weak with laughter, then said: "O.K., let's go," and began climbing up the roof.

"Not so fast," whispered Lonny, "We're safe now."

"Safe?!" I retorted, "Safe! The cops have just been."

"That's why we're safe," said Lonny, "They won't come back. They're probably pissed off answering a false alarm. Lightening never strikes in the same place twice."

"But we can't do anything. The auto-call is still working, isn't it?" I replied, puzzled.

"Yeah, but we don't have to do that one. Let's go along the roof a ways and get down into one of the other buildings."

I was no longer in a laughing mood. "Oh no," I said, suddenly dour, "No, let's go!" The adventure was beginning to pall.

"Look, we've climbed up a bleedin' massive roof like Edmund Hilary and Sherpa Tensing. You pissed yourself; you've farted yourself blind, and now the cops are gone. We can't waste all that work, can we?"

I was silent for a moment then, begrudgingly, I agreed, though not without a great deal of trepidation.

Two dusty, tension-filled hours later, Lonny broke through the ceiling of the street-level shop from the floor immediately above it and jerked back as plaster cascaded onto the counter down below.

After breaking through the roof of the adjacent building, we'd traveled down three floors, inch by inch, in the gloom—three dirty, dusty, empty floors full of rat shit and junk—and now we were at ground level peering through the broken ceiling of the shop.

"What is it?" I asked, aching in every joint and weary of the whole business.

"It's a shop—a sweet shop."

"Oh Christ!" I muttered sarcastically, "I could really do with a Mars Bar, I tell you! That's what I came for!"

A friend and I walked into a general store on the Dock Road to find a malevolent-looking youth filling his pockets with anything he could take from the shelves. He glanced at both of us and said: "Shut yer mouth! I've sent the shopkeeper looking for a bar of Palmolive soap. He has to go down the cellar, see? So—" He clenched his fist in a warning.

When the shopkeeper returned, my companion, who hitherto had come in to buy cigarettes, said expressionlessly to the shopkeeper: "Have you got a bar of Palmolive soap, please mate?"

179

"Naah," said Lonny, "There's a cash register down there—and there'll be cigarettes. We can always sell cigarettes."

I peered down into the hole. The shop was fairly well lit by the light from the front windows, lights which streamed from the pub directly across the road.

I was not happy, particularly as I realized that in three hours, though we had covered a terrifically arduous distance up and down, in terms of horizontal distance, we had, in fact, only moved fifty yards, ending up facing the pub.

"It's too bright down there," I said anxiously as the shadows swirled and flickered with the passage of a pedestrian on the pavement outside.

"No. Anyone looking in can't really see," said Lonny, "It's brighter outside. Unless you get close to the glass, no one will see us."

"I hope so."

"Don't be so windy[2]," said Lonny with a grin. He levered himself through the hole and dropped lightly onto the counter and then onto the floor.

I sighed; but we'd got this far and it seemed pointless to turn back, so I levered myself over the hole and dropped through and stood for a moment on the counter, knees bent. A man passed in front of the shop window. Hastily, I jumped off the counter and crouched by Lonny's side.

Then the dog started barking.

My nerves thrummed taut at the sound. Hidden in the gloom at the far end of the aisle behind the counter, the dog snarled and yipped vociferously.

Courtesy Brendan McCormack

The young man in this picture, walking hastily past Aruthur Dooley's statue of the crucifixion, has just 'acquired' the tire—hence his lack of desire to be photographed

"Shut it up! Shut it up!" I cried in anguish.

Just then, a burly shape loomed up against the window and I ducked back, frozen in fear. It was a policeman; a street constable.

"Yip, yip, yip," went the high-pitched barking.

We went rigid underneath the counter as the looming shape at the window suddenly blossomed a light. The flashlight played across the shelves, the rows of lemonade bottles and the cardboard boxes behind us.

"Shit!" I whispered into Lonny's ear, "What if he sees the hole?!" For once Lonny was silent. In the gloom, I could see that he was just as apprehensive as I was.

The light suddenly snapped off. Footsteps echoed dully on the pavement then gradually faded away. The dog's yipping escalated.

"That bleedin' dog!" I muttered, "Christ! Shut it up, Lonny, shut it up!"

"Yip, yip, yip," went the petulant, insistent bark.

"You shut it up," snarled Lonny.

"What?! You're the hard case, man!" I said, "Shut the fucking thing up before someone else comes!"

"I can't " said Lonny, "Not a dog. I can't "

My nerves rose to a snapping point, exasperated by this unforeseen event: Lonny, who had cheerfully waded his way through the blood and bone of half of Liverpool 8's youth, was reduced to a nervous wreck at the idea of hurting a defenseless dog.

"Oh Jesus Christ!!" I cried. With a moan that was somewhere between anguish and self-hate, I hefted a full lemonade bottle, then swung it in an arc and sent it soaring, full force, into the shadows.

The bottle collided with a dull, meaty thud. There was an anguished yelp. Then silence.

"You've killed it, you bastard!" came Lonny's stricken whisper, "You killed it!"

"Oh Christ almighty!" I said wearily. Not only had I committed the heinous deed but now I had to put up with this! "Lonny, lay off! For Christ's sake, man!!"

I crawled forward across the hard linoleum until I reached the patch of gloom where the dog lay. I extended a quivering hand and jerked it back when something warm and wet touched it. It was the dog's tongue; it had licked my hand. I put out my hand again. The dog began licking at it furiously. I ran my fingers over the pathetic little body. It was warm but shivering with fear; a scrawny, little thing. I chucked it under the chin and whispered words of concern: "C'mon feller, it's O.K....we're O.K....sorry, we didn't want to hurt you." Inside, my heart died with remorse.

Lonny crawled alongside me. "Is it O.K.?" he whispered fearfully.

"Yeah, just frightened. I don't think I hit it properly—it would have killed it. C'mon, let's go." I crawled alongside the counter until I found a door in the wall.

Lonny stood up, punched the cash register, and the drawer slid open with a clang that made me cry out in fear: "Lonny!!"

"Nothing," muttered Lonny, "It's been emptied. C'mon, let's get some cigarettes and get out."

But my nerves were gone completely. I stood silently as Lonny made a hasty search. But the only thing that Lonny could find was candy—candy and soda pop.

"Shit! What a friggin' stupid deal!" I muttered, "Hey, what are you doing!"

Lonny was piling box upon box of sweets up on top of each other: Mars Bars; Kit-Kats. "We can take these," he said, balancing the unwieldy pile against his chest and reaching for another box to put on top.

Despite my irritation, I grabbed a handful of boxes and carried them to the back door of the shop.

It proved much easier getting out than it had been getting in. We simply opened the back door to the alley—and we were out. I peered down the darkened alley. I was loaded with boxes right up to my chin. Lonny at my side carried a similar load.

Nothing. The alley was empty.

At a wordless signal, we stepped into the gloom of the alley and began cat-footing through the rubble and piles of dog shit towards our destination: the huge ring of tenement buildings that loomed up ahead of us blocking out the dim light from the stars.

A noise behind us made me turn. I stopped and peered back as something flashed white in the gloom. "Oh no!" I groaned.

It was the dog. It trotted after us, tail wagging furiously; a little, grayish-white mongrel with an eager, rat-like face and a lolling tongue.

"Shoo!" I hissed, making half-hearted kicking motions with my legs. "Piss off! Go ...! Go...!" I glanced around, fearful of making too much noise, desperately thinking of ways to get rid of the dog other than strangling it. But this was not even a remote possibility. I was so full of remorse that I'd probably have been arrested rather than attempt any further violence on the little creature.

"Here!" cried Lonny sotto-voce. He opened a box and pulled out a Mars Bar. The dog sniffed it appreciatively and made an attempt to snatch it from his hand. But Lonny threw it down the alley as far as he could. The dog ran off into the gloom eagerly, and Lonny tossed three more Mars Bars after it. "Well," said Lonny scooping up his boxes, "That should keep it busy for a while."

"I'm glad you think so," I snorted, "Because—"

Before I could finish, Lonny suddenly bounded into a darkened doorway, shoved his boxes in the corner, grabbed my stack and plonked them down in the gloom.

"Hey, what's up?!" I cried as Lonny squashed me in the corner and clutched me in a very, very, amorous embrace, pressing his cheek against mine. "What's up with you??!!" I cried, my voice muffled by Lonny's cheek. I began to resist furiously, startled by this sudden erotic turn of events.

Lonny's eyes rolled white and wild and he said in a very unromantic voice: "Just bleedin' well shut up!" He held me in a fierce grip that looked like a lover's embrace but felt like a wrestler's death grip.

Then I heard it: The unmistakable, solid tread; boots against cobblestones; the requisite 'two to four miles per hour' of the Bobby-on-the-beat; the citizen's friend; the criminal's curse. The cop was back.

Locked in Lonny's arms, I froze rigid in the gloom of the doorway as the moment heightened in clarity. I could smell Lonny's sweaty skin; the acrid soot and dust from the climb in his hair. I could feel the ache of my bruised knees and, despite the chill of the night, the sweat trickling down between my buttocks.

The doorway suddenly seemed very, very shallow and far too bright for concealment. Wide-eyed, I peered over Lonny's shoulder. All I could see from my love-locked position was the vertical rectangle of the doorway which framed the worn, brick wall opposite that displayed a portion of graffiti: 'Eddie Mac is a...'. I couldn't even move my head the inch or so sideways that would have revealed, once and for all, what it was that Eddie was.

An impossibly tall silhouette blocked out the light as the policeman stopped and peered into the gloom, his shape elongated by his tall helmet.

Lonny grasped me closer in an embrace that would have done justice to Rudolph Valentino and, with his bristly chin raking across my face, he nibbled feverishly and romantically at my neck.

"Alright you two," came a gruff voice.

My bowels gave a heave and may have opened on the spot, save that the policeman chuckled and said: "I don't want to see you two here when I get back. Take 'er home to her mother, lad."

"Yes officer," mumbled Lonny through a mouthful of my hair.

We remained in amorous but fearful stasis as the policeman's boots rang out on the cobblestones. When the footsteps had died away completely, I jerked back from Lonny, spluttering with disgust: "Eagh!!" I pulled a face and flapped my hands about as if they'd been immersed in excreta. "Oh Jesus Christ!! Phaagh!!" I spat on the ground several times and rubbed my face and neck. "Jesus Christ!! You ugly bastard!!"

Lonny grinned at my antics. "C'mon asshole features, cut the crap. It worked, didn't it?" He scooped up the boxes, peered out of the doorway, then hissed, "C'mon, let's go!" We both ran down the alley towards the tenement and safety. "You know, Pittsy," giggled Lonny breathlessly as we ran, balancing the boxes beneath our chins, "There's no doubt about it, you'd probably make someone a real, nice boyfriend!"

"Shut it!" I fumed in embarrassment and exasperation, trying desperately not to drop my less-than-precious load.

It took me almost a week to get over the episode, and, eventually, I met Lonny in a downtown pub. There was no doubt about it. Unpleasant as it had been at the time, it had been an adventure.

Lonny bought me a pie and a pint, then pulled out some money. "There, I sold the sweets to me brother-in-law for his kids. Here's half the money." He shoved the notes into my palm.

I opened my hand and stared at the money: two pounds! I lifted my gaze to Lonny's cheerful face, my mind full of snap-shot memories: the hole in the ceiling; skeetering down the roof; the cop car; the dog; the cop at the window.

I called to the barman for two more pints. But an inner decision had been made; the two pounds had clinched it: My career in Arch Criminality had ended forever—a very fortunate decision on my part.

The Fey Quality Of The Celts

18

The Fey Quality of the Celts

One of the contributing factors to the unique musical scene in Liverpool is the Celtic quality.

This quality—"the fey quality of the Celts"—was captured quite succinctly by Fran Flavelle, a Liverpool lass now working in Canada with *The Canadian Journal of Physics*.

Fran said: "The quality implies an ardent pursuit entered into for its own sake; a passion that is self-perpetuating and all-consuming without a thought of success or an end goal."

In searching for an example that encapsulates all of this, no one seemed to fit it better than Brendan McCormack, former lead guitarist for Rikki and His Redstreaks, the Memphis Three, founder of the International Guitar Festival of Great Britain and one of England's finest classical guitarists.

Brendan's story is many-faceted, and his open spirit and quiet generosity is a study in the best aspects of the fey Celt.

John Lennon's Favorite Guitarist—Brendan McCormack

John Lennon is quoted as saying that a Litherland group called Rikki and His Redstreaks was his favorite, which has caused many Beatle fans to ask who on earth they were. They, in fact, mainly played north-end venues (like Lathom Hall and Litherland Town Hall) where they enjoyed a solid and loyal following.

Bob Wooler

Courtesy Spencer Leigh

The album cover of *Home Is Where The Heart Is* by Jackie Lomax. John Lennon is credited as "Rhythm guitar: Rikki Redstreak".

Brendan McCormack was John Lennon's favorite guitarist.

Billy J. Kramer

In the early rock days of the Merseybeat Sound, Brendan was one of the few guitarists who really understood rock, especially Chuck Berry. It was his raw drive that attracted John Lennon's attention. In fact, so much so, that John was to record as Rikki Redstreak on the album *Home Is Where The Heart Is* in a session with Jackie Lomax of The Undertakers.

In the interview with Bob Wooler (see Chapter 8, *The South Discovers Liverpool*) John is quoted as naming the Redstreaks his favorite band. There is no doubt of John's admiration for Brendan. In fact, after the Beatles broke up, it was debated amogst themselves whether they could appear incognito as Rikki and His Redstreaks.

Brendan was a very early veteran of the group scene, moving from the Redstreaks to the Harlems with drummer Gibson Kemp. All in all, he did about forty gigs with the Beatles and there was a great deal of time for John Lennon to watch his style. Brendan had drive. In particular, he could play a Chuck Berry solo like nobody else, and it was probably this drive which attracted John, who was a "raw" player himself. Brendan often chatted with the Beatles, in particular

Jackie Lomax of the Undertakers

Paul, who shared many of his hopes, fears and aspirations with him in the band room. Brendan recalls:

Brendan McCormack when he was playing with the Memphis 3, 1962

"Sadly, I can't recall any of the conversations, which is probably a good thing because we were, at the time, just two Liverpool lads from local bands sharing the kind of mundane conversation that takes place between all teenagers. The Beatles were good, but in Liverpool, they were, at the start, just another band, another four Scousers, just like us.

Brendan was somewhat unusual in Liverpool in that he went deeply into classical music, transcending his guitarist origins and becoming something more than just a guitar player—a musician in his own right. In fact, he is currently scoring for the London Philharmonic Orchestra. On the following pages, we see some of his multifaceted abilities

A typical Liverpool Irish lad, Brendan was brought up in Scotland Road where the police had to walk in threes, it was so violent. Brendan was a lad who, more than once, had to defend his honor with fists and boots.

Prompted solely by that fey quality described above, Brendan locked himself away in a little room above his mother's pub with a bust of Bach and Beethoven and assiduously taught himself classical guitar. It makes an interesting tale.

Brendan playing Bach at the Irish Center, 1965

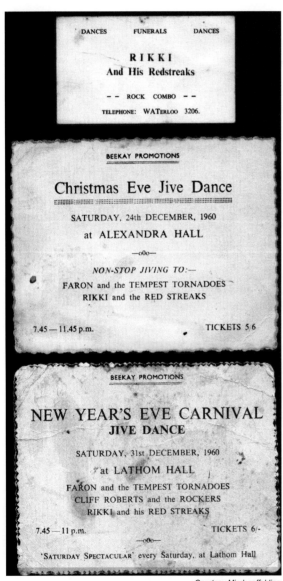

**Some programs from Brendan's rock 'n roll days with
Rikki and the Redstreak**
Note: They even played for funerals

Brendan as an exponent of the lute

"Ma McCormack's", as the Wilbraham was known affectionately, was a pub famed on the grapevine for staying open after-hours. Every night, sing-songs went on until the early hours, fueled by much heavy drinking. Along with the Irish laborers and shift workers was a sprinkling of night people—musicians, artists, actors—drawn to the drink and camaraderie, both quite illicit at that hour.

John Slater, a famous English actor from London, was one such thirsty artiste who found his way to Ma McCormack's after a night's performance at the Royal Court Theater in Liverpool. Mrs. McCormack recognized John, cornered him, and began telling him what a wonderful guitarist her son was. Overwhelmed by the Proud-Ma syndrome, John diplomatically agreed to hear Brendan out. What else could he do? He was surrounded by Irish laborers, Mrs. McCormack was the proprietor and John, after all, was drinking quite illegally. The staple of the music on the pub record-player was, of course, C&W, Irish songs like *My Mother's Eyes* and *The Green, Green Grass of Home* by Tom Jones, so it was not with a great deal of enthusiasm that classicist John viewed Brendan's forthcoming performance. Slater was astounded when Brendan sat down on a stool in the noisy pub and, amidst the smoke, the cigarette packets, the smell of beer, played with exquisite timing a number of Bach preludes on a lovely, handmade guitar.

Courtesy Mindscaffolding

Brendan with guitarist Charlie Byrd (right) and John Duarte

Courtesy Mindscaffolding

Brendan with George Benson at the Montreux Jazz Festival, 1996

Courtesy Mindscaffolding

Brendan with Julian Bream, 1969

John left, quite amazed at this unexpected find. He returned at a later date and this time brought back a BBC camera crew. They did an entire program on Brendan, along the lines of the metaphor 'the rose of culture amidst the debris of the city'.

And, corny as it sounds, it was true.

Thus, fame and fortune lay at Brendan's feet. John invited Brendan down to London. Yet, in typical fey, Celtic fashion, Brendan declined. The reason: "I didn't feel like going," he recalls.

Courtesy Mindscaffolding

Ma McCormack's Pub, the Wilbraham

Though he turned his back on the bright lights of London *that* time, talent will out, and Brendan went on to become one of the chief exponents the of classical guitar (and lute) in the north of England. He is also the founder and organizer of the Annual International Guitar Festival of Great Britain.

Brendan is the founder and director of the annual International Guitar Festival of Great Britain.
The artists featured on this brochure are (top left to right):
Row 1: Chuck Berry, Cephas and Wiggins, Gordon Giltrap and Martin Taylor
Row 2: Hill/Wiltschinsky duo, Martin Pleass
Row 3: Jaleo flamenco troupe, John Pearson, Wulfin Lieske
Row 4: Eduardo Niebla and Antonio Forcione, Raphaella Smits, Jill Nott-Bower and Robert Spencer

Recently, Brendan, who is also one of the core organizers of such events as the Liverpool Beatles' Festival, was featured in a series of interviews with Astrid, the girlfriend of the former Beatle Stu Sutcliffe who died in the '60s. Brendan's insight into the founding period of Liverpool music is quite acute. When asked to comment on the unique character of Liverpool musicians, he came up with the following. He is also a talented calligrapher.

Liverpool 1956.
A drizzly November night and from the docks
the smell of maize and molasses in the air.
I'm outside the music shop with a guitar —
my first and with only enough to buy 2 strings.
You get the picture?

I decide on a 5th and 6th Cathedral brand
and make do with electrical cable core
for the remaining four.

Within 3 weeks I'm in business; 6 real
strings, sore fingers, no chords yet,
but the sound of Rock'n Roll in my ears.

At that time in Liverpool the spirit of
Django Reinhardt was very much alive and
the Jazz Guitarists' Litany of Eddie Lang,
Kress and McDonough and Lonnie Johnson
was fueled by tales of visits by Les Paul
and Big Bill Broonzy.

But on my near horizon was Sun Records,
Chuck Berry and my first electric guitar.

In 1964 I did some recording for Tony Hatch and did a stint in Hamburg at the Star Club: 2 hours on and 1 off in 12 hour shifts [4p.m – 4a.m.] helped develop a solid Rhythmic Style which was the core of the "Mersey Sound" at that time.

I also remember the Star Club as being the first house P.A. System to use Reverb and this coupled with decent Sennheiser Mics made things seem very exotic.

I returned home and had some lessons with Terry Usher [late Prof. R.N.C.M.] and later with Emilio Pujol in Lerida.

I've played solo classical guitar ever since.

For the past 5 years I've been Director of The International Guitar Festival of Great Britain and have yet to put to proper use a good working knowledge of the early lyrics [1956–59] of Chuck Berry!

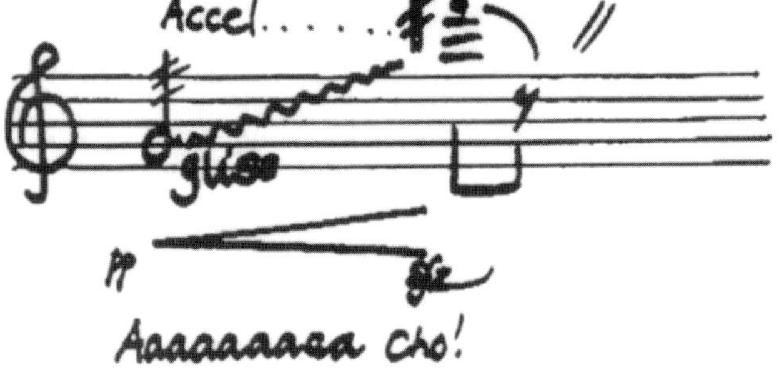

Accel . . . . . .

gliss

pp

Aaaaaaaaa cho!

Brendan's history also throws another interesting sidelight on our story.

The fact is that in the early '60s there was not a black guitarist in sight. Well, there was one—even, perhaps, two. It is a puzzling fact and quite contrary to the recent claims made by young up-and-coming blacks in the British media. This is not hearsay—it is a fact. In a city with over 350 bands, *none* of the players were black. And there is a very distinct reason for this.

Not A Black Guitarist In Sight

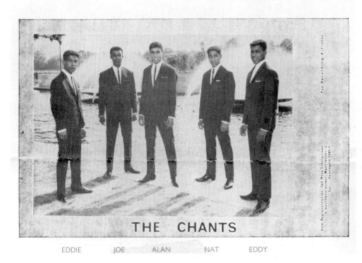

The Chants, one of the few all-black groups in Liverpool

The existence of The Harlems—an all-white group led by guitarist Brendan McCormack—backing up an all-black singing group, The Chants, points to an interesting factor at the root of the Merseyside sound.

It is something that is covered in fascinating detail by Ben Sidran in his accomplished book *Black Talk.* Ben shows that the primary urge in black music—an urge stemming from its African tribal roots—is the oral tradition. This is not the place to delve in depth into this fascinating story, but simply put, throughout the history of black music in America, these transposed Africans have manifested the oral tradition in their music—even when they played instruments. Their primary instruments were the trumpet (breath) and saxophone (breath)—and singing (breath).

Another interesting sidelight is that The Chants, a black do-wop group, were being backed by white Liverpool Irishmen, The Harlems. When they toured Ireland in the '60s, the Irish thought The Chants were white singers in blackface, as they'd never seen black men before!

The Liverpool blacks were exactly the same: they leaned towards the oral traditions of group singing.

The fact is—and it is an indisputable fact—that though the Mersey Sound was built on black music, it was white guitarists emulating black Americans—and not the Liverpool blacks—who formed the basis of the music revolution.

Courtesy Mindscaffolding

The Harlems, Brendan McCormack far left

Liverpool Blacks

Liverpool Blacks

Courtesy Bernie Wenton

The Queen's Coronation, June 1953
The young Bernie Wenton is standing in the front row, far left

Liverpool's black history is rather unique in that the city had a very strong black presence even before the large influx of Caribbean blacks in 1952.

This Coronation street scene is dated 1953 and yet there are a number of blacks present who are obviously well integrated into the local scene. Also, notice how happy everybody is. Street celebrations were a rare event and life was so spartan that when such an occasion arose everybody threw themselves into it with gusto.

Liverpool was a sea port on all the major trade routes, thus, what took place was a natural migratory drift. Blacks had been arriving in Liverpool sporadically since the turn of the century. Some of them were even American in origin—slaves who had been given freedom in return for fighting for the English during the War of Independence.

In fact, during the second half of the nineteenth century, the St. James Parish register recorded a number of these former slaves being baptized. A 1911 census of Liverpool showed a black population of

3,000 in a city of 750,000. By 1920, there were 5,000 and by 1948, 8,000. And all this occurred *before* the McCarren-Waler Act which brought in the sudden influx from the Caribbean.

Interestingly enough, the first blacks lived in and around Pitt Street but slum clearance and war-time damage meant a move to the Granby Street area which, incidentally, is where the author was born.

Furthermore, after World War 2, there were no restrictions on entry into Britain from Commonwealth countries. The first ship load of immigrants came on the Empire Windrush in 1949.

Courtesy Charlie Jenkins

The Whitehouse Pub, 1963
Charlie Jenkins, left, with Les Smith, guitarist, George Pierce, drummer, and John McLean, guitarist

CHARLIE JENKINS is a gem of a man and a fine guitarist. A black Liverpudlian, he can trace his origins back over 200 years. Charlie is a connoisseur of the Liverpool clubs that existed before rock 'n roll. He was primarily a jazz guitarist, though he did play other genres. His grandfather was a well-known figure in Liverpool. The only work for black people at that time was either as a self-employed shopkeeper or a seaman and, Edward Jenkins, who ran his own business, became quite a celebrity such that he entertained other prominent blacks like Paul Robeson and the Deep River Boys when they came to Liverpool.

Charlie's life is a veritable who's-who of the black and white club owners

Courtesy Charlie Jenkins

Charlie Jenkins and some Welsh waiters playing skiffle at a holiday camp in Prestatyn, North Wales, late '50s

who run Liverpool's social scene. He even, at one time, played skiffle with a group of waiters in nearby Prestatyn, North Wales.

St. James School Boxing Team, 1944

St. James was a non-denominational church school in Liverpool that took in many of the ethnic groups: Norwegian, Pakistani, Indian and African. The local Catholic school would not take any ethnic boys. As an act of almost poetic justice, a boxing team was formed at St. James and prominent in the team were a number of strapping young blacks. They then took away the boxing title from the Catholic school which had hitherto refused the admission of ethnic minorities, and continued to trounce them every year.

Holy Trinity was another non-denominational school that accepted ethnic minorities. Three of the boys in this picture went on to become seamen and, sadly, they were all torpedoed in World War 2.

Holy Trinity School, 1933
Back row, second on the right is Charlie Jenkin's father. Charlie was a skiffle player on the Liverpool scene before the Merseybeat started. He belonged to the old school of jazz players and he has played clubs in Liverpool for almost 50 years

The Mandoline Club,, 1961

Charlie's photograph album presents an incredible picture of the mixture of Irish whites and immigrant blacks who thronged to Liverpool's numerous clubs. Charlie tells of one poignant scene which was a regular event on Saturday nights in Stanhope Street, Liverpool 8:

> *When you arrived on a Saturday night, it looked like there was a war on. The streets were milling with black soldiers from the nearby American air base at Burtonwood. You see, these black soldiers were segregated on the base. They were not allowed to go to the white American soldiers' dances, so they would come to the black area in Liverpool to the clubs where blacks and whites mixed. They could also buy cheap wine over the counter. It was the one place they could enjoy themselves without that segregation thing taking place.*

The fact is, though no nation is ever totally free of racism, it can be seen from the photographs that blacks and whites met on equal terms in the pubs.

Above, Joey Ankara of The Chants is seen in the Mandoline Club with an equal sprinkling of blacks and whites. The chap looking at the camera is Terry Wenton, the father of boxer Richie Wenton who won the Lonsdale Belt.

However, tales of Liverpool blacks will, of necessity, give the wrong impression to an American reader. For, although they abound with violence and aggression, there is a qualitative difference to this. Even in the

Stanley House club, Parliament Street near the author's home, 1958

The blacks got down with whites. This picture shows Ronnie Thomas strutting his stuff with a white girl in a magnificent velvet dress while two middle-aged, white Liverpudlians look on.

197

The Bedford Club, early '60s

From left to right: Archie Dawson, Stan Ballard, Charlie Jenkins, Sid Lyon, owner of the Flamingo Club, Eddie Jenkins, Charlie's Dad and Harry Evans, famous snooker player

riots in Liverpool during the Seventies, the significant factor was economic depression and not racism—poor whites were as equally involved in the uprising.

The violence and crime in Liverpool was not symptomatic of racial hostility but poverty and the contradictions of a consumer society which affected poor blacks and whites alike.

Sixties England was, in fact, more of a socialist country than is often realized. Transport a black American back to the England of the Sixties and they would realize, very quickly, that they'd never had it so good.

Of course, racism does exist in England, but it does not suffer from that intense racial bitterness and paranoia that expresses itself in the urban areas of America; the legacy of slavery.

Furthermore, the blacks, themselves, are a different breed. Apart from the influx described above post-war, other blacks arriving were either West Indian or African and, as such, have a different slang, lifestyle and attitude to their cousins in America.

The West Indians are very proud of their Britishness and many of them occupy key positions, particularly in hospitals and the medical services. Unlike their American counterparts, they have never had to regard themselves as inferior. There is not the deep-rooted stigma of slavery and oppression that haunts the American Black. They have a very distinctive culture which is Jamaican or Trinidadian, with their own music, language and lifestyle, while, at the same time regarding themselves as subjects of the Queen.

The royal tradition is one which goes very deep with the blacks, springing from tribality. West Indians, when it comes to group accolades, are right there in the front line, cheering on the Royal family with a mixture of veneration and joy.

Similarly, the Africans who come straight to England from Africa have a high esteem for the English and its royal tradition. The fact is that tribally, they come from a royalist tradition, too. Thus Africans have taken readily to English society, and it is not an uncommon experience to be treated in an English hospital by an African surgeon with an Oxford accent—and tribal scars on his cheeks.

Thus, given these social factors, in Liverpool it was possible to break down barriers between

Charlie Jenkins, left, playing at the Mona Club, Berkley Street, 1962

black and white through drugs, music, dance—and heart. But this is all relative, and an Englishman, who's never experienced the bitter and ruthless racial hatred in America, might think differently. He may mistakenly think that the much watered-down racism he experiences in England is equivalent to the racism in America—but it is definitely not so.

The main problems arose, as always, from the second and third generation black youths who didn't know *what* they were. Their language was an odd patois of their own Liverpool slang and a corrupt West Indian which was unintelligible to the uninitiated. Their subculture revolved around dance and music, and their musical talent, though considerable, was often outweighed by their inability to communicate or to fit into the predominantly white world of the music-recording business.

In Liverpool, it was wonderful to hear and to watch black performances, often conducted spontaneously in the streets and in the pubs—as mentioned in the opening chapters. But, the rough, aggressive and illiterate nature of these blacks told against them. Despite their ability, during the Liverpool boom of the Sixties, their crudeness made promoters back off, and these talented blacks were left behind in Liverpool.

It was an odd paradox. It was the poor Liverpool whites who took the American black music, injected it with working-class venom and returned it to America "with its balls back", while the black musicians in England could not find a place in the U.S. pop scene simply because it was still impossible in America for a black to "sing with balls in the Sixties". That was not to come 'til much later with rap music.

The fact is, when blacks arrived in Liverpool, they were held in deep admiration by Liverpool musicians. They seemed so cool. As teenagers, we wanted to *be* like them; to walk, talk and dance like them. Of course, we could not. But some of their hip blackness did seep in by osmosis.

In Liverpool 8 there was a tremendously characterful woman Member of Parliament named Bessie Braddock who was adored by the poor. She took an active interest in all the kids and though she was white and middle-aged she began to help the Chants when they got their first recording contract with Pye. Bessie, a wonderful woman did what she could to help the Chants. Of course in retrospect it is obvious why, despite their musical talents, which were considerable, the group broke up without any major successes. However, two members of the group did do quite well as part of the soul group The Real Thing.

The fact of Charlie Jenkin's existence as a black guitarist does not change the fact that the rock 'n roll era in Liverpool was paved by white Liverpool guitarists playing black American music.

Charlie's tradition, and that of his cohorts, belonged to the era before rock 'n roll although Charlie was contemporary with it. It was an era of American big band music, of Django Rheinhart, or those early guitar heroes like Eddie Lang or Charlie Christian when jazz was played traditional style on big-bodied guitars. Charlie was as modern as anyone and, in fact, he was one of the first to ever use an echo chamber in Liverpool.

However, the two or three black guitarists who were active on the Liverpool club scene were hardly anything when compared to the 1,000 or so working white guitarist who belonged to the 350+ bands in Liverpool.

As Roger Glover of *Deep Purple* said: "We are the last generation to remember what life was like before rock 'n roll."

Charlie Jenkins and his colleagues can actually bear witness to both the before and the after, spanning, as they did, two major musical epochs.

The Deckers at Stanley House, 1956

The Deckers at the Pergasus Club, Liverpool, 1964
Left to right: Les O'Connor (husband of Mary), Robbie Devine, Charlie Jenkins and Mary O'Connor

Courtesy Charlie Jenkins

Some of the clubs that Charlie Jenkins frequented and played in, early '60s

Courtesy Charlie Jenkins

Charlie Jenkins and his first cousins, 1944
The ready integration of blacks and white post-World War 2 is revealed in this family picture taken on the steps of his family home where Charlie sits with his many cousins, some with corn-blonde hair, others jet black.

Courtesy Charlie Jenkins

A racially mixed Liverpool Elementary School in 1946

The following anecdote is an attempt to show the breadth and nature of the black experience in Liverpool in real-life anecdotes. To reiterate: the violence which was precipitated was less an agent of black-white relationships and more a reflection of the violence lying beneath the surface ready to explode at any time in Liverpool, black or white, because the divisions between poor black and poor white were blurred.

A Black Odyssey: From Lightest Coffee to Deepest Black
—A Personal Anecdote—

I was playing chess—sort of.

Lunchtime. New Year's Eve in The Grapes, the pub in the narrow alley opposite The Cavern and I was playing chess.

I had just finished a raucous, pumping, ear-splitting set at the Cavern; a pre-New Year's Eve special arranged by Ray McFall the manager and hosted by an elegantly-clad, highly-articulate Bob Wooler. And now it was relaxation time.

But I could not relax. And though the pub was crowded, to me it felt empty—empty of support.

At the next table sat my hero, a huge giant of a youth dressed in a large Teddy-Boy suit, his hair swept back in a gigantic quiff. This was Kingsize Teddy Taylor, leader of The Dominoes. I was an ardent fan of The Dominoes. Though I had never talked to Teddy Taylor, the lead singer, I'd watched hundreds of their sets, afire with admiration for Kingsize's raunchy style, his massive frame huddled over a guitar rendered diminutive by his bulk while he wrenched guttural chords from the neck of his semi-acoustic guitar.

At that moment, Teddy was sitting, quiet and serene, talking to a fellow musician. Teddy was a fine singer and performer who served his time in the grueling gigs in Hamburg. He was also able to offer posterity some of the earliest Beatles' recordings because the Beatles swapped some of their Hamburg tapes for a few pints of beer during their impecunious days. At the time, that's all the tapes seemed worth because no one ever dreamed of the incredible fame that would be bestowed upon the four lads and, by association, anyone who knew them.

But such doubtful accolades were yet to come, and the future for Teddy was a gauzy veil, as it was for the musician with whom he was chatting—Pete Best, the Beatles' drummer..

I had a passing acquaintanceship with Pete and had visited Pete's mother's club, The Casbah, a few times. At that moment, Pete sat chatting quietly, dressed in the German leather pants and black jacket that was later to propel, not he, but the rest of the band to world fame.

I strained my ears to catch the conversation between Pete and Teddy. They were talking albums, licks, new releases, muso's gossip, the stuff that made my heart sing. But, unfortunately, I could not just walk over and join them as I was playing chess.

But this was a game of chess strictly

The Grapes, the pub where the incident on the following pages took place

While touring with Chuck Berry, so the story goes, Teddy, being a big man, preferred the back of the tour coach. Apparently, so did Chuck Berry, and Teddy allegedly remarked: "You're the first black man I've ever met who tried to fight his way to the *back* of the bus."

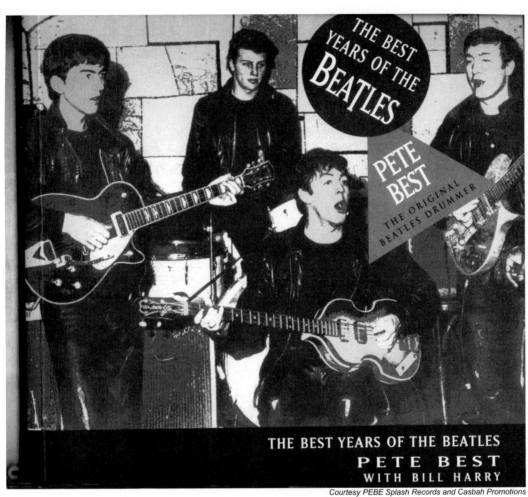

The cover of Pete Best's book, *The Best Years of the Beatles*, 1999

Courtesy PEBE Splash Records and Casbah Promotions

Pete Best's "firing" has been argued over many times and many theories abound. This, in itself, should give rise to the thought: why *should* there be so much argument? And, because the root causes are still so vague, the answer may be simple. After all, we were dealing with young 18 year-olds who are naturally inarticulate about their true wants and desires in the group situation. Who, at age 18, would know what really made them tick?

The facts are that Paul and John were two budding alpha males and George, much younger, followed in the rear with not much say at all at the time. There was little room for a third strong, moody personality (Pete was very much like an early James Dean with his looks and charm) —and much revered by the girls. In the end, perhaps his greatest sin was that he was too good looking. I mean, look at his replacement (no offense intended—I love Ringo!)

in the metaphysical sense. A game of abstract maneuvering, careful consideration and lightening moves which took an immense amount of skill. I was balancing on egg-shells.

In other words, I had been dragged into conversation with Jo-Jo.

Jo-Jo was a fearsome sight. He was as black as the ace of spades with a shaven head and a lean and handsome face marred by a feral watchfulness that promoted instant fear in all whom he surveyed. Jo-Jo loved to play with his prey, cat-and-mouse, before moving in for the kill. And it was the kill that I was trying to avoid. Jo-Jo had not asked me to sit down—it had been an order. Knowing which side my bread was buttered, I had obeyed.

I knew that I was being toyed with. I also knew that as I was a musician and, amidst the crafty mind-games being played by the psychopathic Jo-Jo, there was a spark of genuine interest. There were few options for me in this game apart from a split lip and four missing teeth—or worse. So, with heartfelt trepidation, I had to play along with Jo-Jo.

The maneuvers were difficult. Jo-Jo's questions were tricks designed to trip me into some false statement. The Catch 22 was that sometimes a truthful reply would also be sufficiently confrontational to precipitate Jo-Jo into violence. This was the chess game that Jo-Jo played so adroitly, a murderous smile playing about his thick lips while he watched me through narrowed eyes.

We were surrounded by a watchful circle of black faces and Ted, a white who, having been born in the same house as Jo-Jo, had a certain, though not inviolable, immunity. Ted watched the game somberly with a weary compassion, knowing there was nothing to do but wait until it played itself out or Jo-Jo tired of it.

My tension increased as Jo-Jo goaded me with another facile, insincere question. By this time, I was so fed up that I was near to throwing caution to the winds and letting the inevitable happen. But my racing mind fixed on a possible solution in an echo of Moo's words: "When the going gets tough, remember you're with the band."

It would be a dangerous move, but I was weary and frustrated. All I wanted to do was move over to Kingsize Taylor and Pete Best to chat about music and here I was roped into a conversation about dope, about fighting, about gangs I'd never heard of, with people I didn't care about, by a black psychopath who was watching my every move with cruel enjoyment.

Suddenly, I broke out of the game. "Yeah, of course, that's your deal," I said.

Jo-Jo stared at me through narrowed eyes. "What?" he said. The syllable cut through the smoky air like a cold blade.

"Fighting, man," I said, "You guys like to fight, you're good at it-"

"How about you?" said Jo-Jo in a deathly cold challenge, his fist clenching involuntarily on the table. But Jo-Jo was curious; waiting to see the drift of the conversation.

I shrugged. "If someone jumps me, that's it—you gotta do something. But I don't mean that. What I mean is everyone's got his thing. Like Jerome " I jerked my thumb over to the corner where a long-haired youth was leaning across a table talking urgently to a blonde girl, "He's into chicks." I pointed at Ted, "An' Ted, he's into dope, man."

"Who isn't?" sneered Jo-Jo.

"Yeah, who isn't—right," I said. "But, like, Ted does it, man. He sells it, he buys it, he uses it. It's, like, when he's doing something with dope, he's satisfied—it's his life. And it's the same with you," I shrugged, "You fight, and that's what you do—like it's your job. You know this guy Picasso? Well, his thing is painting, man. And he concentrates on it, like, night and day. And that's what I mean about you and fighting."

Jo-Jo's eyes flashed. "Yeah—so what?" He eyed me through slit eyes as he thought about it.

"Well, that's it. That's your thing, man."

Suddenly it got through.

"Yeah, man!" said Jo-Jo, two hundred pounds of trained, fit, homicidal muscle and bone, "I LIKE that! Fighting's my thing -yeah!" With a short laugh, he whipped a knife out of his pocket and stropped it on his rock-hard calf muscle. "Like my knife—I chose it special, man, not like one of these divvies[1] who buys it in a pawn shop. Check it out—strong, clean." He whistled it through the air, "Beat that!"

The other blacks around the table whipped out their knives for comparison and I relaxed as they began an animated conversation about knives—speed; size; effectiveness—in which I was temporarily forgotten.

Taking advantage of this, I leaned over to the other table and said to Pete: "How's it going, man?"

Pete grimaced, "Hey, man... I dunno...."

I stood up and nodded at Jo-Jo who was still stropping the large blade on his leg. "Catch you later, man," he said.

"Yeah," grinned Jo-Jo, "You got style, man. I like that."

I nodded deadpan as my belly de-contracted like a rusty spring and I went off to where I belonged—with the musicians.

3 P.M. New Year's Eve. Huskission Street

And by a freak of chance, the sun is shining. Its wan, wintry yellow cuts across a pale, blue sky that hinted at far more extreme weather. But, for the moment, the watery sunshine gave an unlikely illusion of warmth to the well-muffled gossipers who sat on the steps of the crumbling, terraced houses around Faulkner Square, the center of Liverpool 8.

I had walked there from the pub, pushing through the New Year's Eve shopping crowds that milled on the downtown pavements. Now I sat contentedly on the first step of my sister's house, flushed on four pints of bitter, watching the kids play ring-a-rosie, hop-scotch and other involved, complex skipping games accompanied by hoots, chants and litanies that have become part of the Liverpool street culture.

On the other side of the road, the pub door burst open, spilling out four black youths who had taken advantage of the New Year's extended pub hours to get in early drinking before the night rush. They all wore black, pork-pie hats, sunglasses (though the sun was usually very little in evidence), narrow-shouldered, long, black overcoats that reached below their calves, and short, tight black pants hovering a good six inches above their shoes and socks. They were my next-door, West-Indian neighbors, sons of Shelley.

At first, the West Indian accent was a source of misunderstanding. Freddie, the Trinidadian who owned my house in Huskisson Street, the black area, came to my door one morning asking for an Oxo which, in England, is a beef stock cube. Confusion reigned for ages until I realized he was asking for a "hacksaw". Similarly, I often wondered why the black guy next door had a girl's name - Shirley - until I realized it was Shelley said with a West Indian accent, "Sher-ley".

Dutch Eddies, 1961
A club in Stanhope Street, Liverpool 8, that both blacks and whites frequented

Courtesy Charlie Jenkins

One of them had a shiny, cheap transistor looped around his neck, and they bopped, skipped and finger-clicked their way across the street to the tinny music. They threaded their way adroitly through the hordes of disinterested kids, black and white, playing skipping games, side-stepped grubby, snotty-nosed boys, then mounted the steps of the next-door house.

"Hey, hey Pittsy!" one of them shouted, swaying his shoulders in time to the music, "Happy New year, mon!"

I nodded, and, pursing my lips, pushed them forward in the traditional West Indian acknowledgement. Then the four were gone.

My sister's voice called from behind. It was dinner time, one of her gargantuan snacks. My belly rumbled. "Coming!" I called.

Bernie Wenton (right) and his brother Bobbie
Look at their shoes—they are obviously hand-me-downs, just like the author's shoes were

New Year's Eve. Seven o'clock. Too nearly to celebrate; too late to sleep off the effect of the gargantuan meal. Anticipating a night of Bacchanalian celebration, I was off to score.

I rounded the corner of Upper Parliament Street and into the momentary blaze of lights at the Rialto intersection. The Rialto, an old, regal-style cinema, was boarded up, but from inside came the rasp of an electric guitar and the multiple harmony of a black singing group.

Blacks. Practising. A harmony group.

Despite the cold, there were more blacks out on the pavements than whites: old blacks; young blacks; stooped or limber; dull-faced, sharp-eyed; cool-suited youths with broad shoulders. They eyed me as I turned and sauntered down the narrow street that would take me to the Gambling House. They all knew what I wanted.

The Gambling House was, strictly speaking, black territory. But, in general, they only ripped off strangers or idiots. I had a certain immunity because my sister's mother-in-law had married a black man, but I still had to watch my body language. To act too cool, with too much self-confidence, was an open invitation to be jumped. The way in which you walked was very important in these areas of inter-ethnic truce.

The Gambling House was an ordinary terraced house on a dark corner. A very, very dark corner, simply because, at this point, all the street lights had been deliberately broken by the blacks. Thus, the entrance to the Gambling House—from which the front door had been removed—was a bright rectangle of yellowish light set in the inky blackness. And, as such, anyone approaching or leaving the Gambling House could be seen quite clearly by the watchers in the gloom.

I knew there were any number of eyes watching me turn into the doorway. But it was O.K.—no one emerged from the shadows to stop me. I loped up the grimy, unpainted stairs, turned a corner, and, reaching the top, stepped cautiously into a large room, and paused.

Lit only by a number of lamps which hung down low over a worn, green billiard table, the room was full of blacks. Scattered around on wooden benches and creaking chairs, sat black men—fat, thin, young, old—intent on the green baize table. Beneath its lights, sweating, grim-faced Negroes leaned over, rattling dice in one hand, clutching money in the other.

Everyone knew I was there the moment I stepped into the room, but no one looked at me. This was their territory and, as such, they were at ease. I was the intruder.

It was a unique establishment; a little piece of

Linguistic Variation

When the West Indians arrived in Liverpool, they brought with them their culture - and their slang. This was absorbed into Liverpudlian idiom, often without Liverpudlians realizing where it came from. Tompy, spliff, etc., were marijuana terms and other terms such as the obscenities "raas-clat", "ofay", "bomba-claat" were used by white Scousers as often as any other vulgarity.

When I went to London years later, I was at first greeted with puzzlement and hostility by the West Indians there because they thought I was imitating jive-talk—until they realized I didn't know that these were West-Indian terms and that I was just swearing "naturally" because of my black Liverpool upbringing

ACHIEVEMENTS

M any talented people have emerged from the community. Their different achievements are all an expression of the community's spirit.

50 James Clarke, local 'coloured' swimming champion in 1908.

54 John Conteh, world heavy-weight champion in 1974.

52 The Chants, a vocal act from the Upper Parliament Street area. They performed in the Cavern in the early '60s. One of their promoters was local MP, Bessie Braddock.

49 John Archer was born in Blake Street, Liverpool, in 1863. After his marriage he went to live in Battersea, working as a photographer. He became a Councillor and in November 1913 Mayor of Battersea - the first Black person in Britain to occupy such a position. In 1919 he visited the Mayor of Liverpool to discuss the race riots. He was involved in the Pan-African movement, radical politics and in local community action. He died in 1932.

53 Levi Tafari, rap poet.

55 Howard Gayle, footballer, who now plays for Blackburn Rovers.

56 Cathy Tyson, who shot to fame in the award-winning film 'Mona Lisa' and Craig Charles, poet and TV-personality.

57 Derrie Wilkie, vocalist and pioneer of the Black Liverpool music scene in the '60s. Renowned for his lively stage shows.

58 Toxteth Community Radio, the popular local channel.

51 Ludwig Hesse, community activist and organiser of the 'Coloured Seamen's Union', in 1948.

Charlie Jenkins, right, and Tommy at Dutch Eddies, 1961

West Indian culture transplanted wholesale to Liverpool. Gambling was illegal, but the police, tired of trying to suppress it, had turned a blind eye. Anyway, no one gambled with dice in Liverpool—except blacks—as no one else knew the rules.

I waited a moment until I caught the eye of a heavy black man with a rotund belly. With barely a discernible flicker of his eye-brows, the man called me over and pursed his lips in the unspoken West Indian question: "What is it?"

At Dutch Eddies, 1959
Codie, left, Renee, Wilf Johnson, Esme and Oddie Taylor

"Got any tobacco, man?" I asked.

The black man nodded then, suddenly, his expression changed; a frown crossed his face and he said in a loud voice that made me go red with embarrassment: "Too-bacco mon?! Too-bacco? Hey, raas, what do yo tin' dis is? A fockin' sweet shop?"

Laughter rocked the room and feeling like a white slug, I backed away, my face burning. I shuffled down the stairs gnawing my lip in agitation.

As he did so, a wiry black of about forty followed me, caught my arm and steered me into the toilet. It stank—a bowl over-flowing with excrement, cigarette butts and toilet paper—but neither of us was concerned about that.

"What you at, man?" said the black man. His accent was Liverpool, not West Indian.

I hesitated, then answered truthfully: "I just wanted to score," I shrugged, "What's the problem?"

"The problem is, the owner is here—and he don't want any trouble. Scorin's O.K., but not in front of him. You know what happened...eh?"

I nodded. I *did* know. The owner had, it seems, achieved the impossible: He had *shot* a white tax man in court, won his plea of insanity and was now out and about—free—though exercising a certain degree of understandable caution. "Yeah, sorry, man," I muttered, "I didn't know... I understand."

"Here, what do you want?" said the man extending his hand.

I hesitated again, then sighed. The man heard the sigh and knew the unspoken statement was: '*O.K., here you go, you can rip me off if you want—I won't do anything. But wouldn't it be nicer if you didn't?*' There was a heartfelt message in the sigh. And, oddly enough, the man responded. I gave him the money, he disappeared upstairs and returned rapidly a moment later to press a wad of brown paper into my hand.

"Split, man," he whispered, "You didn't get it here."

"Hey," I said, "Thanks."

The man gripped my hand and grinned, knowing that I meant '*thanks for not ripping me off*', then disappeared into the gloom.

When I got to the bottom of the stairs, I couldn't resist taking a brief peak inside the packet. I was visible from the street and a West Indian voice floated up from the gloom: "It's charas, mon," followed by a deep chuckle, "What else?"

I nodded amicably towards the unseen voice. The man was wrong, it was grass, but I wasn't going to argue, and I sauntered off towards the lights of the main street set for a night of New Year's revelry, Liverpool style.

R.A.A.S.

The swear word "raas-clat" (meaning "your ass cloth") is used frequently by West Indians, and, to them, it is very vulgar. When they arrived in Britain, the word was unknown to middle-class Brits. So, mischievously, a group of London West Indians formed an organization which was called something like "The Revolutionary Anti-Apartheid Society" so that the huge initial letters on the building spelled out "R.A.A.S". When posh British announcers with plummy British accents would talk on TV about the "Membahs of the West-Indian Society RAAS..." (they pronounced it "rarse") the West Indians would fall over laughing. To understand the joke, just imagine that the initials of such an organization spelled out something like A.S.S.H.O.L.E.

9 P.M.. St. James' Cemetery.

The joint glows like a minute brazier, flickering red in the gloom. Seeds pop, and I inhale deeply from the thick, three-paper spliff rolled faithfully to West Indian standards. It is huge, it is nasty, it is acrid, but I inhale it with all the joie-de-vivre of a wine connoisseur imbibing a Nuit St. George.

The gravestone is cold on my back. I am alone in the vast pit of St. James' Cemetery which lies below the massive bulk of the huge Anglican Cathedral. Above me, the outlines of the cathedral rise into the sky like the head and shoulders of a giant.

Above me is Gambier Terrace, the once exclusive houses of the gentry, now split into scores of low-rent apartments mainly occupied by students. In the end apartment resides a not-yet-famous John with a still-living Stu Sutcliffe.

But, oblivious to posterity, I draw contentedly on my joint, eyeing the cranes silhouetted starkly against the city sky; cranes that have been perched over the cathedral for as long as I could remember; a symbol of the lack of funds and the work that ceased more than fifteen years before.

The walls of the graveyard are steep and deep—fifty feet, in places. They are criss-crossed with ramparts and pitted with caves like the dwellings of Pueblo Indians. Some of them have been used as catacombs; others have become a trysting place for street urchins and illicit lovers, who, in the warmer weather, are

Mike Evans of the Liverpool band, Clayton Squares, playing his sax in the St. James Cemetry, early '60s

numerous. For, in Liverpool, all love is illicit, and apartments are few, so the parks, back alleys and the graveyards, themselves, are the scene of many a briefly-snatched courtship.

I inhale deeply and my cannabis-inspired thoughts swell and rise to the stars as I muse on the poetic twist of socio-economics that could force a whole city's youth out into the graveyards to make love. The options were few: a stand-up knee-trembler in a back alley; a furtive finger-pie on the carpet in front of the fire, parents snoring abed; or the park, patronized by perverts or policemen; and finally this, the eerie mystery of the cathedral graveyard.

The cathedral graveyard was a favorite romping ground in the summer, day and night, owing to its proximity and accessibility to the city. Many a Scouser had had his snorting, beery way with fair maidens on the very grave-stone on which I now lay so nonchalantly staring at the vast gloom of the cathedral through charas-inspired eyes.

"It is fitting," I think, "That life should begin and end here; the dead below, the quick above, rorting and rasping their way to a climax on the cold interface of marble that separates them from the crumbling corpse." I mutter out loud in charas-inspired poetry: "And out of life there shall spring death."

Thoughts waft through my mind like the fragrant scents of exotic blossoms. In the distance, I hear the lowing of a ship's horn; the long, drawn-out clank of trains shunting in the railway sidings; and, very faintly born on the air by a freak of the wind, children's voices lifted in song. Children, yes, albeit snotty-nosed and mercenary, but children all the same and the verses are redolent with an illusory innocence that momentarily touches my swelling heart.

"Eh!! Yew!!" A guttural Liverpool voice growls out from the darkness, deep with authority, dashing my fragile sentiments to a thousand pieces.

Hastily, I stand up and grind my foot into the glowing butt of the joint.

A figure steps from the gloom. Coat buttons glisten metallically in the dim light; something black and sinister swings in the man's hand; and there is a fleshy thwack, then another. A policeman looms over me, slapping a large truncheon in his fleshy palm menacingly.

The fact registers slowly on my THC-ridden brain but a flood of adrenaline raises me to a semblance of wariness. The cops did not normally enter the cemetery at night.

The policeman prods me with the night stick, holding me at arm's length. Then he walks around me slowly, studying me from all angles.

My heart is thudding in my chest and I am painfully aware of the stench of cannabis. I pray that the policeman is, as usual, oblivious to the implications of this acrid smell—a smell which was to become much more widely recognized by the police in later years.

The policeman finishes his scrutiny and slaps his thigh whimsically. "Naah," said the policeman, "You're O.K.—just."

"What's up?" I stutter, relieved.

"Girl was attacked up on the street, just now," says the cop nonchalantly, "But unless you bleached your bleedin' face, son, it wasn't you."

I let out a deep breath. It is the wrong move; the suspicious edge returns to the cop's voice: "Anyway, what *are* you doing down here this time of night on New Year's Eve?" The policeman moves closer and peers into my face. "Not a bleedin' queer, are you?" he says, eyeing my long hair with distaste. I back away, acutely aware of my cannabis-laden breath.

The policeman wrinkles his nose and sniffs as he catches the acrid odor. I freeze as the policeman's face suddenly floods with realization: "Christ almighty! That smell! So that's it, eh?"

"Done for!" I think desperately.

The policeman taps my breast bone with the night stick. "Listen, next time you want a crap, use a public toilet. There's one down by Bold Street. It's a long way, I know, but better than this bleedin' place. Now git."

I almost burst into giggles, so immediate is my relief. But I stifle them and sputter: "Yeah...sure," and sidle away.

The policeman's voice drifted back through the gloom, punctuated with a chuckle: "Lay off the draft Guinness, lad, your guts are rotten ....!"

11 P.M.. The Nigerian Social Club, Parliament Street, Liverpool 8

I am in full swing. I stomp the floor in time with the music, sweat pouring down my face. A sea of black faces swirls around me. Colorful kaftans—red; blue; green; and yellow—merge with extremely sober suits, school ties, razor-sharp creases and pin-stripe pants.

Author and Abayomi Ajilawura (Abby), both nurses at the South Liverpool Psychiatric Annex. Abby was a prince in his own country and had tribal scars

The Nigerian Social Club. Tonight is a special event: The party of my good friend Abayomi Ajilawura, a noble warrior from Nigeria who is royal in spirit and in ancestry; a prince in his own country. Abayomi was once a colleague at the Psychiatric Annex; now he drives a bus, but this does not detract one whit from his princely status or his regal bearing.

A solid man with a barrel chest and ham-like fists, Abby is also a trained boxer and fighter; he still bears the tribal scars of initiation on his cheeks. But Abby is a mild, soft-spoken, gentle person and I have never even seen him raise his voice or fist in anger.

Moo and I are the only white people there. Except for Denise.

Denise is Moo's friend. A dark-haired girl with pretty eyes, Denise has one of those unfortunate glandular dysfunctions which defy all the laws of thermodynamics: if Denise partakes of a mere fifty calories in food, five pounds will blossom as solid adipose tissue on her hips. Somehow, Denise's body, much to her chagrin, is living proof of the Transmutation of Matter—a secret which defied medieval alchemists for years—but here the end-product is fat and not gold. And fat girls in Liverpool don't have much fun—except with Africans, who love it.

Tonight she has the Midas touch, and she is happier than she has been for years. Her body is girded prettily in a large cotton dress and she sports a silk flower in her hair; a splash of red against her dark locks.

Denise, despite her two hundred pounds, is a good mover. Her thwarted sexuality has stored up a great deal of energy. This sexual energy finds its release in her dancing, much to the awe and admiration of the members of the Nigerian Social Club.

Thus, on the eve of the birth of a New Year, Denise she has

Courtesy Derek Massey

Sugar Deen (of the early '60s band, The Valentinos) with Natalie and Nicol, two of his six children

become an African goddess. Pop-eyed African men hover around her solicitously; some openly salacious, completely mesmerized by this radiant, white woman gyrating so sensually in their midst.

No one gives a second glance at Moo. Moo is typical Sixties, typical Liverpool: delicate, small-breasted, with straight, blonde hair, long, slim hands and the narrow buttocks and concave thighs of the androgynous.

It dawns on me that here the sexual standards are reversed: Denise is a raging beauty; Moo is something less—far less. At first I am puzzled. During the introductions, African women—bulky, swaying bundles of sexuality in cotton breast wraps and long skirts—stare at Moo quizzically and then at me. The expression in their eyes is wonder. The men shake my hand gravely, with a certain solicitude, as though each is saying silently, "I'm sorry", much as one would wordlessly comfort the recently bereaved. Abby, gravely as a friend will, voices his concern: "Your girlfriend has been ill, no?" he says to me.

"Ill ...?" I eye Moo, who is gyrating on the floor alone, oblivious to the empty space around her and the crowd of Africans compacted around Denise.

"Yes," continues Abby, "She is so emaciated. Some wasting illness, perhaps?" says Abby in his clipped, neo-Victorian English.

I grin as I realize. "Well, I guess she's a bit thin by your standards."

Unaware that there *are* other standards, Abby understands this to mean that I don't want to discuss Moo's 'wasting disease'. He nods sagely, pats me on the shoulder solicitously and, having said his piece, returns to the bar.

Nigerian high-life music: all brassy trumpets and jagged, syncopated rhythms flood the room. The men whoop and strut, grunting as if they are constipated, pounding the floor with the flat of their feet and sliding in the time-honored high-life style; all shuffles and pelvic thrusts.

Denise is radiant. She struts, gyrates and shakes her money-maker for all its worth, aware of the fact that every man's eyes are fixed on her with awe and open lust. This New Year's Eve, Denise, the daughter of a merchant banker who dis-owned her after an unwanted pregnancy, has discovered her true milieu—a black club down Parliament Street.

Then Comfort finds *me*.

Comfort looks...comfortable. A smooth, round

Africans who did manage to make it to England were often the sons and daughters of African princes. Their English had been learned in schools with archaic books so that their conversation was almost Dickensian. Basil Ogbeama was a wonderful, ingenuous African kid who studied at the same time as me—most assiduously—to get into university. He told me that when he first arrived in England, he got a taxi in London and asked to be taken to Liverpool. It was a mammoth journey by British standards - and very costly. The Cockney taxi driver said: "You mean Liverpool Street Station," because it was unheard of to travel to Liverpool, 200 miles away, at local taxi rates - and the fare would have to be paid for the return trip, which was incredible. "No," said Basil. The taxi man complied and the fare was gargantuan. When I asked Basil why he did this, he replied in Dickensian English: "For fear of brigands."

face, mischievous eyes, she is coffee-colored rather than black. She bears an ornate, cotton turban on her head and her ample body is bedecked with gold, lots of it—West African gold: sweeping chandeliers of earrings; heavy, multiple necklettes, bangles, bracelets and rings. With every lilt in the music, glinting yellow flashes and Comfort resounds with a hundred metallic tinkles.

She has been watching me—this I don't know—but she sways, twitching her ample bottom seductively, half-turns and catches sight of me sitting drinking bottled Guinness with Moo. We are resting, both bathed in sweat after a long stint on the floor.

An interesting light on the lack of awareness of skin color in Africans was revealed when, one day, I invited Basil to the beach. We had both been studying intensively to try to get into university - a very competitive examination in the U.K.. We were both stressed and fed up, with massive headaches, so I suggested a little R&R in the way of going up the coast to Formby, which had a beach and sand dunes. When I got to the sand dunes, I stripped down to my shorts. Basil wore a dark suit, collar and tie despite the heat, which was intolerable to me.

Puzzled, Basil asked me what I was doing.

"Sunbathing," I replied.

"Sun bath-ing?" he echoed (he pronounced it with a flat "a" as in bath - sun bath-ing).

"Why do you do this?" he asked, most puzzled.

"I want to get brown." I replied.

I thought Basil was going to choke at this revelation. Tears running down his cheeks, his eyes bugging, he fell over, he was laughing so hard, repeating over and over, "Sun bath-ing! Ho, ho, ho!!"

For weeks after he would look at me and mutter: "Sun bath-ing!" and giggle derisively.

Comfort stops dancing. She pauses, one hand on a curvaceous hip, emphasizing the low cut of her cotton sarong. She purses her lips and grins, revealing a row of shiny, white teeth dotted with gold. "C'mon!" she beckons, trilling her fingers in an eloquent gesture, "Come go with me."

I look around, surprised, not sure of whether she is talking to me.

There is a flurry of brassy trumpet peals as a new song leaps to life on the juke box. The lilting, syncopated rhythm begins and, with an impudent smile, Comfort beckons again. "C'mon!"

I don't move, so she strides forward, grabs my arm and pulls me onto the floor. The dance begins in earnest.

The song is deceptively simply, but its rhythms are not. With my musician's ear, I adjust and begin to dance in time. Comfort sways in front of me with many a coy glance, though her breast movements and hips are anything but coy.

She mimes the song with coquettish twists and pouts of her full lips, emphasizing each word. She sings to me as if I'm the only man in the room. Each line of the song culminates in a drum beat which Comfort emulated with a 1-2-3 rapid twitch of her huge bottom:

> "I want to know (dum-de-dum)
> I want to know (dum-de-dum)
> I want to know why he loves me."

She slides up close to me and this time, emulates the drum beat by grinding her pubic bone into my crotch. I am half titillated, half embarrassed. "Hey, you white boy," she says insolently, "You dance good. Ah's Comfort," she announces, making it sound like an abstract quality rather than her name, "Who are you?"

"Pittsy," I say.

"Hey, Pittsy. mon, you like Comfort?" She sways just out of reach and gives an emphatic twitch of her buttocks.

I don't want to offend her, but I feel this is going a bit too far. "Yeah- no- Well, I ..." I stutter uneasily. I glance back to where Moo is sitting on the bench, her gold-rimmed glasses two gleaming circles in the half-light fixed rigidly on me.

The music ends and Comfort gives a mocking, uneven curtsey that despite her intended parody is pure, liquid grace: "Thank you."

"Er, thank you," I say awkwardly, and return to Moo.

Unfortunately, that is not the end of the Comfort Zone, for Comfort puts the record on again and repeats the whole manoeuvre. She drags me, unwillingly, back onto the dance floor.

This time when I glance back to the bench, it is deserted save for Moo who sits, shoulders hunched, head down and jaw set. Whether it is a trick of light, I cannot tell, but her glasses seem to glitter like a car's head-lights on a frosty night.

"Uh oh... Look, er, Comfort, I need to go." I shuffle backwards, withdrawing my crotch from Comfort's attempts at vertical orgasm, and mutter apologetically, "I should join my...girl friend." And, with as much grace as I can muster, I leave Comfort on the dance floor.

But Comfort follows me. She slides onto the end of the bench alongside me and, cocking her head to one side like an intent child, glances across at the set face of Moo staring straight ahead. "Hey, Pittsy, is this your girlfriend?"

"Er, yes," I say, uncomfortably aware that Moo is now taking agitated swigs from a Guinness bottle in a manner that boded no good.

"Pittsy, you wanna sleep with me?" asks Comfort mischievously, still cocking her head to one side so she can see both me and Moo. We are busy looking everywhere except at each other.

"Comfort," I say, flustered, vaguely wondering if this is normal African courtship protocol, "You know, you're very nice. But Moo is my girlfriend and…" I spread my hands helplessly.

"That's O.K.," says Comfort musically, the devil in her eyes, "We all sleep together. But me first, O.K.?"

I splutter and then say: "No. No, I—"

But it is too late. The thin red line has definitely been crossed. Moo's eyes blaze behind her glasses and, with a quick twist of her wrist, she swings the bottle by the neck and brings it round in a vicious arc to slam right into my face, snarling: "You bastard!!"

Reflexively, I put my hand up before my face and the bottle hits my palm with a dull thud that smacks my knuckles against my teeth. The impact knocks me backwards over the bench. I lie there fingering my bruised mouth, relieved to find my knuckles are bleeding but my teeth are intact.

Suddenly, from nowhere, an irate African appears, shouting and screaming. Abby materializes beside me and helps me to my feet.

"Who's that?" I whisper to Abby

The black man rages and screams, shaking his fists.

"Comfort's husband," says Abby drily.

I am suddenly very aware of the fact that I'm the only white man in the room. But, to my surprise, the husband ignores both me and Moo. His wrath seems to be aimed entirely at Comfort, who undergoes a dramatic change of personality: She stands with her fists clenched and her head thrust forward, screaming back at her husband, her face a mask of rage. And in this little vignette, I see the truth: I was simply a pawn in Comfort's obvious hostility to her husband and definitely *not* a major black-babe magnet.

Without warning, the husband grabs Comfort, twirls her rapidly and toes her up her ample rump. Comfort bellows and screams, but, by dint of repeated kicks, the husband propels her out of the door, much to the amusement of the onlookers. He ejects Comfort, slams the door and returns to the room, his face filled with indignant wrath, and stomps off towards the bar.

Courtesy Derek Massey

Eddie Amoo (second left) with his wife and four daughters

216

Courtesy Charlie Jenkins

Joe Bygraves of Liverpool, the World Heavyweight Boxing Champion, early '60s

The crowd surges back onto the floor, laughing and clapping. The music resumes, and the moment is gone.

"What did you do that for?!" I hiss at Moo, who is still glaring at me, "Idiot! You can't do that here! We'll get lynched!! Christ, you nearly knocked my teeth out!!"

"Serves you right!" cries Moo furiously.

"I didn't do anything!" I say defiantly.

"Yes you did!" says Moo gritting her teeth.

"What?! She asked me if we could go to bed and I said no!"

"You paused!"

"What?!"

"You paused," says Moo, "You didn't say no straight away—you hesitated. I watched you. You hesitated, you didn't say no like you meant it!"

"Oh shit!" I mutter wearily. There is obviously no reasoning with her at this moment. "That's it. I'm getting another drink." I push my way across the floor. Still wary of my rather vulnerable position—the only white man in the room—I approach Abby who stands serenely watching the dancers, a bottle in his large, black hand.

"Sorry Abby," I say, "I really am."

"Sorry?" replies Abby taking a swig from his bottle, still watching the dancers.

"Sorry. It's your party and I didn't want to spoil it."

Abby's eyes seem to half shut and his shoulders begin to heave, then his chest, then his belly. He is laughing. "Ho ho... Sorry..." he says, mimicking my voice in a mock-mournful tone. His whole body pulses jelly-like with the laughter.

I stare at him confused. "Well, it's just that I didn't want to spoil you New Year's Eve, that's all..."

"My friend," says Abby with a broad smile. He puts his hand on my shoulder and speaks softly as if advising a child, "If there is not *this*, there is *no* party." Solemnly, he ushers me over to the contrite Moo and, with a meaty arm around both of us, whisks us off to the bar and buys us both a drink.

I have just had my first lesson in the meaning of celebration—African style.

Princess Road, Home of the Black Clubs—New Year's Day: 2 a.m.

Courtesy Bernie Wenton

Richie Wenton, winner of the Lonsdale Belt and son of Terry Wenton

I am in the lap of the gods. I weave along Princess Road among the late-night crowds streaming out of the black clubs. I am drunk. No, that is far too mundane a word for the Valhalla-like heights to which I have risen. Draft Guinness, Double Diamond, Higsen's Bitter and cannabis—a nefarious concoction of psychoactive substances—all were at work on my spirits at that moment.

I looked good, too, resplendent in a rather unusual garment, handcrafted by Moo. It is my New Year's present; a present which was given to me without the usual grace at 12:05 a.m.[2] Though recovering slowly, Moo is still annoyed about the incident at the Nigerian Social Club. It is a midnight-blue overcoat fashioned in corduroy. Moo is a seamstress of no little prowess and I am rightly proud of my coat, despite the spirit in which it was given.

We have been to the Ethiopian Club, the Stage Door club and the Blue Angel owned by dear old Allan Williams (the man whose doubtful claim to fame was that he gave the Beatles away; popularly known as the Manager of the Month), and now I am drunk and happy, having danced my heart out at Allan's club which was filled to the brim with not-yet-famous musicians. And, like all the other not-yet-famous musicians, be it Ringo Starr or Cilla Black, I was indulging in the time-honored and frustrating Liverpool occupation of Trying-To-Get-A-Taxi-On-New-Year's- Morning.

Moo is not as happy. After the incident with a black lady at the Nigerian Social Club, in which I was, in fact, totally innocent. Though Moo is a little drunk too, its effects seem to lower her spirits rather than raise them.

"Happy New Year everybody!!" I cry, doing a little dance on the pavement and waving at a group of revelers that pour out of a club across the street.

One of crowd waves back: a thin, white-faced youth carrying a guitar. With his long hair and tight, black trousers, he is an unlikely companion for the dour-faced Irishman at his side, who still manages to look like a laborer, despite his blue suit, white shirt and tie. It's Alan James, a would-be muso.

"Hey, Pittsy!!" shouts Alan, "There's a party at my place! Wanna come?!"

I light up, then I catch sight of Moo's face. I shout back: "'Ow long are you going to be here?"

"Oh, ten minutes or so," shouts Alan, "We're waiting for a taxi."

"Taxi?!" I shout full of doubt.

"Yeah, we ordered it at twelve o'clock this afternoon," grins Alan, "We can give you a lift if you're going to come. You'd better make up you mind soon!"

Courtesy Charlie Jenkins

Stan Leon at the Palm Cove club, 1962

"Coming?" I say to Moo.

"You go," she answers sullenly, "I'm going home."

"Moo! I can't go if you don't go!"

"I'll walk," says Moo with a toss of her head.

"Moo! Don't be an asshole! C'mon, I can't go without you! You know I won't let you walk!"

"Asshole, eh?!" says Moo, her ill-temper suddenly finding a cause, "I'm the asshole now! Huh!" She stands with her hands on her hips. "You had a good time tonight, though it wasn't your asshole that Miss Africa was pressing up against!" She glares down at my crotch, "I bet you loved it!"

"Moo! For Christ's sake!" I say wearily. I was quite truly a victim of Miss Africa's libido, not my own.

But Moo stalks off down the pavement, her glasses flashing like twin moons.

I raise my eyes in irritation, muttering: "Bitch!" then go to follow her but, instead, I bump into someone.

A small Chinese youth blocks my path. He stares at me contemptuously and says: "You swear at that chick?"

Preoccupied with Moo who is fast disappearing into the distance down the pavement, I push past the youth.

"Don't push!" says the Chinese youth coldly.

"Hey man," I'm still preoccupied with Moo, "No problems, hey?" I crane my neck to catch sight of Moo amongst the late-night revelers on the pavement, but something pokes me in the chest.

It is the youth's finger.

"Hey! Don't do that!" I say, annoyed by Moo's behavior; my nerves are already on edge.

Then it begins

Caught off balance by the rapid events, I am in it up to my neck before I have time to stop it.

"You swore at my sister," says the Chinese youth, "I heard you."

"Your sister!" I turn, fully aware of the youth for the first time. I stare at him warily. "She's white, man. She's not your sister."

"Hey, I've seen you around," says the Chinese youth softly, "You a hard case[3]?"

"No, I'm not. Look, leave it out, man." I begin to back away. The youth follows me, poking me provocatively in the shoulder with his finger. My nerves are fraying. "Look! Don't do that! I tell you, leave me alone, man! Don't do it!"

"Yeah? And what?" sneers the youth and deliberately pokes his finger right into my face.

My nerves snap completely and I cry out: "I told you!!" I swing my fist back

But it never connected. Something thudded into my back and sent me sprawling on the pavement. I rolled instinctively and leapt up, my back against a wall, to find myself staring at the grinning face of the Chinese youth—and three of his black buddies. I'd been conned into a fight—they'd been following behind all the time he'd been goading me, waiting for the moment.

Then they were on me, kicking and punching. Insane with rage at the injustice of it, I whipped around in circles as they tried to land a solid blow. "Bastards!!! Cowards!! Assholes!!" I screamed, whirling.

They grabbed hold of my coat and danced around me. The coat shredded down the seams and the three whirled like may-pole dancers with me in the middle, a twirling pole of insane, blue

219

The Windsor Street Rovers, 1955

Courtesy Charlie Jenkins

energy, while they kicked and lunged at me.

I broke free and ran across the road, ignoring the blaring horns of the cars. All three ran after me.

A crowd stood outside the club opposite; drunken revelers having a late-night club gossip before the long walk home. I burst in amongst them like a blue tornado, my prized overcoat in tatters, like some latter-day clown in motley clothing. I was incensed by the cowardice of it and I made a very unwise move: I ducked through the crowd, agitated, searching for a familiar face.

Lonny stood there idly, his hands in his pockets, chatting to a girl. I came bursting through the crowd: "I just got jumped by three guys, Lonny!!"

Lonny didn't even answer. In a reflex action, he turned and ran back the way I had come. I ran with him. We reached the corner of the street just as the three black youths swaggered into sight. The youths stood stock still as we burst from the crowd. The last thing they expected was to see me running towards them.

"This them?" cried Lonny.

"Yeah!" I cried.

And with the full impetus of the run behind him, Lonny hit one youth on the jaw. He bounced off the intricately ornate door of the pub and went down, pole-axed. I piled on top of the Chinese youth, punching him repeatedly. A crowd gathered around me, but I was oblivious as I pummeled the startled youth, punctuating each blow with an oath. "Bastard!! Coward!!"

Lonny had rapidly dispatched the other two, who lay sprawled on the pavement. But he had disappeared into an alley where he was retching—fifteen pints of Guinness are not a good basis for late-night acrobatics.

There was a brief pause in the action. I backed away, staring at the three youths groaning on the ground. Time to split.

But it was too late. All hell broke loose and I realized that I should have kept running when I could. Suddenly, I was surrounded by black youths with shaven heads and very grim faces.

Lonny was hauled out of the alley by three of them. I saw them tear his jacket off.

Surprise rendered me inactive for a second. Then, the night sky whirled and the ground seemed to leap up and slam itself in my back as I was knocked to the ground. Something thudded dully with a hollow noise, and I realized it was someone kicking me in the head, though I didn't feel a thing. I rolled over and covered my head instinctively, and from the corner of my eye, I saw Lonny whirl through the air and go down amidst a forest of legs and arms. Then it all went hazy.

220

Photo-stills impinge on my blurred vision; I am dimly aware of a frantic blaring. It is the traffic lined up, stationary—taxis, buses, cars—as the battle rages across the black, glistening tarmac of the main road. I glimpse the crowd inside a double-decker bus, their faces pressed to the windows like gold fish in a bowl. Then the gang is on me again and the night explodes into stars and thuds.

I keep rolling; keep moving. I duck and bob with that incessant energy of survival. Hands grab me; feet fly by my ear; boots thud into my side. Then, in a moment of clarity, I see Moo standing on the pavement, her face stricken. "Moo!!" I yell, "Get!! Go!!" I roll to find myself sprawled half underneath a taxi. I dodge around it and for a moment am free. I scream at Moo again: "Get out of it!!!"

But Moo is mesmerized by the traffic horns and the black youths kicking and punching blindly.

The fight swirls in front of my vision. Then there is a break in the crowd and I see the Chinese youth—the first youth who started it all—suddenly bob up beside Moo. Moo stares at him, bewildered. He mouths words of rage, his eyes rolling, his face contorted. He whips his arm up and punches Moo in the side of the head, full force. Her glasses bob up and down on her nose with the impact; her expression is startled.

And I'm up and running through the crowd, dodging, twisting. I'm at Moo's side. And with all my strength, I knock the youth backwards. Then I'm pulling Moo and screaming: "Go!! Go!! Go!!" But still she does not leave. And the gang is on me again, kicking, punching.

It was the sheer numbers that saved us from serious injury. If the odds had remained at four to one instead of ten to one, we might have been very, very seriously hurt. But there were so many black youths in uncoordinated action that none of them managed to land a really decisive blow. They kept getting in each other's way. However, our luck could only hold out for so long. The decisive factor in the fight came from a totally unanticipated source.

The noises have faded. I squat against an alley wall slightly removed from the periphery of the fight. My breath is harsh, my chest heaves. My coat hangs in tatters; one sleeve is missing completely, torn away. I am totally spent. My face is bleeding from a dozen minor cuts, and there is a large lump on the side of my head. But, apart from that, I am miraculously unscathed. I don't know where Lonny is, or even Moo, but I have reached exhaustion level and can't even think. The world is reduced to a few details: a brick wall; my ragged breath; the filthy gutter. Then I realize I'm staring at a pair of jean-clad legs.

I straighten up to see it is Jo-Jo.

Jo-Jo is alert, balanced; his fingers curved ready for action. But his expression is puzzled. He stares at me and, wordlessly, I read the signs: Jo-Jo wants a fight; Jo-Jo wants to take out this white shit.

"Why did you try to come the odds, la'?" says Jo-Jo in a deceptively soft voice.

It is an eloquent question with all the terseness of the black Liverpool dialect. Translated, Jo-Jo is asking if I was so confident of my fighting ability that I could take on twenty youths with the support of only one other man. The curiosity is tinged with a cruel anticipation: perhaps, thinks Jo-Jo, this is a real opponent; perhaps he can have some fun with such an opponent.

Despite my exhaustion, I know Jo-Jo is waiting for the slightest wrong move. "No," I say. I keep my head bowed. I make no rapid motions. This is the right thing to do, but it is weariness that lends it conviction.

It is obvious I am finished. Jo-Jo narrows his eyes coldly—but he is still puzzled. He cocks his head to one side in an unspoken question.

"Look, I don't fight," I say, "I'm a musician, man, it's not my scene." I shrug. "One of those guys did my girlfriend—for nothin', I tell you. He slugged her. A Chinese guy... A little guy..."

"Yeah? What for?" says Jo-Jo in disbelief.

"He slugged a girl 'cos he lost the fight. Check it out, man." My voice has the ring of truth.

Jo-Jo watches me for one, dangerous moment, then says coldly: "Why don't you piss off." He jerks his thumbs, "Git!"

"Yeah, yeah," I say, "That's all I want." I stand up and limp past the looming bulk of Jo-Jo, expecting to be knocked down.

But Jo-Jo doesn't make a move. He lets me limp off down the road then decisively whirls on the balls of his feet and strides off towards the waiting throng of youths, silent now among the bystanders on the sidewalk.

As with all real-life situations, for the participants, there is no drama: I limp down the road, my eyes vacant, empty of feelings. My numbed senses have shut off in the whirl of action and I want to go home.

Moo and Lonny wait at the corner.

Lonny has his coat on now. His white shirt is drenched with blood. Moo is fearful and silent. Awareness flickers in my brain: the danger is not over. I limp up to them stiffly, still acting on instinct. "You O.K.?" I say to Lonny.

Lonny nods and inexplicably grins. "£10 worth of Guinness and I puke it up in the bushes," he says ruefully, "What a waste."

The wry humor causes my eyes to flood with tears in a sudden, nervous relief. I link my arm into Moo's who, though white-faced, is sufficiently composed to keep her emotions in restraint. "O.K. Moo, walk," I say gruffly, "Slow. Just walk away slowly." I do not have to tell Lonny—Lonny knows exactly what to do already.

We begin to walk slowly away from the corner to safety, aware of the eyes of the group of youths burning into us from behind. A sudden cry makes us turn.

Jo-Jo is standing glaring at the Chinese kid who had punched Moo in the face. Jo-Jo's lips are curled in a snarl. We cannot hear the Chinese kid, but his arms are out and his palms up in a pleading gesture; he is talking very fast. Jo-Jo's expression is bleak.

> Though Jo-Jo was psychopathic with males, when it came to females he was oddly chivalrous. I found out later that he'd had a white girlfriend who'd committed suicide.

Jo-Jo's figure suddenly blurs in an incredibly fast motion, then is still again. And, as if by magic, the Chinese kid is sprawled full-length on the ground, unconscious. Jo-Jo kicks him a few times for good measure, rubs his knuckles and saunters towards the crowd of youths, his shoulders erect. He glowers at them to provoke some retaliation. But they part slowly like the Red Sea to allow Jo-Jo to stride through their midst without reprisal.

Meanwhile, we make themselves very, very scarce.

Prologue

I could not operate in my own district anymore—even with Jo-Jo's intervention, I knew that the gang would be looking for me in some dark alley on some dark night. So, after a week of fretted nerves and peering over my shoulder, regretfully I decided I had to leave Liverpool for a while until the whole affair had cooled off.

Thus, I took Moo and headed off for Bristol, a town that, ironically enough, like Liverpool, had figured prominently in the slave trade. And, it certainly turned out that, despite its large black population, Bristol was definitely not ready for the blues.

The Blues & Liverpool

20

The Blues and Liverpool

Soul is like electricity—we don't know what it is but its force can light a room.

Ray Charles
Ebony Power Thoughts

There is, without a doubt, no more searing or poignant story than that of the blues. If a Hollywood writer were asked to imagine the most exotic extravaganza of the human spirit, he could not come up with a story more biting—and bizarre. The most overwhelming factor about the history of the blues is that it took place at all. Not only did it take place, but it was to have a profound effect upon the very structure of American civilization in the twentieth century.

Of the millions of slaves transported from West Africa, less than seven percent came to America. The principal villain in this tragic drama was not America, but Portugal, with Great Britain and France following closely behind.

Jemas Rawley
The Transatlantic Slave Tradee

It is a sobering thought that, if the Americans had not entered into the slave market, the face of the western world would be significantly different. The slave trade has left its legacy on both sides of the Atlantic. America not only grew more rapidly because of black labor, but the course of its history has been affected by the presence of blacks—the American Civil War being the most dramatic illustration of this truth.

Total Figures for the Slave Trade		
Grand Total	9,556,000	100.00%
Old World	175,000	1.00%
North America	651,000	6.80%
Caribbean Islands	4,040,000	42.20%
South America	4,700,000	49.10%

Jemas Rawley
The Transatlantic Slave Tradee

What is not widely known is that America was a minor carrier of slaves. America came late to the slave trade and withdrew early. The Atlantic trade was almost three centuries old before America started a significant market.

Though America has, historically speaking, been the object of greatest denigration over its slave problem, in the western hemisphere, America's slave population was in the minority.

This is not to deny the fact that hundreds of slaves were transported to the New World not as men but as chattels, having no more dignity than field animals. Furthermore, for years after slavery was abolished, blacks were segregated in America—and beaten, tortured, murdered, mutilated and subjected to all the whims of man's inhumanity to man.

"Downtrodden, humiliated, the Negro sough out his only release, his one form of expression," says the sociologist in a statement nonetheless dramatic because it's true, "And it arose in an odd blending of African rhythms, Elizabethan music, early European and American folk songs—as the blues."

Samual Charters
Musicologist

Despite it all, the black man sang—and sang. It is a poignant fact which has led to a great deal of literature on the subject of black music.

In their summation of the blues' story, ethnographers, historians and musicologists point immediately to the African rhythms, the call-and-response system, the field grunts, hollers and shouts of work songs which became the mark of the early blues and gospel songs. Learned musicians point to the flattened 3rd and 7th of the diatonic scale which is the innovation of the blues' scale. Researchers like the late Samuel Charters traveled the length of America recording songs, shouts, hollers and blues, some of which have now become so ingrained in America's heritage that few people realize where they originated.

It was from these unlikely origins that the nerve-tingling riffs, slides and moans arose—the haunting refrains of an entirely new musical genre. The blacks were introduced to the guitar, an instrument itself a bastardization of the Elizabethan lute, and literally just picked it up and played it. Some were able to work out the traditional European tuning, but most of them simply turned the pegs "until it sounded right".

The answer to the question of why or how the blacks achieved all this under such oppressive conditions is simple: it was not a matter of choice—they had to. Whatever it is in the human spirit that cries out to be heard, to be respected found its outlet in the only way it could. It was a true cry from the soul—perhaps the purest one that America ever experienced.

And it was heard.

There is a belief among musicians, classicists, rockers and sophisticated jazzers alike; a view which is becoming more and more prevalent: Namely, that it is immaterial how technically adept a musician is. For a musician to "swing", there has to be something else; something to do with the place from which he plays. When a musician does not play from this place, even a non-musician feels something lacking; it puzzles him that the music seems so empty. (This is what is happening to a lot of overproduced Nineties' music).

Now of course, we have a word for this phenomenon; it is simply called *soul*, and it is so common as to have become a cliché. But in its context of black history, it is not clichéd at all: it is a singular and fundamental truth about the human condition.

Robert Johnson only recorded enough songs for one and a half albums, having been killed young, allegedly by a jealous girlfriend. He was self-taught, like many black musicians. He just took off with a guitar and a year or two later, turned up again with the guitar incredibly-overstrung in a taut and unlikely open chord, playing with a broken beer bottle on his little finger. The sound that resulted was unbelievable: shrill; nerve-racking; rich with the impossibly-complex rhythms of his Africa heritage. Eric Clapton was to say of Johnson's music: "He still scares me." Johnson's blues is so close to its native origins that, in its raw form, it does not suit everybody's palate. But it was to become the cornerstone of western pop music. Every rock and jazz musician in the twentieth century has been influenced by Robert Johnson's playing, most of them without knowing it.

Blues in Liverpool, Blues in America

The American public came late to the blues when compared to England, even though the blues originated in America. The reason is simple: America did not have the Englishman's distance from racism, because America, unlike England, was deeply ensconced in race problems.

Liverpool, in particular, took the blues to its bosom wholeheartedly, not just in its derivative forms—like the blues-related styles of Chuck Berry, Muddy Waters and the later R&B artists—but in its pure essence.

Music, dance, religion do not have artifacts as their end products, so they were saved. These nonmaterial aspects of the African-American culture were impossible to eradicate. And these are the most apparent legacies of the African past.

LeRoi Jones, Blues People
Ebony Power Thoughts

There was, amongst the Liverpool musicians, a subgroup who were as busy totting up the albums of rare blues' artists (on the Storyville label) as the jazz aficionados were busy collecting Blue-Note albums. Years before Robert Johnson's album *King of the Mississippi Delta* was released on Columbia, the Liverpool Blues Society (a small group of aficionados, myself included) arranged for one hundred pressings of the album and paid an exorbitant price for it...willingly.

Guitarists like Lance Railton (Earl Preston and the TTs) absorbed every riff, every nuance of such diverse guitar styles as those of Big Bill Broonzey; Lightening Hopkins; Furry Lewis; Blind Lemon Jefferson; Blind Gary Davis. Stephen Grossman, it is true, has always been a pioneer of the acoustic blues in the U.S.A., but he was (and is) still largely ignored, although Aurora Block, his female accompanist, has received a modicum of attention.

The most prolific American annotator of the blues, ethnologist Samuel Charters, made a vast collection of field recordings, and, significantly, in the early Seventies, donated the whole collection, not to an American but to an English University, Sussex University in Brighton—because no American university wanted it!. A sore loss for America.

America, of course, is not to blame. While a nation is making history, it is difficult to appreciate it. But one significant point about the blues and its derivations has been largely overlooked by mainstream America.

Recently, Johnson's illegitimate son, who is in his 80s, won a claim to inherit the fortune that has been generated by the sales of Johnson's albums. The son threw some light onto the attitudes of some of Johnson's contemporaries towards the blues. Johnson visited his "wife" and her parents wouldn't let the son talk to Robert or even touch him because they said he was "playing the devil's music". One of the reasons for the limited proliferation and acceptance in America of the blues in its early forms was that many Church-going blacks and whites alike thought it was taboo, the devil's music—attitudes that prevailed for a long time as a relic of Puritanism.

Although most Americans are aware of the blues as a musical form and structure, in particular the twelve bar, its most pertinent aspect has largely been neglected. That is, its role as an oral tradition in providing a safe outlet for socially-disruptive behavior in the blacks.

It is necessary to distinguish between the musical form and its proponents. The artists who practiced the blues in the Sixties and Seventies, particularly those who came across to England in the blue's caravans—Sonny Terry; Brownie Magee; John Lee Hooker; Lightening Hopkins; even Big Bill Broonzey—had become, like any other musicians, entertainers, and not, as many people thought, musical revolutionaries.

Studs Terkel in a *Folkways* record interview, milked Bill Broonzey for all he was worth, interrogating him melodramatically about the blues (a word he draws out for maximum effect as in: "Bill, tell us what style you're agonna play the Belloooze.").

Bill Broonzey, a very down-to-earth man, well aware of the vast distance that separates him from his brothers who'd toiled in the field, answered dryly: "Nightclub style."

Liverpool, then, was very closely allied to the blues and this owed not a little to the proximity of the poor whites and the West Indians and African blacks. It has nothing whatsoever to do with Liverpool having once been the economic center of the slave trade. Though hundreds of ships sailed from Bristol and Liverpool to convey slaves to the New World, none of the slaves stayed in England. They were not needed there; the climate was too bad and England already had its slave population—the lower-class whites. It was in the arduous conditions of the indigo and cotton fields that the black slaves were to be used.

So, nearly three and a half centuries later, the circle became complete. The passing of the McCarren-Waler Immigration Act in 1952 meant that those Caribbean blacks denied access to America came instead to England. Of course, by virtue of shipping routes and economic grouping, they ended up in Bristol and Liverpool.

And this underlines a major point: the blacks in Bristol did not integrate into the white society as they did in Liverpool. There was an essential difference in the spirit of the two cities.

Historically, black music has been a constraining factor, keeping racial aggression within safe boundaries. This finds its correlation in Rap music; and KRS, a Rap artist was to say in 1989: "It is a fact that, without the outlet of Rap, there would be a significant increase in violence in America."

The MacNeil, Lehrer Newshour
June 28, 1989
PBS Special

I Get to Meet Sonny Boy Williamson
—A Personal Anecdote—

As a starry-eyed rock guitarist and blues collector, I was to become acquainted first-hand with the vast gulf between the traditional role of the blues in black culture and some of its less-than-enlightened proponents. My first taste of groupie shock occurred when Sonny Boy Williamson gave a rare performance at the Cavern in the Sixties. I was thrilled, especially as my rank as rock musician gave me the rather doubtful privilege of entering the grubby hole of a band room in which the Beatles sweltered nightly in their leather garments, watched over by Bob Wooler, the erstwhile and articulate M.C..

And there was Sonny Boy, a giant figure on the Cavern stage, sporting a long, black overcoat which flapped about his gaunt frame as he danced about like an animated scarecrow, wailing away on his blues harp.

Despite the "no booze" rule in the Cavern, he had a full pint of Johnny Walker Whisky thrust into each pocket like two six-guns (after all, he was a Blues Artist, wasn't he?). With his black, sweaty skin shining under the lights and his reptilian fingers scrabbling at the harp, he blew up a storm. The audience went wild: Not only was there a blues' legend on stage, but in the booze-free Cavern, there he was drinking whisky!!

At last the great moment came and, with heart pounding, I pushed through the door into the dripping cave of the band room to pump him for first-hand information about the American Blue's legends.

Sonny Boy stood swaying, taking vast swigs of whisky while a meaty-bodied, white bodyguard stared at me with unconcealed hostility.

Finally I found my voice: "Sonny Boy, you took your name from the other Sonny Boy, didn't you? And you got your style from him."

SONNY BOY:	Vast burp; swig; no answer.
ME (desperately):	"What do you think of Big Bill Broonzey as a guitarist?" [1]
SONNY BOY (red-eyed; notices me for the first time):	"Huh! I buried dat cunt!" (swig)
ME (ignoring feelings of stupidity):	"Do you like any of the earlier blues harp players? I mean, not the rhythm and blues, but people like—"
SONNY BOY (cutting me short):	"A load of shit, all of it—and them."

There is a moment's silence in which I realize that, far from being enthused and inspired, Sonny Boy is treating me like some latter-day groupie who asks questions like "do you like Hagen Daas ice cream?" Rebellion wells within and, deadpan, in true Liverpool style, I asked: "Do you like raw carrots?"

Sonny Boy stared at me blearily and gives the first (almost) concise answer I'd had so far: "Naah, I never heard of the son of a bitch."

I giggle somewhat nervously. Tension breaks and Sonny Boy's brow furrows as the significance of the remark sinks in—he's been had! He roars in anger: "Who de fuck are you??!!" and whirls to the beefy bouncer: "Who de fuck is dis cunt anyway?!"

By way of answer, the bouncer ceremoniously bundles me out, thus ending my first (and last) encounter with the Blues-Artist-In-The-Flesh—from which I deduced the theory that: "The blues ain't nothing but an asshole getting drunk", a statement which, fortunately, never left a lasting impression either on me or on the world of music at large.

In fact, as a mitigating factor, it turns out that Sonny Boy was a sick man and, shortly after he returned to the U.S.A., he died in Arkansas.

You can take the man out of Africa but
you can't take Africa out of the man

One of the factors which has prevented the African American from enjoying some of his cultural richness is the well-meaning attempts by liberal whites to avoid racial stereotypes. This stems in a large part from a lack of exposure to Africans and African culture—which is much more available in a U.K. context.

There is often a tendency to misconstrue cultural identity with stereotyping. An example of this is the Denver, Colorado, girl who was shocked when I said African Americans are good dancers. This is not racial stereotyping any more than saying the French are good cooks. Rhythm, group singing and movement are an essential part of the African-American cultural heritage, as witnessed in gospel singing or the incredible adroitness of hip hop and break dancing.

I had a wonderful experience of the vocal and dance ability of blacks in Sheffield, of all places, a dour part of northern England near Liverpool

A Personal Anecdote

Courtesy Charlie Jenkins

The Hill Street Church Mission, Liverpool, 1947

The gray streets and walls were wet with drizzle as I walked somberly along an unknown street after a gig had been canceled at a working men's club. It was a miserable Sunday morning and I was a bit glum. I noticed a splash of color ahead and saw a group of little black girls clad in bright blue, pink and yellow dresses. Their hair was in braids tied with brightly-colored ribbons. Eagerly, they descended from a van and ran into an old building at the side of the road.

I stopped and listened. I could hear the sound of a ratchety old electric guitar slightly out of tune drifting from an open front door. Throwing caution to the winds, I entered the building.

In a huge hall were about 200 black people of all ages. Some of them wandered about; some of them stood quietly listening to the preacher—for it was, indeed, a church service.

The preacher was a small, round-faced man whose cheeks shone like black moons. By his side, a wheezing old white-haired man was playing an old electric guitar through an even wheezier amplifier.

An elderly black man, dressed in his Sunday best, looked up at me and, without hesitation, smiled and offered me a hymn book. 'Black, white,' his smile seemed to say, 'this is the House of the Lord.'

At that moment, the congregation started to sing and clap, and when they hit the chorus, which was "I clap my hands together for the coming of the Lord", the words and hymn books were forgotten as, in impromptu surge, they all began to clap fiercely, repeating the line over and over in complete disregard of the other ten verses in the hymn book. As the clapping steadied to a solid rocking beat, some of the women, all dressed in Sunday finery, began to shudder and moan and the perspiring preacher yelled: "Is there anyone here who got the Spirit of the Lord?! Is there anyone here who got the Spirit of the Lord?!"

The clapping increased in frenzy, as did the moans from the women. Suddenly, a woman in front of me holding a baby shuddered and convulsed and her wails pierced through the air.

"Sister Mary! Sister Mary, she got the Spirit!" shouted the preacher.

Sister Mary, babe still in her arms, suddenly bolted into a run down the aisle and a short woman, who was about as fat as she was high, obviously Mary's mother, ran alongside her and caught the baby when Sister Mary reached the stage.

Sister Mary wailed and writhed and the preacher smote her with his hand and she fainted clean away. The preacher gyrated and shouted: "Hallelujah! Hallelujah brothers and sisters, hallelujah!"

The whole congregation clapped and stamped, swaying, jigging and crying "Hallelujah!! Praise the Lord!"

Author's collection

The Dobro and National steel guitars were a cornerstone of the blues

When I left the church I was elevated; my gray mood had lifted. I thought about the sober piety of a British church and realized how far these people were from their mother country. Probably Caribbean blacks who'd come post-World War 2. I'd seen a little bit of Africa beneath the gray skies of England and, boy, did it feel good...

This is not racial stereotyping but a beautiful aspect of African or African-American culture. Ben Sidran says:

> The complexity of this rhythmic approach is in part due to the value placed upon spontaneity and the inherently communal nature of oral improvisation.[2]

He reports an example given by a Ralph Ellison who once saw a group of African tribesmen dancing to the back-firing of a gasoline engine.

As they have not had the long history of slavery which ended in a civil war, Europeans have a different attitude to black musicians. Those who tour Europe are met with admiration. Europeans see them as bringing "music from the source". Jazz and blues musicians who visit Europe or England, including the 'Blues Trains' which went to Liverpool and Manchester in the '60s, attest to the reverence and awe with which they are greeted by the audiences. So much so, in fact, that many black musicians ended up living in Europe permanently.

There is another myth which is equally spurious: that only black people can pay the blues or jazz. The fact is, the root of all blues and jazz is a deeply-felt feeling. Painful emotions are a basic part of humanity. So, any person, black or white, who can feel this way and has a grasp of his or her instrument to express it—soul is the term—can play blues and jazz. I have observed that white musicians who play black music, either by disposition or the influence of music, become a little more African. I've never heard any of them complain about it.

There are, however, certain blues' traditions. And for those white British or American blues players who think that 'Sidney Blenkensop Plays The Blues' on an album cover doesn't sound quite right, there is a remedy. And here it is:

Use the first letter of your first name to determine your NEW first name:

a = fat	j = boney	s = blind
b = muddy	k = curley	t = big
c = crippled	l = pretty	u = yella
d = old	m = jailhouse	v = toothless
e = texas	n = peg leg	w = screamin'
f = hollerin'	o = red	x = fat boy
g = ugly	p = sleepy	y = washboard
h = brown	q = bald	z = steel-eye
i = happy	r = skinny	

Use the first letter of your middle (or maiden) name to determine the second half of your first name:

a = bones	j = fingers	s = bad boy
b = money	k = boy	t = baby
c = harp	l = liver	u = chicken
d = legs	m = gumbo	v = pickles
e = eyes	n = foot	w = sugar
f = lemon'	o = mama	x = cracker
g = killer	p = back	y = tooth
h = hips	q = duke	z = smoke
i = lips	r = dog	

Use the first letter of your last name to determine your NEW last name:

a = Jackson	j = Washington	s = Davis
b = McGee	k = Smith	t = Franklin
c = Hopkins	l = Parker	u = White
d = Rivers	m = Lee	v = Jenkins
e = Green	n = Thompkins	w = Bailey
f = Brown	o = King	x = Sinatra
g = Jones	p = Bradley	y = Blue
h = Dupree	q = Hawkins	z = Tubbs
i = Malone	r = Jefferson	

Yes, of course it's a joke. C'mon, lighten up. After all, using this system I ended up as "Sleepy Sugar Bradley"…

Sleepy Sugar Bradley still playing the blues with Guitar Mac and the Delta Bayou Blues band, Sacramento

The Slave Trade
Liverpool & Bristol

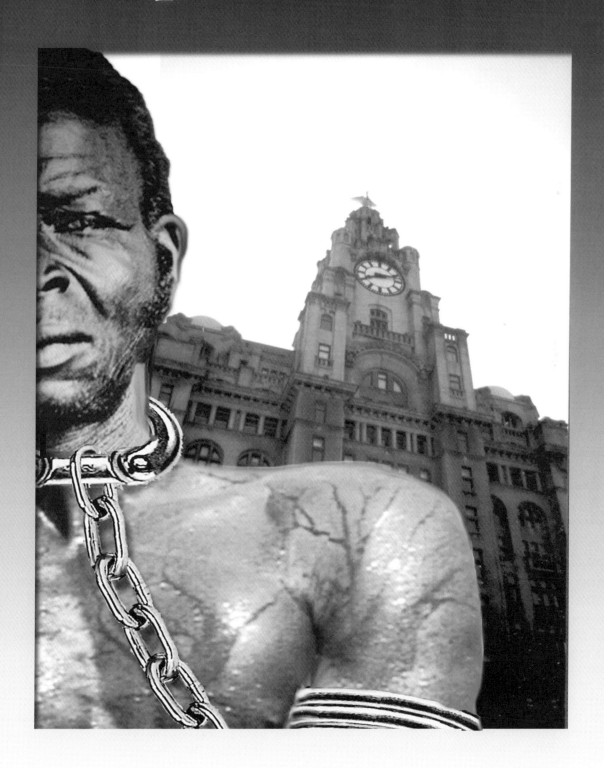

21

The Slave Trade: Liverpool and Bristol

A Brief Historical Digression

Courtesy Bristol Web Site

Bristol

Bristol is a university city situated in the southwest of England on the River Avon. Its population is, at present, not quite as large as Liverpool, but its connections with Liverpool are extensive, particularly as it was once the second major port in England. Daniel Defoe was to say in 1723 that it was the best port in England, London city excepted. Being in the south of England close to Bath, it was historically connected to the aristocracy and the growing merchant classes, in particular the slave traders. Its many links with the early colonization of America are indicated by the claim that the continent was named after a Bristol town clerk, Richard Ameryke.

By 1788, Liverpool had outstripped Bristol as a port, but not without paying dearly for it. The result of this rapid expansion was a tremendous overcrowding which caused Defoe to say: "No place, except London and Edinburgh, confined so many inhabitants in so small a compass"; the buildings were "no longer beautiful," and the streets too narrow "for convenience or health."

Liverpool's suddenly-expanding, multifarious population is a typical frontier story. Though Bristol was in a prime position, with its proximity to wealth and its ties to Bath, the great watering-hole of royalty,

Nearly two-thirds of the ships that sailed for West Africa were from Bristol. But Bristol itself, like Liverpool, did not see blacks until the 1952 influx of black immigrants

Courtesy Bristol Web Site

Early pictures of slaves captured in Africa

Liverpool began to outstrip Bristol and became the "eighteenth century success story"—and it is here, perhaps, that we find the key to Liverpool's unique character.

Liverpool traders used different methods from the London and Bristol traders, methods which relied upon the *personal* approach in negotiating and risk taking. Furthermore, having less experience of commercial life, these entrepreneurial revolutionaries had to develop wealth and business experience very rapidly. James Rawley wrote:

Liverpool slave merchants came from diverse sections of society in the town and country, and from outside Lancashire. (Merchants, manufacturers and businessmen provided one source; landowners another; tradesmen a third; and self-made men a fourth). This diversity of origin perhaps explains the energy and vitality that marked the Liverpool slave-merchant community.[1]

Perhaps here, Rawley has put his finger on the pulse of Liverpool. In the arts, as well as in business, Liverpool has ever been the paysanne parvenue—the upstart peasant—trying to show-off to the big-shots in the city. Even today this energy makes itself felt. Bristol, in comparison, though it was once superior to Liverpool as a port, in character is more of an agricultural community, semi-rural, with a slow wit and an even slower way of talking—a complete contrast to the dynamism of Liverpool.

Bristol has a large black population, but it never integrated them—nor were they segregated. Finding no responsive chord in the community, the blacks kept at a respectful, polite distance. Bristol possesses one of the largest black nightclubs in England, but there are never any whites in it. Nor are there any major problems of racism. In Bristol, each community seems to keep quietly to itself; black and white. The result is a much quieter and sedate though rather colorless society—no pun intended.

In a word, the interchange between white and black cultures which took place in Liverpool did not occur in Bristol because of a radical difference in the sensibility of the Bristolian whites—as I learned when I played the blues there.

Bristol, Scrumpy and the Blues
—A Personal Anecdote—

After my difference of opinion with the collective feet of twenty street blacks, as a safety measure, I moved down to Bristol with Moo for a few months. It was a port. It had a black population. The Bristolians liked to drink. But, for all it had in common with Liverpool, it might have been Mars.

I was, by nature and background, a gregarious soul. But, alas, in six months of touring Bristol's clubs and pubs, I had not made one friend or social contact. I fretted. Unlike my familiar Liverpool pubs where a conversation would occur spontaneously and friends could be acquired overnight, in Bristol, I found that people actually shied away from me. My bouncy Liverpool bonhommie received a cold shoulder from the taciturn Bristolians.

Gloomy, lonely and broke, I did what any Scouser would in my place—turn to drink. Except that I couldn't afford it. Then, fortunately or unfortunately, as opinion may have it, I came across the cheapest, most incredibly potent brew I'd ever quaffed.

Scrumpy is a substance unknown in America, and because of the trouble it foments, it had largely been prohibited in the Bristol pubs of the early Sixties. Like its forerunner, Absinthe—which, Oscar Wilde punned, "makes the heart grow fonder"—it was also reputed to cause stomach ulcers, blindness and brain damage—which is probably true.

A milky-green liquid, Scrumpy is brewed from apples, and each brewer has his own fermentation secrets: nails; copper pennies; dead rats; and sheep carcasses are often thrown into the fermenting brew. Any relationship to the American beverage cider is merely an accident of linguistics. It is no exaggeration to say that it is not merely potent, but lethal. A heavy drinker can, at most, take two pints, though there were exceptions to this rule. I was a heavy drinker, but I was not an exception to the rule—as I was to find out.

It was the wig that tipped me off. Like any Liverpool-Irish drinker, I needed alcohol, and the most I could manage were infrequent trips to the corner bottle shop[2].

The shop owner, a suspicious bewigged man, would take my 20p (about 40 cents) and give me a quart of Olde English Cider, the cheapest and most potent source of alcohol that I could find.

I began to notice that with each of my trips to the shop for further sustenance, the shopkeeper's wig would appear to have rotated slightly, so that by my fifth trip, the wig had usually turned a full 180 degrees. With his round flushed face, this gave the shopkeeper something of the appearance of Moe from the Three Stooges. As the night wore on, the shopkeeper's replies would become monosyllabic gibberish and eventually bore no relationship to my questions whatsoever.

Then, in one fell stroke, I discovered the reason for the shopkeeper's intermittent insanity—and the road to Nirvana.

One night, instead of handing me the usual quart of Olde English, the shopkeeper muttered: "Try this. It's the same price," pointing to a wooden barrel on the shelf.

This turned out to be Scrumpy.

Back in the dour confines of the vast but shabby apartment, I poured a pint from the two-quart bottle. "This may be it," I chortled to Moo, "I bet this is what's sending the friggin' shop-keeper do-larry[3]. We may have cracked the Bristol Boredom syndrome, Moo!"

Moo eyed the murky-green liquid with trepidation but said nothing.

According to my custom, I downed the whole pint in one gulp and, as eager as any medieval alchemist, awaited the results of the bio-experiment:

T + 5 secs:	"JESUS!" I cried glassy-eyed. I felt as if I'd just been hit with a baseball bat.
T + 6 secs:	"What?!" exclaimed a concerned Moo as I gurgled incoherently.
T + 7 secs:	"My nose...it's going numb."
T + 8 secs"	Silence.
T + 9 secs:	Moo, concerned: "Look, maybe you shouldn't have drunk the whole pint."
T + 10 secs.:	I gave a rather lop-sided grin and mumbled: "We've found it, Moo. This is it."
T + 30 secs:	I slumped out, unconscious.

Bristol Harbor

Courtesy Bristol's Web Site

Eight hours later, I awoke, jubilant and refreshed. "Moo," I announced with all the pride of Edmund Hilary after ascending Everest, "We have done it! Our social problems are over."

We discovered a pub, The Coronation Tap, where the Scrumpy was even cheaper. And one fateful night, we made the mistake of downing two pints on empty stomachs. Moo had chided me, saying we should eat.

"Eat?!!" I exclaimed, "We can't eat! It's either eat or drink. And what'll we eat for 25p, eh? Besides, think of all the goodness in this—it's full of nutrition." I held my glass up aloft and eyed the greenish syrup as though it were Chateau Neuf du Pape.

Moo was not so enthusiastic. Nevertheless, circumstances prevailed and she drank.

It was a big mistake.

Light glided by with a distant roaring sound that filled me with a dim perplexity. Something shimmered in front of my eyes; hard; gleaming; cold; and my face felt flat, compressed, as though it were being squashed by a pane of cold glass.

Bewildered, I raised my hand to find it was a pane of glass: I was leaning, face first, on the window of a bus shelter, supported by my cheek pressed against the glass pane. I lurched backwards and my cheek peeled off the glass with a sudden squelch like a suction cup. I focused my eyes with great effort and realized that the lights gliding by were cars. So that was the roaring sound!

I was in the street, somewhere at the top of Clifton Hill. Swaying dangerously on my heels, I tried to remember: How had I gotten here? Where was Moo? What was going on? But all that came to me was a roaring noise in my head as the street lights bobbed up and down.

Bizarre sensations stole up from my extremities: a violent, stabbing in my nose; pins and needles in my feet; and feelings of heat then cold in my buttocks and belly. With a sickly suspicion that I'd been poisoned, I pushed myself away from the safety of the concrete wall.

A huge monster suddenly bore down on me, its eyes aglare, a roaring voice, a cacophony of light and sound that temporarily blinded and deafened me. Had my legs not been like rubber, I would have fled.

It was only a bus. It disgorged two passengers who avoided me in a wide, wary circle as though I were a caged beast. Then they hurried away and I was alone again.

Then I spotted Moo. "Moo... Moo!" My voice was thick in my throat. I tried again: "Hey, Moo!"

Moo came up the hill with the measured, heavy steps of a somnambulist, her granny glasses glittering in the street lights. Her head was held erect and her mirrored eyes were fixed and blank; she stared straight ahead. She resembled nothing less than a bad actor from the *Night of the Living Dead*, and her chalky-white face only added to the ham effect.

"Moo... Oh, Moo! What's happening?" I gurgled. I swayed and clutched the shelter rail, nearly falling over. "Moo!!"

But Moo, at a regular wooden pace of no more than two miles an hour, never even looked at me but stomped past with her fixed, zombie expression.

"Moo!!" I cried in indignation and reached out quivering fingers. But my reach fell short and Moo was gone, her stiff, waxy footsteps carrying her off into the night.

"Moo!!" I yelled in despair and anger, "What the hell?!! Come back, you! What is this?!!"

235

Bristol's Industrial Area

But the only answer was the wail of a fog-horn in the distance and the pounding of my own ears.

With grim determination, I propelled myself from the wall and, with a gait like Douglas Bader's[4] first tentative steps on his newly-acquired prosthetic legs, I staggered off to find Moo.

Something bothered me. It wasn't just the noise in the background or the smells, but the sensation on my forehead—a dull, throbbing pressure. I frowned, then realized that I was sitting forward in a seat with my forehead against the chair in front. I jerked upright and focused blearily:

Singers; guitars; chairs.

I was in a small room over one of the local pubs. Slowly my brain cleared sufficiently for me to recognize it: the Colton Folk Club—a place I hated!

I had no recollection of how I'd got there! I glanced down. There, between my feet, was a full half-pint of Scrumpy nestling amongst the wet sawdust on the wooden floor. Not being sufficiently coherent to realize that therein lay the root of my present predicament, I chortled and raised the glass to my lips, somehow managing not to spill a drop.

Someone had obviously bought me a drink. I grinned amicably at the girl next to me. She sported waist-length, immaculately clean hair, a green blouse and skirt and sandals. Even through my drunken haze, I recognized a 'Folk Music Purist'—a phenomenon that, as a rock musician, normally made my toes curl in embarrassment. But, grateful to my unknown benefactor, I cheerfully raised my glass, thinking it had been her, and said: "Well, thanks for the drink, luv." What actually emerged was something like: "Fangs or a drinkuv."

With a grimace of disparagement, the girl moved and sat down further away, turned her gaze to the stage and resumed the trance-like expression of the Connoisseur-of-Ethnic-Music.

I made an attempt at a disdainful shrug that nearly made me fall off my seat. "Woa!" I cried, fearful for my drink. I regained my balance and turned my attention to the stage—and groaned.

I hated folk clubs simply because everyone was so serious. I also disliked any music without a beat. Most of all, I hated the rapt, enthralled silence with which the audience (who never drank more than a half pint of bitter) would listen to the singer reel off the ethnic history credits of his missive:

> "And now I'd like to sing a ballad discovered by Critchley and annotated in his well-known book, *The Lost Songs of the Association of Woolgatherers and Packers, Middleton-on-the-Weir in The Early 1900s.* This little ditty,

which consists of alternating stanzas in the ABAB pattern, describes how the woolgatherers at the end of the day would congregate around the village church and..."

I stared, glazed and helpless, at the acned youth on the stage, clad in a farmer's smock and leggings, who delivered this vast, rambling pre-amble. Finally it was over and the youth bowed to a thunderous applause.

I sank back with a sigh of relief. But my relief didn't last long. The singer cleared his throat, put one hand on his hip, folk-singer style, put the finger of his other hand in his ear and, striking the traditional Unaccompanied Singer Pose, he began.

The structure of the song was incredible. Notes and glissandos soared along exotic musical routes undeterred by the presence of a musical instrument which may have at least kept the lad within some kind of harmonic structure.

To my musical ear, it was agonizing. I screwed up my face in pain, clapped my hands over my ears and tried to stand up.

"Ssshhh!" Like a punctured steam pipe, a vast hiss of admonishment arose from the crowd. Beaten, I slumped back in my seat.

Someone leant over to me and whispered in my ear: "Do you want to perform, then?" It was the M.C., a rather fat and bellicose youth who eyed my black outfit suspiciously.

"Oh, er...oh yeah...yeah," I spluttered, "Is there a guitar up there?"

"What did ye say?" queried the youth in a broad country accent.

I managed to convey my desires, and the disgruntled youth, concerned about subduing the gushes of steam arising from the "shhing" audience, reluctantly agreed to borrow a guitar for me.

The acned youth finished his 'song' and, seeing this as an opportunity to escape, I staggered up on rickety legs and made for the door. I had almost reached the safety of the Exit when I heard the fat youth announce: "A new artist from, er ... out of town—Peter Pitts!"

It mattered little to me that the fat youth had got my name wrong. What did matter is that I found myself mysteriously propelled away from the Exit by a clapping audience. The noise stopped and, dazed, I found I was standing on the small stage peering into the eager faces of a *Folk Club Audience*, a phenomenon which I had for years decried during long, vast tirades to Moo.

"This is Jonathan, eh," said the M.C.

"Eh?" I said.

"This is Jonathan," the M.C. repeated in a whisper.

Jonathan was a red-faced youth who looked, for all the world, as though he'd just stepped out of the fields. In his right hand he clutched a cheap Hofner guitar with a white, plastic plectrum guard.

My heart sank when I saw the awful piece of non-musical hardware which masqueraded as a guitar. I knew I was in for a difficult time. Any resemblance between this object and a real instrument was accidental, but I realized hopelessly that I'd have to make do.

Jonathan did not relinquish his grip on the guitar immediately. He eyed my hairstyle and tight, black trousers with obvious distaste, then said in a whiny voice: "Now, normally ah don' lend this 'ere guitar out, on account it's my best. But if'n ee uses it now, like, and I unnestands ee's in a bit of a bind at the mooment, well, wipe yer 'ands first, and be sure ye don't scratch it. Now, let me see yer finger-nails... Ooh, I see... Well, they'll have ter do..." Jonathan continued in this way for a full ten minutes, as if he were about to release a Stradivarius into the care of an orangutan. Then, and only then, did he reluctantly hand me the guitar.

With a sigh of relief, I sat down in the performer's seat. Simultaneously, the freshly-imbibed glass of Scrumpy seemed to find its way into my bloodstream with the force of a tidal wave. I went numb and almost fell off the chair.

The author performing solo

With all my might, I focused my eyes on one of the lights and slid my hand around the neck of the guitar. Gritting my teeth, with tremendous effort I managed to grunt out the name of the song: "I'd like to sing an old blues song called *Going Down Slow.*"

The audience clapped and, with a spurt of sheer willpower, I freed myself momentarily from the numbing grip of the Scrumpy and began singing:

> "Well, I have had my fun... (riff)
> If I don't get well no more.... (riff)
> Oh Lord!
> I have had my fun
> If I don't get well no more..."

I was playing and singing on a fully automatic pilot. But even through my addled brain, I realized something was very wrong. I was playing O.K., I thought (considering), even singing O.K. (considering) but, gradually, people were beginning to stand up and head for the door, the bar, the toilet, the pie stand; anywhere, in fact, that was away from me. But with nothing left to lose, I persisted with the song:

> "Lookee over there yonder,
> See a team of white horses coming by.
> Lord, I don't mind dying
> But I hate to see my children a'cryin' ..."

The notes shrilled and surged. As I droned the morbid lyrics, I bent and whined the strings, pulling them halfway across the neck with drunken fervor, counterpointing the heavy, solemn rhythm of the blues. But somehow it wasn't right; something odd and discordant merged and clashed with my voice...something I couldn't quite place.

I'd barely finished, when the M.C. whipped the guitar out of my hand and announced in a shaky voice: "Thank you Peter. And now, we'll take a short intermission and get back to our *regular* artists. So, time for a quick drink, folks."

There was no reply—as everyone had already left. I was perplexed. Still smarting from the indignity of a badly-received performance, I sat shaking my head, wondering what had happened. Hearing a voice at my side, I turned and jerked back from the round face of Jonathan which hovered in front of me like a large, red moon. "What was that?" I asked.

"I said," reproached Jonathan, "Why didn't you tune the guitar?" I numbly followed Jonathan's pointing finger to the neck of the guitar where the strings hung as slack as wet cotton. "I always leaves the strings slack a'fore playin'," said Jonathan, "Makes 'em last longer. Ye didn't tune 'em..."

With a gurgle of self-reproach, I lurched up and headed in the direction I'd wanted to go all night—towards the door. As I reached it, I heard a snicker from behind. It was Jonathan: "Bin drinkin' Scrumpy, eh, Liverpool?"

Though numbed by the Scrumpy, I sensed vaguely that when the drink wore off, tonight's performance was going to make me feel very, very bad.

Of course, being a veteran of many a binge, I did find my way home. But it was only after a nightmare of crashing through hedges, fences, wrong turnings and negotiating psychotic traffic (seemingly intent on nailing me). I found Moo blithely unconscious in bed and I fell beside her and went out like a light. And, yes, when I awoke I did feel very, very bad.

End Note

It should be realized that my reactions as a rebellious teenage rocker to the Bristol scene were a very subjective reaction to the town. I was then singular in my musical tastes, expansive in my consumption of alcohol and primitive in my attitudes. Bristol is, in fact, a lovely place with a lively musical scene and a very positive cultural scene. To my knowledge, Scrumpy is no longer served in the public houses now because, sadly, it caused too much trouble, though I do believe it is secretly brewed and consumed behind closed doors by many a Bristolian. Seeing behind those closed doors might prove very, very interesting.

American Blacks
& Liverpool Whites

22

American Blacks & Liverpool Whites
"Making A Way Out Of No Way"

A lesser people may not have survived at all. The black achievement has been not only to survive, but to do so with style, with grace, irony and irreverence; and an exuberant vitality that demonstrates an exhilarating capacity to affirm, to celebrate life under the most soul-destroying conditions. Black humor, black music and black folklore all reveal this ability to give life significance. They are all a means of "making a way out of no way".

Charles E. Silberman
Criminal Violence, Criminal Justice

Courtesy Bernie Wenton

Slim Gallard, an American keyboard player with the Wenton brothers: Bobbie (far left),Bernie (back, second right), Bobbie (back, right) and Terry (front right). Betty Lowenthal and Mike Fox also joined them for this picture

In America, the oral culture in black music has acted not only as a catalyst for cultural change but, most importantly, was a way of socializing aggressions and hostilities that would otherwise have disrupted the fabric of American society. And this finds a direct correlation in Liverpool wit which is used exactly for the same purpose: to defuse potential violence.

It is a statistical fact that in Nineties' America, violence is on the increase. The blacks' progress has not followed the normal patterns demonstrated by other reviled subcultures: Irish, Italian, Puerto Rican, Mexican, etc.. After an initial period of repression, most minorities in America have moved up the social scale with each generation. (Unfortunately, so it seems, to then persecute the minority that follows.) In the case of the blacks, this pattern has not emerged and generation after generation of blacks do not move up the social ladder.

In this, there was a direct parallel with the poor whites in England: despite the sweeping social changes implemented by the Labour government, it was still social origin which determined exactly who moved into the power positions. Furthermore, such advantages as were gained by the Labour Government have been gradually undermined by the Thatcher administration over the last decade.

The greatest shock for British musicians of the Sixties when they arrived in America was to see the way their black heroes were treated. Keith Richards recalls "I used to see these posters down South that said, 'Don't let your kids buy Negro records. Savage music—it will twist their minds'."

The subjugation of blacks in America and whites in England had an insidious and crippling effect on the economy because crime—as discussed elsewhere—is not simply deviant behavior at all but a very natural reaction to social repression.

The "descent" of the American black into crime is summed up in the old black-American folk song:

"White man goes to college
Nigger to the jail,
White man learns to read and write
Poor nigger leans to steal."

In a word, black crime does not "lie in the genes". The esteemed Mark Twain himself has posited: "There is no distinctly native American criminal class except Congress."

And, contrary to the popular myth of the Black Savage, violence is not something that the slaves brought with them from West Africa. It was something that was generated in America. The black American has been the victim of some of the foulest atrocities in the history of the American nation. Two unique factors preclude this: 1) their entry into American society as a slave (something not shared by Irish, Italian, Puerto Rican or Mexican, no matter how lowly); and 2) blackness.[1]

Given his situation, the black man has had to defend himself and in the early days of slavery and emancipation where violence and retaliation were out of the question, the black's weapons were oral. He learned to duck, bob and weave; to play the "stupid nigger" because his life depended on it. One outcome of this is the harmless, comic farce of the Black Minstrel that proliferated throughout American culture; the ultimate expression of the tragicomedy implicit in the blues.

The so-called laziness of the blacks is a mark not of stupidity but adaptation to an untenable situation, and indicates just how adept the blacks have been in staying alive by manipulating the white man in this fashion. After all, sloppy work and laziness are, in the long run, the only form of sabotage available to a race living under threat of violence or death.

No matter how whites talk about racism, they can never experience it.

Blacks have had to learn to live with rage and, as James Baldwin pointed out, they have had to discover and create ways of channeling this anger as a form of self-protection—for Anger + Rage = Death.

This resulted in a tradition of musical and oral expression largely unknown to the white man because it was only practiced amongst blacks. Other aspects of it have become more public domain. The net result has been an African-American culture of momentous effect that has literally altered the face of America.

John Lennon pointed out that it was the black music that he played while even the blacks in America were laughing at the blues and people like Chuck Berry. "Nobody was listening to rock & roll or to black music in America. We felt like we were coming to the land of its origin, but nobody wanted to know about it."

John Lennon

Noel Redding, the British bass player for Jimi Hendrix, once described an experience of going into a bar in the USA with Jimi and watching a TV report about the Martin Luther King assassination. Men at the bar starting mouthing racial slurs. Jimi kept his mouth shut and stayed cool. Noel, who had never before thought of Jimi as being a black man but simply as a musician, was deeply troubled. For the first time Noel realized that a man could be killed in America solely because of his skin color.

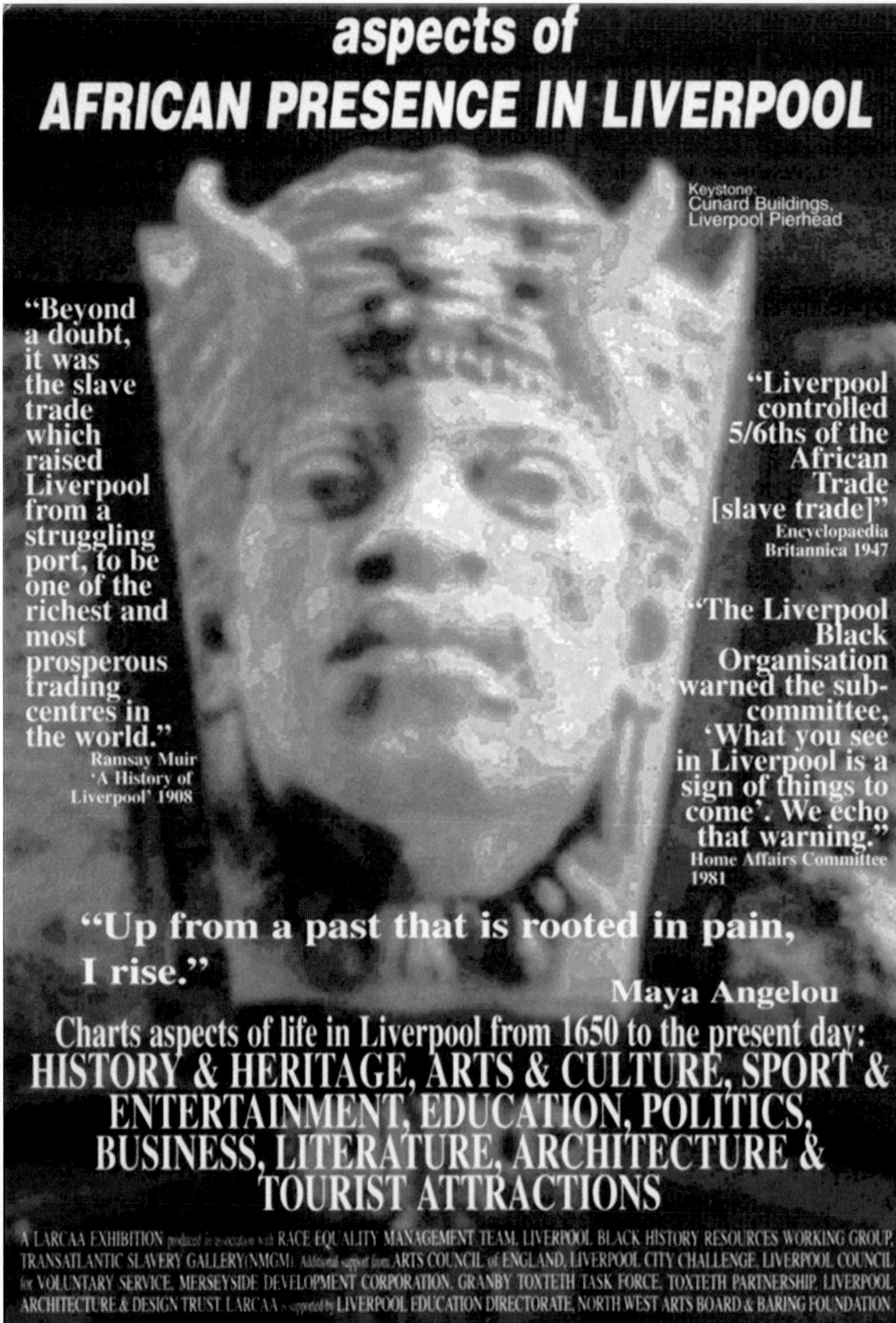

aspects of
AFRICAN PRESENCE IN LIVERPOOL

Keystone:
Cunard Buildings,
Liverpool Pierhead

"Beyond a doubt, it was the slave trade which raised Liverpool from a struggling port, to be one of the richest and most prosperous trading centres in the world."
Ramsay Muir
'A History of Liverpool' 1908

"Liverpool controlled 5/6ths of the African Trade [slave trade]"
Encyclopaedia Britannica 1947

"The Liverpool Black Organisation warned the sub-committee, 'What you see in Liverpool is a sign of things to come'. We echo that warning."
Home Affairs Committee 1981

"Up from a past that is rooted in pain, I rise."

Maya Angelou

Charts aspects of life in Liverpool from 1650 to the present day:
HISTORY & HERITAGE, ARTS & CULTURE, SPORT & ENTERTAINMENT, EDUCATION, POLITICS, BUSINESS, LITERATURE, ARCHITECTURE & TOURIST ATTRACTIONS

A LARCAA EXHIBITION produced in association with RACE EQUALITY MANAGEMENT TEAM, LIVERPOOL BLACK HISTORY RESOURCES WORKING GROUP, TRANSATLANTIC SLAVERY GALLERY(NMGM). Additional support from ARTS COUNCIL of ENGLAND, LIVERPOOL CITY CHALLENGE, LIVERPOOL COUNCIL for VOLUNTARY SERVICE, MERSEYSIDE DEVELOPMENT CORPORATION, GRANBY TOXTETH TASK FORCE, TOXTETH PARTNERSHIP, LIVERPOOL ARCHITECTURE & DESIGN TRUST. LARCAA is supported by LIVERPOOL EDUCATION DIRECTORATE, NORTH WEST ARTS BOARD & BARING FOUNDATION.

Courtesy Mindscaffolding

Support Black History Month in Liverpool

"Until the lions have their historians, tales of hunting will always glorify the hunter."
African Proverb

GOLDEN LEGACY
ILLUSTRATED HISTORY MAGAZINE

GOLDEN LEGACY
ILLUSTRATED HISTORY MAGAZINE

The Saga of
HARRIET TUBMAN
"The Moses of Her People"
Vol. 2

FREDERICK DOUGLASS
PART TWO
Vol. 8

GOLDEN LEGACY
ILLUSTRATED HISTORY MAGAZINE

THE LIFE OF
MATTHEW HENSON
Vol. 5

GOLDEN LEGACY
ILLUSTRATED HISTORY MAGAZINE

THE BLACK INVENTORS
LATIMER & WOODS
Vol. 16

THE LIFE OF
MARTIN LUTHER KING JR.
Vol. 13

GOLDEN LEGACY
ILLUSTRATED HISTORY MAGAZINE

ALEXANDER DUMAS
AND FAMILY
Vol. 6

Above: some of the Golden Legacy series from Fitzgerald Publishing Co., Inc. USA. Right: the first publication from Liverpool's Black History Resources Working Group.

Slavery: An Introduction To The African Holocaust

Suitable For KS3 of The National Curriculum For History

Courtesy Mindscaffolding

243

Music and Oral Tradition As Survival Factors

"Into each life some jazz must fall
With afterbeat gone kicking
With jive-alive a ball for all
Let not the beat be chicken."
Ascribed to Cannonball Aderley[2]

The blacks' catalogue of personal tragedy began with the blues, a tradition of which most Americans are at least aware.

But, it didn't stay there.

With the blacks, as with the poor Liverpudlians—as, indeed amongst any people denied access to power—verbal adroitness has been used as a substitute for prestige. Jokes and repartee are all forms of expression highly prized by the Liverpudlian and, in exactly the same way, the blacks used verbal adeptness as a mark of prestige amongst themselves.

> The African race is like a rubber ball—the harder you dash it to the ground, the higher it will rise.
>
> African Proverb
> Wisdom of Our Elders
> Ebony Power Thoughts

American society has become much richer for this oral tradition, but, more implicitly—as sociologists have begun to point out—the breakdown of this oral tradition and the black social sanctions that accompanied it is one of the reasons for the escalation of black violence in the Eighties.

In *The Cotton Club*, a movie about the famous club in Harlem where black entertainers, paradoxically, played to all-white audiences, one of the black protagonists (played by dancer Gregory Hines) is being coerced into violence by a fellow black. Hines defers, with the remark: "No, we'll kill 'em with our tap shoes." Then follows a beautifully-choreographed sequence where Hines, in foot-blurring action, dances up a flight of stairs while the sequence is syncopated to the rat-tat-tat of a machine-gun assassination taking place simultaneously by white gangsters elsewhere. It is a neat, poetic statement of white violence/black entertainment.

> Yeah, life hurts like hell, but this is how I keep going. I have a sense of humor, I've got my brothers and sisters. I've got the ability to make something out of nothing. I can clap my hands and make magic.
>
> Bill T. Jones, Black Pearls
> Ebony Power Thoughts

In this graphic image lies the key to the black man's socialization of his hostilities and the foundation of black culture.

The Changes of Attitude Revealed in Black Music

If the history of black music is analyzed, it reveals a gradual change of attitude in the black man, both to himself and to American society in general:

The Blues:

The blues was largely tragicomic. Comic, because to draw too much attention to his heartfelt angst would only attract reprisal, even death, to the early slave.

Blues' lyrics were a constant lament; but while they dealt with love, death, drink, women and sex, the enemy was never defined. Robert Johnson sings of "stones in my pathway, hell-hound on my trail." Such references have led early white blues ethnographers to talk about 'the mystical apparition' that haunts the black man's blue's lyrics; a relentless, malevolent force that pursued the black man. There was nothing mystical at all about this hell hound. The tormentor whose face the black singer could not reveal was, simply, the white man.

Big Bill Broonzey was more outspoken and, in an interview with Studs Terkel, he pointed out that he had been criticized for his lyrics in *Black, Brown and White*:

If you're white, you're all right,
If you're brown, stick around,
If you're black, whoa brother,
Get back, get back, get back...

This song was criticized by both blacks and whites. But such explicit forms of expression were uncommon. The early blues' artist had only two strings to his bow of self expression: he could lament incoherently or make the white man laugh.

Soul:

With soul music, a change of stance has taken place. Here, time has allowed the black artist some modicum of respect if not for his skin color, for his music. Thus, he is allowed to indulge an emotion which seems, very largely, the prerequisite of the poor the world over: sentimentality.

In both Liverpool culture and black soul music, sentimentality is rife. Cynicism is an indulgence of the educated, privileged middle class (which by definition, includes most black writers) coupled with rage, aggression and finger-pointing. Sentimentality is the province of a subject race, and is always "the echo of violence."[3] (Ringo, noticeably the most sentimental of the Beatles, was brought up in the violent battleground of the notorious Park Road area.)

Rhythm & Blues:

A further change was to take place with the blending of blues and soul into rhythm and blues, which was then transformed into the hard rhythms of rock. Here we have similar lyrics, the age-old themes of love, sex—and, with the advent of Chuck Berry and Fifties white rock, the teenager's rite of passage—but its primary feel is jungle sex and jungle rhythm.

Rock:

And it is at this point that musical history takes an odd turn: It was largely the Liverpool white musicians who seized upon a factor which was only implicit in black American music—aggression—and indulged it to the full. Though this was there, lurking beneath the surface of the musical genre, its full expression was denied to American black musicians because of socio-political factors.

Not so the Liverpool rock musicians. Pumped up on amphetamines, cocky, feisty, they would take a slightly schmaltzy Ray Charles' number, such as *Hit the Road Jack* or *Sticks and Stones*, with its bland Quincy Jones jazziness, strip it down to its core, then deliver the same number with all the angry force of a trip-hammer. Liverpool responded to the feeling behind black music, absorbed it and regurgitated it with the full force of its illicit emotion: violence.

The black man could not express violence publicly, but he did privately—but it was for black ears only. It is an aspect of the black oral tradition which has received little widespread attention by whites, largely because they were never intended to hear it.

The man who asserts his masculinity and refuses to bow before authority is therefore good. Thus, a bad nigger is one who is so bad, he is good; he is admirable in his defiance. Christina & Richard Milner Black Players	The subject treated is freedom of the body through super-human feats and [freedom] of the spirit through acts that are free of restrictive social mores (or in direct violation of them), especially in respect to crime and violence. Roger D. Abrahams Positively Black

Toasting: (Signifying; Joning; Running Down)

> Got a tombstone disposition
> And a graveyard mind,
> I'm a mean mother-fucker
> And I don't mind dyin'...

One of the significant changes that has taken place in black culture in the last twenty years is the disappearance of the verbal contests that formerly provided an alternative to street fighting. These contests—toasting; joning; playing the dozens (a highly ritualized exchange of obscene rhymed insults directed at the contestants' mothers or other female relatives)—served as a social restraint simply because those who responded to the verbal insults with violence were condemned as the losers. It was a natural control factor because self-control under extreme provocation was essential to blacks in the South.[4]

To some extent, joning and running down has been replaced by jive talk (which is now more a form of machismo) and rap. While rap still serves as a social restraint, the subculture of toasting has become almost obsolete. The earlier tradition of toasting passed by largely unseen by the white man, though some has slipped into popular songs (notably *Stackolee* or *Stagolee*).

The toasting tradition is a fascinating example of a profound fact: that if you sit upon a man's self-respect, it will assert itself elsewhere. The Badman toasts are the most significant because, as the black man was denied a social outlet for his hostility, toasts lauded the ultimate badness of a superhero—a hero who ignored social sanctions, death (his own and others) and familial restraints.

> Bitch jumped up and said, "Baby, please!"
> He shot that whore through both her knees
> A pimp eased up and turned out the lights
> And I heard, "I'm dead" in both my sights
> When the lights came back on poor Billy gone to rest
> With nine of mah rockets in his mother-fuckin' chest.

The most obvious aspect of the toast is inversion: Stacker Lee is B-A-A-D, real BAD, and that is his kudos. Being "good" by the white man's code meant being a "boy", to keep in line, to obey. Thus the reversal in the toasts is that Stacker Lee is good because he's so bad.

The quotes above are from studies of black culture in the early Seventies. In the Eighties, this black slang became the common parlance of rebellious, white youth: bad is good; tough is great; bitchin is better. In other words, the reversals of the toasting songs

But, more significantly, as toasting, joning and signifying died out, something more sinister happened: released of some of the restraints of the white man's suppression, the black man has come to realize, after 350 years of fearing whites, that the white man is afraid of him:

The blues, toasting, the Badman myth, the Trickster stories once worked as unseen outlets for the black man's rage and pain, but in the Eighties, the shift was from myth to reality. In an incredible explosion of mindless violence, the "bad nigger" is no longer a mythical character enjoyed by blacks in the privacy of their own oral culture, but he is now a sobering social reality splashed on the pages of our daily newspapers.

To understand the reasons for crime is not to condone it; and blacks themselves are realizing the extent of the violence which is being released. Former militants like Eldridge Cleaver have begun to ease up, now realizing that black violence is getting out of control. It is not whites who suffer. The rate of black to white murder victims by blacks is about eight to one. And as Cleaver eventually came to remark: "The price of hating other human beings is loving myself less."

Through entertainment, education and social reform programs, the blacks—slow though the process may be—are beginning to move into a stronger position in society. During this transitional period, their culture is in a turmoil and the control factors of the slave mentality are breaking down. But, at present, there is nothing to replace it from within the black community: the black middle class won't live in black areas; the oral tradition no longer provides a safe outlet; and drug money and weaponry have increased the power of formerly economically-deprived groups, East Los Angeles being the prime example.

The crucial factor in the ghetto culture is the lack of strong, male role figures: The alpha males who could act as forces for social restraint either get out of the ghetto or become criminal overlords.

It is the rap artists who are the last bastion of black culture with any kind of stabilizing influence.

In a PBS Special, Rappers who were accused of promoting violence, denied this vehemently. 'KRS One' and 'Ice-T', both media success stories as Rappers, stated quite fiercely that without rap, there would be much more violence.
The MacNeil Lehrer Newshour
June 28, 1989
PBS Special

When a man angers you, he conquers you.
Toni Morrison
Quotations from African Americans
Ebony Power Thoughts

RAP: The Culmination of the Black, Musical Odyssey

Look at me, dude
Listen what I say
Bin a long time comin'
But I'm here to stay...

The black slave could only moan his cry in the dark. But in the Eighties, the black man, fiercely proud and defiant, stood upright on both legs, stared the white man straight in the eye and rapped.

The history of black music is, therefore, a history of the black man's attitude to himself and society, and the culmination of this progressive change, is rap. With rap, the cat is out of the bag, so to speak; now the black is taking an open stand: "I'm here, listen yo!" is the rap message. It is declarative, defiant.

Those who denigrate rap music, who deem it as an incitement to violence, miss one significant point: it is still oral; it is still within the tradition of sublimation; and it is still better than physical action. Rap is intrinsically good. The fact that it could be used to promote violence is simply an indictment of the fact that the violence is there to be promoted, and not of rap itself.

Rap, then, is simply part of a long oral tradition. The word, once again, is out on the street: the black man is "making a way out of no way."

Courtesy Bernie Wenton
Bernie Wenton's grandfather pulling his ticket booth down to the Pierhead where he sold tickets for the ferry from Liverpool to North Wales

The 'mores' of the western world are based on a very deep-rooted conception of right and wrong, embedded in the metaphor of blackness being synonymous with badness.

A black scholar has pointed out that the Oxford English Dictionary gives him "724 ways of insulting himself." Linguistically, the implication of the word "black" is always pejorative (foul; evil-smelling; dirty; sullied); whereas "white" signifies "good, clean, virtuous" etc.. Like it or not, this is so deeply embedded into our collective consciousness that the black man starts life with a unique disadvantage. The well-springs of prejudice against "blackness" run so deep that liberal whites are not aware of the tug of this malign current ever present beneath the consciousness of the most benign liberal——but the black man is.

There is, in this world, no such force as the force of a man determined to rise. The human sould cannot be permanently chained.

W.E.B. Du Bois
My Soul Looks Back Lest I Forget
Ebony Power Thoughts

The Landing Stage at the Pierhead where Bernie Wenton's grandfather set up his ticket booth

Bernie Wenton (second right) and lovely wife (second left) with Ken Dodd, the well-known Liverpool comedian and his girlfriend, early '90s. Bernie has moved a long way from his humble origins.

The American Presence In Europe

The American Presence in Europe

During World War II, Liverpool was a landing stage for American planes and servicemen. This P-51 Mustang minus tail and wingtaps is being towed down Liverpool's main street in 1944 on its way to Burtonwood Air Base to be re-assembled

A nd so, the issues raised at the beginning of this book have, in part, been clarified: why were there 350 groups in Liverpool when there were hardly any in the rest of England? The answer lay in a comparison with the emerging black culture in America. A parallel was drawn between the short-term socio-economic development in postwar England and the longer development in America of civil and social reform factors:

Postwar England saw the demise of the British empire; the rise of public housing and public education; and the partial emancipation of the working class. Postwar America saw the civil rights movements and the partial emancipation of the blacks.

Thus, American blacks and poor English whites both experienced a period of release and emancipation in the Sixties. It was demonstrated that there are more similarities than are commonly acknowledged between poor American blacks and poor English whites. This was revealed by similar attitudes to crime; violence; sport; drink; drugs; and, particularly in the rise of oral traditions as a form of release and self-expression.

Furthermore, it was shown that these forces have been more active in Liverpool than in any other segment of English society. Various factors were examined which explain this: Liverpool's peculiar position as a nexus of cultures—Scottish, Irish, Welsh and English; and the influx of immigrants in the 1950s, to name but two. A comparison was made with other towns (like Bristol) which were also subject to the massive influx of blacks, Asians and other immigrants in the Fifties, a comparison which revealed a degree of empathy and integration in Liverpool that did not exist elsewhere.

On the wider front, national and international events resounded throughout the world, resulting in the great upheavals of the late Sixties and continued in the incredible, worldwide revolutions of the late Eighties.

In America during the Sixties, these manifested themselves as the dream of the civil rights movement. In Sixties England, the parallel was in the rise of the youth movement, the working class and the Beatles.

Only a few more factors needs to be added and the picture is almost complete.

A Few More Strands: (1) The American Presence in England: Air Bases

World War II brought in its wake not only the demise of the British Empire but the legacy of American occupation of England, France and Germany. The effect of their presence was to have significant ramifications for British music.

In many ways, it was the culmination of Liverpool's enchantment with America and black music, both an end and a beginning.

The American air base, Burtonwood, near Liverpool became a source of tribulation to Liverpool parents afraid for their daughters. The girls flocked to the Yanks like bees to honey. For Liverpool teenagers, Burtonwood was an Aladdin's cave and Liverpudlians greedily consumed the largesse generously dispensed by the 'rich' American soldiers and the PBXs: American liquor; chocolates; cigarettes; and, of course, music.

In the Sixties, the disparity between the economy of Northern England and that of America meant that the average G.I. was wealthy in comparison to the typical Liverpudlian who could barely get a job, let alone a wage. This was a source of some envy to the Liverpool males, as the girls, knowing which side of their bread was buttered, made a rush for the Yanks.

One of my fondest childhood memories is of a huge box of candies—chocolate-covered cherries dipped in creme and rum—delivered to our humble Liverpool home by my sister's beau; a smiling, swaggering crew-cut youth (named Eddie Zich—where are you Eddie?) Postwar kids had all been brought up with sweet rationing, so these candies were like ambrosia from the Gods. And, along with the candies came the music.

(2) AFN and Luxie

You didn't know whether they were black or white. It was just an electric sound on the radio. You just got intrigued by the sound of this mystic image, this intriguing sound over the radio.

Paul McCartney

The history of British music and the rise of the Beatles may have been very different without the influence of the AFN broadcasts in Europe and Radio Luxembourg (or Luxie).

In the late Fifties, the Beatles and other Liverpudlian music aficionados would listen to the output of AFN and Luxembourg with awe and delight (there were no commercial radio stations in England), amused and astounded by the American-style advertisements. But that whistling, hissing contact across the air waves was the single most prominent link with up-to-date American music. Significantly, the programming was not just that of white-dominated America, but also the black artists who were only being played on minority radio stations in the U.S.A..

Some of the programming was white pop: Elvis, Buddy Holly, Guy Mitchell. But, there was also something else: rhythm & blues and Chuck Berry.

In fact, if a catalogue were made of the early American musical influences on the Beatles and

Liverpool groups, it would consist largely of the output of these stations; an odd freak of coincidence due to two factors: 1) the Allied Forces occupation of Europe; and 2), the large number of poor blacks who became American soldiers.

Radio Luxembourg: A Great American Source

Without Radio Luxembourg, the story of the rise of British rock may have been very different indeed. In postwar Britain, the BBC still had the monopoly on broadcast programs. There were only three channels: the Light Program (big bands, orchestral music); the Home Program (talk shows, documentaries, popular drama); and the Third Program (classical, highbrow music). This was the sum total of Britain's radio repertoire, with not an Americanism in sight (heaven forbid!). And yet, whenever there was the slightest chance that an American song could be heard, teenagers would be glued to the radio. However, the restrictive programming of the BBC meant that very little American music was to be heard on BBC broadcasts.

Fortunately for the history of British rock, fate intervened in the form of Radio Luxembourg, located in the Grand Duchy of Luxembourg which was free from the broadcasting restrictions of a country.

In 1939, Luxembourg was occupied by the Germans, who used it as a powerful transmitter to disseminate propaganda throughout Europe. But by the mid-'50s, in the hands of the free world once again, it bounced back, broadcasting on 208 meters medium wave.

It began transmission at 7:00 p.m., GMT, every day. It was an exciting concept to the media-starved British who would dial in 208 (which was constantly phasing and fading as it was an extremely narrow waveband) and listen spellbound.

Luxembourg owed its success not just to good timing but to a highly innovative programming philosophy. They were the first to start a Top Twenty show. Furthermore, Luxembourg's policy was to disseminate all styles of music. They played anything: top hits, gospel even hillbilly.

It was to Luxembourg's ethereal, static-laden noise that budding guitarists like the young Paul McCartney and thousands of other enchanted British youths would listen avidly, grasping after anything that came from America. And it did: Chuck Berry, Guy Mitchell, The Coasters, Elvis Presley, Buddy Holly, Duane Eddy—a passport to nightly nirvana in a bleak, postwar Britain.

British music is eternally indebted to this station which is still referred to by British musicians as "Luxie" with an affection reserved for lovers, mothers and families, of which it can be said it was, perhaps, all three, nurturing within its bosom the seeds of '60s music.

(3) Air Bases in France & Germany

T.T.'s return from France

Earle Preston and the T.T.'s have returned from a two-month season in France, where they appeared at four U.S. bases. Female vocalist Wendy Harris was so successful that the group will be including her in their appearances in Liverpool. The group will remain on Merseyside for one month and then return to France for at least two months.

On their last evening in France, they sat in on a jam session with the recording group, Dave D'Coster and the Strollers, which was more successful than the time a French group sat in with them, for the French group had a line-up of trumpet, accordian and drums.

Lance Railton, a folk music enthusiast, introduced a number of folk songs into the performances and they were enthusiastically received.

Article about the Liverpool group Earl Preston and the TTs after a gig in Paris

The American presence in Europe was to give rise to a number of points at which black American music inadvertently touched Great Britain. For example, Lonnie Donegan, a key figure in the birth of British rock was to expand his knowledge of American music and guitars when he served his National Service in Vienna and met American soldiers there.

Also the English groups which began touring American air bases in the early '60s were a key point of communication with black American G.I.s. In particular, the blacks on the air bases loved the Liverpool groups. The reason was simple: the musicians' sets consisted largely of numbers that, in America, were broadcast only by "Race" stations. Because of this, bonds immediately sprung up between these black G.I.s and the young musicians. The Liverpool lads and black G.I.s would swap anecdotes way into the small hours. The black soldiers, estranged from home and their own culture, were simply overwhelmed to hear their own music.

But it was not all wine and roses...

Advertisement in French Newspaper, early '60s

(4) The German Connection
Derry Wilkie, a Liverpool Black Opens the Door for the Beatles
(A Brief Flashback to the Beatles' Pre-Fame Days)

One of the prevalent myths of musical history is that the Beatles went to Hamburg, Germany, refined their style and came back to reintroduce this into the Liverpool rock world. This is not quite true. For a start, they weren't the first (or the only) group to go to Germany. As this account has shown, lots of bands went. The actual facts are a little more subtle than the usual historical gloss.

The man who quite inadvertently started the Liverpool-Hamburg connection was ALLAN WILLIAMS.

Allan was the manager of the Jacaranda, the tiny, dank cellar coffee-bar in Liverpool mentioned earlier where beat poets, the young Beatles and impoverished pill-heads would hang out until the early hours. Just around the corner was a more sophisticated drinking club, the Blue Angel, which was also owned by Williams and his wife Beryl.

The Blue Angel was a little more salubrious than the Jacaranda, and was frequented by the creative and arcane of Liverpool, particularly the more successful bands. Allan was a small, energetic man, constantly misunderstood by all around him as he was an entrepreneur far ahead of his time. (He introduced such novel delights into the Blue Angel as topless barmaids when the world was throwing its arms up at the sight of a belly button.)

Allan's stint as Beatles' manager is, of course, immortalized as part of rock history, the way in which rather mundane events often become so to posterity.

In brief, the facts are that Allan came into contact with a German entrepreneur, Bruno Koschmid who ran The Kaiser Keller in Hamburg, a city which was replete with vice and red-light clubs—in a word, a captive audience for rock 'n roll! Eventually Allan's booking of the Beatles and other groups in his English club led him to take them out to Hamburg, along with his wife Beryl and Lord Woodbine, a West Indian Liverpool character. But the Beatles were not the first to go. In fact, Allan had booked Derry and The Seniors[1] into The Kaiser Keller earlier.

The odd fact is that Derry was the only black group leader in Liverpool and when he got to Hamburg, he literally blew them away. They loved him. But then, even to this day, black rock, jazz and blues singers are more revered in Germany and France than anywhere else in the world. But what an historical footnote: the door to white R&B played by white British guitarists was opened by Derry, a British black. Then the door was closed in his face and Derry, despite being managed by the Epsteins, never hit the big time either in England or in race-conscious America, though he did go on to become very popular in Rome, Italy, of all places.

Hoping to emulate Derry's achievements in Germany, Allan booked the Beatles into The Indra and later on, The Kaiser Keller.

The rest, of course, is history and not without its warts. But still, when was history ever interesting without its warts?

The chief of which was that Derry Wilkie, a black man, paved the way for white Liverpool musicians, then was left by the wayside by posterity; while the groups that followed him went on to

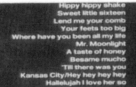

INCLUDES FIFTEEN NEVER BEFORE RELEASED TRACKS

Also available on 8 track cartridges and cassettes.

The Star-Club Album, Hamburg Germany
Look at the variety of music here, all originating from Liverpool

Author's collection

The Tracks on the Star-Club Album (including 15 never-before released):

Hippy, Hippy Shake
Sweet Little Sixteen
Lend Me Your Comb
Your Feets Too Big
Where Have You Been All My Life
Mr. Moonlight
A Taste of Honey
Besarme Mucho
'Til There Was You
Kansas City/Hey, Hey, Hey
Halleluja, I Love Her So
Little Queenie
Falling In Love Again
Sheila
Be-Bop-A-Lula
Red Sails in the Sunset
Everybody's Tryin' To Be My Baby
Matchbox
Talkin' 'Bout You
Shimmy Shake
Long Tall Sally
I Remember You

Hamburg? Memories of Hamburg? Drunken insanity sums it up. You were reduced to a physical wreck after four days, but it was enjoyable to be a physical wreck. It was wonderful lying in the gutter in a whiskey-sodden heap in rain water. I'll never do it again.

Johnny Gustafson

Kingsize Taylor and The Dominoes playing in the Star Club, Hamburg

Courtesy Teddy Taylor

Hamburg-St. Pauli, Große Freiheit 39

CONTRACT

The following contract was signed this day between Manfred Weissleder K.G., 39, Grosse Freiheit, Hamburg-Altona, party of the first part, hereinafter called Employers, and

_____, which includes the following musicians:

party of the second part, hereinafter called the Band.

To wit:

1) The Band will be engaged by the Employers as musicians from _____ until _____. This contract terminates automatically on unless it is extended by mutual consent.

2) The Employers will pay to the members of the Band the following monthly/weekly/daily gross/net salary as follows:—

                                                                 DM

Form this amount, the Employers shall deduct all taxes and social benefit charges required by law and will pay these sums to the appropriate revenue offices.

3) The Employers agree to provide for every member of the Band accomodation for the duration of the contract free of charge at a cost of DM _____ per week.

4) The Employers agree to pay to the leader of the Band the sum of DM _____ for each member of the Band as a travelling allowance. This amount shall be paid only for the trip to Hamburg, no money will be paid for the return trip.

5) All salaries shall be paid on a daily, weekly, monthly basis.

6) Work shall be _____ hours a day. After _____ minutes of playing time, an intermission of _____ minutes will be granted.

   There will be _____ workdays per week.
   The Employers will regulate working hours at the beginning of the engagement. All members of the Band will adhere strictly to these times.

7) In case of a breach of contract by either party, the penalty shall be DM _____, which the defaulting party must pay to the injured party.

8) Without permission of the Employers, the Band, nor any of its members, will accept other engagements during the validity of this contract.

9) The Band nor any of its members will not accept engagements in establishments offering dance music in Hamburg for a period of _____ months following the start of this contract.

10) Hamburg shall be deemed the legal domicile of both parties in case of disputes.

Hamburg, this _____ day of _____, 1962

Courtesy Dave Forshaw

international fame, particularly the Beatles.

The First Time I Saw The Beatles

. . . I didn't even notice them. It was during the period when I was in the Merchant Navy. After a stint down the west coast of Africa, we headed back to Europe and, much to the decadent delight of the crew, went to Hamburg, "Sin City", where the ladies were openly on display in glass windows in the notorious Reeperbahn.

The peggy[2] and I (the young lad pictured here) headed straight for the rock clubs, particularly The Top Ten. We were mesmerized by a volatile musician of considerable talent who was singing half in English, half in German. He sang an up-tempo version of *When the Saints Go Marching In,* which had the crowd going wild. I didn't pay much attention to the backing group. Afterwards, I found out that they were called The Beat Brothers and that their lead singer was Tony Sheridan, an Englishman. The Beat Brothers were, of course, none other than the Beatles.

I may be excused for this perceptual faux pas as, halfway through this event, my buddy disappeared and when I found him, he was battered, bruised and penniless, having been mugged on his way to the toilet. Thus, with our drinking money cut in half, the night ended early.

Author's collection
Author and his guitar (right) with the seaman who got mugged in Hamburg

Tony Sheridan

Another little-known fact is that the Beatles not only honed their style playing the twelve-hour, two-hours on, two-hours off shifts of the German clubs, but that they themselves were highly influenced by TONY SHERIDAN, yet another unsung hero of the rock guitar saga.

Tony's guitar style, his interpretation of American R&B was unique—and inspired. In fact, the Beatles copied much of Tony's style and implemented it in their act—and this was one of the most telling aspects of their music when they returned from Germany.

Unfortunately, Tony was a self-destructive musician who suffered badly from his own antisocial behavior. Oddly enough, his idiosyncrasy would go down very well with today's in-your-face attitudes—perhaps he was thirty years ahead of his time!. One particular night, I witnessed his quirky behavior first-hand at a Hamburg-Meets-Liverpool swap night at the Iron Door, Liverpool, where Tony began singing lengthy 12-bar obscenities and screaming at the audience. It was hair-raising. But it wasn't a send-up—he was really incensed with rage; he seemed to really hate the audience. Not very good for public relations.

The result of his temperamental behavior was that, although Tony achieved a modicum of fame in Germany, elsewhere he faded. Nevertheless, Tony's influence was recognized and acknowledged by other Liverpool bands.

Les Maguire of Gerry and the Pacemakers says: "Tony Sheridan is fabulous, he's a knockout. He influenced so many people that the Liverpool Sound should be called the Tony Sheridan Sound. He did more for the Beatles than anybody else."

What Tony brought to R&B was a radically innovative approach. He would often eschew the original version of the number, rearranging it with his own unique and dynamic chord styles—fast partials laced with rapid bass runs—which he wove

The Beatles owe everything to Sheridan because they copied him to a T. Sheridan was a fantastic guitarist, the governor.

Johnny Hutch of The Big Three

TONY SHERIDAN singt im  Star-Club
Hamburg - St. Pauli

Courtesy Dave Williams

in and out of his electrifying singing. The Liverpool groups, especially the Beatles, copied this wholesale.

Tony's moody personality made him unpopular, not just with impresarios, but the other musicians, too, who often found him very difficult to work with.

Sometimes Tony's antics were funny: like the time a German newspaper asked him for the lyrics to *Skinnie Minnie*, and he obliged by writing out an incredibly obscene, incredibly nonsensical version of the song that was simultaneously disgusting and hilarious. The German groups eagerly incorporated the number into their sets. The effect was stupefying. When the Germans played this number, the British musicians would be rolling on the floor helpless with laughter, realizing the poor Krauts hadn't the slightest inkling of what they were singing.

Paddy Chambers of The Flamingoes, said: "We'd been backing Tony for months. Everybody knew the songs and we really had it down. Then we were booked for a live broadcast of the BBC's Saturday Club. When we got there, Tony started doing strange songs we'd never heard before. It ruined everything."

I saw a lot of dreadful things at the Star Club. One evening before we went on stage some gentleman who hadn't paid his bills was brought in upside-down. He was shaken until his money fell out of his pockets. They took his money and his wallet and threw him out of the back door. It's a bit disconcerting when you're trying to tune up your guitar.

Wayne Bickerton

Having served their time with Tony as The Beat Brothers, the Beatles returned to Liverpool and, via the Beatles, Tony's innovations were added to the stylistic melting pot of Liverpool and, eventually, the world of British rock guitar in general. There's many a guitarist to this day who plays riffs and partial chords without even realizing they came from Tony Sheridan; a talented man who missed his mark.

When Tony took some time off, his backing band went on a tour of the American air bases in France and Germany. And it is here that we get the most telling interaction between American blacks and Liverpool whites in a first-hand anecdote from the guitarist in Sheridan's band, Paul ▶

257

The Beatles — Number One the whole world over

By R. A. Crabtree

THE top disc sellers in America throughout 1963 were the Four Seasons. Using a system based on chart positions of their discs the "Cashbox" magazine credited the group with 1,421 points, 21 ahead of their nearest rivals, The Beach Boys.

These points were accumulated throughout the twelve months of 1963; since January 11th of this year The Beatles have a total of 1,420.

This fantastic feat has been achieved by the appearance of twelve different titles in the U.S. charts most of which have been described as the fastest-selling singles ever. As each new disc is released the previous one loses the title! Five singles so far have passed the million mark in the States alone.

Both "I Want to Hold Your Hand" at number 2 and "Can't Buy me Love" at number 21 have sold over three million each. The current chart topper "She Loves You," "Twist and Shout" and "Please, Please Me" at 3 and 4 respectively are all on the right side of the Gold-Disc winning target.

Although not released in the U.S. "Roll Over Beethoven" has moved up to 40th position through imported copies from Canada and, for the second time in six months "From Me to You" is climbing and is now at number 43.

"Do You Want to Know a Secret" at 75 and "All my Loving" at 80 were released the same week as "Can't Buy me Love" as also was an EP containing "Misery," "A Taste of Honey", "Ask me Why" and "Anna". With two B-sides "I Saw Her Standing There" and "Thank You Girl" in the charts at 14 and 92 respectively as well as the Tony Sheridan disc "My Bonnie" now down to 54. The Beatles have the fantastic total of twelve songs in the U.S. charts.

Incidentally there are only six other British discs in the same Hit Parade.

Their Capitol LP "Meet the Beatles" currently topping the U.S. album charts, is the biggest selling LP and after only two months' sales has sold four million copies. "Introducing the Beatles" on the Vee-Jay label is at number 2 and is expected to earn them another Gold Disc in the near week or so.

Further down the list, at number 103 (!) is an MGM album entitled simple "The Beatles" despite the fact Tony Sheridan is the vocalist. A new album just released will no doubt be soon high in the lists, titles "Jolly What!" it features eight Frank Ifield numbers and four from ... yes, The Beatles.

Meanwhile back in the old country... "Can't Buy me Love" only their sixth single, has become their fifth chart topper, earned them their third British Gold Disc and their fifth Silver single Disc. "All My Loving" has earned them their third silver EP - eight silver, three gold: Cliff has 16 silver and 3 gold.

A look at the rest of the world's hit parades shows that not only the U.K. and the U.S. appreciate our Beatles. Down under for instance, "I Want to Hold Your Hand" was knocked from the top spot by "I Saw Her Standing There" which is likely to be pushed down by "Love me Do" now at number 2.

"Twist and Shout" and "She Loves You" are also in the Australian Top Fifteen, in fact last month these five discs were all in the top ten. "I Want to Hold Your Hand" still tops the charts in places as far apart as New Zealand and The Netherlands.

Courtesy Combo

These articles from Combo Musical Weekly in 1962 sum up the irony of Tony Sheridan's situation: on the left, an accolade for the Beatles who were already world famous; on the right, an advertisement for Polydor and Tony Sheridan who subsequently fell into obscurity.

►Pilnick—for the Liverpool musicians were to meet racial segregation for the first time.

The Circle is Complete: Liverpool Musicians and Black Servicemen

Paul Pilnick is one of Liverpool's most highly-regarded musicians. Not only has he worked with some of the top bands in England, but he was one of the key figures on the Liverpool scene. He replaced Brian Griffiths as guitarist with The Big Three, recorded with Gerry Rafferty, went to New Orleans with Alain Toussaint and he also had some hair-raising experiences backing Tony Sheridan's Big Six in Germany. His interview encapsulates all that happened in France and Germany.

Paul Pilnick in the early '60s

"Ted Easton was the original entrepreneur. He was Belgian, I think; that wasn't his real name, he assumed an English name. Anyway, Bruce McGaskill (later manager of the Average White Band) saw an advertisement to play in the American air bases. He fixed it up and we went across to France in 1962. Ted paid our fares and arranged our accommodation. At first it was in hotels, then we were put up in the bases themselves. It was a fantastic time, as we played all the time. We really became tight. We were supposed to play for a month at one air base, then move onto the next. We started at La Police near La Rochelle then went to Chatteraux and then Angely.

The first thing they made us do was cut our hair, give us G.I. crops. Then we started to play. At first, we backed up Freddy Starr then later Frank Baron. We noticed straight away that when we played only Elvis stuff or country, there

Johnny Hutch welcomes his new guitarist

THE BEAT BOYS

With Alcydon

JOHNNY Hutchinson, Leader and founder of "The Big Three" was most enthusiastic about his new lead guitarist Paul Pilnick when I spoke to him over coffee last week.

Paul, who was approached by "Hutch" when he learned of the break-up of Lee Curtis' All-Stars, was not too confident of his ability to help retain such a big sound as the Three have established in the Big Beat Scene.

But his fears were dismissed by Faron and Hutch when they heard Paul expound his expressive style at a practise they had arranged for the purpose of finding a replacement for Paddy Chambers.

Hutch told me: "Paul is very good and after a while when he gets to "feel" the sound of the group, he should fit in as easily as Griff."

"Griff" was Brian Griffiths, the lead guitarist before Paddy.

The "Three" and their new member successfully recorded four numbers for Decca some days ago. The title of their record is not yet known nor is the release date. But it will be out very shortly.

One of the numbers, Hutch tells me, has a string backing. It should sound good.

Paul, who has already recorded with his ex-group, The All Stars, had no trouble relaxing once he arrived at the studio where, he told me, he found the atmosphere very much like that of the Cavern, sound-wise.

I asked Paul how he felt in his new job and he told me:
"I'm knocked out to be in the group. The material the Big Three include in their programme has always appealed to me, and I feel the group being a trio allows me more scope to play.

"I regard Hutch and Faron as "guvnors" in their instruments and any rut I may have slipped into I will recognise through the others' perfectionism."

He added: "I only hope Big Three fans will accept me with as much enthusiasm as they did Paddy."

Dave Clark

STOPPED off at the Gaumont theatre in Liverpool to see the special preview of "Sound Of A City", the Rank Organisation's Look At Life feature on the beat scene.

The film, technically, was good. But the idea and the theme wandered a little with the result that the whole thing got a little out of perspective.

It actually reached the point where Freddie and the Dreamers were described as one of Liverpool's top groups.

The Cavern shots were wonderful. Some intelligent camera work showed the place as it really is — a technical feat which I think has never before been achieved.

The Escorts were at the Cavern when this film was short and their sound with "Dissy Miss Lizzie" makes you sit up and take note.

I was sitting behind Dave Clark and his Five and when the 10-minute film was finished I asked him for his opinion. "Great", he replied. "But I think it could have portrayed the Liverpool

forced police to evacuate a dance hall.

Five minutes before the bomb was allegedly due to explode, firemen and police invaded the hall as Phill and the boys were halfway through a number.

The group had to drop their instruments and clear out of the building. Fortunately no bomb was found.

Whether going out into the cold night air was the cause or not, Phil and the Crescents have been ill for a couple of weeks with gastric 'flue. They have been passed fit again and have returned to normal bookings.

Kinsley

Dave Preston, drummer with the Harlems — the Chants' backing group — has left to join bass player Billy Kinsley who left the Merseybeats recently.

Billy, who was quoted as saying he was tired of the hectic life led by recording groups, is trying to form a new outfit.

It is belived Paddy Chambers of the Big Three may also join this group.

Sabres

DENNY Seyton and the Sabres have recorded an L.P. for Philips' Mercury label to be released in the states sometime this month.

The LP features Dave Clark's "Bit's and Pieces" and some Beatle numbers.

Courtesy Combo

Paul Pilnick Article in Combo, April, 1964

▶ *wasn't a single black guy in the place. We'd never come across segregation before and didn't really recognize it for what it was.*

Whenever we played there was trouble, and it was always because of the black-white thing. Where it really came out was in Spandau, Germany. This wasn't a Ted Easton gig, though other bands in France had similar experiences. We were The Tony Sheridan Six at that time. Sheridan was off somewhere, so we did this gig at Spandau air base, this time without a lead singer. We did our own material. We did Jimmy Smith stuff, 'Walk on the Wild Side', and so on; we even had a Hammond B57 organ. We did Ray Charles' 'What'd I Say'—all those kind of numbers. Without realizing it, we were doing all black music. This time when we played there wasn't a white guy to be

Paul, left, playing with The Big Three

seen in the hall, just blacks. They went crazy over us; came into the band room, offered us pot. They were, like, acting as if to say, "Hey, not all white guys are shitballs; these guys are cool." We loved it. They loved us. Then this white sergeant comes up and says: "Look, we've got a problem here." He told us to play white music, some country stuff. So we did, kind of...made it up; did some Carl Perkins' stuff, you know. This time there wasn't a black face in the whole room. We thought it was really shitty. So next time we played, we did all the black numbers again. The black guys, man, they came into the band room, they even came onto the bus, our tour bus, in the break. They loved us. The whole bus was full of black guys, talking, laughing, smoking pot. We didn't really smoke pot 'cos we were pillheads. At first we refused, but we got into it. We were smoking their pot and drinking Thunderbird.

Then the white sergeant came in and broke it up. We were really pissed off. The bass player, a guy named Ian Campbell got really drunk—he was always getting drunk anyway—and got up on stage. He picked up an acoustic guitar and started singing a song, which he was making up as he was going along, all about this business of keeping the black guys out. He called it 'The Shame of America'. That was that. Within minutes, the stage was surrounded by military policemen and we were ordered off the base. Within an hour, they had us all packed up, Hammond B57 and all, and we were marched off the base surrounded by MPs. One of them was this great big black guy who had really dug us; he'd even been out on the town with us a couple of times—he'd become a really good friend of ours. He was really upset, man, you should have seen his face. We told him: "No sweat, man, don't worry; you're only doing your job. We understand."

That was it for us at Spandau. But we did what we did because we thought

Paul in the years after his return from the American air bases

*it was wrong. It was an incredible experience. We were really sticking our noses in and standing up for something. It made us sick and **we knew that we couldn't go along with it without being part of it. That's why we did what we did**.*"

Paul Pilnick Interview, USA/UK, 1996

Paul's experience was shared in various ways by other bands who played the air bases in France. Black music had come full circle, and now the Liverpool whites who played it were being persecuted. It was an intensely educative experience for these young lads and they readily sympathized with the blacks. They, too, knew firsthand what it was to be the subjugated segment of a nation.

Of course, the blacks took the Liverpool musicians to heart; feted them, showered them with presents, turned them on—and gave them more music to take home.

These accolades were new to Liverpudlian musicians and it increased their self-esteem and musical fervor enormously. No longer were they starving amateurs playing to sweaty Cavern crowds, only to line up in the dole queue[3] on Friday, but professional musicians appreciated as true artists for the first time.

These groups returned to Liverpool and injected a wave of enthusiasm, skill and professionalism into the Liverpool scene which left no one untouched.

The Beatles did not go to France; they went to Germany—but this is immaterial. The Liverpool scene was both eclectic and competitive, and the power of the bands returning from France made itself felt on all the other bands. Its source

Culture is the sum of your experiences. What you've been through and how you express that in painting, poetry, play writing or however. That is your culture. I think that is the other thing that unifies black people, it is our common culture. In addition to our common oppression, we have a common culture.

Oscar Brown, Wisdom of the Elders
Ebony Power Thoughts

Courtesy Bernie Wenton

Powie and Johnnie Wenton, Liverpool, 1930s

of inspiration: the black American soldiers. Its motive power: the sheer professionalism attained by nights of grinding away hour after hour in the French PBXs.

When the Liverpool bands played the air bases, it was a historical event, though even the Liverpool musicians involved didn't realize just how vast a circle had been completed:

It had begun with a black man whimpering in a dark ship's hold; separated from tribe, culture and family. Once in the cotton fields, the cry became a grunt, a holler, expelled with the downward swing of an axe or hammer. At night it became a drone, a poignant bending of the strings of a bastardized seventeenth century lute—the American guitar. The tribal rhythm became the insistent four-four of the blues beat and this metamorphosed into the grind of the dirty Chicago blues. And, eventually, it came to be the mode of expression of the youth of urban Liverpool; a raw-edged beat with repetitive lyrics that were sometimes little more than nonsense syllables.

But to these Liverpool kids, it spoke volumes; it touched them more deeply than anything they had ever heard. In the wordless way of kindred spirits, it whispered to them of something already nestling within their hearts; of man's inhumanity to man, and the indominitable nature of the human spirit which could "make a way out of no way"—and express it as music.

The ability to experience and communicate emotional content on such a broad level is characteristic of the oral man's failure to "detach" intellectually—to not categorize, specialize or analyze—and is, ultimately, a strong point in the survival of the Afro-American culture. The oral tradition is, even more than a way of experiencing, a manner of presentation. This accounts, in part, for the universality of black music, for the acceptance of this music by peoples of all cultures and, especially, by people who are in some way oppressed.

Ben Sidran
Black Talk

"My challenge to the young people is to pick up where this generation has left off, to create a world where every man women and child is not limited except by their own capabilities"

Colin Powell: My American Journey

Courtesy Charlie Jenkins

Liverpool, present day: Children playing in Egerton Street

I Meet Little Richard & The Rolling Stones

24

A New Era: I Get to Meet Little Richard and The Rolling Stones

There is a joke prevalent in the north of England about a man called Albert Murgatroyd. The nature of the joke is that he seems to pop up everywhere in the presence of famous people. It goes on a bit with repeated incidents of famous people meeting Albert Murgatroyd in the most unlikely places, but the punch line takes place outside the Vatican building where thousands of people are in the square waiting for the Pope to give his blessing. Two figures come out onto the balcony and an onlooker says: "There are *two* figures up there. Who are they?" His friend answers: "Well, I don't know who the other one is, but the guy on the left is Albert Murgatroyd."

Author's collection

Portrait of the author as a young man

That, in a word, sums up Denny Flynn. More than anyone I know, Denny was the archetypal Liverpudlian. He didn't do much besides drugs, rock music and sex, sex, sex, nor was he particularly handsome or impressive. But Denny turned up everywhere. He hung around with the Beatles, he drove in Ray Charles' limousine. Once, I turned over the back of a rock album and there was Denny staring at me from the photograph. Denny—poor, Irish, uneducated— hobnobbed with the stars. In fact, Denny was known throughout the muso's world for being, well, Denny Flynn.

In 1962, my home in the Iron Door ended abruptly when ownership changed hands. Sam Leach lost it to a former partner who was not so benign in his attitude to beatniks. Thus, one afternoon, myself and a crowd of beats and musicians waited in the street outside the famous door as our few precious belongings were thrown into the narrow alley by some very big, very tough security men hired by the new management. Thin, broke, unemployed and forlorn, I didn't know what to do. Suddenly, I was homeless again.

Then Denny approached me, saw I was down and clapped me on the back and asked me if I wanted to

"meet the Stones and Little Richard."

I was overwhelmed, particularly as we didn't have two pennies to knock together. That afternoon, we hitchhiked to Manchester thirty miles away and, good to his promise, we did get to see the Stones—and much more.

And though we didn't realize it then, it was to be a point of demarcation: the end of an era and the start of another.

Where Were You in '62? Little Richard Meets Two Liverpool Louts—And Smiles
— A Personal Anecdote —

The lorry driver disgorged us on the busy Manchester intersection with a great hiss of brakes. The huge rig was angled around the corner, much to the chagrin of the drivers in the lane of traffic behind. Ignoring the blaring horns, the Liverpool driver gave two thumbs-up to us, shouting: "Don't screw anything I wouldn't screw!"

"You bet!" shouted Denny.

Manchester was as drab and dour as Liverpool and though only thirty miles away, it could've been three hundred. But we couldn't have cared less. We were on our way to see the King.

There was a vast queue of girls outside the Manchester Odeon. They yacked like a gaggle of geese; "oohing", "aahing" and smoking cigarettes with great flair, though some of them were only about twelve. I sauntered past the crowd, acting nonchalant, but I experienced a moment of trepidation as I gazed at the poster outside.

German Bonds spielen im ☆Star-Club

The Rattles, a German group from Hamburg

At the bottom of the bill were The Rattles, a German group; next, the Rolling Stones; Bo Diddley; then the Everly Brothers; and, right smack dab on the top, Little Richard, all bouffant hairstyle, smile and mascara.

"Hey, Denny," I muttered, suddenly very aware of my shabby shoes, "How are we going to get in?"

Denny uttered his magic words, music to my ears: "Leave it to me." He pulled open a small shoulder bag and showed me the contents.

"Shee-it!" I said wrinkling my nose as Denny pulled out some black, evil-smelling T-shirts.

"The Stones'..." said Denny glibly, "Left them in the Adelphi Hotel after their Liverpool gig. I'm just bringing them back."

"Christ, Denny!" I retorted, "I bet they threw them away—they stink! You're sure this'll get us in?!"

"Wait here," said Denny with the quiet confidence of the born hustler, "I know the Stones. They'll get us in."

Denny disappeared through the front entrance of the closed theater and I waited outside nervously, eyeing the growing crowd with the disquieting knowledge that, without money, I couldn't even join the end of the queue.

Ten minutes later, we were in.

Dazed and happy, I followed Denny through the empty theater down the center aisle, led by a quietly amicable Bill Wyman of the Stones.

I was in heaven. Stage hands and road managers bustled around sorting out leads, setting up amps, yelling commands to the road crew. Behind the Odeon backdrop, Mick Jagger stood talking to a black sax player while a German musician sitting on a coil of rope blew great bubbles of pink gum nonchalantly. A drummer was setting his traps behind the screen. He flashed me a big grin and gave his bass pedal a welcoming "thud thud!"

Then I heard something that made my heart leap: the musical twang of a southern American accent.

The Rolling Stones

WE have been inundated with requests for a picture of the Rolling Stones since word was flashed around that the wild-looking group with ear appeal would short-ly be appearing in the North. So here it is. The Stones, currently riding high — very high — in the charts, will be appearing at some of the leading best venues in the North, including the Jungfrau at Manchester the Majestic at Birken-head and they will be opening the Cubiklub at Rochdale.

Courtesy Combo

The Rolling Stones, 1963

"Christ almighty, Denny," I said, "It's Phil Everly!" And so it was—Don, too—all vast, Presley hair quiffs, greasy side-burns, smooth faces and amicable, southern manners.

I moved closer and drank in every word. I not only knew every Everly Brother song on the market, but every note of every guitar solo; every harmony. And here they were, talking and laughing like normal people, just three feet away!!

"Hey, Pittsy! C'mon!" shouted Denny who was strolling around the stage acting as if he'd been there for years and owned the Odeon personally, "Let's go down to the Stones' dressing room—everyone's down there!"

Indeed they were. Especially Bo Diddley, who was holding forth at a great rate to a trio of pressmen; mostly, it seemed, talking about Bo Diddley. We steered a wide berth, mainly because Bo was so *loud*.

Courtesy Norman Williams

Mick Jagger performing at the Tower Ballroom, New Brighton, November 1963

Everyone else seemed natural, even self-effacing, but old Bo had the bit between his teeth and he was letting them know that Bo had arrived.

Denny was standing with Mick Jagger. "Make yourself at home," Denny said to me with a nonchalant wave of his hand. I was awestricken. "Wanna beer? Hey, Mick, wanna beer? Denny shoved a beer into my hand and offered one to Mick Jagger, who declined with a quiet smile.

"No thank you, Denny. I'm O.K."

"He talks so posh!" I hissed to Denny, "He sounds like the Duke of Edinburgh!"

"Oh? Oh—Mick... Naah!" said Denny, "He's alright."

Denny was right. Mick was alright; so were the rest of the Stones. I was accustomed to seeing them on stage wailing away or stomping madly to borrowed rhythm & blues numbers and I couldn't quite equate their crazed, rock-style personality with the four likeable lads who moved quietly about the dressing room. They were all silent, unassuming, sober. They moved amongst the other musicians as if they were fans themselves, just visiting, and not a rapidly-growing musical phenomenon in their own right.

I rapped a bit to a very sober, self-effacing Keith Richards. Then Bill Wyman asked us if we'd like to go outside for a coffee: "I like to get away before the show," he explained.

Me, Denny and Bill pushed open the stage door and I experienced my one and only moment of fan-mania. A piercing scream rose from the crowd and the girls crushed forward, grabbing at us. Then they fell back in uncertainty, puzzled, not quite sure who anyone was. Mick Jagger, though famous, was not yet at super-star status, and though the Stones had groupies, the presence of me and Denny confused them. Thus they weren't even sure of Bill Wyman—or, indeed, if it was Bill Wyman at all.

After a moment of milling about, during which me and Denny wise-cracked amicably, the girls parted and let us through.

"It's alright, girls," shouted Denny when we were free from the crowd, "We'll be back. Make sure your underwear's clean!"

That convinced the groupies once and for all that this motley trio couldn't be stars and, with a concerted shrug of disdain, two hundred little girls pouted and turned a collective cold shoulder.

"You'll be sorry!" shouted Denny to their backs.

It was a pleasant interlude in the shabby Manchester tea-room. Denny and I chatted quietly to Bill about science fiction, music, Liverpool, London—and drugs. Bill would not be drawn into any major discussion about drugs though, as the shit had just hit the fan for the Stones on that issue. "Naah," he said, "We don't take drugs. But try telling the Customs that—we're always getting searched." Denny gave me a meaningful glance but said nothing. After all, at times he had actually supplied the Stones with drugs.

Eventually, it was time to return to the theater, and we got back just in time to catch the Rattles who, by German standards, were a fine group, but by English standards were, as Denny put it so judgementally: "Crap!"

Then it was the Stones, and Mick went into his novel foot-shuffling dance; a theatrical innovation at the time. Denny and I cackled as the Everlys, very much amused by this, strutted up and down in the wings like chickens with ingrown toenails, in a merciless parody of Mick's unique strut. This brought a gale of laughter from the musicians backstage, but the Stones were so loud, it didn't matter.

Courtesy Norman Williams

Keith Richards performing at the Tower Ballroom, New Brighton, November 1963

Little Richard, he's the king. I got to play on the same bill as him when he played the Tower Ballroom. What a blast! Little Richard is my vocal hero—always will be.

Johnny Gustafson

Anyway, no one seemed to mind. It was all in good fun, and when it was the Everly's turn Denny and I made a strange pact: we were not going to turn on. "Christ, man, I'm high enough!" grinned Denny, bobbing and weaving to the Everly's music, "Let's save it for after."

"Right, Den," I agreed in an unheard of fit of abstinence. I was, in fact, already soaring with the Gods, mesmerized, as the Everly's lilting, lovely harmonies shimmered through the air in planes of gold and silver:

"Don't want your looooove anymore
Don't want your kisses, that's for sure..."

At this point, Denny whispered to me: "Hey, man, let's go see the King. It's O.K.."

I wouldn't move. I was so close to the Everlys, drinking in every nuance, watching the little interchanges and glances which were part of their well-rehearsed stage act. Eventually, Denny literally dragged me away. He led me down a short corridor behind the stage.

"Oh, c'mon Den," I muttered, "I was having a great time, and—"

I stopped short, for there, sitting in a room that was only as big as a large toilet, was the King—Little Richard.

I forgot all about the Everly Brothers and stood staring at the raw-throated pioneer whose numbers were screamed out nightly by every band in every club in Liverpool; a man who was more loved, respected and admired in the Liverpool scene than any other single artist. I couldn't believe it: there I was standing in front of Little Richard!

There was an awkward silence in

Courtesy Norman Williams

Brian Jones performing at the Tower Ballroom, New Brighton, November 1963

which I became acutely aware of a

factor that distinguished the man from all the others—the Stones; the Everlys; the Rattles: he seemed incredibly calm—and very alone. An air of quiet hung around him like a cloak. I grew aware of other sounds: the Everlys singing; in the distance, the creak of a door; a muttered conversation further down the corridor. I was non-plussed, finding it difficult to believe that this was the raw-voiced visionary who'd thrilled us all with *Tutti-Frutti, Long Tall Sally, Good Golly Miss Lolly*. No one could do it like the King, and here he was, so quiet, so still.

Richard, in turn, stared at us, the two Liverpool louts who stood so solemn and reverential before him. We must have been an odd sight with our pinched, teenage-acned faces; our rusty, black jackets and tight pants. Our wardrobe bespoke of a sort of melodramatic poverty which, fortunately for us, at that time was indistinguishable from 'rock-group grubby chic'.

Then, suddenly, the tension broke as Richard smiled warmly. "What can I do for you guys?"

Denny blurted out: "Oh, Richard! Wow... Please... Please could I have a souvenir? Like, maybe your tie?"

Richard smiled again. "Well," he said, "I'd be glad to do that, boys, but you see, I use my shirt and tie in the act. When things are jumping, I take 'em off and throw 'em in the audience." Denny looked so glum that Richard chuckled. "Hey, I'll tell you what. How about you and me swap ties? Now, that'll work!"

Denny's face lit up and I stared in wonder as Richard unloosened his elegant tie without a wrinkle in it and solemnly handed it to Denny. Denny's own tie, Mod style, had a teeny-weeny knot that sported multiple layers of grease, grime and tobacco stains. It had become as hard and black as greasy wood as Denny always pulled the tie over his head without undoing the knot. Thus, he looked nervous as he slid the tie off because the knot made a noise like a steel cable sliding through an oiled slot.

But Little Richard never even blinked as Denny handed him the greasy, offensive article. Richard just gave over his own impeccable tie graciously and looped Denny's disreputable rag around his bright, clean, white collar, saying: "Fair exchange." Then he shook Denny's hand.

Denny's face was so flushed that I had a momentary thought that he was going to pass out. But, instead, Denny said in a very small voice, "Oh, man! Thanks!"

Our Moment of Bliss

*D*enny and I stand in the wings peering around the curtain at the dark sea that is the waiting audience. Just a few feet away is the grand piano, and lined along the backdrop like soldiers are three sax players, a bass player, the guitarist and two drummers.

The atmosphere is electric.

Bo Diddley and his band have warmed up the audience. Diddley's companions—the buxom Duchess and a black cat who is high as a kite on something—have been the hit of the night. The black cat makes no distinction between Life and the Stage because before the show he'd been bopping in the empty theater, in the toilet, in the dressing room. Right up to the minute they went on, he bopped. He bopped onto the stage, bopped through the numbers and bopped off it after the show. Denny remarks: "He's probably bopping in some nightclub in Manchester at this very moment."

Denny and I are standing behind Little Richard's stage manager. We've never seen anything so cool. God, the man is dressed all in leather—black leather—in the Sixties! Leather shirt, jacket, trousers, a long, leather coat, soft as silk, and a black leather fedora. We'd die to have the world see us standing with this guy at that moment—and it shows in our rapt faces 'cos the stage manager smiles with a flash of very white teeth.

Denny shakes his head: "Oh man!" says Denny, ingenuous in his admiration, "You're so cool, man! Christ! I wish I looked like you!" The black stage manager slaps his thigh at this and his shoulders convulse in the coolest black laugh that we have ever seen. This sets Denny off again: "Oh, fuck, why don't I laugh like that?!" he says in genuine despair. This cracks up the black guy even more. He starts shaking and shuddering with laughter again.

Then the M.C. suddenly bounces onto stage and says: "And here he is, folks! Hang onto your seats! The man you've been waiting for... The King himself: LITTLE RICHARD!!!"

Then, there he is; leaping, capering and cavorting about the stage and the audience goes berserk. Richard bounces up and down, wheels, waves and shouts at them: "You wanna hear it?!!"

"Yeah!!!"

"You gotta hear it??!!"

"Yeah!!!"

"Shall I give it to you??!!"

"Yeah!!!"

Each line is punctuated by a high-pitched yelp from Richard and a drum beat.

Then Richard screams; the scream to end all screams. It is a high-drawn, ululating note that slides up the scale glissando, to terminate in the words: "LOOOOOOOORDY, LOOOOOOORDEEEEEE, YEAH!! Then I gonna do it!!!"

And, lowering his head, he charges pell mell down the stage like a bull about to ram a fence. At the last minute, he executes a move that brings a roar of approval from the audience: He suddenly turns sideways and SLIDES on his polished pumps like an ice-skater and, as he slithers past the piano, he reaches out and executes a perfect arpeggio from the treble right down to the bass and stops DEAD in his tracks with his little finger ringing out the bass note: "Doooong!!"

There is a brief pause, silent save for the sonorous resonance of the key note. Then, just two feet from us two Liverpool louts, to our eternal bliss, HE WINKS AT US, opens his mouth, throws back his head and the walls reverberate with an incredible sound:

"A-WOP-BOP-ALOOMOP-A-WAM-BAM-BOOM, TUTTI-"

On the word "Frutti", three saxes, two drummers, the guitarist and the bass slam down into the first beat of the bar and a wall of sound sweeps across the audience like a tidal wave.

"Oh God!!" I murmur, almost fainting with joy.

"Oh!!!" whimpers Denny, agonized with ecstasy.

Afterwards Denny claims he'd come in his pants.

He probably had.

Aftermath

Somewhere on the East Lancashire Road on a dark-green grassy verge, two madmen cavort beneath the bowl of a starry night. The headlights of the passing trucks sweep over the grass and the drivers squint and wonder at the bobbing shapes and wonder what strange animal it can be.

But it is only me and Denny, crazy with joy; too hysterical to even begin to hitchhike; scrabbling about on the ground insanely.

I am rolling in circles, throwing handfuls of grass in the air while Denny pulls up clumps of wet grass with both hands, crying out: "That black cat! Man oh man! A leather shirt! Fuck, I want one! I want one!"

"Christ, I wanna look like him!" I groaned, "Why aren't I black?! I'll never look that cool! And Richard! Man! He threw your tie in the audience, man! Some chick's gonna have that on her wall thinking it is Richard's! That snotty, greasy rag, man! She'll worship it forever and think it's covered with his egg stains!"

We rolled and giggled in joy, screaming, shouting: "*'Gonna tell Aunt Mary about Uncle John, says he's got the blues but he has a lot of fun…'*" We leapt up and bopped, playing the air guitar with frenetic, adept strokes, screaming with joy. We'd never had it so good. We'd seen the King; we'd talked to the King; he'd given us his tie; and then he'd given us the message, his gospel, personally…

The year was 1962 and on the East Lancashire Road the world stood poised on the brink of a series of apocalyptic events.

There, under the night sky, as we screamed in delirious, delightful happiness, neither of us realized that we, Little Richard, the Beatles, Liverpool—the world—were caught in a tide that had taken centuries to rise; a tide that was about to peak. 1963, the next year, was the year that the world would go mad and nothing would ever be the same.

But we didn't know or even care.

We shouted our joy to the trees, the fields, the passing lorries, the stars; to the universe…not caring whether it was heard or not. Over and over we rendered the sermon the King had given to us personally, with all its eloquent profundity:

"Awop-bop-aloom-whop a-wham-bam-boom!"

And so to 1963 and an uncertain future.

Strange Connections
Our Theme

syn·chro·nic·i·ty

Function: noun
Date: circa 1889
1 : the quality or fact of being synchronous
2 : the coincidental occurrence of events and especially psychic events as similar thoughts in widely separated persons that seem related but are not explained by conventional mechanisms -- used especially in the psychology of C. G. Jung

Merriam-Webster's
COLLEGIATE® DICTIONARY

The Dream

Carl Jung, Psychiatrist

Martin Luther King, Activist

John .F. Kennedy, President

The most massive demonstration ever to occur in the United States was devoid of violence: On August 28th, 1963, some 250,000 Americans of all faiths, races and creeds joined Martin Luther King in an unprecedented demonstration of solidarity, to march on Washington. King delivered the most impressive oration of his career: "I have a dream," he said often during his fiery speech, "A dream of the time when the evils of prejudice and segregation will vanish." Many of those present wept openly.

Encyclopedia of Americana

In 1918, Carl Jung began to conclude that individual dreams might provide a clue to movements in the collective consciousness, foreshadowing future developments in the conscious world. And, of course, particularly in the twentieth century, there are few more revealing windows on the dream life of the age than artistic activity.

The Neophiliacs by Christopher Booker
Gambit, Boston, 1970

November 22, 1963, President Kennedy was shot to death whilst riding in a motorcade in Dallas, Texas.
Encyclopedia of Americana

25

1963: The Year the World Went Mad

"The Fatal Outbreak of Demonic Power"

The threat to the President's life was higher than in any previous years. The total threatening and abusive letters in 1963 reached the staggering and frightening high of 32,000.

Autobiography of Frank J. Wilson,
Former Chief of America's Secret Service

The Queen of England has been booed tonight and I am furious!
Henry Brooke, Home Secretary, 10 July, 1963

With bewildering rapidity during the year 1963, the following events took place in England and America:

- The Profumo scandal topples the Conservatives
- Negro leader Medgar Evers is murdered in Mississippi (June) Four days later, Kennedy presents his Civil Rights Bill to Congress
- Slum landlord Rackman is exposed in England
- The biggest robbery ever in England (The Great Train Robbery)
- The biggest Civil Rights demonstration in America's history—200,000 marchers—in Washington.
- The Beatles establish themselves once and for all as their fourth record, *She Loves You* resounds like a war cry from the top of the Hit Parade: *Yeah, Yeah, Yeah*
- Harold MacMillan resigns in England
- Harold Wilson aligns his party with President Kennedy's 'New Frontier' policy (October)
- November 1: Vietnam finally erupts into open revolt; *and*
- November 22: President Kennedy is assassinated

For days the world was in shock. A pall hung over the civilized world as it mumbled over and over, "no, no, no." Then, into this void came the "yeah, yeah, yeah" of the Beatles, and a shocked and dazed world realized that the Beatles had arrived as, seven days after the President's assassination, the Beatles' fifth record *I Want to Hold Your Hand* went straight to the top of the Hit Parade and stayed there for nearly two months, to become the best-selling British record ever made.

Liverpool had arrived; but the British Empire had fallen.

On December 16, almost as a valediction to the British Empire, Harold MacMillan gave his final speech in the House of Commons from below the gangway. *The Evening Standard* put out a special issue: '1963, The Year of the Beatles'.

In the early part of 1964, the Beatles flew the Atlantic and landed at Kennedy Airport, whilst America was still grappling with post-assassination gloom and uncertainty. It was a momentous event, and the amazing scenes at Kennedy Airport have become part of the world's collective consciousness.

But what no one realized at the time was that the Beatles and their entourage were not alone: they were also bringing Liverpool with them. Nor was anyone to realize that this was the end of one era and the start of another; an era which was symbolized by the ascension of a working-class pop culture in the Beatles, and a grocer's son, Harold Wilson becoming the British Prime Minister.

When his accession to power was confirmed on October 15, 1964, appropriately, Harold Wilson was staying in his Liverpool constituency just a stone's throw away from the Cavern. Why he chose to be in Liverpool is an historical oddity, but it certainly added significance to the event, for,

Liverpool—black with soot and black in name, the most reviled, downtrodden and disenfranchised city in England—was at the height of its tribal glory. In fact, at one point, Harold even made headlines by visiting the Cavern.

The previous two years had been heady ones for Liverpool. Suddenly starlets and politicians were not only accepting the guttural Liverpool accent but even imitating it. Liverpool Football Club had won the League Championship and the fans' war-cry "Ee-ay-addio, we won the Cup!" was now followed by a token to the four Liverpool lads who had put Liverpool on the world map: "Yeah, yeah, yeah!"

The swing to Labour on Merseyside was spectacular, and that night Wilson was elected as Prime Minister by a hair's breadth—an overall majority of a mere five hundred seats. But he did it. Not only did Wilson receive the news in Liverpool, but he began to implement his plan "to get a tired country moving" by utilizing the New Frontier Plan as formulated four years earlier by Peter Shore.

Liverpool was a jubilant as any freed slave. Were they not all they could be and more? Had they not shown the world a thing or two, as well as those "toffee-noses"[1] down in the culturally-glib south? Liverpool was King.

It was a long time before Liverpool began to sit up and think that, in fact, very little had changed. As John Lennon was to remark in the Seventies: "So what have we got? Now it's O.K. to walk around with long hair, that's all."

Liverpool had shown the world how, but the forces of heredity and class were still all-powerful, hidden just below the surface of these sensational events. Subsequent years were to reinforce the cruelty of the joke, "What do you call a black man with two degrees from M.I.T....?" John himself was to make his own personal version of it: "What do you call a Liverpudlian (a Beatle, in this case) who makes ten million a year and mixes with Kings, Queens and Presidents?" The answer is at the end of the third verse of *A Working-Class Hero*: "You're still a fucking peasant."

Yes, we were still "fucking" peasants and it seemed that there was nothing left to believe in, not even the Beatles—as John immortalized in his bitter and ponderous diatribe *God*.

The nostalgia that posterity holds for the Sixties is not simply for the Beatles but for the promise of an entire generation which has petered out into Reaganomics and Thatcher's England. Somehow, the fate of the Beatles seemed to underscore the whole point.

The conclusion of the Beatles' story, at first sight, is not a happy one. Society not only boosted them to mythic status, but then went on to crucify them quite cheerfully.

From their bright beginnings and cheerful, Liverpool optimism, the Beatles' story seemed to take a downhill path. Their vast fortune was hacked apart by predatory businessmen; self-seekers crawled over the spoils like greedy ants. The ever-faithful Neil Aspinall, longtime friend and confidante ended up as custodian of Apple, sadly watching the constant trickle of royalties from the sale of old Beatles' albums. He said: "I'm the custodian of a graveyard."

Each of the Beatles, albeit multimillionaires, must have pined for the days when the music was a joy; when it was performed simply as an overflowing of their love for the rock genre. At the end, they all returned (somewhat sobered) to their original identities as four Liverpool lads:

George married a much more down-to-earth girl and retired into privacy, music, meditation and gardening, only to be shocked at the violation of his security and home when he was knifed by a psychotic fan, a Liverpudlian, nonetheless.

Paul became what he had always been: a middle-class husband with an ideal wife, happy in his marriage and his day-to-day existence—and one of the most sincere, grieving widowers in the world when his wife died. For the second time, the woman in his life succumbed to cancer.

Ringo, like any good working-class lout, drank heavily and watched the TV (the fact that he did it for nigh on twenty years with a millionaire's income only reinforces the point). He has, however, now gone "on the wagon".

And John found ultimately that the mother he was looking for was inside himself—and, contentedly became a house-husband in a brief period of peace before his meaningless slaughter.

Pain; bitterness; exploitation; disillusionment. These seem to be the culmination of the Beatles' tale.

But, it is not so.

If it is any consolation to the Beatles—and to Beatle lovers the world over, from Liverpool to Louisiana—the ending of the Beatles was neither tragic nor unhappy, for it was not an end but a beginning.

When John, Paul, George and Ringo stepped onto American soil in February of 1964, what neither they nor the world realized was that they were carrying a flame.

It was a flame that had gleamed dimly in the holds of West Coast slave ships; had burned in the dark huts of the cotton fields; and had flickered feebly through the history of black music up to the Sixties. Flickered, yes...but it had never been extinguished.

The flame, carried to England by the music of race, flared strongly in Liverpool. The Beatles and their lovers can console themselves with this truth: Not only were the Beatles the bearers of the flame, but it has come to illuminate the most distant corners of the world.

It is not fanciful thinking to say that the momentous events in Tiananmen Square and in Europe—the collapse of the Berlin Wall—owe not a little to mass communication and modern music—in particular, the Beatles.

We opened this book with Carl Jung's thesis:

> *What seems to be the be a wholly senseless heaping up of single, haphazard occurrences...is, for primitive man, a completely logical sequence of omens and of happenings indicated by them. It is a fateful outbreak of demoniac power...'*

The "fateful outbreak of demoniac power"—which manifested itself in the turbulence of the Sixties and found its peak in the Beatles—was nothing else but the human spirit crying out for release, a cry which began in the dark hold of a slave ship bound for the New World.

John's death was not in vain; the hours of dedicated playing by the Beatles were not in vain; nor were Paul's or George's or Ringo's efforts to keep on going. They were moving proof that the cry had been heard in a city which is not black or white, but eternal shades of gray: Liverpool.

It is the cry of freedom, and it still resounds around the world.

He who controls images controls everything.
Robert Townsend
Voices of Struggle, Voices of Pride
Ebony Power Thoughts

Epilogue

Denny Flynn never became famous. You've never heard of him before this account. He couldn't play an instrument, he wasn't in a band. In fact he never did anything much except have a good time. Yet everybody in Liverpool knew Denny. He was a simple Liverpool-Irish lad whom everybody liked.

Above all, Denny loved the Beatles. He was so proud of them, so proud that such a talent came out of the 'Pool. When they became famous and went to America, no one was more disconsolate than Denny Flynn. For Denny, the fan par excellence, no door had ever been closed. Wherever there was scene, Denny could smell it—and he always got there somehow. Now his hometown heroes lay across the great divide of the Atlantic, separated by distance, money, passports, international borders. And the door seemed closed.

But a strange thing happened. Denny, though quite young, was struck down with incurable cancer. As he was dying, his poor Liverpool-Irish family and friends got it all together. They raised the money and, as his last wish, Denny was sent off to America. They even dressed him up in a tuxedo. So Denny, happy as a sandboy[2], got to go to America to see his idols in style—once. Then he died.

Unlike the first Liverpool invasion, there were no crowds awaiting Denny at Kennedy Airport. But his visit, in its own way, was just as momentous, for Denny, in his spirit, encapsulated all that was Liverpool—the fifth Beatle.

In 1986, the great mythologist Joseph Campbell talked to interviewer Bill Moyers at George Lucas' Skywalker Ranch in Marin, California. Campbell said of the extraordinary events of the Sixties:[3]

Campbell: *The Beatles brought forth an art form for which there was a readiness. Somehow, they were in perfect tune with their time. Had they turned up thirty years before, their music would have fizzled out. The public hero is sensitive to the needs of his time. The Beatles brought a new spiritual depth into popular music which started the 'fad', let's call it, for meditation and Oriental music. Oriental music had been over here for years as a curiosity, but now, after the Beatles, our young people seem to know what it's about. We are hearing more and more of it, and it's being used in terms of its original intention as a support for meditations. That's what the Beatles started."*

Moyers: *Sometimes it seems to me that we ought to feel pity for the hero instead of admiration. So many of them have sacrificed their own needs for others.*

Campbell: *They all have.*

Thanks lar........

End Note—A Plea

Please don't bite my finger, just look where I'm pointing

You see, this book has been ten years in the making and has seen many revisions and re-writes through three agents and three publishers. They all had ideas of how to do it and none of them worked. Now I get to do it my way. Some will not like the academic research. Others will prefer the straight musical history. However, the book is a product of who I am, which is exactly *that*—a curious mixture of academic and street kid. When I left Liverpool and went into the world, I didn't know who the Prime Minster of England was or even what the House of Lords was. It has taken an education to enable me to see my own personal history and how my life fitted into a larger social context.

So, I have come at last to relate the personal anecdotes in the first person—originally I wrote them in the third person to conceal the identity of some of the people involved. This may attract or repel. Nevertheless, the stories are not meant to make any point about *me*, though folks will draw their own conclusions. The personal anecdotes are meant to flesh out the points made in the academic research. The price I pay is being exposed. But that would be worth it if this account brings just a few people to a deeper understanding of the meaning of race and the meaning of humanity.

The music which we call "Beatles" has traveled the world—and it can be seen why. Unwavering in their passion and talent, the four lads wove a tapestry of yearning and beauty that incorporated into itself all the multiple issues that were the roots of their history and the paths which its protagonists had traveled over 300 years. Their music has probably touched you, too, which is, perhaps, why you are reading this book.

Racism is a major problem in our country, but unless a deep understanding of the forces at play is brought to bear, the young will continue to be slaughtered and the jails will overflow with our youth. The dream is to give our children something better.

I do not believe children are pure innocence, that is another matter, but certainly no one is born to be a Ku Klux Klanner or a Black Panther—we taught them that.

Yes, *we*. We are all responsible because the problem continues.

There *are* solutions but a radical change in mindset is needed to eradicate the blight at the core of this social problem.

If this book sheds even a glimmer of light onto this issue, I have achieved my aim. Because it's no longer a question of what is right or what is wrong but *what we are going to do about it.*

Do you want your children to live in a world of hate and violence? I don't. I was raised in violence and I don't want that for them.

Remember the children—for the children's sake.

Courtesy Michael A. Joseph

Four Liverpool kids in class, 2000 A.D.

with many thanks to all
who gave so freely.....

Notes

Chapter 1

1   *Togo* is unrefined sugar

2   *Memory, Dreams and Reflections* by Carl G. Jung, Random House, New York, NY, 1963

3   *Essay on Archaic Man* by Carl G. Jung from *The Collected Works of C.G. Jung*, Volume 10, Princeton University Press,Princeton, New Jersey, 1970

Chapter 4

1   *Charas* is the West Indian word for hashish

2   A *shabeen* is an Irish club or pub

3   *John Bull ofay raas clat* is a West Indian obscenity directed at whites.

Chapter 5

1   NEMS stands for Northern England Music and is the largest music store in Liverpool, owned by Briand Epstein's family

2   A *can lad* is a gopher

3   *Scouser or Scouse* is the English slang term for a Liverpudlian (person coming from Liverpool). It is derived from the dish called scouse, a potato stew, which was eaten by the poor.

Chapter 6

1   Carl Perkins' influence on the Beatles was evidenced when George Harrison attended his funeral in Jackson, Tennessee in January 1998.

2   So much so that Irish musician Van Morrison has brought out a new album with him early 2000, entitled *The Skiffle Years*

Chapter 7

1   *Ganga* is the West Indian word for marijuana and *tompy* and *spliff* are West Indian words for joint

2   *Blast* means to smoke a joint

3   A *spade* is a black man

4   A *Teddy Boy* was an early '60's teenager who dressed anachronistically from the Edwardian era, with velvet collars, drainpipe trousers and string neck ties

Chapter 10

1   A *hod* is a wooden, Y-shaped drvice for carrying bricks

2   Under the influence of American movies, this is changing

3   *M.C* means Master of Ceremonies

Chapter 11

1   It should be remembered that the term "working class" in '60's England does not equate with the American term. A better translation for the American would be to read it as "low class".

2   *The Smoke* is a slang term for the city of London

3   *Saville Row* is the location of London's (hence, England's) most refined clothing stores

4   An *Etonian* is a person (male) who attended Eton, one of the well-known private schools for the upper classes

5   *Posh* is slang for upper class, snobby

6   *Two of Us, John Lennon & Paul McCartney, Behind the Myth* by Geoffrey Guiliano, Penguin Group, New York, 1999

Chapter 12

1   A *jigger* is a narrow alley that runs along the back of rows of terraced houses

Chapter 13

1   This was depicted in the movie *Scandal* starring Joanne Whalley-Kilmer, produced by Nick Powell and Joe Boyd, 1989, Miramax Films

Chapter 13 (cont.)

2   Printed in *Private Eye*, May 31, 1963; cartoon by Timothy Birdsall

3   *Man & Woman, Boy & Girl: Gender Identity From Conception to Maturity* by John Money, Johns Hopkins University Press, Baltimore, MD, 1973

Chapter 14

1   *Britain, A Future That Works* by Bernard Nossitter, Houghton Mifflin Co., Boston, 1978

Chapter 15

1   A *brolly* is an umbrella

2   *Dole-ites* are people living off welfare

3   A *Member of the British Empire* is a distinction awarded to ordinary English citizens by Her Majesty, Queen Elizabeth

Chapter 17

1   *Pissed* is slang for drunk

2   *Windy* is Liverpool slang for yellow-bellied, lacking in courage

Chapter 19

1   *Divvies* is Liverpool slang meaning assholes

2   New Year's Day is also my birthday

3   A *hard case* means a street fighter

Chapter 20

1   Big Bill Broonzey, a large man, died of cancer in 1958, his big frame wasting away almost to nothing

2   *Black Talk* by Ben Sidran Da Caop Press, New York, 1971

Chapter 21

1   *The Transatlantic Slave Trade* by James A. Rawley, W.W. Norton & Co, New York, 1981

2   A *bottle shop* is the same as a liquor store

3   *Do-larry* is Liverpool slang for crazy

4   *Douglas Bader* was a famous British air ace in World War II with two prosthetic legs

Chapter 22

1   *Patterns of Murder and Suicide in African Homicide and Suicide* by Bohannan, Editor, Princeton University Press, New Jersey, 1960

2   Remembered orally by author

3   *The Power of Myth* by Joseph Campbell, Doubleday, New York, 1988

4   *Black Culture and Consciousness* by Lawrence Levine, Encyclopedia Americana, CBD New Audio Resource Library, 1977

Chapter 23

1   Derry and The Seniors—a band with which I had a short-lived, disastrous playing stint, an event recorded earlier. Without me, Derry seemed to do much better, I'm sad to say.

2   A *peggy* is the lowest of the low of a ship's crew; the one who cleans the seamen's mess

3   A *dole queue* is a line of people waiting to collect their welfare checks

Chapter 25

1   *Toffee-noses* is English slang for people who are snobs

2   A *sandboy* is a sand flea on a sandy beach

3   *The Power of Myth* by Joseph Campbell, Doubleday, New York, 1988, p. 134

BIBLIOGRAPHY

Abrahams, Roger D., *Deep Down in the Jungle*, Aldine Publishing Co., Chicago, 1970

Abrahams, Roger D., *Positively Black*, Prentice-Hall, Inc., New Jersey, 1970

Ardrey, Robert, *African Genesis*, Dell Publishing Co New York, 1961

Bacon, David and Maslov, Norman, *The Beatle's England*, 910 Press, San Francisco, 1982

Barnfield, Edward, *The Unheavenly City*, Little Brown & Co., Boston, 1970

Bohannan, Editor, *African Homicide and Suicide*, Princeton University Press, New Jersey, 1960

Booker, Christopher, *The Neophiliacs*, Gambit Inc., Boston, 1970

Booth, Wayne C., *The Company We Keep, An Ethics of Fiction*, University of California Press, 1988

Brown, Peter and Gaines, Steven, *The Love You Make: An Insider's Story of the Beatles*, New American Library, McGraw-Hill, New York 1983

Calvocoressi, Peter, *The British Experience 1945-75*, Pantheon Books, New York, 1978

Campbell, Joseph, *The Power of Myth*, Doubleday, New York, 1988

Collier, Peter and Horowitz, David, *Destructive Generation: Second Thoughts About the '60s*, Summit Books, New York, 1989

Jung, Carl G., *Memories, Dreams and Reflections*, Random House, New York, NY, 1963

Jung, Carl G., *Essay On Archaic Man*, from *The Collected Works of C.G. Jung*, Volume 10, Princeton University Press, Princeton, New Jersey, 1970

Hughes, Quentin, *Seaport: Architecture & Townscape in Liverpool*, Lund Humphries, London, 1964

Levine, Lawrence W., *Black Culture and Consciousness*, Encyclopedia Americana, CBD New Audio Resource Library, 1977

Milner, Christina and Richard, *Black Players*, Little Brown and CO., Boston, 1972

Money, John, *Man & Woman, Boy & Girl: Gender Identity From Conception To Maturity*, Johns Hopkins University Press, Baltimore, MD, 1973

Nossiter, Bernard D., *Britain: A Future That Works*, Houghton Mifflin Co., Boston, 1978

Rawley, James A., *The Trans-Atlantic Slave Trade*, W.W. Norton & Co, New York, 1981

Rock, Chris, *Rock This!*, Hyperion, New York, 1997

Sampson, Anthony, *The Changing Anatomy of Britain*, Randon House, New York, 1982

Seabrook, Jeremy, *What Went Wrong? Why Hasn't Having More Made People Happier?* Pantheon Books, New York, 1978

Sidran, Ben, *Black Talk*, Da Capo Press, New York, 1971

Silberman, Charles E., *Criminal Violence, Criminal Justice*, Vintage Books, New York, 1980

Thomson, Elizabeth and Gutman, David, eds, *The Lennon Companion: Twenty-five Years of Comment*, Schirmer Books, 1988

Tyrrell Jr, R. Emmett ed., *The Future That Doesn't Work: Social Democracy's Failures in Britain*, Doubleday & Co., New York 1977

Vigier, Francois, Change and Apathy, *Liverpool and Manchester during the Industrial Revolution*, The M.I.T. Press, Massachusetts, 1970

About the Author

Prem Willis-Pitts brings an unusual insight to the issues covered in this book. He was forced to leave school early and as a teenager was homeless and on the streets. His career is a checkerboard of experiences: sailor, carpenter, salesman, musician, psychiatric nurse, welder and, most unlikely, writer and Senior Staff Producer for the BBC World Service, London, a most distinguished post in the U.K.. Under his own steam he obtained an honors degree in Literature and Sociology from Sussex University and obtained a further post-graduate qualification from London University. He has lectured at universities in Spain, Italy, South America and the U.K.

Most significantly, in 1980 he gave up his career as a BBC producer and came to America. He began working in Vermont as the head of a shooting team for cable TV but finding this too isolating from ordinary American people, he eschewed it for a job selling ice cream in the streets of Boston.

The mixture of his street awareness and his academic knowledge has enabled him to observe American society with an acute eye. He has worked his way around America for over 17 years, from language teaching in Berkeley to carpentry in Oregon. Eventually, he settled down in California and won a wide array of awards for his works which encompass radio plays, musicals, biographies, screenplays, short stories and novels. His latest novel, *A Deadly Shade of Green*, won the National Writers' Association award for Novel of the Year. He moved to Denver, Colorado after the 1989 earthquake and, along with his writing career, is still playing rock 'n roll. He is involved in a number of creative projects of which *Liverpool the 5th Beatle* is one of the most recent. He is pleased to hear from his readers and can be contacted by e-mail at pwillis9@aol.com.

Other books by the author:

Between the Shadows of the Night
Blood Flowers
Chariot
A Deadly Shade of Green
The Link Trilogy:
Book 1: Orphans of the Last Dream
Book 2: Children of the Link
Book 3: The Dreaming Stone
Cassie Jallassie's Adventures in Space & Time:
Book 1: Androids, Arachnoids and Alien Malls
Book 2: In Search of the Android Libido
Starry, Starry Night, A Graphic Novel

Short Story Collections:
Masques, Speculative Fiction of Nightmare & Illusion
The Sacred and Profane, Speculative Fiction of Sex & Religion
Starry, Starry Night, Speculative Fiction of the Heart

Non-Fiction:
Tales of a Liverpool Lad
The Roots of British Rock Guitar
The Fire and the Rose
Lost in America: A Limey on the Loose

For more information on the author and his various works, visit one of these web sites:
Books can be purchased online at either of these sites or by calling 1-800-450-8624

http://www.adeadlyshade.com
http://www.beatlesbook.net

3

4

5

6

7

Samplers

Floral centerpieces

⑧ Instructions on page 42.   41 cm × 37 cm (16⅛″ × 14½″).

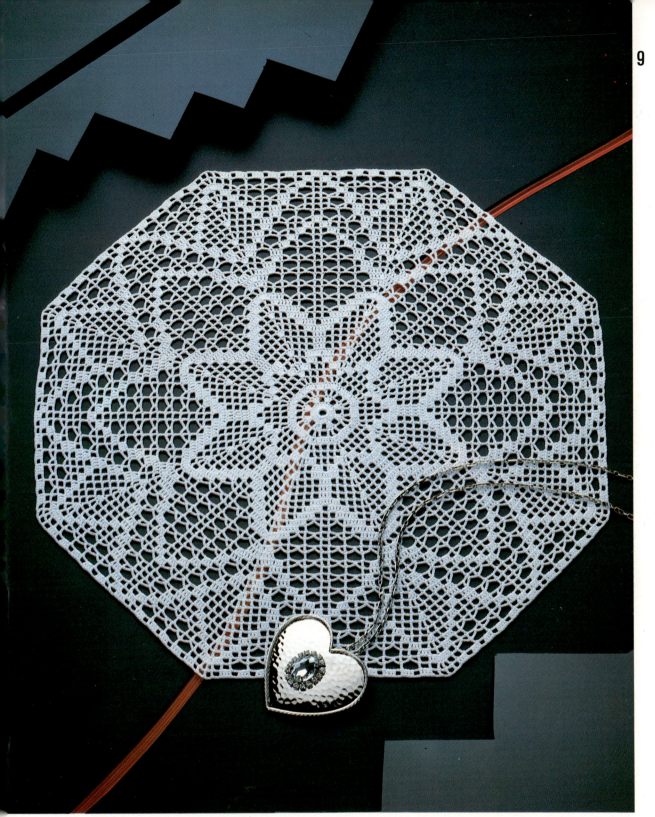

⑨ Instructions on page 43.　34 cm (13⅜″) in diameter.

10

⑩ Instructions on page 44.   34 cm (13⅜″) in diameter.
⑪ Instructions on page 45.   35 cm (13¾″) in diameter.

6

⑫ Instructions on page 46.   29 cm × 44 cm (11⅜″ × 17⅜″).
⑬ Instructions on page 47.   55 cm × 40 cm (21⅝″ × 15¾″).

⑭ Instructions on page 48.   29 cm × 88 cm (11⅜″ × 34⅝″).
⑮ Instructions on page 49.   31 cm × 86 cm (12¼″ × 33⅞″).

14

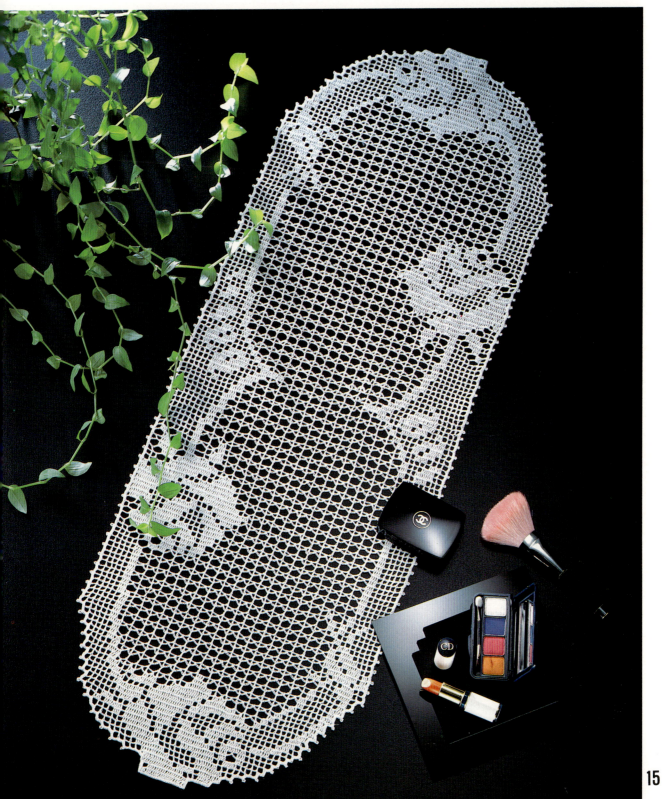

⑯ Instructions on page 50.   42 cm × 73 cm (16½″ × 28¾″).
⑰ Instructions on page 51.   38 cm × 59 cm (14⅞″ × 23¼″).

16

17

18 Instructions on page 52.   65 cm (25⅝") in diameter.
19 Instructions on page 54.   45 cm × 66 cm (18" × 25⅞").

Fairy tales in lace

20

16

21

22

⑳, ㉑, ㉒ Instructions on pages 56 and 57.
⑳ 29 cm × 41 cm (11⅜″ × 16⅛″).
㉑, ㉒ Size of frame 25 cm × 20 cm (9⅞″ × 7⅞″).

29

30

㉓ to ㉘ Instructions on page 58.
㉙ Instructions on page 60.
㉓ to ㉘ 32 cm × 23 cm (12⅝″ × 9⅛″).
㉙ 46.5 cm × 20.5 cm (18⅜″ × 8⅛″).
㉚ 13.5 cm × 12.5 cm (5⅜″ × 4⅞″).

31

32

㉛ ㉜ Instructions on page 64.

㉝ to ㉟ Instructions on page 62.

㉛ 13 cm × 11.5 cm (5⅛″ × 4½″)

㉜ 49 cm × 30 cm (19¼″ × 11⅞″)

㉝ 11 cm × 11.5 cm (4⅜″ × 4½″)

㉞ 47 cm × 30 cm (18½″ × 11⅞″)

㉟ 36 cm × 54 cm (14¼″ × 21¼″)

34

33

35

Lace for charming interiors

㊱ Instructions on page 66.   Size of frame 30.5 cm × 24.5 cm (12″ × 9⅞″).
㊲ Instructions on page 67.   28 cm × 28 cm (11″ × 11″).
㊳ Instructions on page 68.   64 cm (25⅛″) in diameter.

40

④1 Instructions on page 76.   60 cm × 60 cm (23⅝″ × 23⅝″), Frill 5 cm (2″) wide.
④2 Instructions on page 74.   48.5 cm × 47 cm (19⅛″ × 18 ½″), Frill 6 cm (2⅜″) wide.

42

㊹ Instructions on page 78. 90.5 cm × 51 cm (35⅝″ × 20⅛″).

44

㊺ Instructions on page 82.   47 cm (18½″) in diameter.
㊻ Partial pattern of a reference work on page 35.   90 cm × 205 cm (35⅜″ × 80¾″)

㊼ Instructions on page 80.   220 cm × 84 cm (86⅝″ × 33⅛″)

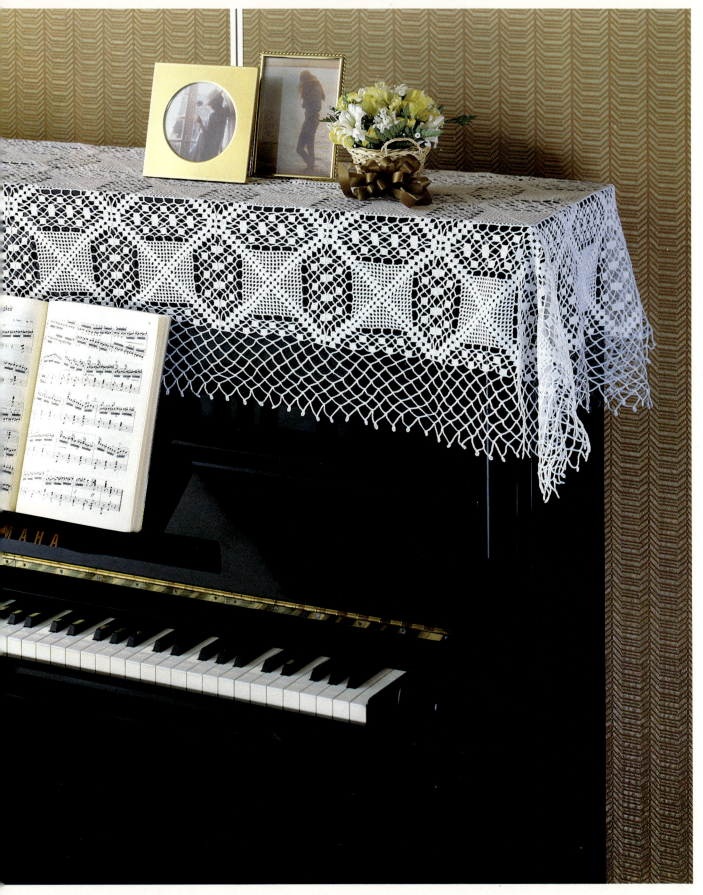

48 Instructions on page 80.   81 cm × 64 cm
(31⅛″ × 25⅛″)

34

Basic Crochet Lace

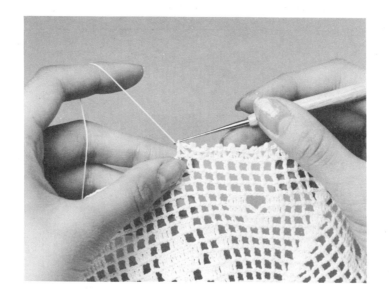

Lace worked with a crochet hook is called crochet lace and is a popular and familiar technique used for several kinds of lace. Matching the crochet hook to thread size is the key to completing a neatly worked piece of lace. Crochet cotton No. 40 is often used in this book, and crochet hook size 0.90 mm (14 steel · U.S.A.) works best with thread No. 40 in general.

Square mesh is widely applicable in any kind of work. You can make a variety of patterns, both floral and geometric, by filling up the spaces freely.

The samplers shown on pages 2 and 3 are the basic motifs. You can make various shapes according to the ways the motifs are arranged and joined. The size of the square or rectangle also depends on the number of motifs.

Edging is worked by repeating single crochet or a small pattern. Select a pattern well matched to the work.

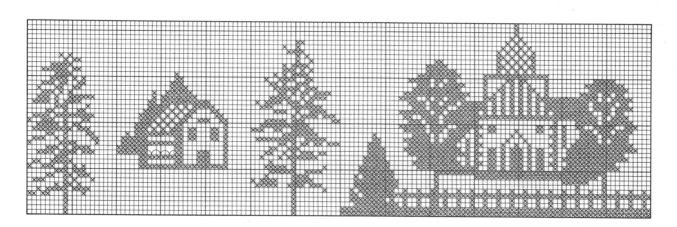

● Symbols Used in Square Mesh Lace and the Basics of Making a Circle

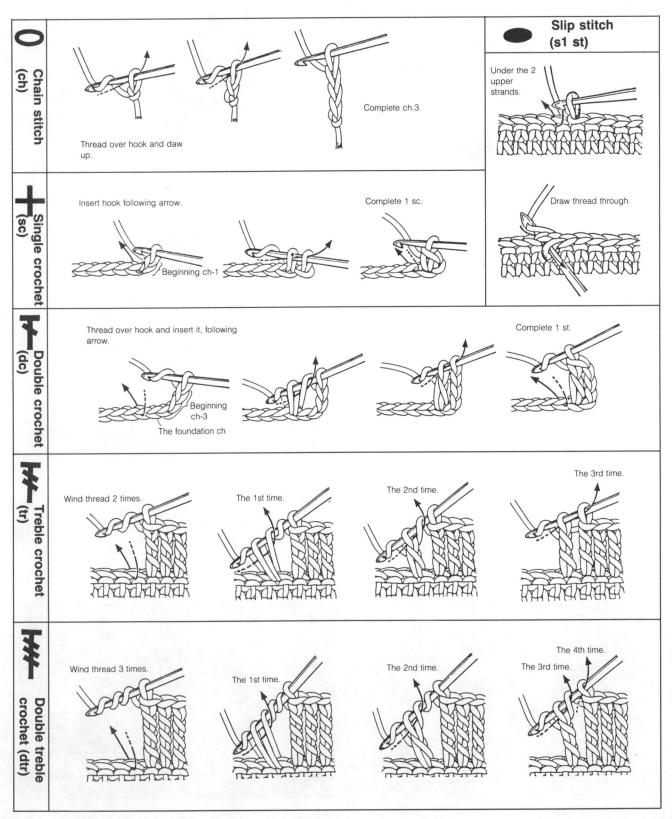

O Chain stitch (ch)

Thread over hook and daw up.

Complete ch.3.

Slip stitch (s1 st)

Under the 2 upper strands.

+ Single crochet (sc)

Insert hook following arrow.

Beginning ch-1

Complete 1 sc.

Draw thread through.

Double crochet (dc)

Thread over hook and insert it, following arrow.

Beginning ch-3

The foundation ch

Complete 1 st.

Treble crochet (tr)

Wind thread 2 times.

The 1st time.

The 2nd time.

The 3rd time.

Double treble crochet (dtr)

Wind thread 3 times.

The 1st time.

The 2nd time.

The 3rd time.

The 4th time.

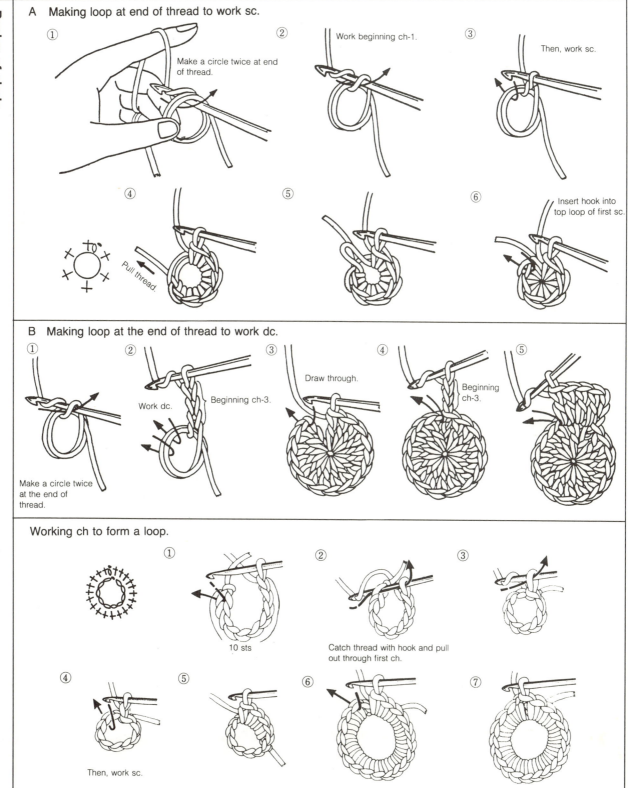

A Making loop at end of thread to work sc.

① Make a circle twice at end of thread.

② Work beginning ch-1.

③ Then, work sc.

④ Pull thread.

⑤

⑥ Insert hook into top loop of first sc.

B Making loop at the end of thread to work dc.

① Make a circle twice at the end of thread.

② Work dc. Beginning ch-3.

③ Draw through.

④ Beginning ch-3.

⑤

Working ch to form a loop.

① 10 sts

② Catch thread with hook and pull out through first ch.

③

④ Then, work sc.

⑤

⑥

⑦

● Basic Square Mesh　　　● Popular Patterns

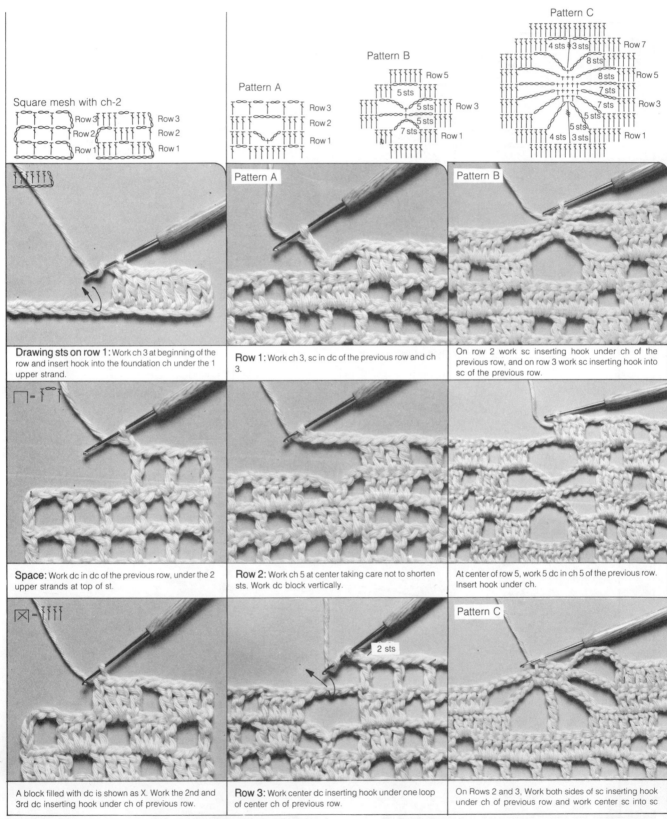

Square mesh with ch-2

Row 3　Row 3
Row 2　Row 2
Row 1　Row 1

Pattern A

Row 3
Row 2
Row 1

Pattern B

Row 5
5 sts
5 sts
5 sts
7 sts　Row 1
Row 3

Pattern C

4 sts 3 sts　Row 7
8 sts
8 sts　Row 5
7 sts
7 sts　Row 3
5 sts
5 sts
4 sts 3 sts　Row 1

Drawing sts on row 1: Work ch 3 at beginning of the row and insert hook into the foundation ch under the 1 upper strand.

Pattern A

Row 1: Work ch 3, sc in dc of the previous row and ch 3.

Pattern B

On row 2 work sc inserting hook under ch of the previous row, and on row 3 work sc inserting hook into sc of the previous row.

Space: Work dc in dc of the previous row, under the 2 upper strands at top of st.

Row 2: Work ch 5 at center taking care not to shorten sts. Work dc block vertically.

At center of row 5, work 5 dc in ch 5 of the previous row. Insert hook under ch.

A block filled with dc is shown as X. Work the 2nd and 3rd dc inserting hook under ch of previous row.

Row 3: Work center dc inserting hook under one loop of center ch of previous row.

2 sts

Pattern C

On Rows 2 and 3, Work both sides of sc inserting hook under ch of previous row and work center sc into sc

38 ● Thick thread is used in photo to make it easy to see each stitch.

● Decreasing and Increasing of Square Mesh

Work No. 14

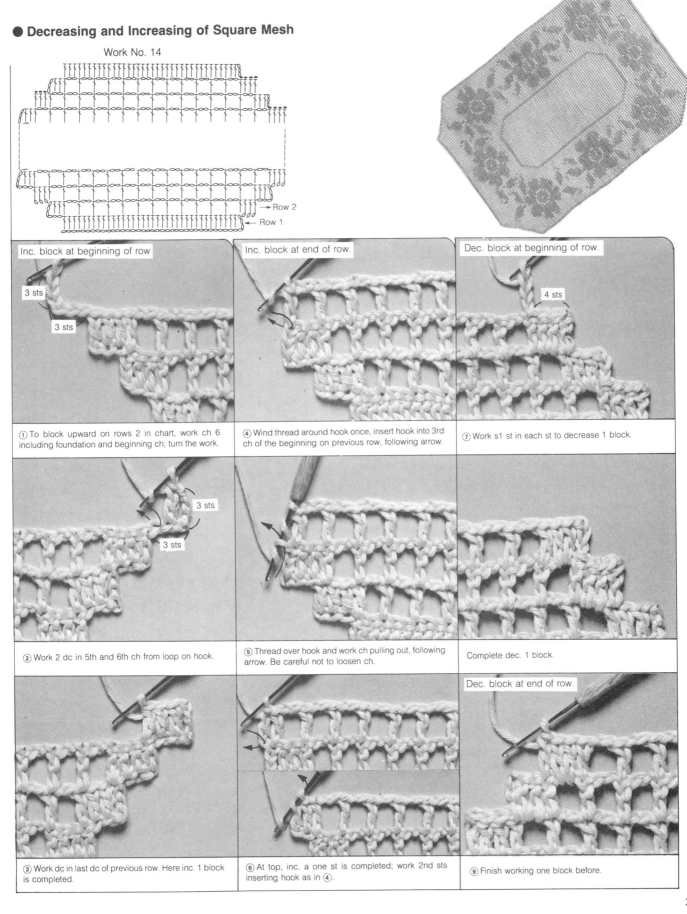

→ Row 2
← Row 1

Inc. block at beginning of row

3 sts
3 sts

① To block upward on rows 2 in chart, work ch 6 including foundation and beginning ch; turn the work.

3 sts
3 sts

② Work 2 dc in 5th and 6th ch from loop on hook.

③ Work dc in last dc of previous row. Here inc. 1 block is completed.

Inc. block at end of row.

④ Wind thread around hook once, insert hook into 3rd ch of the beginning on previous row, following arrow.

⑤ Thread over hook and work ch pulling out, following arrow. Be careful not to loosen ch.

⑥ At top, inc. a one st is completed; work 2nd sts inserting hook as in ④.

Dec. block at beginning of row.

4 sts

⑦ Work s1 st in each st to decrease 1 block.

Complete dec. 1 block.

Dec. block at end of row.

⑨ Finish working one block before.

39

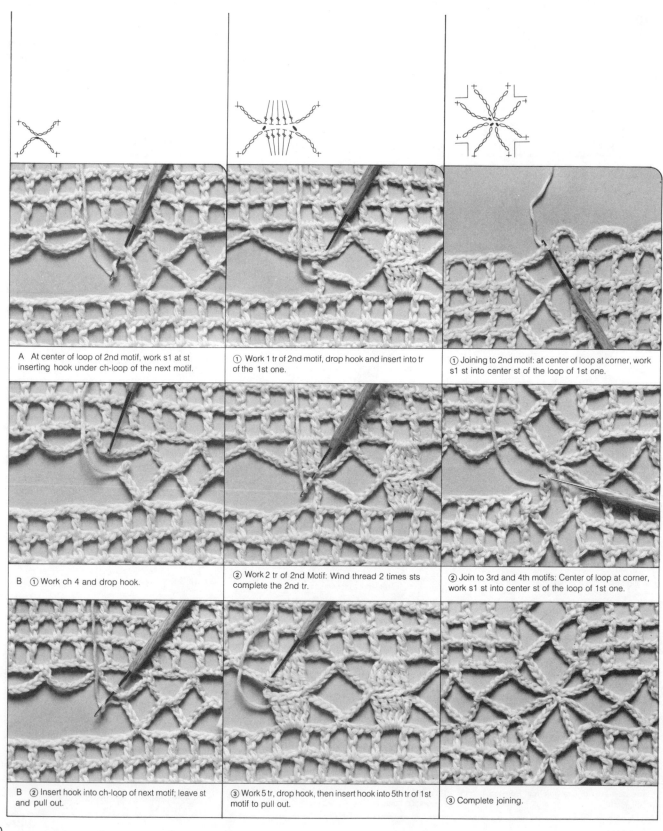

A   At center of loop of 2nd motif, work s1 at st inserting hook under ch-loop of the next motif.

① Work 1 tr of 2nd motif, drop hook and insert into tr of the 1st one.

① Joining to 2nd motif: at center of loop at corner, work s1 st into center st of the loop of 1st one.

B   ① Work ch 4 and drop hook.

② Work 2 tr of 2nd Motif: Wind thread 2 times sts complete the 2nd tr.

② Join to 3rd and 4th motifs: Center of loop at corner, work s1 st into center st of the loop of 1st one.

B   ② Insert hook into ch-loop of next motif; leave st and pull out.

③ Work 5 tr, drop hook, then insert hook into 5th tr of 1st motif to pull out.

③ Complete joining.

1~7

Samplers

Shown on pages 2 and 3. ■

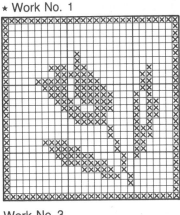

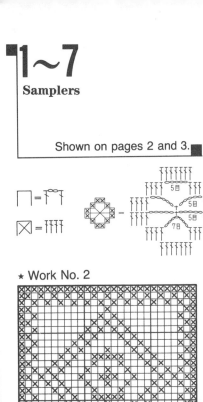

★ Work No. 1

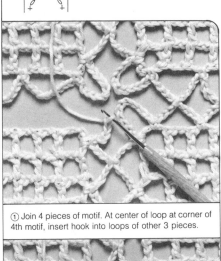

① Join 4 pieces of motif. At center of loop at corner of 4th motif, insert hook into loops of other 3 pieces.

② Draw up at one time and work ch for loop of 4th motif.

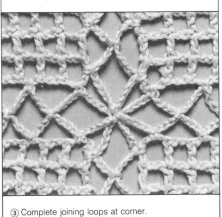

③ Complete joining loops at corner.

★ Work No. 2

★ Work No. 3

★ Work No. 4

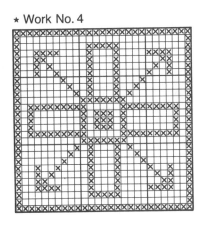

★ Work No. 5

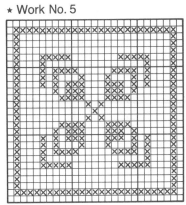

★ Work No. 6

★ Work No. 7

8 Centerpiece

Shown on page 4.

You'll need: Anchor Mercer-Crochet No. 40 White (01) 20 g (¾ oz). Steel crochet hook: Size 0.90 mm (14 steel · U.S.A.).

Finished size: 41 cm × 37 cm (16⅛ × 14½)
Instructions: Work 82 meshes and 82 rows making pattern throughout the work. Make foundation ch 247 and ch 3 at beginning of each row, then work following chart. In any kind of pattern, work dc the same length and work top of dc and ch the same size to make the work look neat. Work edging continuing to last row. Work 3 sts and 2 sts alternately in 1 mesh on both sides.

★ Edging

★ Beginning

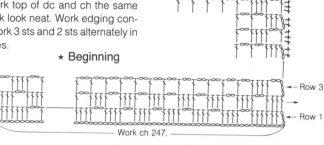

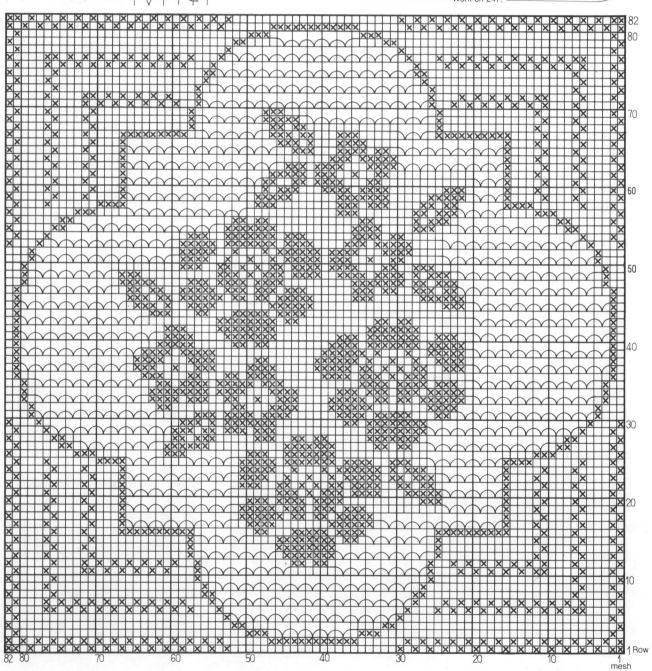

9 Centerpieces

Shown on page 5.

You'll need: Anchor Mercer-Crochet No. 40 White (01) 30 g (1¹⁄₁₆ oz). Steel crochet hook: Size 0.90 mm (14 steel · U.S.A.).

Finished size: 34 cm (13⅜″) in diameter.

Instructions: Work from the center outward. Make a loop of ch 8 at the begin-ning and work ch 3 and 23 dc, inserting hook into ch-loop, then s1 st in the begin-ning ch-3. From Row 2, work ch 3 at the beginning of each row and increase sts at 8 points on every row, then continue working to Row 38 to complete.

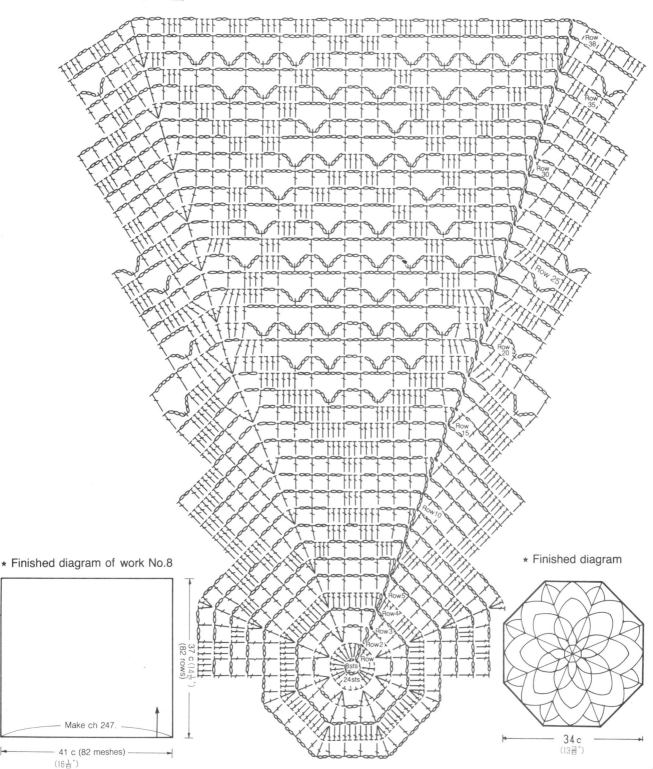

★ Finished diagram of work No.8

Edging 1 row

Make ch 247.

41 c (82 meshes)
(16⅛″)

37 c (14½″) (82 rows)

★ Finished diagram

34 c (13⅜″)

10 Doily

Shown on page 6. ■

You'll need: Anchor Mercer-Crochet No. 40 White (01) 30 g (1¹⁄₁₆ oz). Steel crochet hook: Size 0.90 mm (14 steel · U.S.A).

Finished size: 34 cm (13⅜") in diameter.

Instructions: This is an octagonal centerpiece worked form the center outward. Make a loop of ch 8 at the beginning and work ch 3 and 23 dc, inserting hook into ch-loop, then s1 st in the beginning ch-3. From Row 2, continue working ch 3 at the beginning of each row, increasing sts at 8 points until Row 34. Make flower pattern from Row 14 to 26 and work whole sts for the last row with dc.

★ Finished diagram

34 c
(13⅜")

44

11 Doily

Shown on page 7.

You'll need: Anchor Mercer-Crochet No. 40 White (01) 50 g (1¾ oz). Steel crochet hook: Size 0.90 mm (14 steel · U.S.A).

Finished size: 35 cm (13¾″) in diameter.

Instructions: Work from center outward to form hexagon. Make a loop at the end of thread and work 6 sc inserting hook into loop on Row 1. From Row 2, work ch at the beginning of each row, make flower from Row 10 to 24, and finish by working square mesh on Row 29, then work around pattern with picot on Row 30.

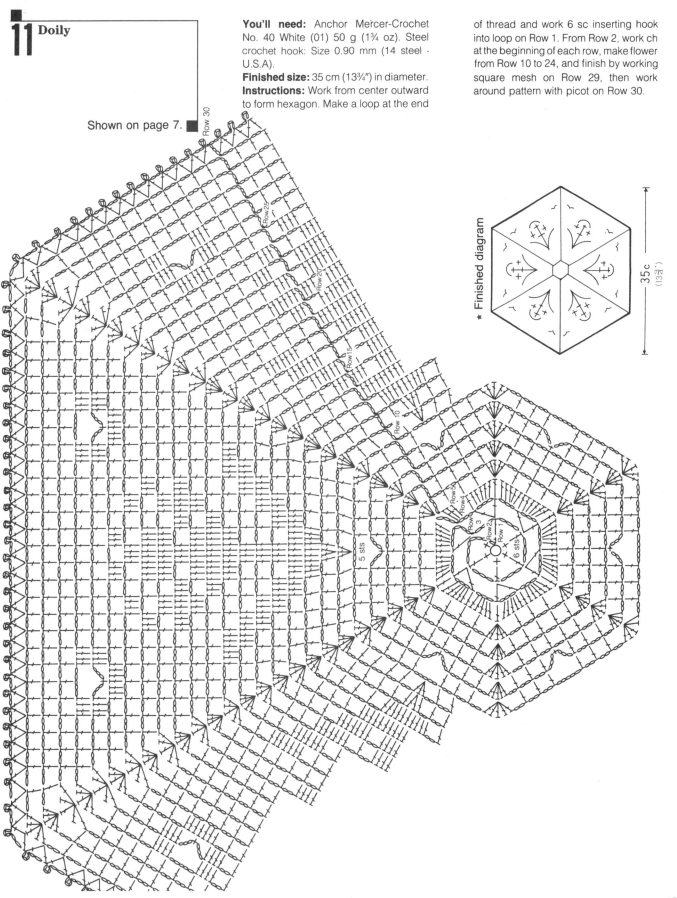

★ Finished diagram

35c
(13¾″)

45

12
Centerpiece

Shown on page 8. ■

You'll need: Anchor Mercer-Crochet No. 40 beige (768) 40 g (1⅓ oz). Steel crochet hook: Size 0.90 mm (14 steel · U.S.A).

Finished size: 29 cm × 44 cm (11⅜″ × 17⅜″)

Instructions: Make foundation ch 187 and work referring to diagram from Row 1 to 8; from Row 9 repeat, working 20 rows as one repeat of pattern. After making 5 flowers vertically, finish repeating pattern on Row 94, and work as shown in diagram from Row 95 to 101. Work edging 2 rows continuing to last row. On first row, inserting hook into dc or under ch of each mesh, work "3 sc in 1 mesh and 2 sc in next one." Work 3 sc in 1 mesh on the lower and upper ends.

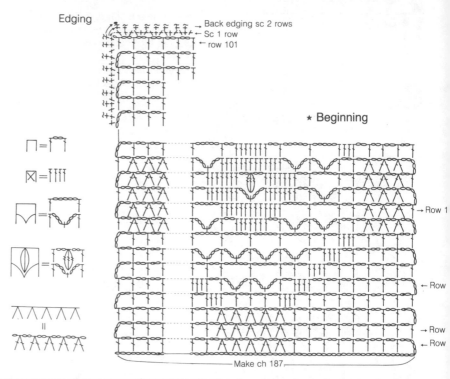

Edging

★ Beginning

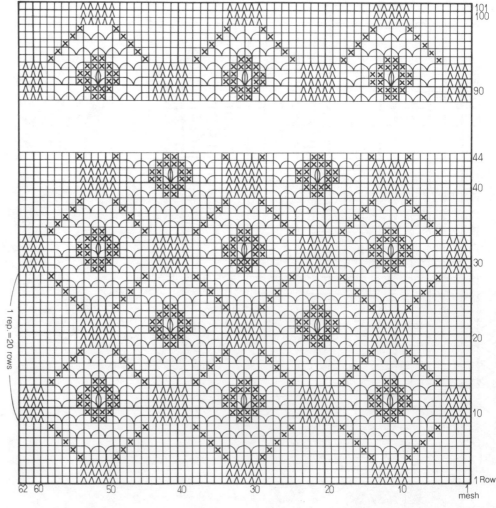

★ Finished diagram

46

13 Centerpiece

Shown on page 9. ■

You'll need: Anchor Mercer-Crochet No. 40 white (01) 70 g (2½ oz). Steel crochet hook: Size 0.90 mm (14 steel · U.S.A).

Finished size: 55 cm × 40 cm (21⅝″ × 15¾″).

Instructions: Make foundation ch 271, from Row 1 to 3 work square mesh with 1 dc and ch 2, then follow diagram from Row 4 to 63. Work ch 3 at the beginning of each row. At 4 corners and center work lacy pattern, matching length of surrounding meshes, and make a rectangle. Work edging continuing to last row. On the 1st row of edging work ch 6 and s1 st-picot with 3-ch and continue working around as shown in chart, but at the other corners work 1 dc instead of the beginning ch-3 to shape corner and complete.

★ Finished diagram

★ Beginning

★ Edging

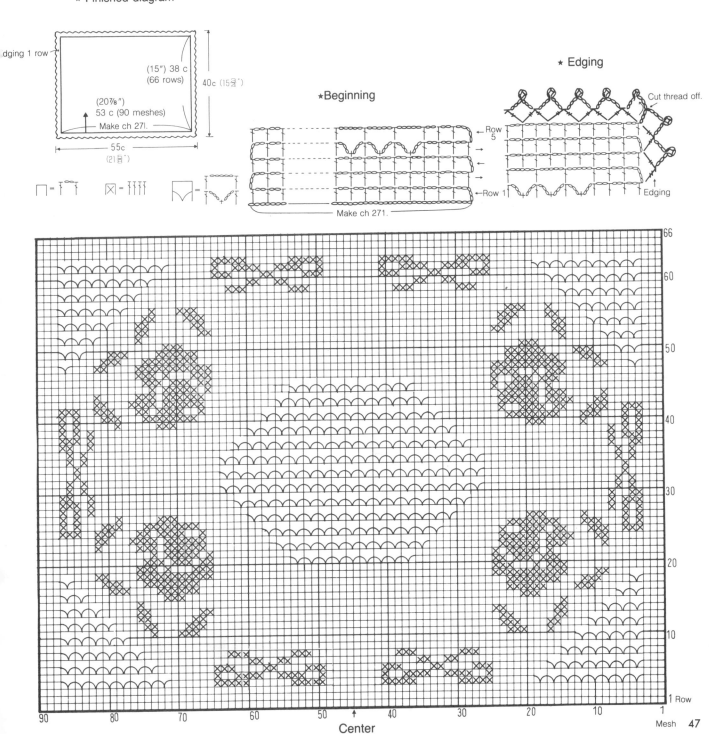

14
Runner

● Chart with symbols on page 54.

Shown on page 10. ■

You'll need: Anchor Mercer-Crochet No. 40 white (01) 70 g (2½ oz). Steel crochet hook: Size 0.90 mm (14 steel · U.S.A).

Finished size: 29 cm × 88 cm (11⅜″ × 34⅝″).

Instructions: In this runner the foundation ch is worked from the center toward both ends. Make foundation ch 151, and from Row 1 work ch 3 at the beginning of every row, increasing or decreasing 1 mesh on each side referring to diagram on right. After completing 82 rows turn the work and diagram; starting again from the foundation ch, work Row 2 to 82 again. Work edging continuing to last row. Work around with sc edging, inserting s1 st-picot with 4-ch at the positions shown as loops in diagram on right.

★ Finished diagram

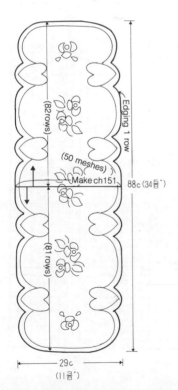

48

15
Runner

Shown on page 11. ■

Instructions: Start runner from center line and work toward both ends. Make foundation ch 157; on Row 1, work the beginning ch 3 and 2 for the first space, then work 5 spaces and block with dc to make flower pattern, referring to diagram. Work ch 3 at the beginning of each row to Row 54; decrease meshes at both sides from Row 55 to 80. At the end of row, work dc and dtr together to decrease neatly. After completing 82 rows, turn the work and diagram and work Rows 2 to 80 again. Work edging continuing to last row. See chart on page 54 for edging. Make loops working s1 st-picot with 4-ch. Work only sc from Row 77 to 80.

You'll need: Anchor Mercer-Crochet No. 40 white (01) 60 g (2⅛ oz). Steel crochet hook: Size 1.00 mm (12 steel · U.S.A).

Finished size: 31 cm × 86 cm (12¼″ × 33⅞″).

● Chart with symbols on page 54.

$\square = $ ⌐⌐⌐ $\boxtimes = $ ││││ ⌣ = symbol

★ Finished diagram

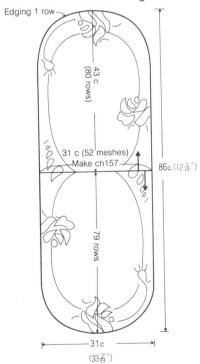

Edging 1 row
43 c (80 rows)
31 c (52 meshes)
Make ch157
86c (12¼″)
79 rows
31c
(33⅞″)

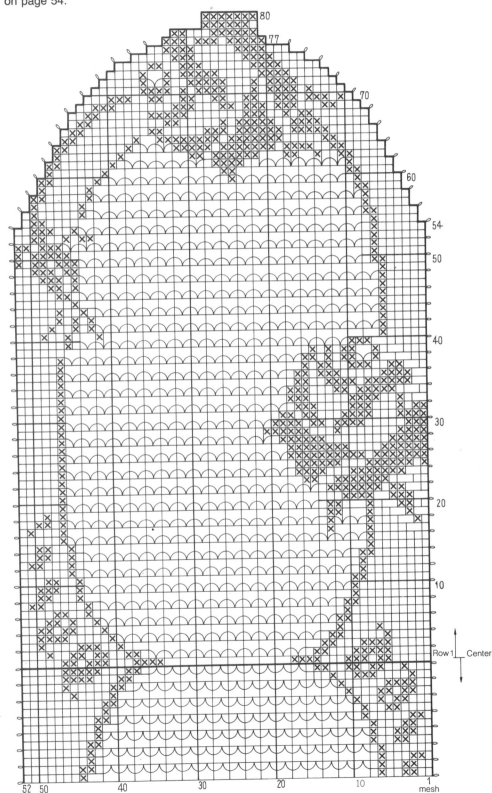

49

16
Centerpiece

Shown on page 12.

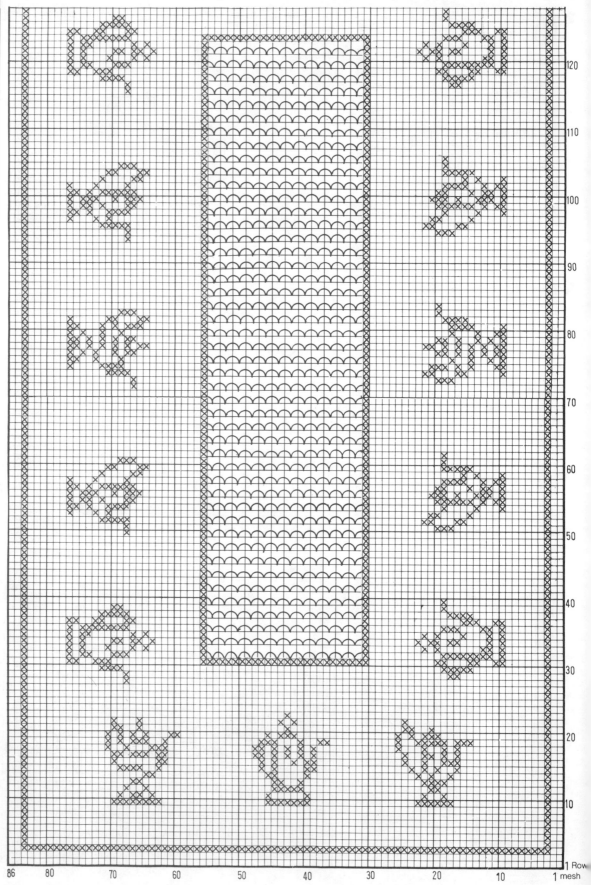

$\sqcap$ =

$\boxtimes$ =

50

You'll need: Anchor Mercer-Crochet No. 40 white (01) 100 g (3½ oz). Steel crochet hook: Size 0.90 mm (14 steel · U.S.A).

Finished size: 42 cm × 73 cm (16½" × 28¾").

Instructions: Make foundation ch 259 and work 155 rows, beginning each row with ch 3. The right side of the work is shown when you work on odd rows. Work edging, continuing to last row. Be careful never to let edge become loose, to keep lace rectangle neat.

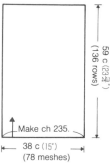

17
Centerpiece

■ Shown on pages 13.

□ = ⌐ ⌐ ⌐   ⊠ = ⌐⌐⌐⌐   ⌐⌐⌐ = ⌐⌐⌐

You'll need: Anchor Mercer-Crochet No. 40 white (01) 85 g (3 oz). Steel crochet hook: Size 0.90 mm (14 steel · U.S.A).

Finished size: 38 cm × 59 cm (15" × 23¼").

Instructions: Make foundation ch 235, begin each row with ch 3 and work dc inserting hook under one strand of the 5th ch from st over hook to continue dc into each foundation ch. One repeat of pattern is 22 rows and work 136 rows repeating from row 2 to 23 of diagram.

★ Finished diagram

59 c (23¼") (136 rows)

Make ch 235.

38 c (15") (78 meshes)

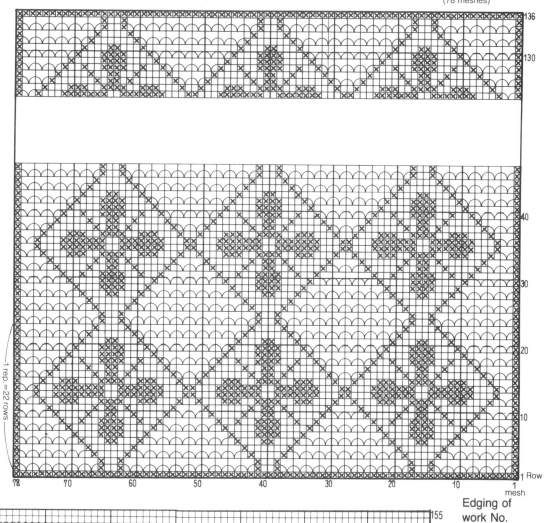

★ Finished diagram of work No. 16

Edging 1 row

73 c (28¾") (155 rows)

1 rep. = 22 rows

Make ch 259.

42 c (16½") (86 meshes)

78 · 70 · 60 · 50 · 40 · 30 · 20 · 10 · 1 mesh · 1 Row

Edging of work No. 16.

Start and end here.

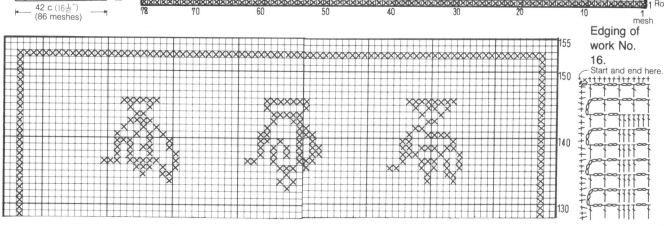

18
Centerpiece

Shown on page 14. ■

You'll need: Anchor Mercer-Crochet No. 40 beige (0387) 100 g (3½ oz). Steèl crochet ·hook: Size 0.90 mm (14 steel · U.S.A).

Finished size: 65 cm (25½″) in diameter.

Instructions: Work from center outward. Make loop at the end of thread as foundation. Row 1: work ch 5 and repeat "1 dc and ch 2" 5 times, then s1 st in 3rd ch of the beginning. Row 2: ch 5 and work 1 dc in s1 st of the previous row, "ch 2, 1 dc in dc of previous row, ch 2, 1 dc, ch 2, 1 dc" 5 times, 1 dc in s1 st of previous row, ch 2 and s1 st in 3rd ch of the beginning. From Row 3 to 57, work in same way as Row 2 at beginning and end of row, referring to chart, and cut thread off. Join thread at each side of hexagon on Row 58 and work to Row 62 as shown, then s1 st in each at on Row 63. At the beginning of Row 58 to 62, work s1 st in each st to continue to the next row.

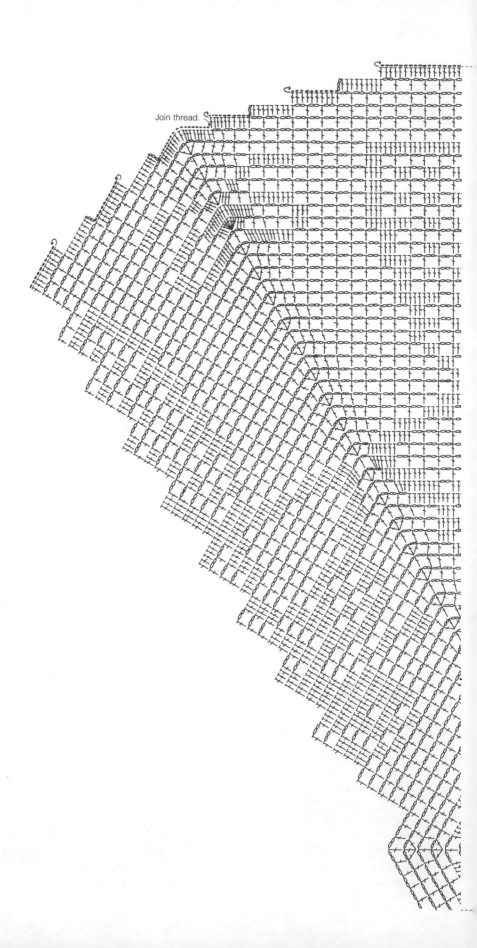

Join thread.

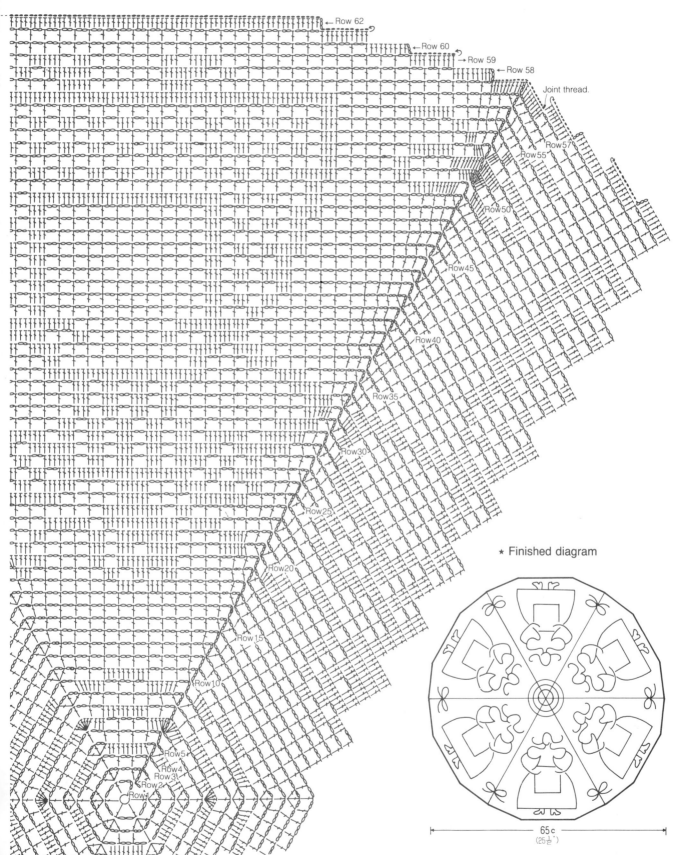

← Row 62

←Row 60

← Row 59

← Row 58

Joint thread.

Row 57

Row 55

Row 50

Row 45

Row 40

Row 35

Row 30

Row 25

Row 20

Row 15

Row 10

Row 5

Row 4

Row 3

Row 2

Row 1

★ Finished diagram

|← 65 c →|
(25 1/2")

★ Chart with symbols of work No.14.

★ Edging

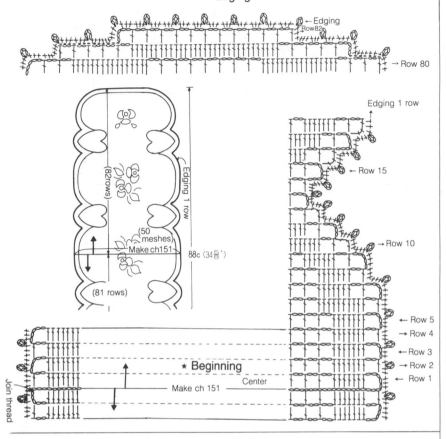

← Edging
  Row 82
→ Row 80

Edging 1 row

← Row 15

→ Row 10

← Row 5
← Row 4
← Row 3
← Row 2
← Row 1

Join thread

(82 rows)

Edging 1 row

88c (34⅝″)

(50 meshes)
Make ch151

(81 rows)

★ Beginning

Make ch 151   Center

★Chart with symbols of work No.15.   ★ Edging

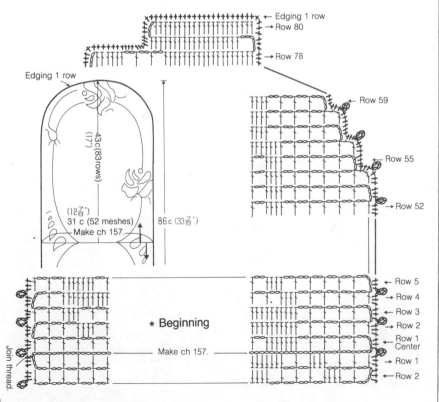

← Edging 1 row
→ Row 80
→ Row 78

Edging 1 row

← Row 59

← Row 55

← Row 52

← Row 5
← Row 4
← Row 3
← Row 2
← Row 1
  Center
← Row 1
← Row 2

43c(83rows) (17″)

(12⅞″)
31 c (52 meshes)
Make ch 157.

86c (33⅞″)

★ Beginning

Make ch 157.

Join thread.

■19
Centerpiece

Shown on page 15. ■

You'll need: Anchor Mercer-Crochet No. 40 beige (0387) 85 g (3 oz). Steel crochet hook: Size 0.90 mm (14 steel · U.S.A).
Finished size: 45 cm × 66 cm (18″ × 25⅞″).
Instructions: Make foundation ch 148; Row 1, ch 3 at beginning of row and work every st with dc as shown in chart; on Row 2 to 15, increase 1 block at both sides on each row, so work extra ch 3 as foundation at the beginning and work referring to page 39 at end of row. Row 55 is the center line. After finishing Row 55, turn Row 1 on diagram upward and continue working from Row 54 to 1. On the latter 14 rows, work decreasing 1 block each to Row 109 and complete. Work 49 sts with dc on the last row.

★ Finished diagram

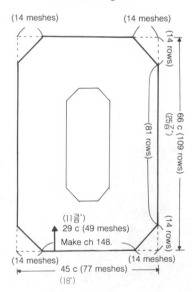

(14 meshes)   (14 meshes)

(14 rows)

66 c (109 rows)
(25⅞″)

(81 rows)

(11⅜″)
29 c (49 meshes)
Make ch 148.

(14 rows)

(14 meshes)   (14 meshes)

45 c (77 meshes)
(18″)

54

★ Beginning and ending

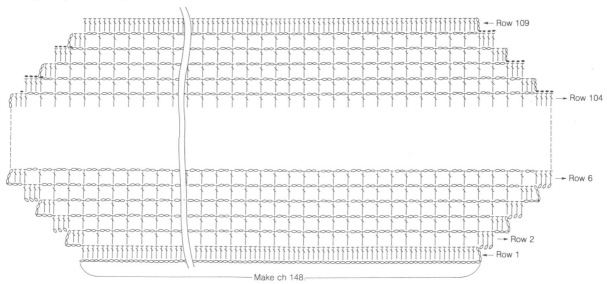

Row 109
Row 104
Row 6
Row 2
Row 1

Make ch 148

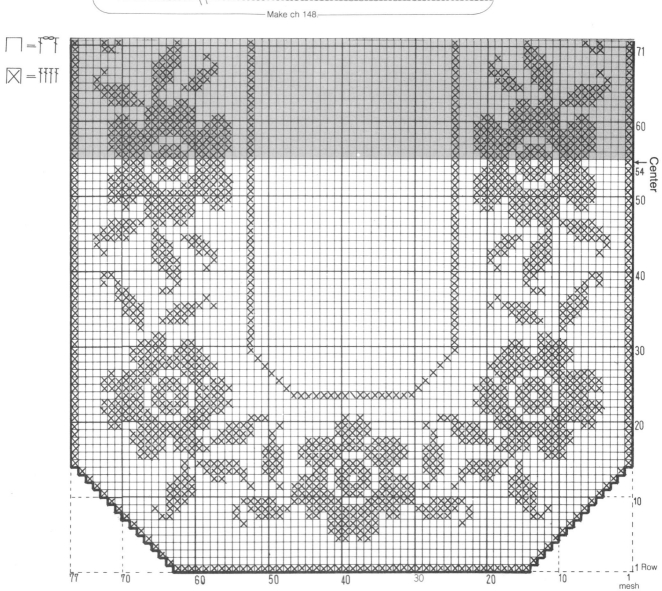

55

20 Wall hanging

Shown on page 16.

You'll need: Anchor Mercer-Crochet No. 40 White (01) 40 g (1⅓ oz). ANCHOR® Embroidery Floss, a bit of blue (133) (930), green (203) (208) (227), pink (76) (50), brown (309) (359), red (47), orange (302) (316), flesh (6), yellow (291) (288) and gray (398). 2 dowel rods, 1 cm (⅜") in diameter. Steel crochet hook: Size 1.25 mm (9 steel · U.S.A.)

Finished size: See the diagram.
Instructions: Make foundation ch 160 and work 7 rows with square mesh; on Row 8, fasten foundation ch and top of Row 7 together by inserting hook into the foundation ch and sts of Row 7. Complete 83 rows and cut thread leaving 60 cm (23⅝") length, hemstitching the top sts of Row 83 to Row 76, forming a carries for rod. Use 6 strands of each color for embroidery.

Darning st on hat (47)

Darning st on boy's hair (309)

Detached open chain st on Girl (359)

① ② ③

3 Out
2 In 1 Out
1 and 3 are the same point.

4 In 3
2 1 5 Out
2 and 4 are the same point.

8 In 7 Out
6 In 5 9 Out
③ shows the work repeating from ①, ②.

Free st of skirt (930, 50)

3 4
5 2
1 Out

work 2, 3, 4 and 5, inserting needle into top of dc.

★ Finished diagram

Rod 1 cm in diameter
Braid for hanging

39 c (15⅜") (69 rows)

41 c (16⅛")

□ =
⊠ =

29 c (15⅜") (53 meshes)
Make ch 160.

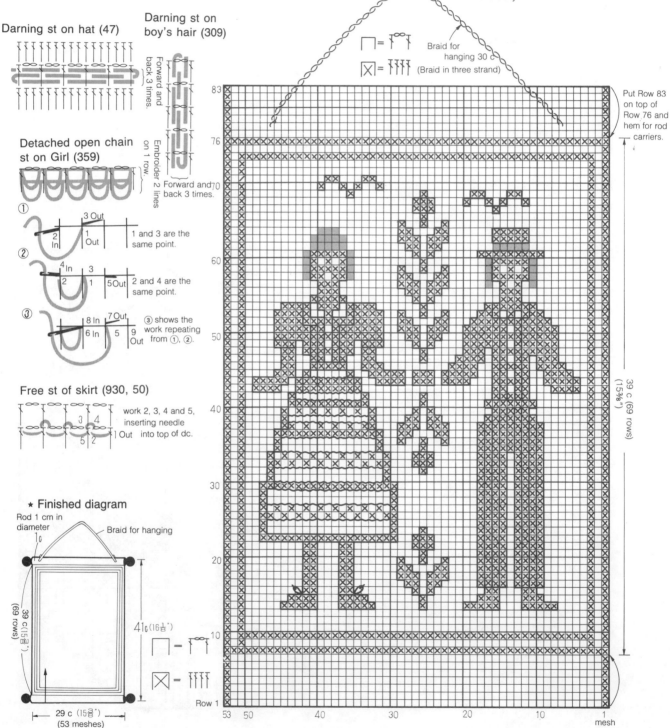

□ = Braid for hanging 30 c
⊠ = (Braid in three strand)

Put Row 83 on top of Row 76 and hem for rod carriers.

39 c (69 rows) (15⅜")

Row 1

53 50   40   30   20   10   1 mesh

56

21·22 Two types of framed lace

Shown on page 17.

Work No. 21
You'll need; Anchor Mercer-Crochet No. 40 White (01) 20 g (¾ oz). ANCHOR® Embroidery Floss, small amount each of 10 colors. Steel crochet hook: Size 0.90 mm (14 steel · U.S.A.). Frame.

Finished size: See the diagram.
Instructions: Work 38 means meshs (make foundation ch 115), making 40 rows with square mesh in advance, work holbein stitch with indicated colors of 6-strand ANCHOR® Embroidery Floss and set it into frame.

Work No. 22
You'll need: Anchor Mercer-Crochet No. 40 White (01) 20 g (¾ oz). ANCHOR® Embroidery Floss, 1 skein of white. Steel crochet hook: Size 0.90 mm (14 steel·U.S.A.). Frame.
Finished size: See the diagram.
Instructions: Work same as No. 21 but embroidery only with white.

★ Finished diagram

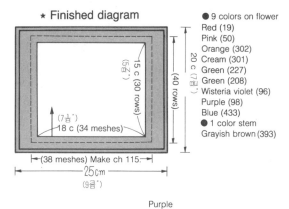

● 9 colors on flower
Red (19)
Pink (50)
Orange (302)
Cream (301)
Green (227)
Green (208)
Wisteria violet (96)
Purple (98)
Blue (433)
● 1 color stem
Grayish brown (393)

15 c (30 rows)
(5寸)
40 c (40 rows)
20 c (7⅞")
(7⅛")
18 c (34 meshes)
(38 meshes) Make ch 115
25cm
(9⅞")

★ Beginning

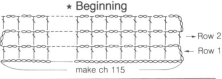

→ Row 2
→ Row 1
make ch 115

Ribbon on boy's hat Darning st (47)
Boy's hair Darning st (309)
Girl's hair Detached open chain st (359)
Girl's apron Cross st and Free st (76)(50)(930)
Girl's shoe string Lazy daisy st (50)
Center border of blouse Cross st (50)
Work holbein st on other parts See photo.

★ Basic techniques

Joining thread.

Ending

End of thread

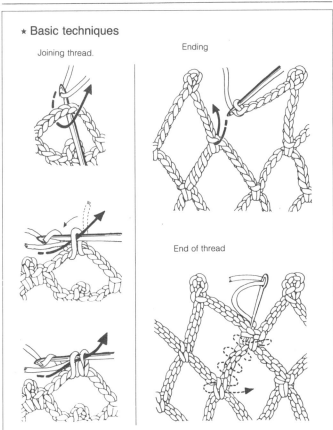

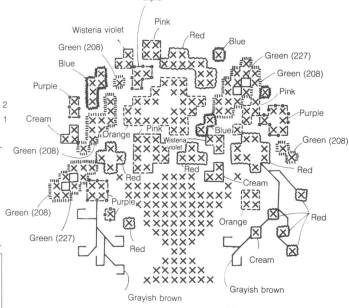

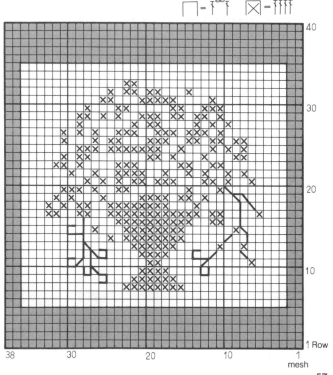

= ▯ = ▨

57

23~28 Placement

Shown on page 18.

For one piece
You'll need: Anchor Mercer-Crochet No. 40 White (01) 25 g (⅞ oz). Steel crochet hook: Size 0.90 mm (14 steel · U.S.A.)
Finished size: 32 cm × 23 cm (12⅝″ × 9⅛″).

Instructions: Make foundation ch 196; from Row 1, ch 3 at the beginning of each row and make square mesh working "ch 2 nd 1 dc" and dc blocks according to design. Complete on Row 43 and work edging 2 rows selecting from pattern A, B or C as you like.

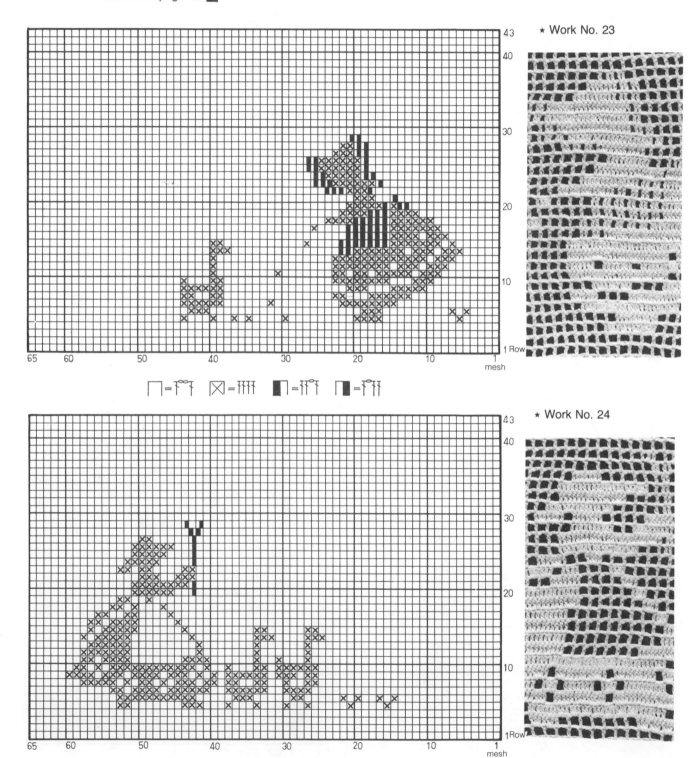

★ Work No. 23

★ Work No. 24

★ Edging A

★ Edging B

★ Edging C

★ Beginning

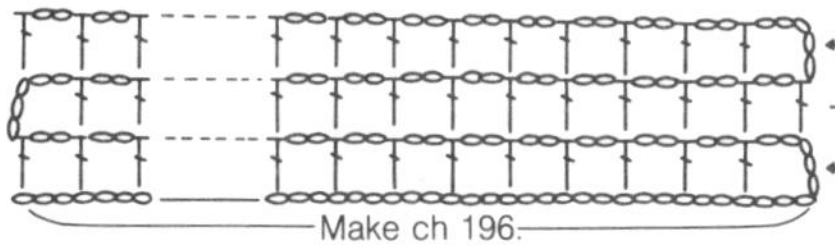

Row 3
Row2
Row 1
Make ch 196.

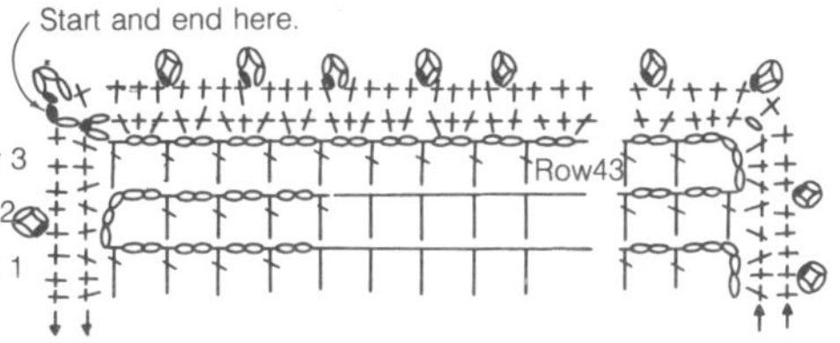

Start and end here.
Row43

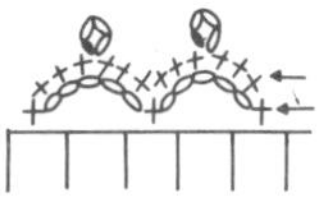

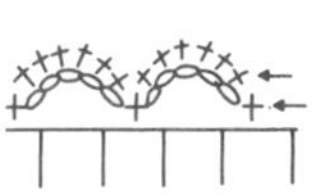

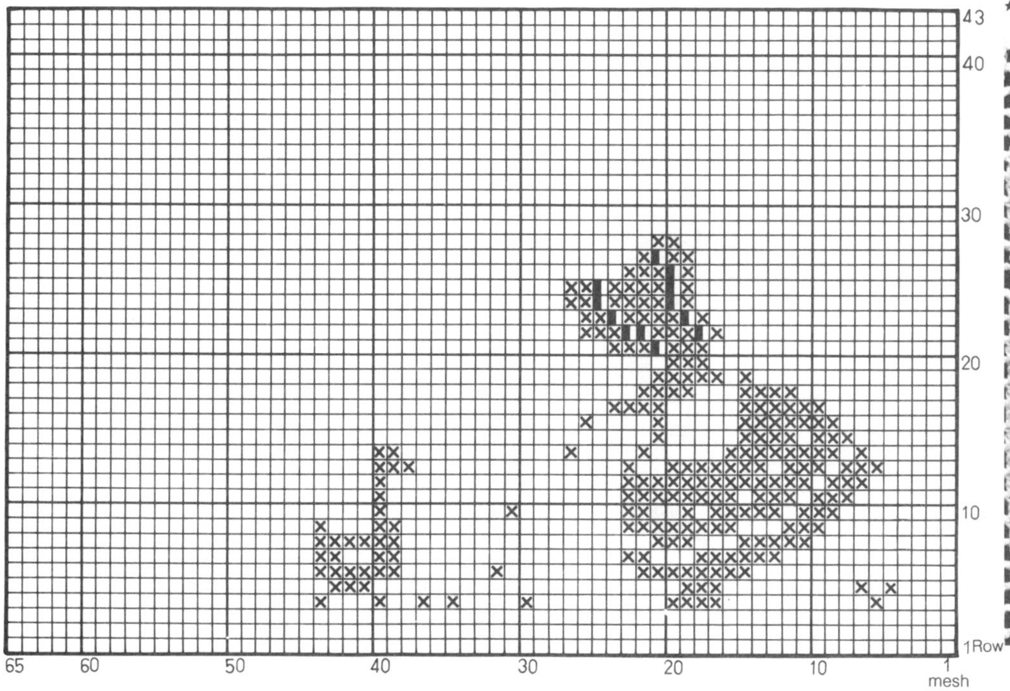

43
40
30
20
10
1Row
65
60
50
40
30
20
10
1
mesh

★ Work No. 25

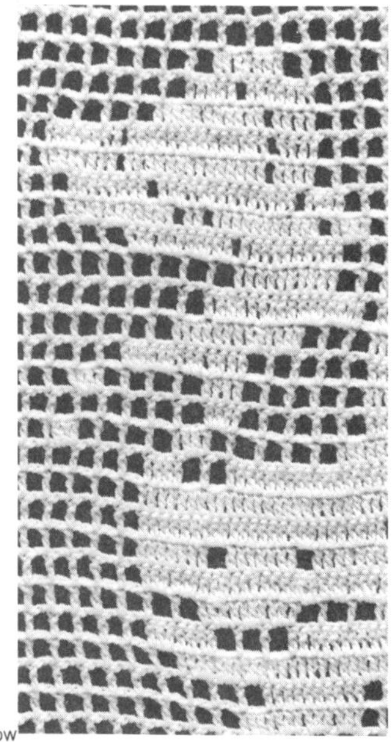

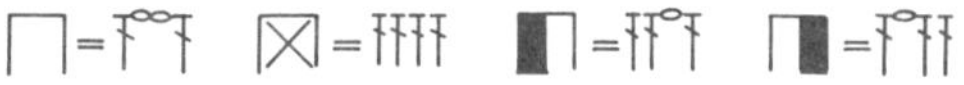

★ Work No. 26

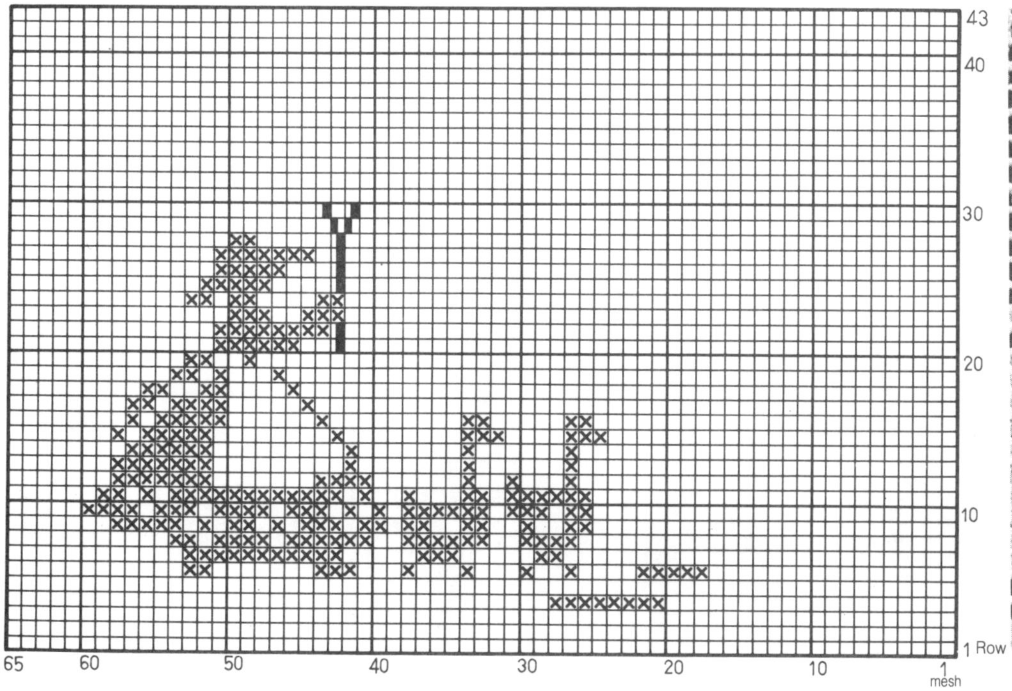

43
40
30
20
10
1 Row
65
60
50
40
30
20
10
1
mesh

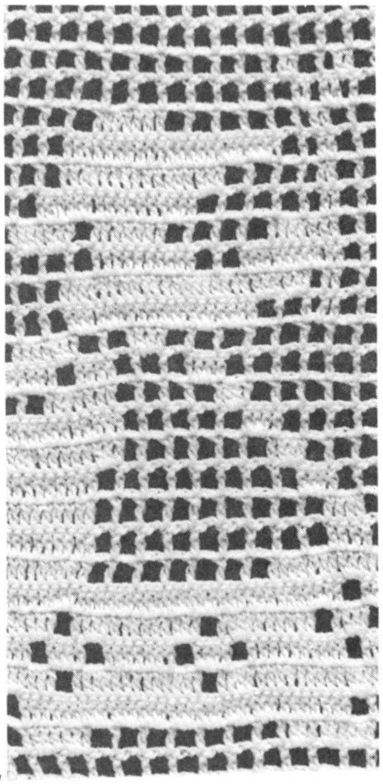

★ Finished diagram

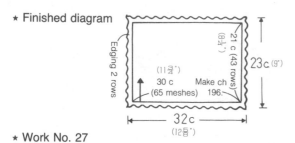

★ Work No. 27

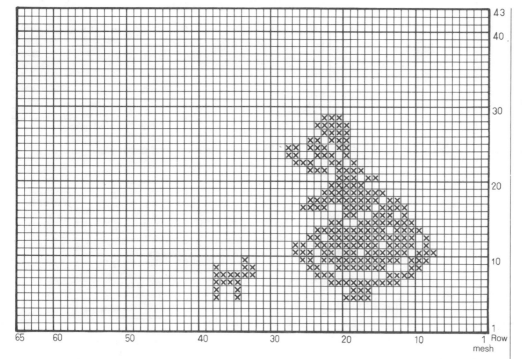

65 60 50 40 30 20 10 1 Row
mesh

⊓ = ‡°‡   ⊠ = ‡‡‡‡

★ Work No. 28

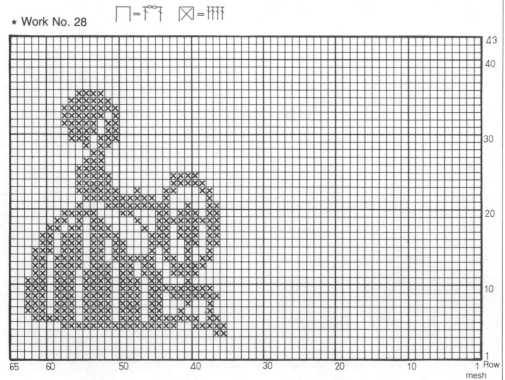

65 60 50 40 30 20 10 1 Row
mesh

■ Shown on page 19.

Work No. 29 Centerpiece
You'll need: Anchor Mercer-Crochet No. 40 White (01) 30 g (1¹⁄₁₆ oz). Steel crochet hook: Size 0.90 mm (14 steel · U.S.A.).
Finished size: See the diagram.
Instructions: Make foundation ch 271, work ch 3 at beginning of each row and continue, referring to diagram. Work edging 1 row continuing to last row and complete.

Work No. 30 One coaster
You'll need: Anchor Mercer-Crochet No. 40 White (01) 5 g (⅛ oz). Steel crochet hook: Size 0.90 mm (14 steel · U.S.A.)
Finished size: See the diagram.
Instructions: Work same as the centerpiece.

★ Finished diagram

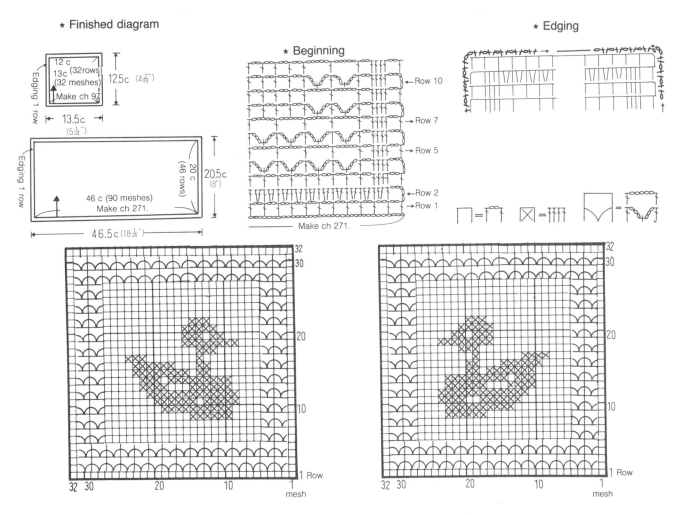

★ Beginning

★ Edging

Make ch 271.

★ Row 10
★ Row 7
★ Row 5
★ Row 2
★ Row 1

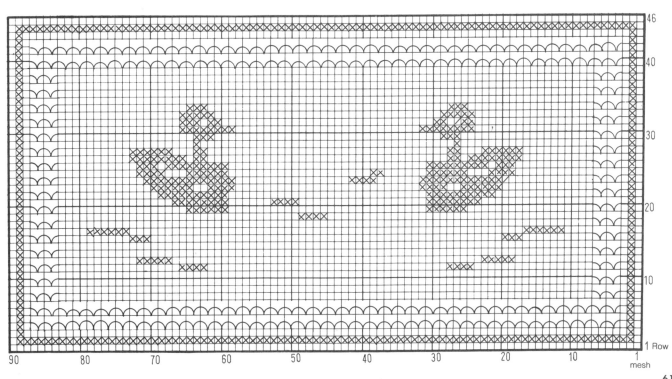

Centerpiece, placemat and coaster 33~35

Shown on page 21.

Work No. 34 One placemat

You'll need: Anchor Mercer-Crochet No. 40 White (01) 50 g (1¾ oz). ANCHOR® Embroidery Floss, 2 skeins each of blue and pink, and a half skein each of green and olive. Steel crochet hook: Size 1.25 mm (9 steel · U.S.A.).

Finished size: 47 cm × 30 cm (18½″ × 11⅞″).

Instructions: Work square mesh with white for the groundwork. Make foundation ch 268, work ch 3 at the beginning of Row 1 and insert hook into 4th ch from hook to work dc, then work dc in each st. From Row 2, work according to chart on top of opposite page, making ch 3 at the beginning and turning lace on every row to Row 63. As width increases on Rows 1, 3, 62 and 64, be careful to finish the width of the lace evenly on the other rows. After completing the groundwork, work embroidery on twigs, stems, petals, and leaves with holbein stitch using colored threads. Use 6-strands of embroidery thread in the colors indicated on the opposite page.

Work No. 33 One coaster

You'll need: Anchor Mercer-Crochet No. 40 White (01) 5 g (⅛ oz). ANCHOR® Embroidery Floss, a bit of yellow, green, and olive. Steel crochet hook size 1.25 mm (9 steel · U.S.A.).

Finished size: 11 cm × 11.5 cm (4⅜″ × 4½″).

Instructions: Work in same manner as 33. With white thread make foundation ch 64, and from Row 1 work ch 3 at the beginning of every row, then continue working to Row 23. Work holbein stitch using indicated colors of thread in 6 strands.

Work No. 35 Centerpiece

You'll need; Anchor Mercer-Crochet No. 40 White (01) 70 g (2½ oz). ANCHOR® Embroidery Floss, 2 skeins of wisteria violet and 1 skein each of green and olive. Steel crochet hook: Size 1.25 mm (9 steel · U.S.A.).

Finished size: 36 cm × 54 cm (14⅛″ × 21¼″).

Instructions: With white thread make foundation ch 202, and from Row 1 work ch 3 at the beginning of every row, then continue working to Row 109 referring to the diagram. Make 7 flowers in same way, filling up block with dc. Work holbein st using 6-strand colored thread.

★ Holbein stitch
The holbein stitch is worked like a running stitch, inserting needle into mesh of 1 row and carrying thread backwards over the stitch to bring needle in. Work twice around the outline of flowers, leaves, and twigs to complete.

★Basic techniques   Chain stitch (foundation stitch)

Hold with thumb.

1 sts   4 sts

Slip stitch picot with 3-ch

★ Finished diagram

Placemat

Coaster

Make ch64

11c (4⅜″) (23 rows)

11.5 c (4½″) (21 meshes)

Make ch 268.

30 c (64 rows) (11⅞″)

47 c (89 meshes) (22½″)

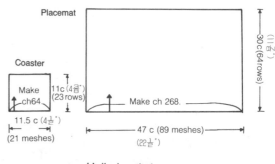

★ Holbein stitch

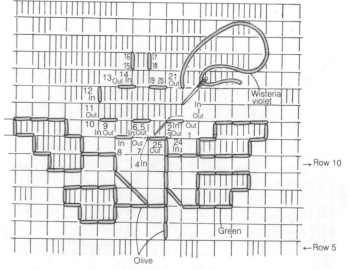

Wisteria violet

→ Row 10

Green

→ Row 5

Olive

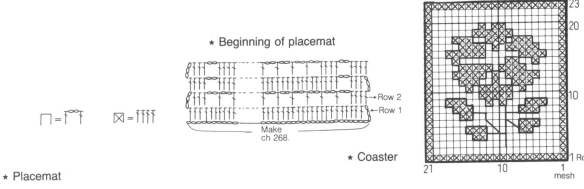

★ Beginning of placemat

Make
ch 268.

→ Row 2
← Row 1

□ =

⊠ =

★ Coaster

21   10   1
mesh

23
20

10

1 Row

★ Placemat

64
60

50

40

30

20

10

1 Row

89   80   70   60   50   40   30   20   10   1
mesh

The work	ANCHOR® Embroidery Floss in 6 strands	Flower	Leaf	Twig and stem
Centerpiece	Anchor embroidery threads	Wisteria violet (96)	Green (266)	Olive (281)
Placemat	Anchor embroidery threads	Left side: Blue (160) Right side: Pink (24)	Green (266)	Olive (281)
Coaster	Anchor embroidery threads	Yellow (290)	Green (266)	Olive (281)

Centerpiece

**Centerpiece,
coaster**

Shown on page 20.

Work No. 31 Coaster
You'll need; Anchor Mercer-Crochet No. 40 White (01) 10 g (⅜ oz). Steel crochet hook: Size 0.90 mm (14 Steel · U.S.A.).
Finished size: 13 cm × 11.5 cm (5⅛″ × 4½″).
Instructions: Use the same motif as for 3. Work referring to diagram on page 41. Make foundation ch 79 and work ch 3 at the beginning of row. On Rows 1, 3, 24 and 26, as lace becomes wider, work tops of dc as tightly as possible for a neat finish.

★ Finished diagram

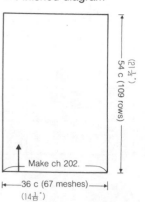

Work No. 32 Centerpiece

You'll need: Anchor Mercer-Crochet No. 40 White (01) 60 g (2⅛ oz). Steel crochet hook: Size 0.90 mm (14 steel · U.S.A.).

Finished size: 49 cm × 30 cm (19¼″ × 11⅞″).

Instructions: Make foundation ch 304, on Row 1 work ch 3 at the beginning and work dc in each st starting from 5th ch from hook. Insert hook under the 2 upper strands of ch. Work to Row 66, taking care to work the width of lace evenly, and finish.

★ Finished diagram

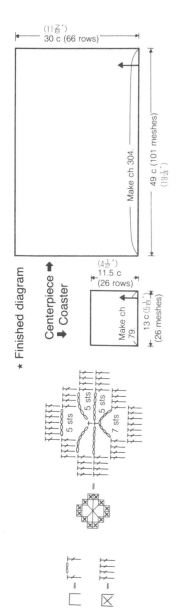

★ Centerpiece

Frame 36

Shown on page 22.

You'll need: Anchor Mercer-Crochet No. 40 White (01) 23 g (⅞ oz). 71 each of milky white spangles 6 mm (2⅜″) in diameter and white beads. Frame 24.5 cm × 30.5 cm (9⅝″ × 12″) in outer size. Steel crochet hook: Size 0.90 mm (14 steel · U.S.A.)

Finished size: See diagram.

Instructions: 1 mesh of lace is 2 sts. Work lace in advance. Make foundation ch 141 and work to Row 50 referring to diagram, then finish with iron. Fix spangles with beads and work double ch cord, then bring the end of cord and the thread left from the beginning to the wrong side to anchor them. Finish with iron and put into frame.

★ How to fix spangles

★ How to work double ch cord

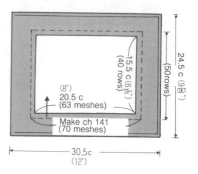

★ Finished diagram

24.5 c (9⅝″) (50 rows)

15.5 c (6⅛″) (40 rows)

(8″) 20.5 c (63 meshes)

Make ch 141 (70 meshes)

30.5c (12″)

$\prod$ = 三角 $\diagup\!\!\!\!\prod$ = 三角

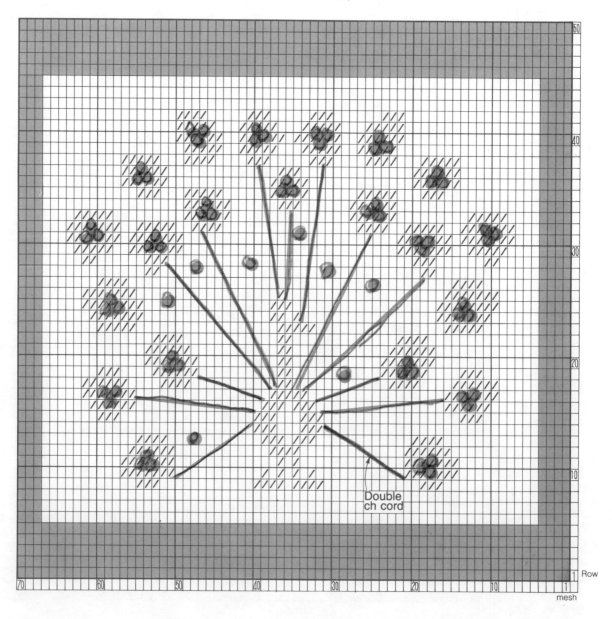

Double ch cord

70   60   50   40   30   20   10   1   Row

60   50   40   30   20   10   1   mesh

66

37
Doily

Shown on page 22.

You'll need: Anchor Mercer-Crochet No. 40 White (01) 25 g (⅞ oz). Steel crochet hook: Size 0.90 mm (14 steel · U.S.A.).
Finished size: 28 cm × 28 cm (11″ × 11″).
Instructions: Make this octagonal doily starting from the base: work foundation ch 64, on Rows 1 to 12 increase sts 1 mesh at both ends of every row and work straight from Row 13 to 33, then on Row 34 to 45 decrease sts 1 mesh at both ends of every row. Work edging 3 rows continuing to the last row.

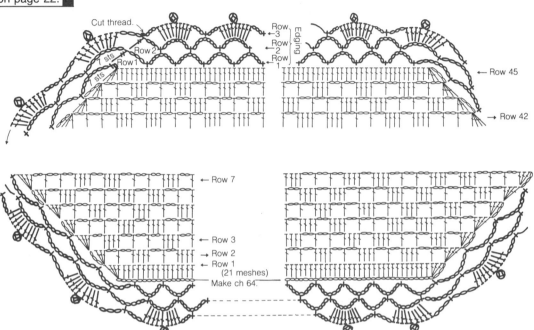

★ Finished diagram

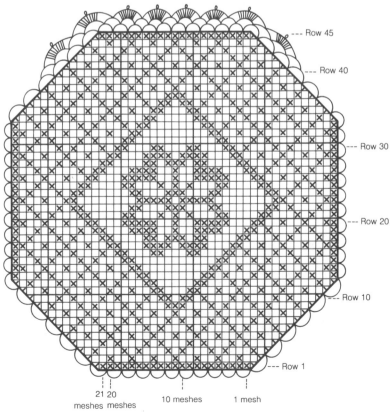

67

Round centerpiece 38

You'll need: Anchor Mercer-Crochet No. 40 White (01) 125 g (4⅜ oz). White linen 43 cm × 43 cm (17″ × 17″). ANCHOR® Embroidery Floss, 1 skein of white. Stell crochet hook: Size 0.90 mm (14 steel · U.S.A.).
Finished size: See diagram.
Instructions: ① cut fabric 40 cm (15¾″) in diameter and 14 cm × 14 cm (5½″ × 5½″) with 1.5 cm (⅝″) seam allowance.

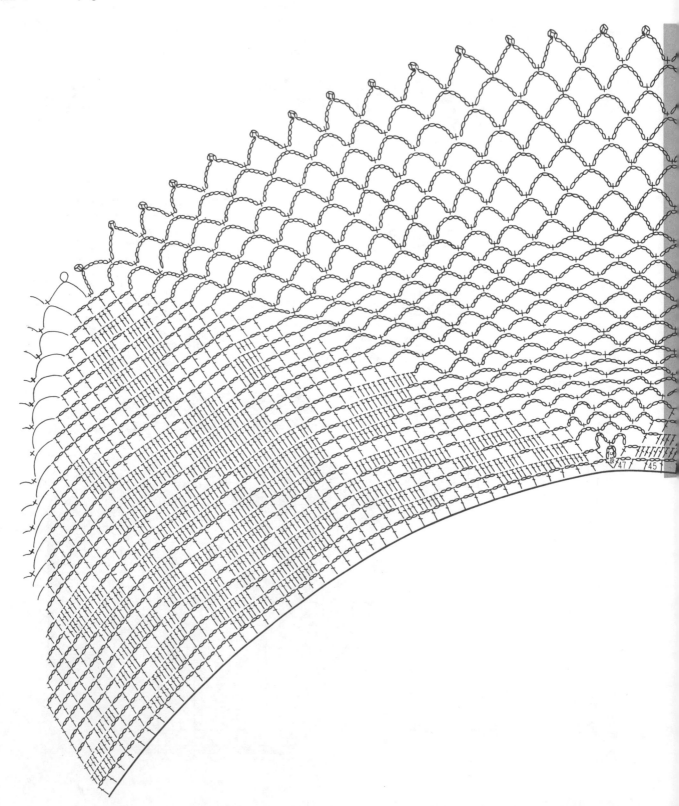

② Fold 1.5 cm (⅝″) seam allowance on 2 pieces of fabric to wrong side and iron, then work buttonhole stitch along fold with 4 strands of embroidery thread.

③ Make square framed lace at center of work. Pick up sts for 43 square meshes from one side. To work evenly, mark with thread at the center and quarter before working. Divide outer fabric into 8 parts for each interval of pattern in same manner as the square one and mark with thread to work 47 meshes as one repeat of pattern.

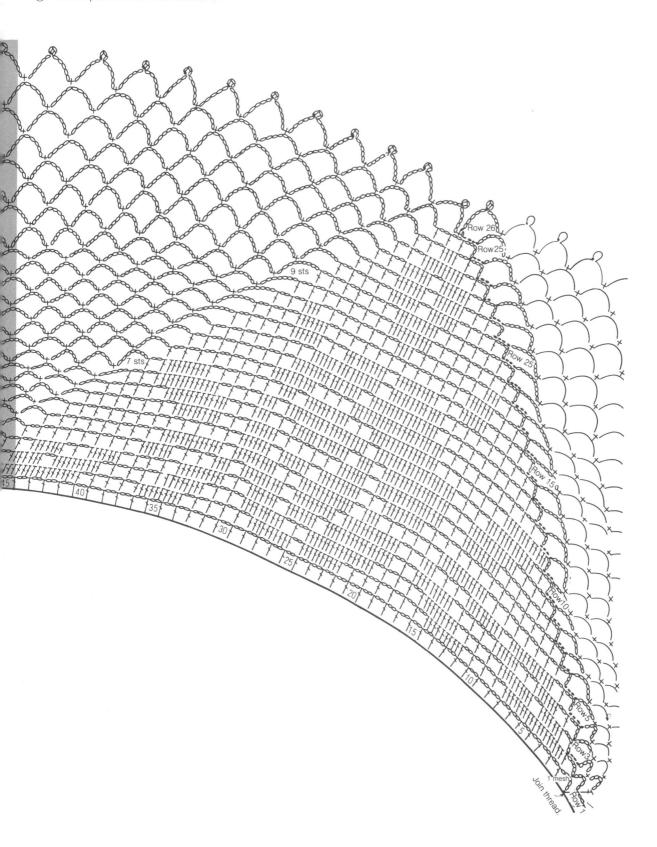

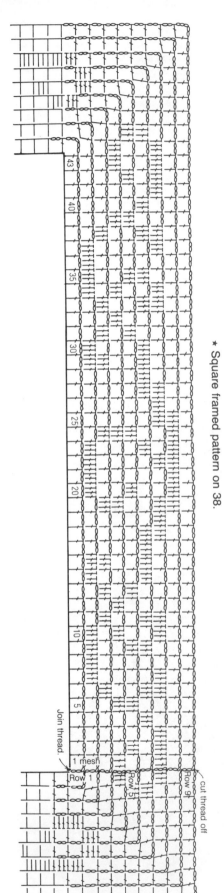

★ Square framed pattern on 38.

④ Work square framed lace first. Join thread in a corner of center and square fabric, working ch 3 at the beginning of every row and 43 meshes on side; at each corner, increase sts inserting hook into center st of previous row, then cut thread off after completing Row 9.

⑤ Join thread at marked point on outer fabric and work square mesh and net st. End with s1 st at each end of row and work s1 st on 1 mesh, then continue working to Row 26. Net st becomes frill.

⑥ Join outer and center fabric together at outer edge of square and finish with iron.

39 Round centerpiece

shown on page 24.

You'll need: Anchor Mercer-Crochet No. 40 White (01) 30 g (1¹⁄₁₆ oz). Steel crochet hook: Size 1.25 mm (9 steel · U.S.A.)

Finished size: 32 cm (12⅝") in diameter.

Instructions: Though the centerpiece is round, start working from the bottom. Make foundation ch 34 and on Row 1 work ch 5, including the beginning ch-3 and ch-2 for square mesh, and dc as shown in chart. From Row 2, increase sts at both sides. Referring to chart, work ch at one side and dtr at the other side. Work dtr the same height as bottom width of one mesh. Increase sts to Row 24 and decrease sts from Row 35. Be careful that decrease sts form the meshes right-angled at each side.

Work edging continuing to last row.

★ Finished diagram

12c
10c
10c
0.2c
Buttonhole st
20c (7⅞")
14c
Fabric
3 c (Row 9)
14c
20c (7⅞")
Fabric
10c
64c (25⅛")
40c (15¾")
40c (15¾")
64c (25⅛")

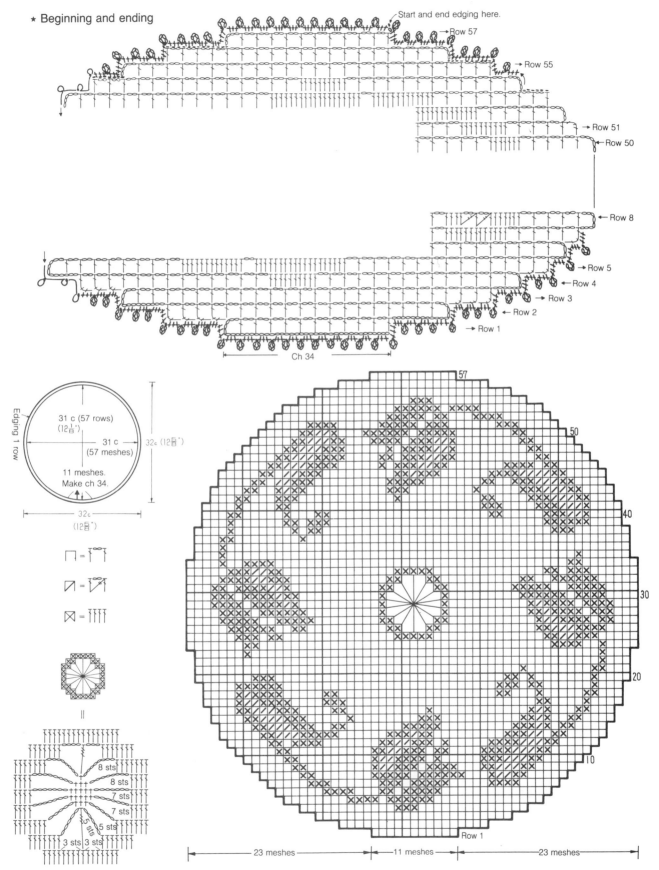

★ Beginning and ending

Start and end edging here.

→ Row 57
→ Row 55
→ Row 51
→ Row 50
← Row 8
← Row 5
← Row 4
← Row 3
← Row 2
→ Row 1

Ch 34

Edging 1 row

31 c (57 rows)
(12⅛")
31 c
(57 meshes)

32 c (12⅝")

11 meshes.
Make ch 34.

32 c
(12⅝")

⊓ = ⌐°°⌐

⊿ = ⌐°°⌿

⊠ = ⏐⏐⏐⏐

‖

8 sts
8 sts
7 sts
7 sts
5 sts 5 sts
3 sts 3 sts

57
50
40
30
20
10
Row 1

23 meshes — 11 meshes — 23 meshes

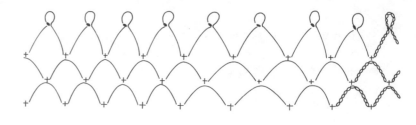

Square tablecloth **40**

■ Shown on page 25.

You'll need: Anchor Mercer-Crochet No. 40 White (01) 280 g (9⅞ oz) white. Steel crochet hook: Size 0.90 mm (14 steel · U.S.A.)

Finished size: 105 cm × 105 cm (41⅜″ × 41⅜″).

Instructions: Work 1 row of edging along sampler motif 4 on page 3 to make square motif sized 17 cm (6⅝″) by 17 cm; join 25 pieces of motif, arranging 5 pieces vertically and 5 pieces across, then make 10 cm (4 ″) of frill with net st to complete square tablecloth. For one piece of motif,

★ Finished diagram

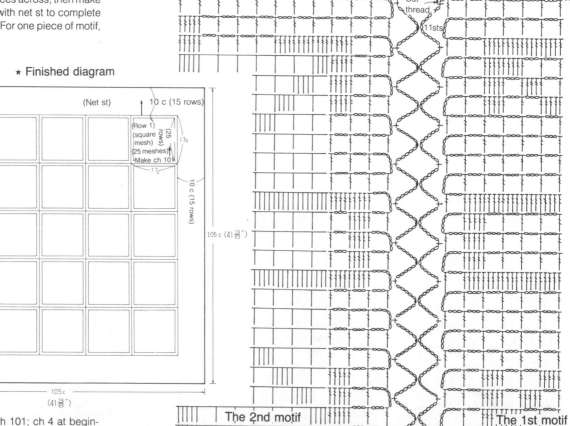

make foundation ch 101; ch 4 at beginning of every row from Row 1 to 25 and work square mesh with "ch 3 and tr" making geometric pattern to Row 25. Make square with 25 meshes lengthwise and across, and work along edging with ch 11, then cut thread. From 2nd motif, join to previous one with s1 st at the center of net st. After finishing 25 pieces make edging, working 14 rows of net st with ch-11 and 1 row of ch loops with picot.

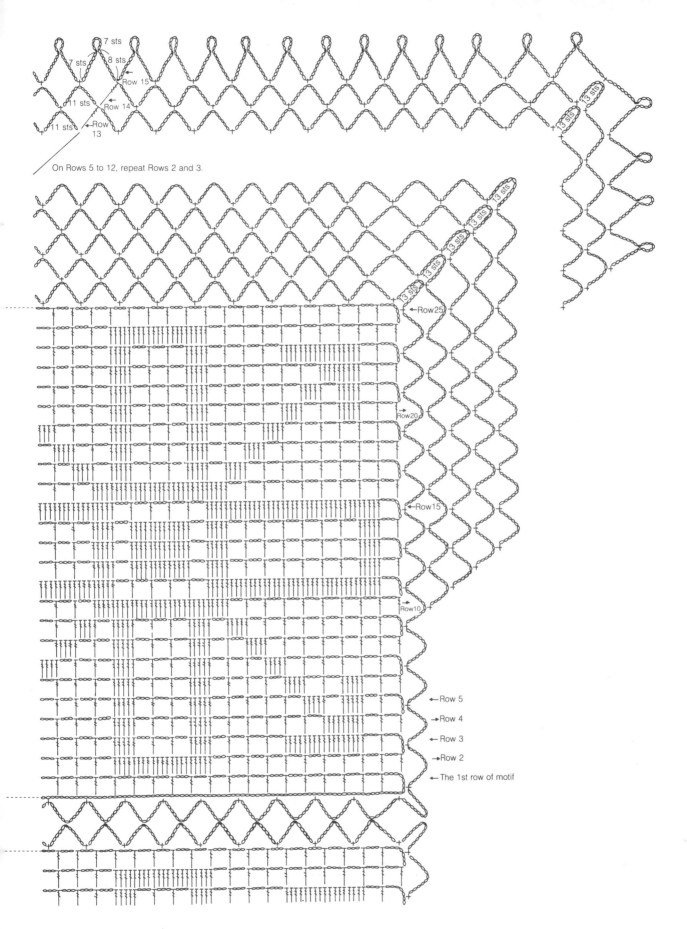

7 sts

7 sts   8 sts

←Row 15

11 sts   ←Row 14

11 sts   ←Row 13

On Rows 5 to 12, repeat Rows 2 and 3.

13 sts

13 sts

13 sts

13 sts

13 sts

13 sts

←Row25

→Row20

←Row15

→Row10

←Row 5

→Row 4

←Row 3

→Row 2

←The 1st row of motif

42

Cushion

■ Shown on page 27.

in width and 50 cm (19⅝″) in length on inner pillow to stuff and put into lace through back opening.

For one piece

You'll need: Anchor Mercer-Crochet No. 40 beige (0780) 200 g (6⅔ oz) 2 pieces of dark brown satin 58 cm (22⅞″) × 58 cm for inner pillow. Stuffing 750 g (26½ oz). One zipper 40 cm (15¾″) long. Steel crochet hook: Size 0.90 mm (14 steel · U.S.A).

Finished size: 48.5 cm × 47 cm (19⅛″ × 18½″). Frill 6 cm (2 ⅜″) wide.

Instructions: Make outer pillow with lace. Work 97 meshes and 104 rows as 1 piece for the right side, and 48 meshes and 104 rows, and 49 meshes and 104 rows as 2 pieces for the wrong side.

Front side: Make foundation ch 292, ch 3 at beginning of every row and work square mesh to Row 104 with ★"ch 2 and dc" and block filled with dc to make flower pattern shown on opposite page.

Back side: Work square mesh with ★ only.

Frill: Make foundation ch 22 and work 960 rows repeating 24 rows as 1 repeat of pattern as shown in the right chart, then join each st of the last row and the foundation ch together with darning. **Finishing:** Place front side lace and 2 pieces of back side together outside out, inserting hook into square meshes along 2 pieces and work 1 row repeating with 2 dc in 1 mesh. Divide 960 rows of frill into 4 parts, mark on the straight edge with thread, and truck to make frill evenly, then fix on outside sc with darning. Attach zipper along opening. Sew 52 cm (20½″) in width and

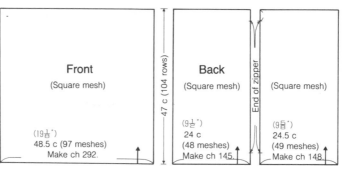

Front
(Square mesh)

(19⅛″)
48.5 c (97 meshes)
Make ch 292.

47 c (104 rows)

Back
(Square mesh)

(9½″)
24 c
(48 meshes)
Make ch 145.

End of zipper

(Square mesh)

(9⅝″)
24.5 c
(49 meshes)
Make ch 148.

★ Frill

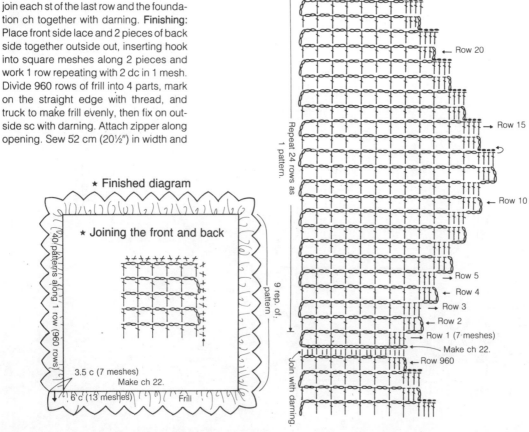

★ Finished diagram

★ Joining the front and back

(40 patterns along 1 row (960 rows))

3.5 c (7 meshes)
Make ch 22.

6 c (13 meshes)   Frill

9 rep. of 1 pattern

Join with darning.

Repeat 24 rows as 1 pattern.

Row 25
Row 20
Row 15
Row 10
Row 5
Row 4
Row 3
Row 2
Row 1 (7 meshes)
Make ch 22.
Row 960

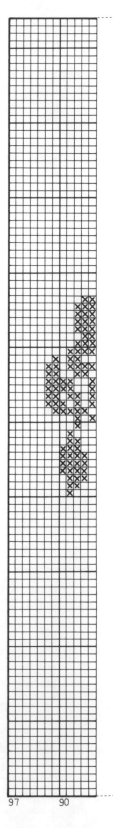

97   90

41

Cushion

Shown on page 26.

You'll need: Anchor Mercer-Crochet No. 40 White (01) 130 g (4⅝ oz). Pink satin for outer pillow and 2 pieces of cotton cloth 66 cm ×66 cm (25⅞″ × 25⅞″) for inner pillow. Stuffing 1400 g (49⅜ oz). Steel crochet hook: Size 0.90 mm (14 steel · U.S.A.).

★ Frill

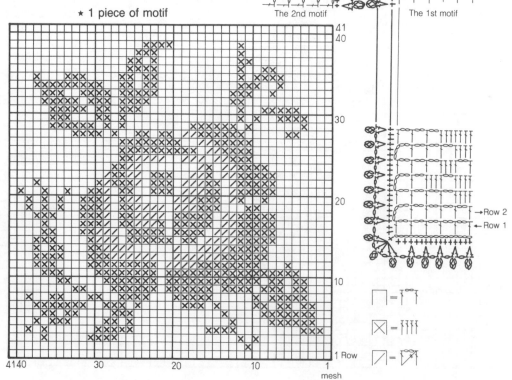

Start here.

Row 1   Row 5   Row 9

★ Finished diagram

5 c (8 rows)

45c

60c

70c
(27½″)

45c

60c

70c
(27½″)

★ Center lace

45c
(18″)

Edging 1 c (2 rows)

20c (41rows)

20c (41meshes)
Make ch 124.

45c
(18″)

★ Motif joining

The 3rd motif

The 4th motif

Join thread

Edging
Row 2
Row 1
←Row 41

The 2nd motif

The 1st motif

Finished size: 60 cm × 60 cm (23⅝″ × 23⅝″). Frill 5 cm (2 ″) wide. Center lace for applique 45 cm × 45 cm (18″ × 18 ″).

Instructions: ① Join 4 square motifs for the lace center. Work 41 meshes and 41 rows with square mesh and work 2 rows edging to complete 1 piece of motif. after finishing 1st motif, work the 2nd and join to previous motif, turning in different direction as shown in chart. ②Finish cushion with pink satin sized 60 cm × 60 cm (23⅝″ × 23⅝″) and fix the lace ① on the center of the front. ③ Start frill making foundation ch 960 (240 cm-94½″) to form a circle. Attach marks of thread at every ch-240 at this time. The positions marked become corners. Work ch 3 at the beginning to make 2 meshes on Row 1,

★ 1 piece of motif

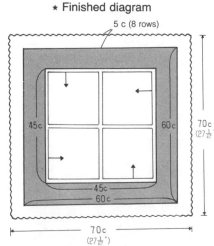

41
40

30

20

10

1 Row

4140   30   20   10   1
mesh

→Row 2
←Row 1

□ =
⊠ =
◿ =

43 Centerpiece

Shown on page 28. ■

You'll need: Anchor Mercer-Crochet No. 40 ivory (0387) 70 g (2½ oz). Steel crochet hook: Size 0.90 mm (14 steel · U.S.A.).

Finished size: 39 cm × 55 cm (15⅜″ × 21⅝″).

★ Beginning

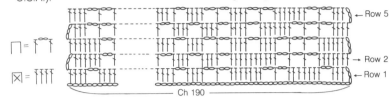

□ = dc

☒ = treble

Ch 190

Row 5
Row 2
Row 1

Instructions: This is a vertical-striped pattern. Make foundation ch 190 and work ch 3 at beginning and dc into 5th ch from hook, then continue working 92 rows with square mesh referring to diagram. Work edging 1 row continuing to last row.

★ Finished diagram

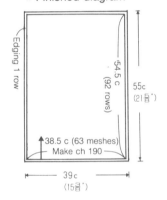

Edging 1 row

54.5 c (92 rows)

55 c (21⅝″)

38.5 c (63 meshes)
Make ch 190

39 c (15⅜″)

★ Edging

Start and end here.

Row 92 →

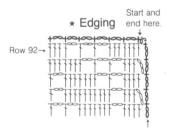

work square mesh 8 rows increasing sts at each corner, then work 1 row of edging. ④ Put seam of cushion opposite the foundation ch of frill and join together with overcasting sts one by one to complete.

92
90

80

70

60

50

40

30

20

10

1 Row

63 60   50   40   30   20   10   1

mesh

44

Centerpiece

Shown on page 29.

You'll need: Anchor Mercer-Crochet No. 40 Ivory (0764) 140 g (4⅞ oz). Steel crochet hook size 0.90 mm (14 steel · U.S.A.)

Finished size: 90.5 cm × 51 cm (35⅝″ × 20⅛″).

Instructions: Make 15 pieces of motif joining 5 pieces across and 3 pieces vertically, and work 3 row of edging. For one piece make foundation ch 101 and work ch 7, including the beginning ch-4 and ch-3 of square mesh, then complete 25 rows working tr as shown in diagram. Work edging along with 9-ch loop on each side continuing to Row 25 work 11-ch loop at each corner. Work 2nd motif joining to the next one with s1 st at center of loop of edging. At corner of 4th motif, join with other 3 loops referring to page 41. After joining 15 pieces, join thread in 11-ch loop at corner and work 2 rows of net st with 9-ch, then work along with "4 sc, sl st-picot with 4-ch and 4 sc" on loops.

★ 1 piece of motif

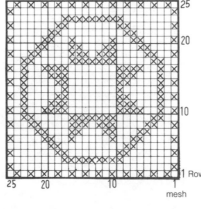

★ Finished diagram

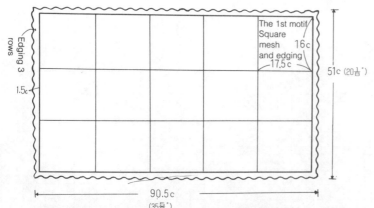

* Work 25 meshes and 25 rows (make ch 101) with square mesh and edging to complete 1 piece of motif.

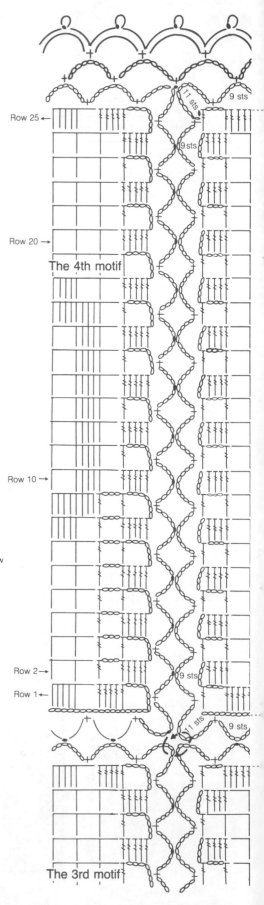

78

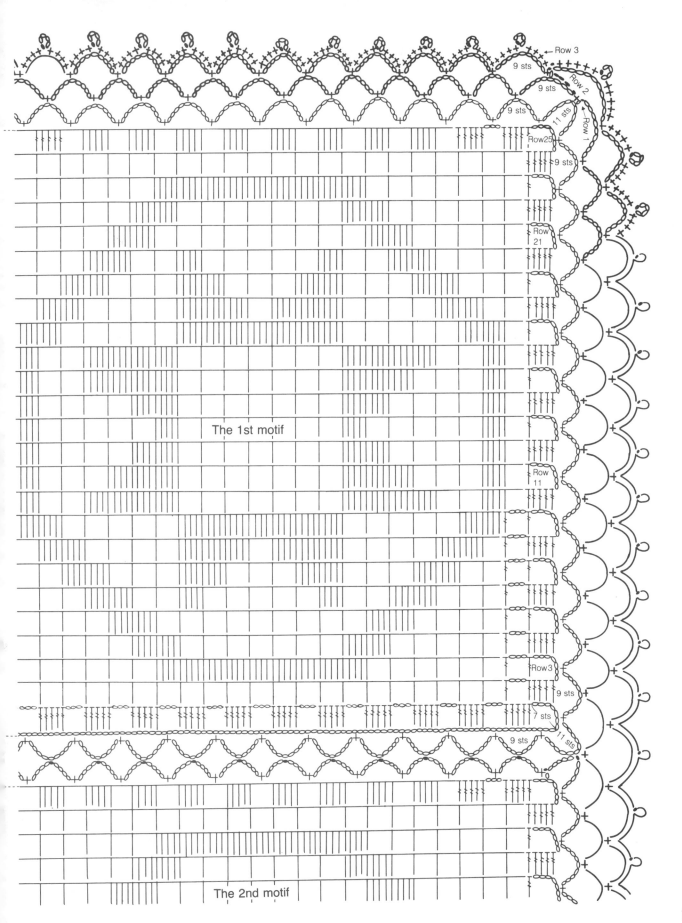

Row 3

9 sts

9 sts

9 sts

11 sts

Row 2

Row 1

Row 25

9 sts

Row 21

The 1st motif

Row 11

Row 3

9 sts

7 sts

11 sts

9 sts

The 2nd motif

Cover for piano and stool

47•48

■ Shown on page 32 to 34.

Work No. 47 Cover for Piano

You'll need: Anchor Mercer-Crochet No. 8 White (0402) 600 g (21⅛ oz). Steel crochet hook: Size 1.25 mm (9 steel · U.S.A.)

Finished size: 220 cm × 84 cm (86⅝″ × 33⅛″).

Instructions: This work, using 17 cm (6⅝″) square motif as 1 piece, joins 12 pieces across and 3 pieces vertically. Make foundation ch 6 to form a loop and work Rows 1 to 9 with square mesh, increasing sts at each corner and from Row 10 to 13 with net st. From 2nd motif work Row 1 to 12 the same as 1st one, but work joining to next one with s1 st on Row 13. See page 40 about s1 st. Work edging with net st to Row 8 and repeat "ch 10, s1 st-picot with 7-ch, ch 10" on Row 9.

Work No. 48 Cover for Stool

You'll need: Anchor Mercer-Crochet No. 40 white (01) 160 g (5½ oz). Steel crochet hook: Size 0.90 mm (14 steel · U.S.A.).

Finished size: 81 cm × 64 cm (31⅞″ × 25⅛″).

Instructions: Use same motif as cover for piano. Complete the 1st motif, and from the 2nd one join work to the previous one on the last row, then make 12 pieces of motif joining 4 pieces across and 3 pieces vertically. Then work 6 rows of edging. Work edging the same as cover for piano from Row 1 to 5. Work Row 6 in same way as row 9.

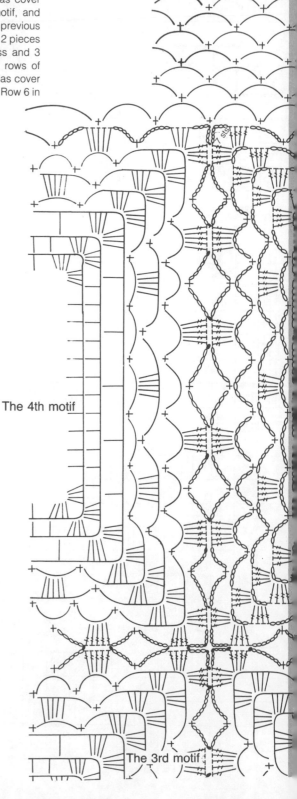

The 4th motif

The 3rd motif

★ Finished diagram

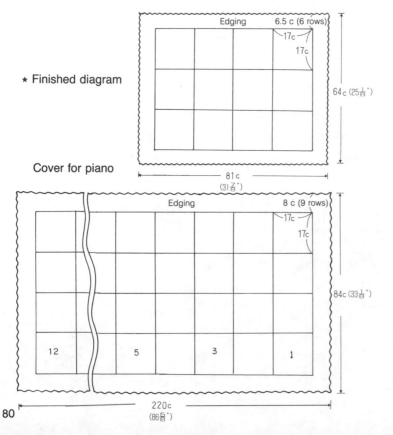

Cover for stool

Edging — 6.5 c (6 rows)
17c
17c
64 c (25¹⁄₈⁻)
81 c (31⁷⁄₈⁻)

Cover for piano

Edging — 8 c (9 rows)
17c
17c
84c (33¹⁄₈⁻)

| 12 | 5 | 3 | 1 |

220c (86⁵⁄₈⁻)

Cut thread.

5 sts
7 sts
7 sts
5 sts
7 sts
5 sts
7 sts

Row 13
Row 10

13 sts

Join thread.

Quintuple tr

Row 5
Row 4
Row 3
Row 2
Row 1

Row 1
7 sts

Row 2
13 sts

Row 3
13 sts

Row 4
13 sts

Row 5
13

13 sts
10 sts
7 sts
10 sts

Row 9

The 1st motif

The 2nd motif

45 Round centerpiece

Shown on page 30.

You'll need: Anchor Mercer-Crochet No. 40 White (01) 40 g (1⅓ oz). Steel crochet hook: Size 0.90 mm (14 steel · U.S.A.).
Finished size: 47 cm (18½″) in diameter.
Instructions: Make foundation ch 15 to form a loop and on Row 1

work ch 5 at the beginning, and repeat "1 dtr, ch 4 and 1 dtr" inserting hook into the loop. Work Rows 2 to 24 around with 10 repeats of flower pattern as shown. Work net st with 7-ch loop on Rows 25 and 26.

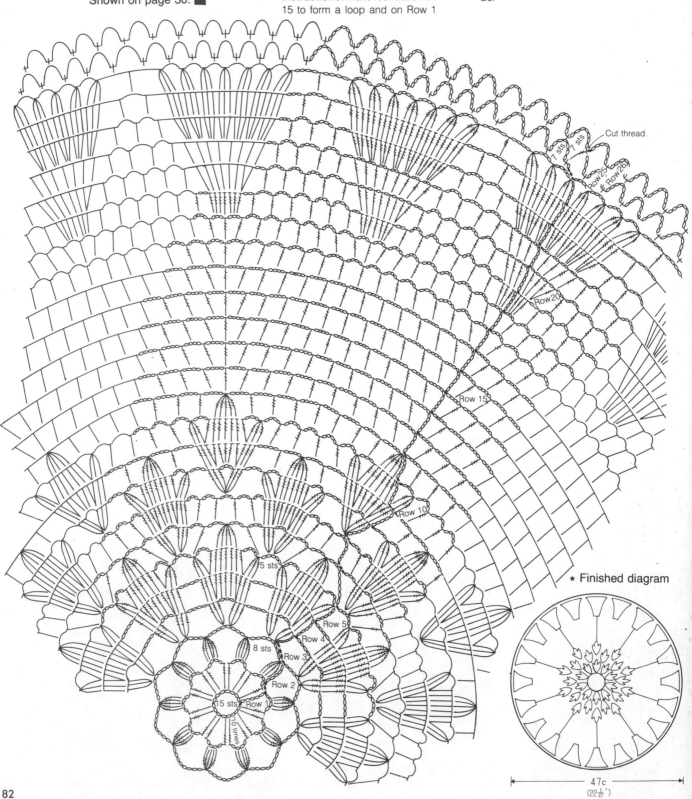

Cut thread.

7 sts 7 sts

Row 25 Row 26

Row 20

Row 15

Row 10

Row 5

Row 4

Row 3

Row 2

5 sts

8 sts

15 sts Row 1

10 times

★ Finished diagram

47c
(22⅛″)